Ready
WITH AN
Answer

Ankerberg&Weldon
JOHN — JOHN

HARVEST HOUSE PUBLISHERS
Eugene, Oregon 97402

Cover by Koechel Peterson & Associates, Minneapolis, Minnesota

Most of this material originally appeared in condensed form in *The Ankerberg Theological Research Institute News Magazine.*

Pages 173-183 are reprinted from *The Creation Hypothesis,* edited by J.P. Moreland, used by permission of InterVarsity Press, P.O. Box 1400, Downer's Grove, IL 60515.

READY WITH AN ANSWER

Copyright © 1997 by Harvest House Publishers
Eugene, Oregon 97402

Library of Congress Cataloging-in-Publication Data
Ankerberg, John, 1945–
    Ready with an answer / John Ankerberg and John Weldon.
       p. cm.
    Includes bibliographical references.
    ISBN 1-56507-618-4
    1. Apologetics. I. Weldon, John. II. Title.
BT1102.A57 1997
239—dc21
                                               96-51535
                                                 CIP

Printed in the United States of America.

97   98   99   00   01   02   /BC/   10   9   8   7   6   5   4   3   2

To those who have faithfully supported
the John Ankerberg Show, with our
sincerest appreciation.

Contents

Charts and Lists

A Note from the Authors

Almost everyone is searching for something beyond themselves to give their lives meaning. However inadequately, many people are searching for the truth. Indeed, there probably isn't a person alive who wouldn't like to know the truth, if that were possible.

Despite the religious, political, moral and philosophical confusions of the modern age, despite the penchant to make personal preference one's truth, people know intuitively there is more to life and they secretly yearn for it.[1] We can see indications of this all around us, in cinema, art, literature, science, philosophy, politics, and just about every other realm of human endeavor.

That is why we have written this book—to help people find the truth. Of course, sometimes the truth is hard to take. But of all things in life, knowing the truth is surely one of the most satisfying. Knowing the truth means knowing that what you believe is absolutely true, and not just true for you alone, but for everybody else as well. Not just true for now, but true forever. That's the truth we are searching for, and that's the truth we are talking about in this book.

This book is written both for Christians to help strengthen their faith and non-Christians to help persuade them that Christianity is the truth.

Naturally, there are relativists who deny truth exists. But what if they are wrong? "A philosophy that denies the possibility of truth is a philosophy that denies its own truth-claims. No one should take it seriously."[2]

This book is designed to take the reader through a progression of logical arguments that we hope will cause him or her to conclude there is a truth and that it can both be known and experienced. What makes the endeavor a bit easier is that in the end, there are only two options for explaining our existence: the natural or the supernatural.

First, there is the supernatural or religious explanation. Is it reasonable to believe that the universe was created by an infinite God? Second, there is the natural or evolutionary explanation. Is it more reasonable to believe the universe arose by chance from nothing, as modern science claims? Interestingly enough, even the natural explanation is a religious one, tantamount to requiring belief in the miraculous. Either way we are forced into the realm of the religious. Further, if a great deal of scientific evidence rules *out* a naturalistic explanation for origins, we have little choice. By default we are automatically required to enter the realm of religious truth claims, at least if we want to know the truth about who we are. And who isn't at least a little bit curious?

The difficulty is that all religions claim to be the truth (even naturalistic ones). Of course, not all religions *can* be equally true. All might be false, or one might be true, but all cannot be absolutely true since they all clearly contradict one another. Indeed, it is somewhat startling that millions of people today claim that all religions *are* true. Everyone knows better. And if all religions *aren't* true, either all are false or *one* is true. There are no other options.

If there is one true God, it is logical to assume there is one true religion. The purpose of this book is to see just how clearly the evidence leads us to conclude that there is only one true God and only one religion that is fully true.

If you really want to examine the case for knowing the truth, you can't afford to miss this book. Like it or not, we all live out our lives more or less consistently with what we think is true. And, depending on what we believe is true, this has major implications for each of our lives. Further, we all die. To live our lives apart from the truth isn't healthy, but to die without the truth is a tragedy.

So, if you are currently of a naturalistic persuasion, and you already believe in one kind of miracle, perhaps it wouldn't hurt you to consider another kind of miracle along the way. If you are currently of a religious persuasion, perhaps it wouldn't hurt you to examine your beliefs more critically.

So where do we begin our search for the truth? Although we will discuss other religions and philosophies, our emphasis in this book will be to examine the evidence for the truth of biblical Christianity.

Why?

Simply because this is the most logical starting point. There is little need to examine 500 different religions in A to Z fashion (even if that were possible), when there is one religion that stands out from all the others in almost every respect.

Christianity is the only religion that is simultaneously most likely to be true and, given its claims, the easiest to disprove if false. Given this, there is no better place to begin.

If biblical Christianity proves true, then we have found the truth.

If it proves false, then the search is still on. . . .

If nothing else, we hope this book will be a challenge to you personally to spend some time in the most important endeavor in life.

There is no greater adventure.

"You are a king, then!" said Pilate.
Jesus answered, "You are right in saying I am a king. In fact, for this reason I was born, and for this I came into the world, to testify to the truth. Everyone on the side of truth listens to me."
"What is truth?" Pilate asked.

−John 18:37-38a

Part 1

Jesus Christ

The Most Unique Man in History

Chapter 1

Why Christianity?

"Every tiny part of us cries out against the idea of dying, and hopes to live forever."
    −Ugo Betti in *Struggle to Dawn* (1949)

The Issue of Truth

In our increasingly hectic world, it seems as if most people have substituted convenience for truth. Despite the unhappy exchange there is nothing more important in life than finding truth, nor is there any more valued possession. Throughout history both the famous and men of letters have had some interesting things to say about truth:

Man passes away; generations are but shadows; there is nothing stable but truth (Josiah Quincy);

A sincere attachment to truth, moral and scientific, is a habit which cures a thousand little infirmities of mind (Sydney Smith);

God offers to every mind its choice between truth and repose (Emerson);

To love the truth is to refuse to let one's self be saddened by it (Andre Gide);

So little trouble do men take in their search after truth; so readily do they accept whatever comes first to hand (Thucydides);

Without truth there is no goodness (Matthew Henry);

17

> For most of us the truth is no longer part of our minds; it has become a special product for experts (Jacob Bronowski);
>
> Truth matters more than man . . . (George Steiner).[1]

If knowing truth is in one's best interest, then the claim of Christianity to have the truth and the claim of Jesus Christ to be the truth is worth investigation.

For those who do not share our Christian worldview, why might they consider openly evaluating the Christian religion?

First, because it is good to do so. As noted, the honest search for truth is one of the most noble philosophical endeavors of life. Plato declared, "Truth is the beginning of every good thing, both in Heaven and on earth; and he who would be blessed and happy should be from the first a partaker of the truth."

Any religion or philosophy that makes convincing claims to having absolute truth is worth consideration because only a few do. More to the point, any religion that claims and produces solid evidence on behalf of an assertion that it alone is *fully* true is worth serious consideration for that reason alone. Only Christianity does this.

Second, the kind of existence Christianity offers in life is one of deep and abundant satisfaction, regardless of the pain and disappointment we may have to experience. Jesus claimed He would give us what we really want in life—true meaning and purpose now, and everlasting life in a heavenly existence far beyond our current comprehension. The noted Oxford and Cambridge scholar, C. S. Lewis, correctly understood one of the most heartfelt yearnings of mankind when he wrote, "There have been times when I think we do not desire heaven but more often I find myself wondering whether, in our heart of hearts, we have ever desired anything else."[2] Jesus declared, "I came that they might have life and have it abundantly" (John 10:10) and "I am the resurrection and the life. He who believes in me will live, even though he dies" (John 11:25). He also said, "I am the truth" (John 14:6).

Everyone likes a good adventure and, this side of death, life is undoubtedly the greatest adventure of all. The reason is obvious. Most people live their lives not really knowing why they were born—or what happens when they die. Most moderns would consider it too presumptuous to claim any final answers to the mysteries of life and death. But what if, in spite of all the questions, there really were an answer? What if Jesus Christ claims He *is* the answer and that anyone who wishes could determine the truth of His claims to their own satisfaction?

Third, Christianity is not just intellectually credible, whether considered philosophically, historically, scientifically, ethically, or culturally, but from an evidential perspective, it is actually superior to other worldviews, secular or religious. If Christianity were obviously false, as some skeptics charge, how could such esteemed intellectuals as those quoted below logically make their declarations? Mortimer Adler is one of the world's leading philosophers. He is chairman of the board of editors for *The Encyclopædia Britannica,* architect of *The Great Books of the Western World* series and its amazing *Syntopicon,* director of the prestigious Institute for Philosophical Research in Chicago, and author of *Truth in Religion, Ten Philosophical Mistakes, How to Think About God, How to Read a Book,* plus over twenty other challenging books. He simply asserts, "I believe Christianity is the only logical, consistent faith in the world."[3] How could Adler make such a statement? Because he knows it can't rationally be made of any other religion.

Philosopher, historian, theologian, and trial attorney John Warwick Montgomery, holding nine graduate degrees in various fields argues, "The evidence for the truth of Christianity overwhelmingly outweighs competing religious claims and secular world views."[4] How could an individual of such intellectual caliber as Dr. Montgomery use a descriptive phrase as "overwhelmingly outweighs" if it were obviously false? His fifty-plus books and one hundred-plus scholarly articles indicate exposure to a wide variety of non-Christian religious and secular philosophies.

The individual widely considered to be the greatest Protestant philosopher of God in the world, Alvin Plantinga, recalls, "For nearly my entire life I have been convinced of the *truth* of Christianity."[5] On what basis can one of the world's greatest philosophers make such a declaration if the evidence for Christianity is unconvincing, as critics charge?

Dr. Drew Trotter is executive director of the Center for Christian Studies at Charlottesville, Virginia. He holds a doctorate from Cambridge University. He argues that "logic and the evidence both point to the reality of absolute truth, and that truth is revealed in Christ."[6]

If we are looking for obvious truths, then perhaps we should consider the words of noted economist and sociologist George F. Guilder, author of *Wealth and Poverty*, who asserts, "Christianity is true and its truth will be discovered anywhere you look very far."[7]

Alister McGrath, principal of Wycliffe Hall, Oxford University, and author of *Intellectuals Don't Need God and Other Myths*, declares that the superior nature of the evidence for Christianity is akin to that found in doing good scientific research: "When I was undertaking my doctoral research in molecular biology at Oxford University, I was frequently confronted with a number of theories offering to explain a given observation. In the end, I had to make a judgment concerning which of them possessed the greatest internal consistency, the greatest degree of correspondence to the data of empirical observation, and the greatest degree of predictive ability. Unless I was to abandon any possibility of advance in understanding, I was obliged to make such a judgment. . . . I would claim the right to speak of the 'superiority' of Christianity in this explicative sense."[8]

The noted Christian scholar Dr. Carl. F. H. Henry wrote a three-thousand-page, six-volume work on the topic of *God, Revelation and Authority*. After his exhaustive analysis, Henry declared, "Truth is Christianity's most enduring asset. . . ."[9]

Such accolades could be multiplied repeatedly. While testimonies *per se* mean little, if they are undergirded by the weight of evidence they can hardly be dismissed out of hand. Indeed, as Norman Geisler comments, "In the face of overwhelming apologetic evidence, unbelief becomes perverse. . . ."[10]

Fourth, as we will see, Christianity's founder, Jesus Christ, is utterly original and totally unique when compared to every other religious leader who has ever lived. In the words of an article in *Time* magazine, His life was simply, "the most influential life that was ever lived."[11] In addition, the Christian Bible itself is clearly the most influential book in human history. As we will see, the evidence in favor of its divine inspiration and the inerrancy of its autographs is formidable, even to many former skeptics. But if Jesus Christ and the Christian Scriptures continue to exert an unparalleled influence in the world, shouldn't they be considered worthy of an impartial investigation? If objective evidence points to Christianity alone being fully true, then it seems that only personal bias can explain a person's unwillingness to seriously consider the claims of Jesus Christ on his or her life.

A final reason secularists and those of other religious persuasions should be receptive to Christianity is because we live in an increasingly poisonous age. In our pluralistic and pagan culture, almost anyone is a viable target for conversion to a wide variety of false beliefs which are far more consequential individually than Christianity—from various cults and New Age occultism to solipsism and nihilism. Philosophies of despair and potent occult experiences can convert even those who think they are the least vulnerable: "There is a great deal of research that shows that all people, but especially highly intelligent people, are easily taken in by all kinds of illusions, hallucinations, self-deceptions, and outright bamboozles—all the more so when they have a high investment in the illusion being true."[12] In other words, even in this life it is the personal welfare of the non-Christian that may be at risk.

Chapter 2

Great Minds Speak About Jesus

"The contemplation of things as they are, without substitution or imposture, without error or confusion, is in itself a nobler thing than a whole harvest of invention."

— Francis Bacon

Today, most people who are unfamiliar with the facts concerning Jesus Christ tend to place Him in the same category as other great religious leaders and prophets. They assume Jesus was no different from the rest. Most people also believe that religion everywhere is largely the same and that it doesn't make a great deal of difference what one believes. A recent poll indicated that even 43 percent of born-again Christians had apparently adopted our culture's relativistic outlook. They agreed with the following statement: "It does not matter what religious faith you follow because all faiths teach similar lessons about life."[1]

Those having such an outlook usually assume that all paths lead to the same God. If there is an afterlife, almost everyone is going to get there regardless of his or her beliefs, as long as he or she was not a terribly evil person. So it really doesn't matter what one believes religiously, and perhaps whether or not one believes at all.

In light of such assumptions, many people wonder if any religious prophet or leader could have significant relevance for today. Aren't these prophets dead and gone? And do their teachings really offer anything unique or special? Can't their instruction be summed up by the fundamental principles of moral living that everyone already knows? Why should anyone be interested in someone like Jesus who lived 2,000 years ago and has no apparent relevance for us today?

The Influence of Jesus

In response to this, we must consider why non-Christians should become informed about Jesus Christ. First, no one can logically claim to be a truly educated person if he does not understand who Jesus is and the influence He has exerted upon humanity. That means many atheists, agnostics, and skeptics apparently aren't very well-educated. Christ's influence in the world and His claims on people's lives are unparalleled. As Dr. D. James Kennedy points out in *What If Jesus Had Never Been Born?* "Jesus Christ, the greatest man whoever lived, has changed virtually every aspect of human life—and most people don't know it. . . . Nineteen centuries have come and gone, and today He is the central figure of the human race. All the armies that ever marched, all the navies that ever sailed, all the parliaments that ever sat, all the kings that ever reigned, put together, have not affected the life of man on this earth as much as that one solitary life."[2] (Indeed, on April 8, 1996, something unique happened in the history of secular publishing. All the three major news magazines—*Time, Newsweek,* and *U.S. News & World Report*—carried cover stories on the same person: Jesus Christ.)

He is undoubtedly the single most commanding person in the entire history of mankind. It is not too much to say that if Jesus Christ had never been born, you and I and this entire country, and our entire Western Civilization, would not exist as it does. The influence of Christ and Christianity in helping the poor, in the founding of America, in expansion of civil liberties, in education and science, health and medicine, economics, the family and morality, the arts, music, and other areas is far greater than the average person ever suspects. (To illustrate this influence in e.g., the founding of America, we have prepared a brief chart at the end of this chapter.)

Even the death of Jesus was unique. "His death, beyond any question of dispute, was the most famous death in human history. No other death has aroused a fraction of such intense feeling over so many hundreds of years. Few can be passive about Jesus. No other human being has been so loved and so hated, so adored and so despised, so proclaimed and so opposed. Yet if the records of Jesus are true, then unquestionably there is no greater truth to be found anywhere in the universe."[3]

Can anyone deny that because of Jesus, Christianity has become the largest religion in the world? That it has a membership of almost two billion? That geographically it is the most widely diffused of all religions? That it has positively altered individuals, countries, and cultures?

The second reason to be informed about Christ is of paramount importance to each individual personally. As we will see, Jesus Christ makes stupendous claims upon each person's life. These claims compel us to conclude that your relationship to Christ, or lack of it, will dramatically affect your present and future existence. His life is far more vital to your life, as well as the lives of your friends and family, than you may realize. Jesus Christ is that important, and the evidence backs it up.

Let us illustrate some small portion of the impact Christ has had by citing the comments of many famous and noted people—kings, scientists, poets, theologians, lawyers, members of other religions, and philosophers alike.

We will begin with a concise sampling of declarations made by Jesus Himself. (These will be examined further in the next chapter.) In light of these statements, the ones below are all the more incredible if Jesus really were *not* who He claims. In evaluating the claims of Jesus, readers should understand that even skeptics can't logically deny that the four Gospel biographies of Christ are based on accurate historical reporting and that at least two, Matthew and John, were written by those who knew Christ personally and traveled closely with Him for more than three years. Luke asserts that he "carefully investigated everything from the beginning" in completing his biography (Luke 1:3), and it is generally agreed that Mark got the information for his biography directly from the Apostle Peter. For those and other reasons (see chapter 16), we know the Gospels constitute reliable historical reporting.

The kind of scholarly nonsense we find in skeptical endeavors like the "Jesus Seminar" is all too common today, and, despite its consequences in the lives of the uninformed, believer or unbeliever, only serves to discredit the skeptics own credibility and make plain his prejudices.* Due to advances in textual criticism and other areas, it is now considered a historic fact that Jesus said and did what the Gospel writers claim He said and did. In other words, when we read the Gospels—Matthew, Mark, Luke, and John—we are, in fact, reading what Jesus Himself actually said, taught, and did.[4]

What Did Jesus Claim?

As you read the words of Jesus, ask yourself, what kind of mere man would say them?

> I am the light of the world. Whoever follows me will never walk in darkness, but will have the light of life. (John 8:12)

> I am the resurrection and the life. He who believes in Me will live, even though he dies. (John 11:25)

> No one has ever gone into heaven except the one who came from heaven—the Son of Man. (John 3:13)

> For the bread of God is he who comes down from heaven and gives life to the world.... I am the bread of life. He who comes to me will never go hungry, and he who believes in me will never be thirsty. (John 6:33,35)

> "I tell you the truth," Jesus answered, "before Abraham was born, I am!" (John 8:58)

> When a man believes in me, he does not believe in me only, but in the one who sent me. When he looks at me, he sees the one who sent me. (John 12:44-45)

> You call me "Teacher" and "Lord," and rightly so, for that is what I am. (John 13:13)

> And if I go and prepare a place for you, I will come back and take you to be with me that you also may be where I am. (John 14:3)

> I have overcome the world. (John 16:33)

---

*See, e.g., Michael Wilkins and J. P. Moreland (eds.), *Jesus Under Fire: Modern Scholarship Reinvents the Historical Jesus* and Gregory Boyd, *Cynic, Sage or Son of God? Recovering the Real Jesus in an Age of Revisionist Replies* (InterVarsity).

My teaching is not my own. It comes from him who sent me. If anyone chooses to do God's will, he will find out whether my teaching comes from God or whether I speak on my own. (John 7:16 -17)

I and the Father are one. (John 10:30)

Anyone who has seen me has seen the Father. (John 14:9)

All that belongs to the Father is mine. (John 16:15)

You are from below, I am from above; you are of this world, I am not of this world. (John 8:23)

Now, what did Jesus declare of such brazen assertions? Only that, "My testimony is valid" (John 8:14), and "I am the one I claim to be" (John 8:28), and "You are right in saying I am a king. In fact, for this reason I was born, and for this I came into the world, to testify to the truth. Everyone on the side of truth listens to me" (John 18:37). Throughout history, untold millions have believed these claims were true. Even those in the first century who either knew Him personally or critically examined His claims believed what Jesus said. Considering the incredible nature of such claims, perhaps that is the most amazing thing.

The Apostle John—"This is the disciple who testifies to these things [about Jesus] and who wrote them down. We know that his testimony is true." (John 21:24)

The physician Luke—"I myself have carefully investigated everything from the beginning.... so that you may know the certainty of the things you have been taught...." "After his [Jesus'] suffering, he showed himself to these men [apostles] and gave many convincing proofs that he was alive. He appeared to them over a period of forty days and spoke about the kingdom of God." (Luke 1:3,4; Acts 1:3)

Former skeptic and Jewish leader, Saul of Tarsus—The Apostle Paul told King Herod Agrippa II that, while he formerly persecuted believers in Christ, condemning them to death (Acts 26:9-11), Jesus had now personally appeared to him, confirming Jesus' resurrection and messiahship (vs. 12-19). Paul then said, "But I have had God's help to this very day, and so I stand here and testify to small and great alike. I am saying nothing beyond what the prophets and Moses said would happen. . . . What I am saying is true and reasonable. The king is familiar with these things, and I can speak freely to him. I am convinced that none of this has escaped his notice, because it was not done in a corner." (Acts 26:22, 25b-26)

The Apostle Peter—"We did not follow cleverly invented stories when we told you about the power and coming of our Lord Jesus Christ, but we were eyewitnesses of his majesty." (2 Peter 1:16)

Significantly, unlike any other religious leader, Jesus frequently appealed to His ability to *prove* His claims by predicting the future or performing dramatic miracles, such as healing those born blind or raising the dead:

I am telling you now before it happens, so that when it does happen you will believe that I am He. (John 13:19)

Believe me when I say that I am in the Father and the Father is in me; or at least believe on the evidence of the miracles themselves. (John 14:11)

What Leading Thinkers Have Said About Jesus

Now in light of such claims by Jesus, consider what informed and great people historically and today—believers and unbelievers alike—have said about Him. Could all of them, down to the last one, be mistaken? Certainly if men and women, as those listed below, felt it was vital to be informed about Jesus Christ, perhaps you should also become informed. Can you read *all* of the statements in the following chart and still believe investigating Jesus is not a worthwhile endeavor?

Blaise Pascal, French philosopher and scientist, author of the classic work *Pensées*	"Jesus Christ is the centre of everything and the object of everything, and he who does not know Him knows nothing of the order of nature and nothing of himself."
Ralph Waldo Emerson, American poet and transcendentalist	"The unique impression of Jesus upon mankind—whose name is not so much written as ploughed into the history of the world—is proof of the subtle virtue of this infusion."

Augustine of Hippo, church theologian and philosopher

"Christ is not valued at all unless He be valued above all."

Napoleon Bonaparte, Emperor of France

"I know men; and I tell you that Jesus Christ is no mere man. Between Him and every other person in the world, there is no possible term of comparison. Alexander, Caesar, Charlemagne, and I have founded empires. But on what did we rest the creations of our genius? Upon force. Jesus Christ founded His empire upon love; and at this hour millions of men would die for Him. . . . There is not a God in heaven, if a mere man was able to conceive and execute successfully the gigantic design of making Himself the object of supreme worship, by usurping the name of God. Jesus alone dared to do this."

Pope John Paul II

"Christ is absolutely original and absolutely unique."[5]

Robert Louis Stevenson, Scottish novelist and poet

"When Christ came into my life, I came about like a well-handled ship."

Alfred Lord Tennyson, English poet

"The Lord from Heaven born of a village girl, carpenter's son, Wonderful, Prince of Peace, the mighty God."

Lew Wallace, American lawyer, soldier, and author of *Ben Hur*

"After six years given to the impartial investigation of Christianity, as to its truth or falsity, I have come to the deliberate conclusion that Jesus Christ was the Messiah of the Jews, the Savior of the world, and my personal Savior."

H. G. Wells, English novelist and historian, author of *The Time Machine, War of the Worlds,* and *An Outline of History*

"The Galilean has been too great for our small hearts."

Malcolm Muggeridge, English novelist and critic

"The coming of Jesus into the world is the most stupendous event in human history . . . What is unique about Jesus is that, on the testimony and in the experience of innumerable people, of all sorts and conditions, of all races and nationalities from the simplest and most primitive to the most sophisticated and cultivated, He remains alive. That the resurrection happened seems to be indubitably true. Either Jesus never was or He still is."[6]

Albert Einstein, American physicist who originated the theory of relativity

"I am enthralled by the luminous figure of the Nazarene."

Sir Lionell Luckhoo, listed in the *Guiness Book of Records,* the world's "most successful lawyer," knighted twice by the queen of England

"I have spent more than forty-two years as a defense trial lawyer appearing in many parts of the world. . . . I say unequivocally the evidence for the resurrection of Jesus Christ is so overwhelming that it compels acceptance by proof which leaves absolutely no doubt."[7]

George Barlow

"The example of Christ is supreme in its authority."

Vance Havner

"Jesus was the most disturbing person in history."

John M. Mason, American educator; provost, Columbia College

"He who thinks he hath no need of Christ hath too high thoughts of himself. He who thinks Christ cannot help him hath too low thoughts of Christ."

G. Campbell Morgan, British preacher, author

"Everything that is really worthwhile in the morality of today has come to the world through Christ."

Sholem Asch, Polish novelist and playwright

"Jesus Christ is the outstanding personality of all time. . . . no other teacher—Jewish, Christian, Buddhist, Mohammedan—is *still* a teacher whose teaching is such a guidepost for the world we live in. . . . He became the Light of the World. Why shouldn't I, a Jew, be proud of that?"

William E. Biederwolf, American educator and evangelist

"A man who can read the New Testament and not see that Christ claims to be more than a man, can look all over the sky at high noon on a cloudless day and not see the sun."

William Ellery Channing, Unitarian leader and abolitionist

"I know of no sincere enduring good but the moral excellency which shines forth in Jesus Christ."

Joseph Ernest Renan, French nationalist and skeptic, humanist historian of religion

"Jesus was the greatest religious genius that ever lived. His beauty is eternal, and His reign shall never end. Jesus is in every respect unique, and nothing can be compared with

Him. All history is incomprehensible without Christ... Whatever may be the surprises of the future, Jesus will never be surpassed. ...All ages will proclaim that among the sons of men there is none born greater than Jesus."

P. Carnegie Simpson

"The face of Christ does not indeed show us everything, but it shows the one thing we need to know—the character of God. God is the God who sent Jesus."

Phillips Brooks, Harvard-educated preacher and bishop of Massachusetts who preached before Queen Victoria

"That Christ should be and should be Christ appears the one reasonable, natural, certain thing in all the universe. In Him all broken lines unite; in Him all scattered sounds are gathered into harmony."

Jean Baptiste Lacordaire, French prelate and revolutionary

"Whatever motives Jesus Christ might have had against calling Himself God, He did call Himself God; such is the fact."

Bishop William Quayle

"This calm assumption of Jesus that He is not a sinner will take hold of the wrists of any thoughtful mind and twist them till it must come to its knees."

Leonce De Grandmaison

"Either Jesus was and knew what He was, what He proclaimed Himself to be, or else He was a pitiable visionary."

W. A. Visser't Hooft, Dutch ecumenical, grand secretary of the World Council of Churches

"The Christian Church stands or falls with this simple proposition: that Jesus is nothing less than God's self-communication to men, and the only certain source of our knowledge of God."

Fulton J. Sheen, Roman Catholic bishop and broadcaster

"If we are to find the secret of His Timelessness—the simplicity of His Wisdom, the transforming power of His Doctrine, we must go out beyond time to the Timelessness, beyond the complex to the Perfect, beyond Change to the Changeless, out beyond the margins of the world to the Perfect God."

Dorothy Day, American writer and social reformer

"Christ is God or He is the world's greatest liar and impostor."

Herbert E. Cory

"The witnesses for the historical authentication and for the proofs of the Divinity of Jesus, from the earliest days, are far more comprehensive

	than the testimonies for the existence of many famous historical characters we accept without question."
P. T. Forsyth, Congregationalist theologian who rejected his earlier liberalism and, according to E. Brunner, became the greatest British theologian of his day	"An undogmatic Christ is the advertisement of a dying faith."
Charles Lamb, English essayist and critic, author of *Tales from Shakespeare*	"If Shakespeare should come into this room, we would all rise; but if Jesus Christ should come in, we would all kneel."
C. F. Andrews, Anglican missionary to India	"The supreme miracle of Christ's character lies in this: that He combines within Himself, as no other figure in human history has ever done, the qualities of every race."
F. R. Berry	"The Humanist suggestion that Jesus was 'morally right, but religiously mistaken' defies all psychological probabilities."[8]

All this is no mean testimony, but it could be multiplied many times over. Still, there are many people and groups today claiming false things about Jesus, and many others who reject or oppose Him. This includes liberal theologians who reject His deity, religious cults like Mormons and Jehovah's Witnesses who claim to honor Him and accept His teachings but do not, and those in other world faiths who reinvent His message to conform to their own.[9] Because such misinformation is widespread today, even the one who names the name of Christ needs to be thoroughly versed on what history and Scripture teach about Him and why contrary views are invalid.

Did the Founding Fathers Believe Christianity Was the Basis of American Government?

Do you think our Founding Fathers believed in God and founded America as a Christian nation? The Supreme Court answered this question in 1892 and cited fifty historical examples to prove America was indeed a Christian nation. These are just a few:

Governor Bradford, in writing of the Pilgrims' landing, describes their first act: "Being thus arrived in a good harbor and brought safe to land, they fell upon their knees and blessed the God of heaven. . . . "

The New England Charter, signed by King James I, confirmed the goal of the first settlers to be: "to advance the enlargement of Christian religion, to the glory of God Almighty."

The goal of government based on Scripture was affirmed by individual counties, such as is found in the **Rhode Island Charter of 1683**, which begins: "We submit our persons, lives and estates unto our Lord Jesus Christ, the King of kings and Lord of lords and to all those perfect and most absolute laws of His given us in His holy Word."

Benjamin Franklin stood and addressed the Continental Congress with these words: "In the beginning of the contest with Britain, when we were sensible of danger, we had daily prayers in this room for divine protection. Our prayers, sir, were heard and they were graciously answered. All of us who were engaged in the struggle must have observed frequent instances of a superintending Providence in our favor. . . . Have we now forgotten this powerful friend? Or do we imagine we no longer need His assistance? I have lived, sir, a long time, and the longer I live, the more convincing proofs I see of this truth: that God governs in the affairs of man. And if a sparrow cannot fall to the ground without His notice, is it probable that an empire can rise without His aid?"

George Washington, in his inaugural address to Congress as the first president of the nation stated: "No people can be bound to acknowledge and adore the invisible hand which conducts the affairs of men more than the people of the United States. Every step by which they have advanced to the character of an independent nation seems to have been distinguished by some token of providential agency. . . . "

One of **George Washington's first official acts** was the first Thanksgiving proclamation, which reads, "Whereas, it is the duty of all nations to acknowledge the providence of Almighty God, to obey His will, to be grateful for His benefits, and humbly implore His protection and favor . . . " It goes on to call the nation to thankfulness to Almighty God.

Thomas Jefferson said: "Indeed, I tremble for my country when I reflect that God is just, and that His justice cannot sleep forever."

President John Quincy Adams: "The first and almost the only book deserving of universal attention is the Bible."

Andrew Jackson: "Go to the Scriptures . . . the joyful promises it contains will be a balsam to all your troubles."

From **President Abraham Lincoln's Proclamation for a National Day of Fasting, Humiliation, and Prayer, April 30, 1863:** "We have been the recipients of the choicest bounties of heaven. We have been preserved, these many years, in peace and prosperity. We have grown in numbers, wealth and power, as no other nation has ever grown. But we have forgotten God. We have forgotten the gracious hand which preserved us in peace, and multiplied and enriched and strengthened us; and we have vainly imagined, in the deceitfulness of our hearts, that all these blessings were produced by some superior wisdom and virtue of our own. Intoxicated with unbroken success, we have become too self-sufficient to feel the necessity of redeeming and preserving grace, too proud to pray to the God that made us! It behooves us, then, to humble ourselves before the offended Power, to confess our national sins, and to pray for clemency and forgiveness."

The Supreme Court Decision 1892—Church of the Holy Trinity Vs. The United States: "Our laws and our institutions must necessarily be based upon and embody the teachings of The Redeemer of mankind. It is impossible that it should be otherwise; and in this sense and to this extent our civilization and our institutions are emphatically Christian. . . . This is a religious people. This is historically true."

President Woodrow Wilson: ". . . the Bible . . . is the one supreme source of revelation of the meaning of life, the nature of God and spiritual nature and need of men. It is the only guide of life which really leads the spirit in the way of peace and salvation."

In spite of these statements, many people today say that the Founding Fathers never intended for religious principles to be part of public life or public affairs. They add: Doesn't being a Christian nation really threaten pluralism? Interestingly, the Founding Fathers discuss that and they felt that it enhanced it.

Patrick Henry made a very clear statement: "It cannot be emphasized too often or too strongly that this great nation was founded not by religionists but by Christians; not on religions but on the gospel of Jesus Christ. . . . It is for this reason that people of other faiths have been afforded asylum, prosperity and freedom of worship here."

It must be concluded that our Founding Fathers *did* believe in God and founded America as a Christian nation. (For documentation see The John Ankerberg Show transcript, *Did the Founding Fathers Establish America as a Christian Nation?*)

Chapter 3

What Does the Bible Say About Jesus Christ?

"Truth is truth, to th' end of reck'ning."
—Shakespeare

As noted, today almost everyone has an opinion of who Jesus Christ is. These opinions vary widely and are often contradictory, and contrary opinions can't all be true. How then do we determine who Jesus really is and whether or not He truly is the person of paramount importance He claims to be? The only way is to frankly examine His claims and explore the quality of evidence that exists to support them. It is our hope that this more lengthy chapter will help our readers understand the real Jesus Christ.

We can begin by noting that *history* is defined as follows: "A continuous methodological record of important or public events; the study of past events, especially of human affairs" (*Oxford American Dictionary*). Notice there is no declaration here that miracles cannot be part of history, despite their uniqueness. So when we encounter supernatural events in the life of Christ, the only issue is whether or not they occurred. If competent eyewitness testimony indicates miracles happened, then they must be considered part of history. Obviously if God has intervened in history, then miracles could be expected. Thus, the true historian should be concerned with what actually did happen, based on careful and impartial investigation of the evidence, not with upholding a bias against the supernatural.

Seven Crucial Facts About Jesus

It is once again important to note that the Gospels constitute accurate historical reporting. It is no longer logically possible to argue that Jesus did not say and do the things His biographers recorded of Him. In light of this, there are at least seven key things the Bible teaches about Jesus Christ. These stand alone; in no other religion on earth do we find anything similar:

1. Jesus is the prophesied Messiah who was predicted hundreds of years in advance through very specific prophecies.

2. Jesus is unique in all creation; in all history and religion there has never been another like Him;

3. Jesus is virgin born, and morally perfect, i.e., sinless.

4. Jesus is deity, the only incarnation of God there is or will be.

5. Jesus is the world's only Savior, who died for our sins on the cross and offers eternal salvation as an entirely free gift.

6. Jesus rose from the dead as proof of His claims.

7. Jesus is the Final Judge: He will return and personally judge every person who has ever lived on the Last Day.

In no other person of history can we see his life and nature prophetically outlined 400 to 1,000 years before his birth. Of no other individual this world has known is it possible to differentiate between their birth and origin or to speculate over their nature. The world has never known any other virgin-born and truly sinless person. No other man ever claimed to be God and convinced literally billions of people throughout history he was telling the truth. No one else ever claimed he would die for man's sin and that he personally could freely offer humanity *eternal* life. In no other man do we find the audacity to specifically predict on many occasions his own time and method of death (to the very day) or to predict his rising from the dead. No man ever said he would visibly return from heaven to judge the world and decide the eternal fate of every individual. The well-chronicled life of Jesus Christ offers a wonderful opportunity to examine His claims.

Let's briefly explore the previous seven points.

Is Jesus the prophesied Messiah predicted centuries in advance in the Old Testament?

> *"It is one thing to wish to have truth on our side, and another to wish sincerely to be on the side of truth."*
> *—Richard Whately*

The Hebrew Scriptures are unique among those of the world's religions in that they contain scores of prophecies about a predicted future Messiah. These prophecies extend over a period of 1,000 years and many are given in specific detail. The final prophecy was given 400 years before Christ was ever born. In our book, *The Case for Jesus the Messiah: Incredible Prophecies That Prove God Exists*,[1] we discuss more than a dozen of these prophecies, at length, proving that only Jesus Christ fulfills them, and therefore, that only He is the predicted Jewish Messiah (cf., John 5:46). For example, in the anguished imagery of King David's prayers, Psalm 22 accurately describes a crucifixion—yet this description is given hundreds of years before the method of execution by crucifixion was devised. No other Psalm fits the description of Christ's crucifixion better than Psalm 22, explaining why it is the most frequently quoted Psalm by New Testament writers. Yet this Psalm was written 1000 years before Jesus was even born. Significantly, Jesus quoted the first verse of this Psalm while on the cross. Whatever one thinks of this Psalm, no one can deny that it describes what happened to Jesus on the cross an entire millennium later, for example, "They have pierced my hands and my feet. I can count all my bones; people stare and gloat over me. They divide my garments among them and cast lots for my clothing" (Psalm 22:16-18; cf. Matthew 27:35).

In Isaiah 9:6-7, written 700 years before Christ, the prophecy of the coming Messiah concerns a child to be born who will also be God and who will have an everlasting kingdom. In the Gospels, Jesus claimed that He was that incarnate God and that He would have an everlasting kingdom (Matthew 16:28; 26:64; Luke 22:30; John 6:38-42, 62; 8:42; 10:30, 36-38; 18:36; cf., 2 Peter 1:11).

In Isaiah 53:4-12, the Messiah is prophesied to be crushed and pierced for our transgressions; that God will lay upon Him the iniquity of all mankind. In the Gospels, Jesus claims to fulfill this prophecy (Matthew 20:28; 26:28; cf. Isaiah. 53:12). In fact, Jesus repeatedly claimed He was the predicted Messiah by continually claiming He was fulfilling Old Testament prophecies: "You diligently study the Scriptures because you think that by them you possess eternal life. These are the Scriptures that testify about me" (John 5:39; see also Matthew 26:24, 54, 56; Luke 24:25-27, 44).

In Micah 5:2, written 700 years B.C., the Messiah is said to be eternal, the ruler over Israel, and that He will be born in a very specific location, Bethlehem Ephrathah. No one denies that Jesus Christ was born in Bethlehem Ephrathah, and none can logically deny that He claimed He was Israel's King and the eternal one (John 5:18; 8:58; Mark 14:60-63).

In Daniel 9:24-27, written 500 years before Christ is born, the Messiah is prophesied to be killed at the exact time Jesus Himself is put to death. (See note 2.)

In Zechariah 12:10, also written 500 years before Christ, it is prophesied that God Himself will be pierced by the inhabitants of Jerusalem, who will mourn over Him. The Hebrew word means pierced as with a spear, just as Jesus was pierced by the Roman spear during His crucifixion and had others mourn over Him (John 19:34-37). What is interesting about this prophecy is that God, as Spirit (John 4:24) cannot be physically pierced; hence this prophecy must refer to an incarnation of God.

If we look at the list of prophecies we discuss in our book, we see that Jesus Christ fulfilled all of them. Remember, no one can logically deny that the following are predictions made hundreds of years before He was even born. Whatever one's view of the Old Testament, one fact is unassailable: The Septuagint, the Greek translation of the entire Hebrew Scriptures, was completed by 247 B.C. Therefore, even critics must acknowledge these prophecies were in existence at least 250 years before Christ was born. Consider these prophecies:

Genesis 3:15—Jesus defeated Satan but was wounded during the crucifixion.

Genesis 12,17,22—He was the literal descendant of Abraham, Isaac, and Jacob in whom all the world was blessed.

Deuteronomy 18—He was the "prophet like Moses."

Psalm 22—He was mocked, insulted, and crucified. His garments were gambled for and His bones were not broken.

Psalm 110:1—He was David's Lord. (Jesus used this psalm to prove the Messiah would be both God and man, cf. Matthew 22:41-46.)

Isaiah 53—He was perfectly innocent and without sin, yet He atoned for the sin of the world. He was resurrected from the dead.

Jeremiah 23—Because He was God and "justified many," His proper name is "Jehovah our Righteousness."

Daniel 9—He arrived at the specific time given by the prophecy, 483 years after Artaxerxes' decree to rebuild Jerusalem.[3]

Micah 5—He was eternal, yet He was born in Bethlehem.

Zechariah 9—He was the King of Israel who brought salvation; He entered Jerusalem riding on a donkey.

Zechariah 12—He was Jehovah; He was pierced.

Malachi 3—John the Baptist prepared the way for Him as He suddenly came to His temple.

Had we space, there are dozens of other prophecies we could discuss that are just as specific. For example, the Bible tells us:

1. He would be born of a virgin (Isaiah 7:14; see Matthew 1:23).

2. He would live in Nazareth of Galilee (Isaiah 9:1-2; see Matthew 2:23; 4:15).

3. He would occasion the massacre of Bethlehem's children (Jeremiah 31:15; see Matthew 2:18).

4. His mission would include the Gentiles (Isaiah 42:1-3, 6; see Matthew 12:18-21).

5. His ministry would include delivering those captive and the performing of miracles (Isaiah 29:18-21; 35:5-6; 61:1-2; see Luke 4:16-21; 7:20-23).

6. He would be the Shepherd struck with the sword, resulting in the sheep being scattered (Zechariah 13:7; see Matthew 26:31, 56; Mark 14:27, 49-50).

7. He would be betrayed by a friend for 30 pieces of silver (Zechariah 11:12-13; see Matthew 27:9-10).

8. He would be given vinegar and gall to drink (Psalm 69:21; see Matthew 27:34).

9. He would be hated without a cause (Psalm 69:4; Isaiah 49:7; John 7:48; John 15:25).

10. He would be rejected by the rulers (Psalm 118:22; Matthew 21:42; John 7:48).

Who is the only Person who has fulfilled all of these prophecies—and many more?[4] Only Jesus Christ. There is no way to avoid this fact. Old Testament scholars Delitzsch and Gloag have rightly stated: "So far as we can determine, these prophecies refer to the Messiah only, and cannot be predicated of another. The ancient Jews admit the Messianic character of most of them; although the modern Jews, in consequence of their controversy with the Christians, have attempted to explain them away by applications which must appear to every candid reader to be unnatural... these and other predictions have received their accomplishment in Jesus of Nazareth... the combination of prophecies is sufficient to prove that Jesus is the Messiah..."[5]

In fact, as we show in chapter 11, the calculations of mathematical probability reveal these prophecies could have been fulfilled only in the manner they were through the power and omniscience of a sovereign God. The odds of any one man fulfilling just 48 of them are 1 in 10^{157}—infinitely beyond the limits of probability.[6]

Remember, in John 4:25-26 and Mark 14:61-64, Jesus Himself undeniably claimed He was the prophesied Messiah. In order to disprove this claim, one only need find a single prophecy (out of scores in the Old Testament) that proves Jesus was wrong. Because no one has yet done this, and because Jesus filled all of the prophecies relating to His incarnation, and because He resurrected from the dead, no one can logically deny that He was and is the prophesied Jewish Messiah.

Is Jesus really unique in all creation and all religious history? Has there never been another like Him?

> *"It is morally as bad not to care whether a thing is true or not, so long as it makes you feel good, as it is not to care how you got your money so long as you have got it."—Edwin Way Teale*

> *"Truth, like surgery, may hurt, but it cures."—Han Suyin*

The average non-Christian, and even many Christians, have little understanding of how unique Jesus really is. Messianic prophecy is only a small part of Jesus' uniqueness. In all the world and throughout all history, there has never been anyone like Him. There never can be. One only need to read His words and of His deeds to plainly see this.

Anyone who wishes can also read the world's greatest religious and philosophical literature—the *Analects* of Confucius, the *Koran* of Mohammed, the *Vedas* of the Hindus, the teachings of the Buddha, or of Taoism, Shinto, Zoroaster, or any of the great philosophers like Plato, Socrates, Wittgenstein, Aristotle, Descartes, Kant, Hume, Bacon—or any of the greatest scientific minds such as Einstein or Alfred North Whitehead. One who does this will realize that they pale in comparison to the words and deeds of Jesus. One could almost argue that all the literature of the world combined hardly matches the quality, character, uniqueness, and truth of the words of Jesus, because, compared to the words of Christ, the words of anyone else are almost lifeless. It is a chasm that somehow seems to separate the infinite from the finite, even as the words of God are separated from the words of men. In John 14:10 Jesus even declares that His *words* are the works of God (cf., John 6:63; 8:47; 12:48-50). If Jesus really *is* God incarnate, then this is what one expects. Listen to the response of those who actually heard Him speak and act, believer and unbeliever, friend and enemy, alike:

> "You have the words of eternal life. We believe and know that you are the Holy One of God." (John 6:67-69)

> The Jews were amazed and asked, "How did this man get such learning without having studied?" (John 7:15)

> "No one ever spoke the way this man does," the guards declared. (John 7:46)

> "The crowds were amazed at his teaching because he taught as one who had authority, and not as their teachers of the law." (Matthew 7:28-29)

Those with open and closed minds alike should frankly study His words and acts if for no other reason than to prove their uniqueness. Reverent study of the words and deeds of Christ and comparison to any or all other religious teachings or teachers should logically make one a follower of Jesus.

Probably tens of thousands of commentaries have been written about the words and deeds of Christ and should humanity survive millennia more, tens of thousands more will be written. That His words and deeds can never be exhausted is a testimony to their uniqueness.

In fact, when we look at the *person* of Jesus and compare Him to Buddha, Mohammed, Confucius, and others, it becomes difficult to even gauge the gap. It is like comparing the sun and the light bulb, the ocean and the glass of water, the universe and the atom. Even these comparisons seem somehow inadequate. Co-author John Weldon majored in philosophy in college for two years, has an M.A. degree in Christian Evidences, another master's in Biblical Studies, and a Ph.D. in Comparative Religion. Additionally, he has studied some 70 minor religions and cults. For 25 years he has examined or studied competing religions and philosophies. He asserts without the slightest possibility of ever being proven wrong that there is no one anywhere like Jesus; nothing comes close to the glory and majesty of Christ.

The Bible also teaches that there is no one who has ever lived who is like Jesus. In John 3:16-18, Jesus Himself declares:

> For God so loved the world that He gave His *one and only* Son, that whoever believes in Him shall not perish but have eternal life. For God did not send His Son into the world to condemn the world, but to save the world through Him. Whoever believes in Him is not condemned, but whoever does not believe stands condemned already because he has not believed in the name of God's *one and only* Son.

The words translated "one and only" are translated from the Greek *monogenes*, which literally means "one of a kind." This word emphasizes the unique nature of the one spoken of. In all human history there is no one else like Jesus because *only* Jesus is the literal Son of God. In John 5:18, where Jesus "was even calling God His [very] own Father," the Greek literally means that God the Father exists "in a special relation to Jesus which excludes the same relationship to others."[7]

Because Jesus Christ is God's only Son, the Apostle Paul discusses His supremacy and preeminence over all creation: "He [Jesus] is the *image* of the invisible God, the firstborn over all creation. For by Him all things were created: things in heaven and on earth, visible and invisible, whether thrones or powers or rulers or authority; all things were created by Him and for Him. He is before all things and in Him all things hold together. And He is the head of the body, the church; He is the beginning and the firstborn from among the dead, so that in everything He might have the supremacy" (Colossians 1:15-18).

The Greek word translated "image" is *eikon*. Like the word *charakter* in Hebrews 1:3, it mean Jesus "is the express image of " or "of identical nature with" God.[8] Further, when Jesus is described as the firstborn over all creation, the word translated "firstborn" is *prototokos* and stands in contrast to *ktizo* (created). By using the word *prototokos*, the Apostle Paul was emphasizing Christ's preeminence, priority, and sovereignty over all creation, as the context reveals. Paul was not stating, as Jehovah's Witnesses and some others have maintained, in the attempt to deny

Christ's deity, that Jesus literally came into existence at some point in time. If that had been His intent, He would have used appropriate Greek words teaching that Christ had a beginning.

If the Bible itself teaches that Christ is unique, that there never has been and never will be another like him; if Christ's own teachings, actions, character, and resurrection prove this is true, and if one-fourth to one-half of the world has recognized this fact to varying degrees, then the burden of proof must clearly rest with the critic to prove otherwise. Isn't it significant that in 2,000 years no critic ever has?

There are some other ways in which Jesus Christ is unique. First, we have already seen some of the amazing statements Jesus made that leave us few options as to His nature; He was either who He claimed, God incarnate, or absolutely crazy.

Jesus made many statements like the following which, upon reading, most people 2,000 years removed rarely understand the weight of. For example in John 14:7, Jesus says of God the Father, yet referring to Himself, "From now on you do know him and have seen him." Jesus' whole point is that the disciples have *seen* God the Father in *His* own person. Noted commentator William Barclay remarks, "It may well be that to the ancient world this was the most staggering thing that Jesus ever said. To the Greeks, God was characteristically *The Invisible.* The Jews would count it as an article of faith that no man has seen God at any time." As the biblical scholar Leon Morris remarks: "He is claiming something far, far greater than anyone else had claimed."[9]

Consider some of the other powerful statements made by Jesus. In Matthew 12:8 He claims He is actually the Lord of the Sabbath. In other words, if the Sabbath came from God and if He can overrule the laws of the Sabbath, He must be God. In Matthew 13:41 and 24:31 He claims that He, the Son of Man, will actually send out *His* angels at the final judgment of humanity. In Matthew 18:20 He declares He is omnipresent—present everywhere. In Matthew 24:35 He declares that the universe would pass away but His words *never* pass away. In John 5:28-30 He claims He will one day raise *all* the dead, that is, literally billions, perhaps trillions of people, *Himself.* In John 12:32 He says that when He is dead He will "draw all men to myself "! Surely, no other man ever made such statements. In John 15:26 He says He will *send* God the Holy Spirit. In John 18:36-37 He declares He is a king and that His kingdom is not from this world but "from another place." In Matthew 25:31-34 He declares He is, quite literally, the King of the universe.

Further, consider Jesus' use of the phrase *ego eimi*. In the Gospel of John alone, the phrase *ego eimi* ("I Am") is used 30 times when recording what Jesus said. What is significant is that, according to the Greek language, when you see the word *Am* you know the subject is *I;* this is not something that is immediately known in the English language, but it happens constantly in the Greek. For example, when Jesus says "I Am the bread of life," all He really needed to say was "Am the bread of life." But what *he* wanted to do was to emphasize the subject, so he used the pronoun. This emphasis upon "I Am" instead of just "Am" is unique. What did God name Himself to Moses in Exodus 3:14? "I Am who I Am." When Jesus made these statements He was deliberately using the personal name and style of God. Further, Griffith Thomas points out, "There is scarcely a passage in the gospels without a self-assertion of Jesus coming out in connection with His teaching. His message and His claims are really inextricable."[10] In other words, the only logical choice is to take all of Jesus or none of Him. To reject His claims is to reject His teachings is to reject Him.

Another unique aspect of Christ is His impact on the Roman world. It is a historic phenomenon that Jesus transformed the Roman empire and yet, by Roman standards, was a Jew, a despised Jew, a criminal Jew, and a crucified Jew. The fact that Jesus alone could begin a movement that within 300 years had literally converted the most powerful empire in the world is a miracle of history—especially since "the Jews among whom Jesus lived and died, were a strange, remote people, little understood and little liked by most Europeans of the time, more often the butt of Roman humor than of serious interest."[11] (So why should anyone be surprised that Jesus received such little attention in the Roman history books?) In spite of this, within three centuries the entire Roman empire had bowed the knee to Jesus.

Not by military conquest, as was true for Islam, but solely by preaching a message of God's love for mankind!

A further unique aspect of Jesus is that during His lifetime, He made predictions about the future that no one else would have dared to make unless they were God—and, in fact, no one else in history ever has made. With predictions like these it is impossible that, had even a few failed, the disciples could ever have trusted Jesus to be the Messiah, let alone God. The nature of these predictions are such that after the disciples heard the predictions they would have seen them proved false and *known* Jesus could not have been who He claimed.

For example, Jesus frequently told people that their friends or family had been healed, even at great distances. The Roman centurion's servant who lay at home paralyzed was "in terrible suffering." Jesus healed him immediately, "Then Jesus said to the centurion, 'Go! It will be done just as you believed it would.' And his servant was healed at that very hour" (Matthew 8:13). Concerning the Canaanite woman who begged Jesus to cure her daughter from demon possession, "Then Jesus answered, 'Woman, you have great faith! Your request is granted.' And her daughter was healed from that very hour" (Matthew 15:28). When Jesus was in Cana in Galilee a royal official's son lay dying at Capernaum. The official asked Jesus to heal his son and, "Jesus replied, 'You may go. Your son will live.' The man took Jesus at His word and departed. While he was still on the way, his servants met him with the news that his boy was living. When he inquired as to the time when his son got better, they said to him, 'The fever left him yesterday at the seventh hour.' Then the father realized that this was the *exact time* at which Jesus had said to him, 'Your son will live.' So he and all his household believed" (John 4:50-53).

If Jesus had never really healed these and hundreds of other individuals, everyone would have known it. It would have proved Jesus false. Instead, their accuracy is more evidence of His deity.

Jesus also predicted momentous things about His own future and things about others, both of great weight and little import. On many occasions He predicted His own trials before the authorities and His own suffering and death by crucifixion (e.g.,

Matthew 17:12). In Matthew 26:2 He accurately foretold His crucifixion would happen exactly two days later. He accurately predicted He would be betrayed in Jerusalem (by Judas, his own disciple), to Jewish leaders who would condemn Him to death, turn Him over the Gentiles who would mock, flog, and crucify Him. Yet He would be raised from the dead (Matthew 20:18-19; 26:21-25; Mark 10:33-34, cf., Matthew 12:4-7; 17:9). In Matthew 20:28 and 26:28, He predicted He would be dying for the sins of the world. In Matthew 24:4-44 He has the boldness to make numerous detailed predictions concerning the events surrounding His claimed return to earth at the end of history. Even before the Sanhedrin, under solemn oath, He declared He was the Messiah and that He would return again: "The high priest said to him, 'I charge you under oath by the living God: Tell us if you are the Christ, the Son of God.' 'Yes, it is as you say,' Jesus replied. 'But I say to all of you: In the future you will see the Son of Man sitting at the right hand of the Mighty One and coming on the clouds of heaven'" (Matthew 26:63-64).

In Matthew 26:56, Luke 4:21, and elsewhere He claimed to be the fulfillment of extremely specific prophecies. In Matthew 24:2 and Luke 19:41-44 and 21:6, He predicted the destruction of the massive Jewish temple in Jerusalem. Here He was predicting the military siege by the Roman commander Titus that was literally fulfilled forty years later. As the NIV study note for Matthew 24:2 comments concerning His prediction that not one stone of the temple would be left on top of the other, "Fulfilled literally in A.D. 70, when the Romans under Titus completely destroyed Jerusalem and the temple buildings. Stones were even pried apart to collect the gold leaf that melted from the roof when the temple was set on fire. . . . Excavations in 1968 uncovered large numbers of these stones, toppled from the walls by the invaders."

Consider His prediction to His own disciples. In Matthew 17:24-27, to pay the Roman taxes, He told Peter to go to the lake, take the first fish caught, open its mouth, and there, in the fish's mouth, Peter would find a four drachma coin, the exact tax amount required! What do you think Peter, a fisherman, thought of this?

Despite their protests, He predicted in Matthew 26:31 and Mark 14:27 that *all* the disciples would forsake Him. In Matthew 26:34, despite Peter's staunch protests, He predicted Peter would disown Him three times. In Luke 5:4-7 He predicted to Peter that a great amount of fish would be caught after an entire night of not catching even a single fish. In Luke 10:17-20 Jesus promised the disciples that He had given them power over demons and, elsewhere, promised them that they could perform miracles in His name. Is there anyone who thinks that the disciples could not easily have determined such claims were false? Either they could do these things or they couldn't. And obviously, they couldn't do them before they met Jesus.

In John 20:27, *after* Jesus had died, we have the account of Thomas placing his hand into Jesus' sword wound and his fingers into Jesus' crucifixion wounds. Does anyone think that Thomas wouldn't have denied this claim far and wide if it were false?

In John 11:3, 11-14 Jesus predicted Lazarus' death and resurrection four days before it occurred! We are told in verses 18-19 and 45-46 that *many* believers *and* unbelievers saw Lazarus come back from the dead and saw the grave clothes unwrapped from him. How easy it would be for something like this to be proven wrong and for the word to get out that the foolish Jesus *tried* to raise the dead but couldn't. But no one could deny that these things really happened (see John 12:17-19).

Does anyone think that the account of Jesus raising Lazarus and other people from the dead would not have been denied far and wide if these things never really happened and the apostles had reported them falsely? But again, even the Jewish leaders who were Jesus' enemies couldn't deny them:

> Therefore many of the Jews who had come to visit Mary, and had seen what Jesus did, put their faith in him. But some of them went to the Pharisees and told them what Jesus had done. Then the chief priests and the Pharisees called a meeting of the Sanhedrin. "What are we accomplishing?" they asked. "Here is this man performing many miraculous signs. If we let him go on like this, everyone will believe in him, and then the Romans will come and take away both our place and our nation" (John 11:45-48).

In John 21:5-6, after Jesus had risen from the dead, we read, "He called out to them, 'Friends, haven't you any fish?' 'No,' they answered. He said, 'Throw your net on the right side of the boat and you will find some.' When they did, they were unable to haul the net in because of the large number of fish" (John 21:5-6). Again, the disciples had not caught a single fish all night (verse 3). Jesus does the same miracle after His death and resurrection that He did when He was alive. What could be more convincing as to Jesus' resurrection and deity to a group of fishermen?

In John 10:11-18 and 16:16-20, 32, He gives very specific information concerning His death and resurrection and what will flow from it. And in John 7:33, 8:21, and elsewhere He tells the Jews that they will try to find His body but will be unable to do so, for example, "Jesus said, 'I am with you for only a short time, and then I go to the one who sent me. You will look for me, but you will not find me...'" (John 7:33). And in John 8:21, "Once more Jesus said to them, 'I am going away, and you will look for me...'" Obviously they would look for His body in an attempt to disprove the disciples' claims that Jesus had resurrected from the dead. And just as obviously, they never found it.

Now the point of all this is to give some sense of how easy it would have been for Jesus to have been proven wrong on many different occasions. "He predicted something here, but it never happened." "He tried to do a miracle there but couldn't." Why would anyone write all the things we find in the Gospels, miracle after miracle after miracle, if they were obviously false and could so easily be proven false by talking to the crowds who followed Jesus? These things either happened or they didn't. If they happened, Jesus is who He claimed to be. If they didn't, we would have known it once and for all 2,000 years ago.

Finally, if we look at the other miracles of Jesus we also see how utterly unique He was. The chart on page 1596 of the NIV study Bible lists Jesus' miracles and their reporting in the different gospels: He healed a man with leprosy, Peter's mother-in-law, the Roman Centurion's servant, two men from Gadara, a paralyzed man, a woman with bleeding, two blind men, a man mute and possessed, a man with a shriveled hand, and a man blind, mute, and possessed. He healed a Canaanite woman's daughter who suffered greatly, a boy with a demon, two other blind men (one named), a deaf mute, a man possessed in the synagogue, a blind man at Bethsaida, a crippled woman, a man with dropsy, ten men with leprosy, the high priest's servant, the official's son at Capernaum, the sick man at the pool of Bethesda, and a man born blind. He had complete control over the forces of nature. He calmed storms, walked on water, and fed 5,000 people here, and 4,000 people there from just a few loaves and fish. He withered a fig tree, turned water into wine, and produced miraculous catches of fish. He even brought the dead back to life including Jairus's daughter, the widow's son at Nain, and Lazarus. And, as the Apostle John emphasizes, those were only a few of Christ's miracles (John 21:25).

Is there anyone else in human history who did miracles like this? Again, if Jesus never did these miracles and yet the early apostles and Christians falsely claimed He did, don't you think everybody would have known the claims were false since all the miracles were claimed to have been done publicly, often with large crowds around? When Jesus Himself claimed that the miracles proved Him to be God and Messiah, don't you think this would have proven Him a fraud had they never really occurred? To those who skeptically asked if He was the Messiah, "Jesus answered, 'I did tell you, but you do not believe. The miracles I do in my Father's name speak for me...'" and "Jesus said, 'I have shown you many great miracles...For which of these do you stone me?'" and "Do not believe me unless I do what my Father does. But if I do it, even though you do not believe me, believe the miracles, that you may know and understand that the Father is in me, and I in the Father" and "Believe me when I say that I am in the Father and the Father is in me; or at least believe on the evidence of the miracles themselves" and "If I had not done among them what no one else did, they would not be guilty of sin. But now they have seen these miracles, and yet they have hated both me and my Father" (John 10:25, 31-32, 36-38; 14:11; 15:24).

The truth is that Jesus hasn't left us any choice.

What about the founders of other world religions?

"The truth is always the strongest argument."
—*Sophocles*

When we consider all the great religious teachers, leaders, and prophets who have ever lived, who is the equal of Jesus? Not Moses, Confucius, Buddha, or Lao Tse (Taoism), who never claimed to be anything other than sinful men. Not Mohammed, Joseph Smith, Zoroaster, or Guru Nanak (Sikhism), who never gave any evidence they were true prophets of God. Not Brahma, Vishnu, Shiva, or Krishna, who were only mythical deities. Not Mahavira (Jainism), the leaders of Sufism (e.g., Jalal-ud-Din Rumi), or the founder of any other religion the world has known has ever been like Jesus. Neither animism, Buddhism, Confucianism, Hinduism, Islam, Jainism, Judaism, Mormonism, Shintoism, Sikhism, Sufism, Taoism, Zoroastrianism, or any other religious belief outside Christianity has anything that can even be slightly compared to Jesus. With the psalmist we can only respond, "My whole being will exclaim, 'Who is like you, O LORD?'" (Psalm 35:10 NIV).

Thus, if we examine the specific claims of the founders of the great religions, we find none of them claims what Jesus does. In *The Koran* the Muslim prophet Mohammed states, "Muhammad is naught but a messenger" and "Surely I am no more than a human apostle."[12] In fact, several times in *The Koran*, Mohammed is acknowledged as sinful, asks forgiveness from God, or is even rebuked by God.[13]

If Mohammed confessed he was sinful, Jesus claimed He was sinless. If Mohammed only claimed to be a prophet of God, Jesus claimed to be God. If Mohammed was rebuked by God, Jesus was never rebuked by God; in fact, He said, "I always do what pleases Him" (John 8:29).

Consider the Buddha as a more in-depth illustration. The Buddha simply claimed to be an "enlightened" man, one who could show others how to escape the futility of this world and find eternal release from suffering in a state of individual nonexistence called "nirvana." After his alleged enlightenment, the Buddha said he realized the importance of maintaining an attitude of equanimity toward all things because this attitude helps one to end the cycle of rebirth, attain permanent release from the human condition, and "enter" nirvana: "Monks, I'm a Brahmana [enlightened being], one to ask a favor of, ever clean-handed, wearing my last body. I am inexorable, bear no love nor hatred toward anyone. I have the same feelings for respectable people as for the low; or moral persons as for the immoral; for the depraved as for those who observe the rules of good conduct. You disciples, do not affirm that the Lord Buddha reflects thus within himself, 'I bring salvation to every living being.' *Subhuti* entertain no such delusive thought! Because in reality there are no living beings to whom the Lord Buddha can bring salvation."[14]

Noted professor of religion Houston Smith in *The Religions of Man* comments about the Buddha, "Notwithstanding his own objectivity toward himself, there was constant pressure during his lifetime to turn him into a god. He rebuffed all these categorically, insisting that he was human in every respect. He made no attempt to conceal his temptations and weaknesses, how difficult it had been to attain enlightenment, how narrow the margin by which he had won through, how fallible he still remained."[15]

Clive Erricker, a lecturer and prolific writer in the field of religious studies with a special interest in Buddhism, writes of the Buddha in *Buddhism*, "Indeed, he did not even claim that his teachings were a unique and original source of wisdom... [citing John Bowker in *Worlds of Faith*, 1983]. Buddha always said, 'Don't take what I'm saying [i.e., on my own authority], just try to analyze as far as possible and see whether what I'm saying makes sense or not. If it doesn't make sense, discard it. If it does make sense, then pick it up.'"[16]

If Buddha claimed merely a personal enlightenment designed to escape human nature, Jesus claimed (in His *own* nature) to *be* the Light of the world. If Buddha claimed it was wrong to consider him one who brings salvation to men because men, having no permanent reality, do not finally exist, Jesus taught that He came to bring salvation to all men and to dignify their existence eternally. If the Buddha promised to give others "enlightenment" so that they might find nirvana, a state of personal dissolution in the afterlife, Jesus promised to give men abundant life and eternal personal immortality in heaven. If Buddha had the *same* feelings for good and evil, Jesus exalted righteousness and hated evil.

Confucius said, "As to being a Divine Sage or even a Good Man, far be it for me to make any such claim."[17] If Confucius denied that he was divine or even a good man, Jesus claimed He was divine and morally perfect.

We can proceed to examine all the world's major religions in detail and never find anyone like Jesus. Zoroaster only claimed to be a prophet, "I was ordained by Thee at the first. All others I look upon with hatred of spirit."[18] Lao-tze and Guru Nanak sum up the attitude, at one time or another, of all the great religious founders when they confessed their humanity and even their ignorance. For example, Lao-tze the founder of Taoism said, "I alone appear empty. Ignorant am I, O so ignorant! I am dull! I alone am confused, so confused!"[19] Even in the latter part of his life, Guru Nanak, the founder of Sikhism, still struggled to achieve enlightenment and lamented over his own spiritual darkness: "I have become perplexed in my search. In the darkness I find no way. Devoted to pride, I weep in sorrow. How shall deliverance be obtained?"[20]

In *The World's Living Religions,* Professor of the History of Religions Robert Hume comments that there are three features of Christian faith that "cannot be paralleled anywhere among the religions of the world."[21] These include the character of God as a loving heavenly Father, the character of the founder of Christianity as the Son of God, and the work of the Holy Spirit. Further, "All of the nine founders of religion, with the exception of Jesus Christ, are reported in their respective sacred scriptures as having passed through a preliminary period of uncertainty, or of searching for religious light. All the founders of the non-Christian religions evinced inconsistencies in their personal character; some of them altered their practical policies under change of circumstances. Jesus Christ alone is reported as having had a consistent God-consciousness, a consistent character himself, and a consistent program for his religion."[22]

If the claims of men mean anything, or have any implications, and certainly they must, whether true or false, then no one else in history ever claimed and did what Jesus did. He says, "I am the light of the world. Whoever follows me will never walk in darkness, but will have the light of life" (John 8:12). How many other men have ever said that? Jesus claimed, "I am the way, the truth and the life. No one comes to the Father except through Me" (John 14:6). How many other men have ever claimed that? As we saw, Jesus even claimed that 1,500 years before His birth, Moses wrote about Him, and further that the entire Old Testament bore witness to Him (John 5:46-47; Luke 24:27, 44).

Jesus commanded men to love Him in exactly same way that they love God—with all their heart, soul, and mind (Matthew 22:37-38). Jesus said that God the Holy Spirit would bear witness of Him and glorify Him (John 16:14). Who ever made such a claim? Jesus said that to know Him was to know God (John 14:7). To receive Him was to receive God (Matthew 10:40). To honor Him was to honor God (John 5:23). To believe in Him was to believe in God (John 12:44-45; 14:1). To see Him was to see God (John 8:19; 14:7). To deny Him was to deny God (1 John 2:23). To hate Him was to hate God (John 15:23). Did any other religious founders in history ever make such statements?

In Mark 2, Jesus claimed He could forgive sins—something all religions concede is reserved to God alone. In John 10:28 and 11:25, He said He could give all who believed in Him eternal life. How can a mere man, indeed anyone less than God, give eternal life to creatures who die? Yet Jesus raised the dead even in front of His enemies—not in some dark alley, but before scores of eyewitnesses (Luke 7:11-15; 8:41-42, 49-56; John 11:43-44). Who ever did that?

He did other miracles that amazed those who saw them:

"Nobody has ever heard of opening the eyes of a man born blind." (John 9:32)

"We have never seen anything like this!" (Mark 2:12)

In Matthew 25, Jesus said that He would actually return at the end of the world and that He Himself would judge every person who ever lived; that He would personally raise all the dead of history and that all the nations would be gathered before Him. He would sit on His throne of glory and judge and separate men from one another as a shepherd does the sheep from the goats (Matthew 25:31-46, cf. John 5:25-34). Just as clearly, Jesus taught that every person's eternal destiny depended upon how they treated Him (John 8:24; Matthew 10:32). Who has ever made such claims? All these statements and many more like them, leave us little choice. Either Jesus was who He said He was—God incarnate—or else He was absolutely crazy. But who can believe *that*?

Was Jesus Christ virgin born and sinless?

"Before they came together, she was found to be with child through the Holy Spirit." —Matthew 1:18

Many people today scoff at the idea of Jesus' virgin birth. But the virgin birth of Christ is one of the most crucial doctrines of Christianity. In fact, if Jesus were *not* virgin born, there would be no Christianity. Why? First, if Jesus is not virgin born, then He was born just like every other man. This would prove He was *only* a man. But if so, then His claim to be God was a lie and He was self-deceived. In other words, if He was only a man, He could never be the incarnation of God, as He claimed.

Further, if Christ was not virgin born, neither could He have been the Savior of the world. As a man, He would have inherited a sinful nature from His parents. But if He Himself were sinful, He could not have been an atoning sacrifice for the sins of the whole world (1 John 2:2). If He were only a man, how could His sacrifice on the cross, the sacrifice of a mere finite being, satisfy the infinite justice of a holy God offended by human sin and evil? Only if Christ was both sinless man and fully deity could He properly serve as the atoning sacrifice for the world's sins in the face of an infinitely holy God. Therefore, the virgin birth not only undergirds the doctrine of Christ's deity, it also undergirds the doctrine of Christ's sinlessness and His role as the world's Savior. This is why the virgin birth of Christ is an absolutely essential doctrine.

But does the Bible clearly teach that Jesus was born of a virgin? Yes. In Isaiah 7:14, written 700 years before Christ was born, it prophesies, "Therefore the Lord Himself will give you a sign: The virgin will be with child and give birth to a son, and will call him Immanuel." The word *Immanuel* means "God with us." When Matthew describes the birth of Christ from the Virgin Mary, he declares this prophecy of Isaiah was fulfilled in Jesus, "All this took place to fulfill what the Lord has said through the prophet [Isaiah]: The virgin *[parthenos]* will be with child and will give birth to a son, and they will call Him 'Immanuel'— which means, 'God with us'" (Matthew 1:22,23). The Greek word *parthenos* has only one meaning: virgin.

Because Jesus was virgin born, He was also sinless. He even challenged His own enemies to prove otherwise—"Can any of you prove me guilty of sin?" He asked (John 8:46). In John 7:18 Jesus said, "He who speaks on his own does so to gain honor for himself, but he who works for the honor of the one who sent him is a man of truth; there is nothing false about him." The apostles who lived intimately with Jesus for three years were able to examine His life in critical detail. Their unanimous confession was that Jesus was sinless. The Apostle Peter said He was "one who committed no sin" (1 Peter 1:19). The Apostle John said, "And in Him is no sin" (1 John 3:5). Even the former skeptic, the Apostle Paul, said of Jesus, "He knew no sin" (2 Corinthians 5:21). The author of Hebrews said that Jesus was "holy, blameless, pure, set apart from sinners" as well as "one who has been tempted in every way, just as we are—yet without sin" (Hebrews 4:15; 7:26). The Roman governor Pilate, after examining Jesus, said he could find no fault in Him (John 18:38; Matthew 27:23-5; Luke 23:13). Herod concluded the same (Luke 23:13-15). Even Judas, who betrayed Him, confessed, "I have sinned in betraying innocent blood" (Matthew 27:4).

No one can logically deny reliable eyewitness testimony and other evidence that shows Jesus is the only perfect and sinless man who ever lived. But to be without sin means one is *incapable* of lying or deceiving others. This means Jesus was incapable of having any kind of unethical attitude or act. Nor could He have any ersatz philosophical bias because He could always, only, proclaim the truth. If Jesus *was* sinless, then logically, what He said about Himself *must* be true. And if He was perfect and sinless, shouldn't we assume that what He has to say is important to us, regardless of what we may now think about Him?

Is Jesus Christ really God? Is He the only incarnation of God there is or will be?

"The high-minded man must care more for the truth than for what people think."—Aristotle

In what other religion in the world do we find an incarnation like that of Jesus—or even an incarnation at all? At best, there is the idolatrous religion of Jainism which claims, unconvincingly, an incarnation (from a polytheistic heaven) of its god and founder, Mahavira. But, in fact, Mahavira himself denied theism and condemned the practice of praying to or even having discussions about God. The only other conceivable shadow of the biblical concept of incarnation is found in Hinduism, but here the incarnations are of mythical gods, forever cyclical, and just as forever meaningless. According to the influential *advaita* school of Vedanta, the Hindu gods' incarnations are, finally, also part of the duality and *maya* (illusion) of the world and thus never redemptive in the sense of a true propitiatory atonement. There is no concept of incarnation in Buddhist belief unless we consider the later Mahayanists belief in an alleged Buddha nature, supposedly inherent in all men, to be an "incarnation" of a mythically deified Buddha. Judaism has no incarnation; in Judaism the idea of Jesus as the incarnate Son of God is adamantly rejected. Taoism has only an impersonal principle, the Tao, as an ultimate reality and no need or place for an incarnation. In Sikhism, Guru Nanak taught that God is unborn and non-incarnated; in Parsism (Zoroastrianism) the god Ahura Mazda is not incarnated; and in Islam the thought of an incarnation is blasphemous. In Confucianism, Confucius acknowledged himself as only a sinful man. Although he was later worshipped, he was never incarnate. Of the 11 or 12 classical world religions, there is no concept of incarnation except in Jainism and Hinduism, and both of these involve only myths.

In the words of G. K. Chesterton in *The Everlasting Man*, the incarnation of Christ "makes nothing but dust and nonsense of comparative religion."[23] Thus, Chesterton was right when he asserted that only the Apostles have good news for the rest of the world: "Nobody else except those messengers has any Gospel; nobody else has any good news, for the simple reason that nobody else has any news."[24]

This *is* the gospel, the good news—that we can know God. The Creator of the universe is, obviously, worth getting to know. As J. I. Packer states, "Knowing God! Is there any greater theme to study? Is there any nobler goal to aim at? Is there any greater good to enjoy? Is there any deeper longing in the human heart than the desire to know God? Surely not. And Christianity's good news is that it can happen! That is why the Christian message is a word for the world. To know God is the biggest and best of the blessings promised in the gospel."[25]

If the incarnation is true, then men can know God. Jesus Himself declared, "This is eternal life, to know Thee, the only true God, and Jesus Christ whom thou hast sent" (John 17:3, NASB). Further, if the incarnation is true, men have no other option than to know Christ and accept His claims on their life. People cannot refuse the claims of God on their life and think it will never matter. If Jesus is the only incarnation of God ever to appear, He absolutely must be listened to (cf. John 3:16, 18; 10:1-13, 25-30).

Adherents of other religions often claim that their religious founders are unique, but the uniqueness is either invented or contrived. Where is the proof of uniqueness? There is none because the founders of other religions all acknowledge themselves as sinful men, despite the subsequent worship or deification not infrequently given them by their followers. "Certainly one might at least ask whether or not such embellishment is fair. Is it expressing adequate reverence for one's own religious founder to make him into something he never claimed to be, and, indeed, would probably be horrified to learn of?"[26]

Because Jesus Himself so clearly and uniquely proved that He was God incarnate, the authors of the New Testament writings frequently stressed this unparalleled assertion. First, Jesus clearly claimed to be God. In John 10:30, he said, "I and the Father are one." The word *one* in the Greek *(hen)*, according to Greek authority A. T. Robertson, means not just one in the sense of agreement, but that Jesus was saying He and God are "one essence or nature."[27] Second, Jesus' claim to be God was understood by all men, including His enemies. Jesus said, "I showed you many good works from the Father; for which of them are you stoning me?" (John 10:32). The response of His enemies was, "because you, being a man, make yourself out to be God" (John 10:33). In John 8:58, Jesus said, "Before Abraham was born, *I am.*" Jesus was referring to Exodus 3:13-14 where God identified Himself as the "I am." As we saw, Jesus applied the unique divine name to Himself, not only on this occasion but many others. That His hearers understood His claim to be God is evident when they again tried to stone Him to death (John 8:59). His continual identification of Himself with God and His ascribing to Himself divine prerogatives and attributes leave us little choice. Jesus clearly claimed He was the God of the universe: "'My Father is always at his work to this very day, and I, too, am working.' For this reason the Jews tried all the harder to kill him; not only was he breaking the Sabbath, but he was even calling God his own Father, making himself equal with God" (John 5:17-18). Jesus, the perfect man, was the incarnation of God.

Is Jesus Christ the world's only proven Savior who died for our sins on the cross and who offers eternal salvation as an entirely free gift?

> *"Jesus Christ is the centre of all, and the goal toward which all tends." —Blaise Pascal*

In spite of the many claims by people today that there are many "saviors," many "gurus," and many paths to God, Christianity teaches that Jesus alone is the way to God. Why? First, because Jesus Himself taught that only He was the way to God. He declared, "I am the way, the truth and the life, *no man* comes unto the Father but by *me*" (John 14:6). He emphasized, "I tell you the truth, *I am* the gate for the sheep. . . . *I am* the gate; whoever enters through *me* will be saved. . . . I have come that they may have life, and have it to the full. I am the good shepherd. The good shepherd lays down his life for the sheep" (John 10:7-11).

Second, Jesus clearly claimed that He was an atoning sacrifice for the world's sin when He said, "the Son of Man did not come to be served, but to serve, and to give his life as a ransom for many" (Matthew 20:28) and "This is my blood of the covenant, which is poured out for many for the forgiveness of sins" (Matthew 26:28). Because Jesus is the only incarnation of God, His only begotten Son, when Christ died on the cross for human sin, He became the only possible way of salvation for men and women. In other words, no one else paid the penalty of divine justice against human sin. This is why the Bible teaches, "Salvation is found in *no one else*, for there is *no other name under heaven* given to men by which we must be saved" (Acts 4:12). Further, "This is good, and pleases God our Savior, who wants all men to be saved and come to a knowledge of the truth. For there is one God and *one* mediator between God and man, the man Christ Jesus, who gave Himself as a ransom for all men—the testimony given in its proper time" (1 Timothy 2:3-6). Perhaps all this is why Jesus Himself warned, "if you do not believe that I am the one I claim to be, you will indeed die in your sins" (John 8:24).

In addition, Christ offers a salvation unlike that in any other religion. Forgiveness of sins and eternal life are *freely* given without cost to the benefactor. Indeed, Jesus claimed that He would personally raise all the dead and give eternal life to those who had believed on Him:

> For my Father's will is that everyone who looks to the Son and believes in him shall have eternal life, and *I will raise him up at the last day.* (John 6:40)

> For just as the Father raises the dead and gives them life, *even so* the Son gives life to whom he is pleased to give it. (John 5:21)

> I tell you the truth, whoever hears my word and believes him who sent me *has eternal life and will not be condemned;* he has crossed over *from death* to *life.* (John 5:24)

> I tell you the truth, he who believes *has everlasting life.* (John 6:47)

> This righteousness from God comes through faith in Jesus Christ to *all who believe.* There is no difference, for all have

sinned and fall short of the glory of God and are justified *freely by his grace* through redemption that came by Christ Jesus. (Romans 3:22-24)

He saved us, not because of righteous things we had done, but because of *his mercy.* (Titus 3:5)

In the history of mankind, nothing like this has ever been proclaimed outside biblical Christianity. As Martin Luther once correctly noted, there are finally only two religions in the world: the religion of works and the religion of grace. Only biblical Christianity is a religion of grace, because only biblical Christianity is a revelation from God.

Some people may find it difficult to believe that among the different world religions, Christ alone is the way to God, and that men must believe in Him for salvation if they are to be saved. But if Jesus was correct when He said, "All authority in heaven and on earth has been given to me" (Matthew 28:18), then no other option remains. It's not a matter of what we might personally wish to believe; it's a matter of what is true. Even a relatively brief examination of what other religions teach indicates the necessity for such a conclusion. In *Knowing the Truth About Salvation—Is Jesus Christ the Only Way to God?* we discuss this issue in more detail. We show that this exclusivism is not as difficult a concept as it seems at first glance, nor is it at odds with our general experience in life. Usually, for success in any endeavor, the important things in life must be done properly—especially if there are consequences for doing things wrong. Jesus is the only way to God, whether we like it or not.

Did Jesus Christ actually rise from the dead?

> *"He who does not bellow the truth when he knows the truth makes himself the accomplice of liars and forgers."*—Charles Peguy

If Jesus really is the only man in the history of the world to rise from the dead, then who can ignore Him? How do we know Jesus rose from the dead? No other credible alternative exists, as we will see in chapters five through eight. In these chapters we will examine the testimony of both former skeptics and leading lawyers throughout history and today. *All* concluded that the evidence for the truth of Christianity and its view of Jesus and His resurrection was compelling. The formerly committed skeptics abandoned their skepticism and embraced Christ as their risen Lord and Savior—no mean testimony. The lawyers unanimously declared the evidence for Jesus' resurrection would stand cross-examination, even in a modern court of law. Men of skepticism and intellectual caliber as those cited simply do not believe in Christianity apart from sufficient evidence. So whether one is a Christian or not, given the claims of Christ and the historical reality of His resurrection, one cannot logically maintain that Christ is irrelevant to one's life. Indeed, if Christ truly rose physically from the dead, it means that a free gift of eternal life is available to anyone who asks for it.

So how do we know He rose from the dead? On numerous occasions Jesus predicted His own crucifixion, down to the very day (Matthew 26:2). He also predicted His subsequent resurrection three days later (Matthew 17:22-23; Mark 8:31; Luke 18:31-33; John 2:19,22). Before any of the events had occurred, Jesus made no less than ten specific predictions about His death and resurrection, all of which came true.[28]

Even critics agree Jesus was crucified and died at Roman hands and that the location of His tomb was public knowledge. Nor can anyone logically deny that a one- to two-ton stone was rolled over the face of the grave, or that a trained military guard was set at the grave to prevent anyone from stealing the body. And even critics agree the tomb was found empty Sunday morning. Further, no theory to explain this fact has ever proved satisfactory except the Christian one. In part this is because of the numerous resurrection appearances of Christ after His death. He appeared to many different people—to disciples who did not believe it at first, to a crowd of 500, to selected individuals. He appeared to them in many different ways, locations, and circumstances. These appearances eventually compelled belief, as the accounts reveal.

It doesn't take a rocket scientist to conclude that if Christ had died (and everyone agreed He did) and if He was seen alive by large numbers of credible eyewitnesses (and this cannot reasonably be doubted), then the Christian view of the resurrection is established. The very existence of the Christian religion is, literally, historic proof of the resurrection. Why? Because, as we will see in Chapter 5, apart from the resurrection, the Christian religion could never have begun.

Is Jesus the final judge: The One who will personally and visibly return to earth and judge every person who has ever lived on the Last Day?

> *"The modern world, because it is indifferent to dogmatic truth, has logically become indifferent to ethical truth."—Bertrand L. Conway*

> *"Pure truth, like pure gold, has been found unfit for circulation, because men have discovered that it is far more convenient to adulterate the truth than to refine themselves."—Charles Caleb Colton*

No man can claim to determine the eternal destiny of his fellow creatures, but this is just what Jesus claims. Because Jesus is God and because He was the very one who died for the world's sin, He is also the one who will judge each man and woman who has ever lived and make the final determination of each one's destiny:

> Moreover, the Father judges no one, but has entrusted all judgment to the Son, that all may honor the Son just as they honor the Father. He who does not honor the Son does not honor the Father who sent Him. I tell you the truth, whoever hears my Word and believes Him who sent Me has eternal life and will not be condemned; he has crossed over from death to life. I tell you the truth, a time is coming and has now come when the dead will hear the voice of the Son of God and those who hear will live. Do not be amazed at this, for a time is coming when all who are in their graves will hear His voice and come out—those who have done good will rise to live, and those who have done evil will rise to be condemned. (John 5:21-29)

Jesus also taught:

> When the Son of Man comes in His glory, and all the angels with Him, He will sit on His throne in heavenly glory. All

the nations will be gathered before Him, and He will separate the people one from another as a shepherd separates
the sheep from the goats. He will put the sheep on His
right and goats on His left. Then the King will say to those
on His right, "Come, you who are blessed by my Father;
take your inheritance, the kingdom prepared for you since
the creation of the world...." Then He will say to those on
his left, "Depart from me, you who are cursed, into the
eternal fire prepared for the devil and his angels."... Then
they will go away to eternal punishment, but the righteous
to eternal life." (Matthew 25:31-34, 41, 46)

These teachings of Jesus are why the New Testament emphasizes the fact that Christ will judge the entire world. The Apostle
Paul referred to his living "In the presence of God and of Christ
Jesus, who will judge the living and the dead..." (2 Timothy
4:1). The Apostle Peter emphasized that God "commanded us
to preach to the people and to testify that He [Jesus] is the One
who God appointed as judge of the living and the dead" (Acts
10:42). Indeed, God promises each of us that the *proof* of coming
judgment can be found in Christ's resurrection. In other words,
the future judgment is just as certain as Christ's own resurrection: "In the past God overlooked such ignorance, but now he
commands all people everywhere to repent. For he has set a day
when he will judge the world with justice by the man he has
appointed. He has given *proof* of this to *all men* by raising him
from the dead" (Acts 17:30-31). Indeed, the Bible has warned
everyone:

We must pay more careful attention, therefore, to what we
have heard, so that we do not drift away. For if the message
spoken by angels was binding, and every violation and dis-
obedience received its just punishment, how shall we
escape if we ignore such a great salvation? This salvation,
which was first announced by the Lord, was confirmed to us
by those who heard him. God also testified to it by signs,
wonders and various miracles, and gifts of the Holy Spirit
distributed according to his will.... Nothing in all creation
is hidden from God's sight. Everything is uncovered and
laid bare before the eyes of him to whom we must give
account. (Hebrews. 2:1-4; 4:13)

In light of this, perhaps non-Christians should reconsider the "win-win wager" of the brilliant Christian philosopher Blaise Pascal: If the Christian God does not exist, then because of its positive teachings, the Christian loses nothing by believing in God; but if God does exist and he believes, he gains everything in eternal life.

Of course, if God exists and the non-Christian rejects Him, then everything is forfeited in an eternal hell. There will be nothing worse for the unbeliever if Christianity turns out to be true. As Jesus warned, "What good will it be for a man if he gains the whole world, yet forfeits his soul? Or what can a man give in exchange for his soul?" (Matthew 16:26-27)

In our next chapter we will offer a final illustration of why Jesus Christ does not leave us any option other than making Him our Lord and Savior. Before doing that let us summarize a few key points and offer our conclusion:

1. Is Jesus unique when compared to anyone else?

2. Did He establish His claim to be the prophesied Jewish Messiah and God incarnate?

3. Did He physically resurrect from the dead?

4. Have a large number of former skeptics and those expertly trained in evaluating truth claims and the quality of evidence declared He did?[29]

The answer to these questions is an undeniable *yes.*

If Jesus is God incarnate, utterly unique, and rose from the dead as proof of His claims, then who is there who believes they will escape a personal appointment with Him after death? At that moment, each of us will either face Him as Savior or Judge. It's not an issue of what anyone *thinks,* it's entirely an issue of who Jesus *is.*

To establish their counterclaims, skeptics (or higher critics that run theological lotteries like the so-called "Jesus Seminar") have to provide real evidence in support of their beliefs, not just conjecture, biased opinions, or foolishness. One can only wonder why it is that in 2,000 years some of the best minds humanity can muster have never been able to prove their skeptical theories,

or seem to offer a convincing defense of them. For example, the
alternate theories put forth to explain away the resurrection, despite their cleverness, constitute, quite literally, nonsense. The
problem is not that arguments against Christianity never seem
convincing initially, it's that they aren't convincing at all when
examined in light of the contrary evidence. In fact, trial lawyer
and theologian Dr. John Warwick Montgomery's comments on
higher criticism generally could equally be applied to skeptical
theories at large: "I have pointed out again and again that such
'assured results' are non-existent, that redaction criticism, documentary criticism, and historical-critical methods have been
weighed in the balance of *secular* scholarship and found wanting,
and that the burden of proof remains on those who want to justify these subjectivistic methods, not on those who take historical documents at face value when their primary-source character
can be established by objective determination of authorship and
date."[30]

Jesus Christ claimed to be God, and the facts support Him. In
our next chapter we will show why even critics of Christianity, if
they are fair with the evidence and allow logic its due, have little
choice other than to conclude that Jesus is God.

Chapter 4

Could Christ Be
Who He Claimed?

*"Truth is tough. It will not break, like a bubble, at
a touch; nay, you may kick it about all day like a
football, and it will be round and full at evening."*
—Oliver Wendell Holmes, Sr.

There are only four logical choices we have concerning Jesus Christ. As we examine the following material, the reader should decide for himself the one option *most* likely to be true:

1. Jesus Christ was a liar and deceiver.

2. He was insane, mentally ill, or a lunatic.

3. He was only a legend fabricated by the disciples.

4. Jesus Christ was and is who He claimed to be—incarnate Lord and God.

As we proceed to examine these four options, we shall demonstrate that the fourth alternative is the only one that a thinking person can logically arrive at.

Was Jesus Being Purposely Deceptive?

As far as we know, hardly anyone of sound mind has seriously maintained that Christ was a liar and deceiver, even among the most fanatical atheists. Jesus' ethical teachings are the highest mankind has and His personal moral character was above reproach. Even His enemies could not convict Him of sin, dishonesty, or deceit.

It is morally impossible that someone of the highest ethical character would knowingly deceive people concerning the most vital aspect of his teaching—his own identity. Even the great nineteenth-century British historian, W. E. H. Lecky, a committed opponent of organized Christianity, wrote the following sentiments about Jesus, which have been repeated many times over the centuries by men of all and no religious persuasion. In his *History of European Morals from Augustus to Charlemagne,* Lecky noted:

> It was reserved for Christianity to present to the world an ideal character which through all the changes of eighteen centuries has inspired the hearts of men with an impassioned love; has shown itself capable of acting on all ages, nations, temperaments and conditions; has been not only the highest pattern of virtue, but the strongest incentive to its practice, and has exerted so deep an influence, that it may be truly said, that the simple record of three short years of active life has done more to regenerate and to soften mankind, than all the disquisitions of philosophers and than all the exhortations of moralists.[1]

Who then, can imagine that Jesus deliberately lied concerning His own nature? And is it possible that a man of such noble character and exemplary moral persuasion would frequently claim He would rise from the dead, knowing this was a lie? Contemporary philosopher and theologian John Warwick Montgomery asserts, "To answer anything but an unqualified 'No' is to renounce sound ethical judgment."[2]

Eminent Christian historian Philip Schaff argues:

> How, in the name of logic, common sense, and experience, could an imposter—that is a deceitful, selfish, depraved man—have invented, and consistently maintained from the beginning to end, the purest and noblest character known in history with the most perfect air of truth and reality? How could he have conceived and successfully carried out a plan of unparalleled beneficence, moral magnitude, and sublimity, and sacrificed his own life for it, in the face of the strongest prejudices of his people and age?[3]

Further, James Sire, author of *Why Should Anyone Believe Anything at All?* offers other reasons to reject this option:

> There is simply no evidence that Jesus did not think He was telling the truth. He taught with a sense of great personal authority; everyone, even those who did not believe Him, noticed that. He presented a consistent picture of God, Himself and others. When liars elaborate or answer the same kinds of questions repeatedly, they are easily caught in inconsistencies. There is in Jesus a unity of teaching: the stories, the clever sayings, the constant compassion for people, the obvious wisdom of His teaching, the ethical depth of both His teaching and His character. No fault could be found in Him. At His trial, His accusers contradicted themselves, but Jesus stood at His trial with the same integrity as He did on city streets.
>
> The most telling reason for Jesus' not being a liar is that if He was lying, He was lying about the most important issues of life: how to please God, how to inherit eternal life, how to be blessed, how to live well among both your friends and your enemies. If He was lying, He would be selling a salvation He knew to be fake. In fact, He would be no better than the worst religious huckster we know of today, no better than Baghwan Shree Rajaneesh or Jim Jones or David Koresh. No one can call the Jesus of the Gospels that kind of bad man. It fits with none of the evidence whatsoever.... [Critics argue] Maybe Jesus was right about a lot of things... but wrong about who He was.... The problem here is that this kind of delusion is no small matter. This is a delusion about ultimate concerns.... The fact is that religious megalomania is usually accompanied by paranoia— a fear of those outside one's own fold—an anti-social behavior... [However] Jesus gave every appearance of being a psychologically normal person who so surprised people with what He did and said that it took a long time to figure out who He really was.[4]

No one can logically maintain Jesus was a liar and deceiver. Alternative one is ruled out.

Was Jesus Innocently Deluded?

Our second option is even more difficult to believe than our first. Was Jesus mentally ill or psychotic? For someone to be convinced that he is God when he is only a man is the height of psychosis. Was Jesus so psychologically crippled that He had deceived Himself into believing that He was God Incarnate— even though He was only a deluded man? Mental illness or psychosis is defined as an inability to identify reality and to distinguish it from fantasy. The fifth edition of *Introduction to Psychology* describes psychosis in this way: "the psychotic has to some extent given up [his personal] struggle [to cope with reality] and *lost contact with reality*. He may withdraw into his own fantasy world frequently; his thought processes are disturbed to the extent that he experiences delusions (false beliefs) or hallucinations."[5]

But what insane man could ever deliver a self-portrait and teachings that are the epitome of sanity and mental health? Psychiatrist J. T. Fisher observes:

> If you were to take the sum total of all authoritative articles ever written by the most qualified of psychologists and psychiatrists on the subject of mental hygiene, if you were to combine them and refine them and cleave out the excess verbiage—if you were to take the whole of the meat and none of the parsley, and if you were to have the unadulterated bits of pure scientific knowledge concisely expressed by the most capable of living poets, you would have an awkward and incomplete summation of the Sermon on the Mount. And it would suffer immeasurably through comparison. For nearly two thousand years the Christian world has been holding in its hands the complete answer to its restless and fruitless yearnings. Here rests the blueprint for successful human life with optimum mental health and contentment.[6]

Dr. John Warwick Montgomery further explains:

> But one cannot very well have it both ways: if Jesus' teachings provide "the blueprint for successful human life with optimum mental health," then the teacher cannot be a lunatic who totally misunderstands the nature of his own

personality. Note the absolute dichotomy: if the documentary records of Jesus' life are accurate, and Jesus was not a charlatan, then he was either God Incarnate as he claimed or a psychotic. If we cannot take the latter alternative (and, considering its consequences, who really can follow this path to its logical conclusion?), we must arrive at a Jesus who claimed to be God Incarnate simply because *he was God*.[7]

No man can logically maintain Jesus was psychotic. No one who reads His words and carefully examines His clarity of thought, incisive argumentation, or penetrating insight into human nature can possibly think so. Alternative two is ruled out.

Was Jesus Simply Invented by the Disciples?

Our third option is the least credible of all. Everyone but a few diehard atheists agree that Jesus was no invention. No less an authority than the *Encyclopædia Britannica* points out, "These independent [*non-Christian*] accounts prove that in ancient times even the opponents of Christianity never doubted the historicity of Jesus, which was disputed for the first time and on inadequate grounds by several authors at the end of the 18th, during the 19th, and at the beginning of the 20th centuries."[8]

This theory requires that the disciples falsely invented Jesus' teachings and lied about His resurrection. Such men must be classified as deceivers or crazy. But this is impossible, because none of the disciples had either the motive or the ability to invent Jesus. There was no reason for them to do so, nor were they capable of inventing such a being portrayed in the Gospels. No one could invent such a man. Historian Philip Schaff again argues:

> This testimony [of the disciples], if not true, must be downright blasphemy or madness. The former hypothesis cannot stand a moment before the moral purity and dignity of Jesus, revealed in his every word and work, and acknowledged by universal consent. Self-deception in a matter so momentous, and with an intellect in all respects so clear and so sound, is equally out of the question. How could he be an enthusiast or a madman who never lost the even balance of

his mind, who sailed serenely over all the troubles and persecutions, as the sun above the clouds, who always returned the wisest answer to tempting questions, who calmly and deliberately predicted his death on the cross, his resurrection on the third day, the outpouring of the Holy Spirit, the founding of his Church, the destruction of Jerusalem—predictions which have been literally fulfilled? A character so original, so complete, so uniformly consistent, so perfect, so human and yet so high above all human greatness, can be neither a fraud nor a fiction. The poet, as has been well said, would in this case be greater than the hero. It would take more than a Jesus to invent a Jesus.[9]

Even the church collectively could *never* have invented Jesus. As Walter A. Maier points out in his *Form Criticism Reexamined* (Concordia, 1973, p. 38), only the historical Jesus could explain the Jesus of the gospels:

In the first place, with regard to the discourses attributed to Jesus, it should at once be realized that a community cannot create such sayings. We know from experience that a saying must come originally from an individual. A community can only adopt, transmit, and preserve a saying, but the saying itself must first exist. Now the sayings attributed to Jesus in the gospels are by common consent of a singular nobility, loftiness, and power; elevated in character and style. If it be held that in some way the Christian community originated these discourses and statements, then it must follow, as scholar Burton Scott Easton argues, that the Palestinian church either had in its midst a single, brilliant thinker "from whom the sayings all proceeded, but whose name and very existence has disappeared from history—something well-nigh unthinkable—or else there were a number of gifted individuals all fired with the same superlative genius and all endowed with the same exquisite style—an even more difficult conception."

The simple fact is that there is not the slightest indication in New Testament or secular history of the existence of such an anonymous, dynamic, prophetic leader, who would surely be greater and wiser even than ancient Solomon; or of a group of such leaders, gifted with the capacity of creating original discourses such as are found in the gospels.

> The only plausible explanation for these sayings is that they originated, as the evangelists declare, with Jesus; the life situation from which they stem is assuredly to be found in Jesus Himself.

Again, the Jewish disciples would not and could not have engaged in such deliberate fraud as to invent, or lie about, Jesus. First, they did not expect their Messiah to rise from the dead; and once Jesus was crucified, they had abandoned their hopes that He was their Messiah. There was no motive to continue on. Second, almost all of them died as Christians because of their conviction He *did* rise from the dead. Further, their own Jewish ethical code and moral character would have prevented such a massive conspiratorial deception. But even if we thrust aside their ethical standards, the disciples were psychologically incapable of such fraud. As Montgomery points out, Jewish Messianic speculation was at variance with the Messianic picture Jesus gave of Himself; therefore, He was a singularly poor candidate for actual deification on the part of the disciples. As Jews, the disciples' own Jewish beliefs and theology would have prohibited them from deifying Jesus unless the resurrection had already proved to them beyond doubt that Jesus was God.

It is impossible that the person of Jesus could ever have been manufactured or invented.[10] Alternative three is ruled out. One alternative remains.

Was Jesus Lord and God?

It is impossible to maintain that Jesus was either a liar, a lunatic, or a legend. Our only option is that He was God incarnate, e.g., both our Lord and God. This is why the famous Oxford scholar C. S. Lewis concluded:

> The historical difficulty of giving for the life, sayings and influence of Jesus any explanation that is not harder than the Christian explanation, is very great. The discrepancy between the depth and sanity and (let me add) *shrewdness* of his moral teaching and the rampant megalomania which must be behind his theological teaching unless he is indeed God, has never been satisfactorily gotten over. Hence, the non-Christian hypotheses succeed one another with the restless fertility of bewilderment.[11]

Elsewhere, Lewis expands on the idea and shows why the non-Christian really has no logical alternative but to accept that Jesus is God:

> "I'm ready to accept Jesus as a great moral teacher, but I don't accept his claim to be God." That is the one thing we must not say. A man who was merely a man and said the sort of things Jesus said would not be a great moral teacher. He would either be a lunatic—on a level with the man who says he is a poached egg—or else he would be the Devil of Hell. You must make your choice. Either this man was, and is, the Son of God; or else a madman or something worse. You can shut him up for a fool, you can spit at him and kill him as a demon; or you can fall at his feet and call him Lord and God. But let us not come with any patronizing nonsense about his being a great human teacher. He has not left that open to us. He did not intend to.[12]

In conclusion, the very claims of Jesus Himself are evidence for His deity. No man in his right mind would make such claims unless He knew they were true. Little is left to the skeptic but to accept that Jesus was who He claimed He was. Indeed, had He *not* resurrected, we would not have the option of discussing His identity. For many reasons, His name would have dissipated into the mists of historical obscurity 2,000 years ago. But if Jesus is God, then the Christian faith is verified: "If Jesus is who He thought and said He was, Christianity is true. The best explanation for Jesus is that He is who He thought He was. So Christianity has a major claim to be considered true.... When the Gospels are considered in depth, the outlines of the pattern are filled in, and the evidence for the truth of the Christian faith is seen to be very strong indeed."[13]

The Power of Invisible Realities

"When all treasures are tried truth is the fairest"
—*William Langland*

Jesus Christ is important to each of us personally, regardless of what we may now believe about Him. We can argue about the events of His life, but that will not change the reality that He is Lord.

All of us are familiar with AIDS, the fatal disease that destroys the body's immune system. No one can afford to be unconcerned with this modern plague that will eventually kill tens of millions of people worldwide. Everyone knows that infection with the AIDS virus leaves no initial symptoms. No one can know if they are infected with this fatal virus unless they have specific testing to determine exposure. Now consider this question: How important do you think these testing procedures are? Because we are dealing with life and death issues, they are vitally important. Especially if the possibility of a cure is found should the virus be detected early enough.

Now, the fact is, no one can argue with an HIV virus. It simply exists, and it produces certain effects in the body. People may deny they have it, they may argue against it, but it changes nothing. Living their day-to-day lives in ignorant bliss only allows the virus to continue its deadly march.

In the same way, no one can deny it is a historical fact that Jesus lived, made particular claims for His own deity, and was resurrected from the dead. People may argue against these historical facts, but it will not change them. They may live their lives as if Jesus never existed, but this only allows a different virus, a virus of ignorance, to continue *its* deadly march.

Jesus was born in Bethlehem, grew up in Nazareth, preached to tens of thousands of people in Israel, performed dramatic miracles, was arrested and tried by Roman authority, was crucified, and rose from the dead. He appeared physically after His death to 500 people at a single time, as well as a dozen distinct appearances to His own disciples. These occurred on many different occasions and places over a period of six weeks. Today, 2,000 years later, Jesus continues to dramatically impact the modern world. To deny these facts is equivalent to denying the existence of the AIDS virus.

What one does with either of these facts is crucial. If a person knows about the AIDS virus, then he can take certain precautions to protect himself. Ignorance of the fact of an AIDS virus will only increase one's chances of infection.

In a similar manner, what one does with historical facts surrounding Jesus Christ is also vital. If Christ was who He said He was, then what we do with Him personally will determine not only the quality of our lives here, but also the quality of our lives after death, extending into eternity.

Everyone would agree that to deny the truth concerning the existence of the AIDS virus is a foolish and futile endeavor. Likewise, saying false things about the AIDS virus—for example, that it is not transmitted sexually or is no more serious than a common cold—would be equally foolish. Everyone knows better.

In the same manner, to deny the historical facts concerning Jesus Christ is both foolish and futile. To say Jesus was only a good man or of no import to our lives today is precisely what we must not say. To falsely interpret His words or to distort them is equally unwise. Again, nothing is changed.

The truth is that the issue of Jesus Christ's identity is just as important to people's lives—indeed, far more important—than any modern concern they may have over the AIDS virus, whether or not they are infected.

One day, every person who has ever lived will stand before Jesus Christ and be judged by Him. If so, then it is of the utmost importance for people to understand who Jesus is and what He requires of them: "Then I saw a great white throne and him who was seated on it. Earth and sky fled from his presence, and there was no place for them. And I saw the dead, great and small, standing before the throne, and books were opened. Another book was opened, which is the book of life. The dead were judged according to what they had done as recorded in the books.... If anyone's name was not found written in the book of life, he was thrown into the lake of fire" (Revelation 20:11-12,15).

From all that we have discussed about Jesus, from what the Bible teaches of Him, and from Jesus' own words we can understand *why* He makes demands on each person who has ever lived. This is why He emphasized the personal necessity of trusting in Him alone for salvation: "Whoever believes in Him is not condemned, but whoever does not believe stands condemned already because He has not believed in the name of God's one and only Son. This is the verdict: Light has come into the world, but men loved darkness instead of light because their deeds were evil" (John 3:18, 19).

Jesus taught that unless a person was "born again" (spiritually reborn or made alive through receiving Christ as their personal Lord and Savior), it would be impossible for them to enter heaven: "I tell you the truth, no one can see the kingdom of God unless he is born again.... I tell you the truth, no one can enter the kingdom of God unless he is born of water and the Spirit" (John 3:3,5). "Yet to all who received him, to those who believed in his name, he gave the right to become children of God" (John 1:12). And to those who received Him He said, "My Father will honor the one who serves Me" (John 12:26).

He also said to believer and unbeliever alike:

> When a man believes in Me, he does not believe in Me only, but in the One who sent Me. When he looks at Me, he sees the One who sent Me. I have come into the world as light, so that no one who believes in Me should stay in darkness. As for the person who hears My words, but does not keep them, I do not judge him. For I did not come to judge the world, but to save it. There is a Judge for the one who rejects Me and does not accept My words; that very word which I spoke will condemn him at the Last Day. For I did not speak of My own accord, but the Father who sent Me commanded Me what to say and how to say it. I know that His commands lead to eternal life. So whatever I say is just what the Father has told me to say. (John 12:47-50)

Finally:

> Anyone who believes in the Son of God has this testimony in his heart. Anyone who does not believe God has made him out to be a liar, because he has not believed the testimony God has given about his Son. And this is the testimony: God has given us eternal life, and this life is in his Son. He who has the Son has life; he who does not have the Son of God does not have life. I write these things to you who believe in the name of the Son of God so that you may know that you have eternal life. (1 John 5:10-13)

This, then, is what the Bible teaches about Jesus Christ—that He is the prophesied Messiah of the Old Testament; He is absolutely unique in His person in all creation; He was virgin born and sinless; He is the only incarnation of God ever to exist;

He is the world's only Savior who died for our sins on the cross and rose from the dead; and He is the only and final judge of all humanity.

How vital, then, that we be ready to meet Him.

Chapter 5

What Former Skeptics Say

Evidential Distinction

We have seen that among the religions of the world, Christianity is unique in many ways. One area of uniqueness concerns the evidence supporting its basic claims. As lawyer, theologian, and philosopher, Dr. John Warwick Montgomery points out, "The historic Christian claim differs qualitatively from the claims of all other world religions at the epistemological point: on the issue of testability."[1] In other words, only Christianity stakes its claim to truthfulness on historical events open to critical investigation. And only this explains the number of conversions by skeptics throughout history. For example, Viggo Olsen, M.D., author of *Daktar: Diplomat in Bangladesh,* and his wife were both skeptics who "decided to embark on a detailed study of Christianity with the intention of rejecting it on intellectual grounds. Little by little, as they studied works that deal with data common to apologetics and evidences, all the while as unregenerate individuals, they were led step by step to see the truthfulness of Christianity. Their study was no minor investigation or casual perusal. It was an exhaustive search into many of the deepest issues that are treated in textbooks on Christian apologetics."[2]

Indeed, other religions in the world are believed *despite* the lack of genuine evidence supporting their truth claims; only Christianity can claim credibility *because* of such evidence. Regrettably, what is often overlooked in the field of comparative religion today is that no genuinely historical or objective evidence exists for the foundational *religious* claims of Hinduism, Buddhism, Islam, or any other religion.[3] As scientist, Christian apologist, and biblical commentator Dr. Henry Morris observes, "As a matter of fact, the entire subject of evidences is almost exclusively the domain of *Christian* evidences. Other religions depend on subjective experience and blind faith, tradition and opinion. Christianity stands or falls upon the objective reality of gigantic supernatural events in history and the evidences therefore. This fact in itself is an evidence of its truth."[4]

Evidence is defined in the *Oxford American Dictionary* as, "1. anything that establishes a fact or gives reason for believing something. 2. statements made or objects produced in a law court as proof or to support a case." One of the most interesting evidences for the truth of Christianity and, in particular, the resurrection of Jesus Christ, is the testimony of former skeptics, many of whom, like the Olsen's above, set out to disprove the Christian faith. In this chapter we will supply over a dozen examples. We hope this will not only be an encouragement for Christians to take their faith seriously, but that it will spur non-Christians to earnestly examine the claims of Christ on their own lives.

We know the Gospels constitute accurate historical reporting, so it must be recognized that "of all the miracles of Christ, the resurrection receives the most careful and extensive coverage in the Bible. If the Gospels are historically accurate, then the most carefully documented event in the Gospels should be accurately reported."[5] Indeed, were the evidence clearly *insufficient* to establish the resurrection, this chapter and our next three chapters could never have been written. Thus, our concern is not to offer historical evidence that Jesus died, for again, everyone agrees He did and His death may safely be considered a fact of history. Nor will we prove that the tomb was empty, since this is also generally conceded and critics themselves have to agree Jesus' enemies were never able to produce the body. We will not spend a lot of time on the evidence of the resurrection appearances (see the chart), since only their reality can logically explain the disciples' conversion from doubt to belief, their claims to being eyewitnesses, and their willingness to suffer great persecution and death. Indeed, the great variety of Jesus' appearances, their physical nature and other factors make *disbelief* in the resurrection the greater wonder. In the chart below, in almost every case, the disciples both saw and heard Jesus and in at least five cases they either touched Him, saw His death wounds, or Jesus offered to be touched, or He ate with them. In four cases, they saw the empty tomb and empty grave clothes.

The Resurrection Appearances

1. To the women as they returned from the tomb after having seen the angel, who informed them that Christ had arisen (Matthew 28:1-10).

2. To Mary Magdalene at the tomb, during her second visit to the tomb that morning (John 20:10-18; Mark 16:9-11).

3. To Peter sometime before the evening of the resurrection day but under circumstances the details of which are not given (Luke 24:34; 1 Corinthians 15:5).

4. To Cleopas and another disciple on the road to Emmaus on Easter afternoon (Luke 24:13-35; Mark 16:12-13).

5. To ten of the apostles with others whose names are not given (Thomas is absent), gathered together at their evening meal on Easter Sunday (Luke 24:36-40; John 20:19-23; Mark 16:14-18).

6. A week later to all eleven apostles, including Thomas (John 20:26-28).

7. To some of the disciples fishing at the Sea of Galilee, the time undesignated (John 21:1-23).

8. To the apostles on a specific mountain in Galilee (Matthew 28:16-20).

9. To James, with specific information as to time and place not stated (1 Corinthians 15:7).

10. To the apostles on the Mount of Olives at Jerusalem just prior to the ascension (Luke 24:50-52; Acts 1:3-8; Mark 16:19).

11. To 500 additional believers all at once (1 Corinthians 15:6).

12. To Paul on the Damascus road (1 Corinthians 15:8; Acts 9:1-9).

(Adapted from Norman L. Geisler, *The Battle for the Resurrection* [Nashville, TN: Thomas Nelson, 1984], p. 141, references added.)

However, as only one of a dozen lines of evidence, we will show here why merely the existence of Christianity is proof of the resurrection.

The Church as Proof of the Resurrection

Could the Christian Church ever have come into existence as a result of what had become, after Jesus' crucifixion and death, a group of disheartened, frightened, skeptical apostles? Not a chance.

Only the resurrection of Christ from the dead can account for motivating the disciples to give their lives to preach about Christ and nurture the Christian Church the Lord had founded. It can hardly be overestimated how devastating the crucifixion was to the apostles. They had sacrificed everything for Jesus, including their jobs, their homes, and their families (Matthew 19:27). Everything of value was pinned squarely on Jesus: all their hopes, their entire lives, everything. But now He was dead, publicly branded a criminal.

The apostles were dejected and depressed in their conclusion that Christ was not their expected Messiah (Luke 24:21). In such a condition, they can hardly be considered the subjects of hopeful visions and hallucinations. These were not men ready to believe. The very fact that Jesus rebuked them for their unbelief indicates that Thomas was not the only one who was a hardheaded skeptic. At one time or another Jesus rebuked all of the eleven apostles for their unbelief in His resurrection (Matthew 28:17; Luke 24:25-27,38,41; John 20:24-27). This proves they were finally convinced against their will.

As the Gospels show, they rejected the first reports of Jesus' resurrection. It was only after Jesus appeared to them again and again, talking with them, encouraging them to touch Him, to see that He had a physical body, showing them the wounds in His hands and His side, that they became convinced (John 29:20, 27). If they *had* expected a resurrection, they would have been waiting for it. But they weren't, *and* they needed a lot of convincing when it did happened (Acts 1:3).

The record is also clear that none of the disciples understood the necessity for the resurrection. This is seen both from Peter's rebuke to Jesus when He predicted His death and resurrection (Matthew 16:21, 22), and from Christ's prediction of His resurrection after the transfiguration (Matthew 17:9, 22-23). Mark says of the disciples, "But they did not understand this statement, and they were afraid to ask Him" (Mark 9:32). Thus the disciples not only didn't believe in the resurrection, they didn't even understand the implications. For example, after Jesus spoke of His rising from the dead in Mark 9:9, we are told, "And they seized upon that statement, discussing with one another what rising from the dead might mean" (Mark 9:10).

On another occasion when Jesus spoke of His resurrection, it was recorded of the disciples: "And they understood none of these things, and this saying was hidden from them, and they did not comprehend the things that were said" (Luke 18:34). So, how do we account for the disciples coming to believe in something that was completely unexpected unless it really happened?

As Michael Green comments: "It is clear from all the accounts that the disciples were utterly disheartened men. They were anxious only to run away, hide, and forget all about the whole affair. They had been on a wild goose chase in following Jesus of Nazareth, and the crucifixion had dashed all their hopes. They had no thought of carrying on His cause. Resurrection never entered their heads."[6]

In light of all of this, how then do we account for the beginning and spreading of the Christian Church?

Philosopher of religion Dr. William Lane Craig discusses how a mysterious "something" *must* be proposed to account for it:

> It is quite clear that without the belief in the resurrection the Christian faith could not have come into being. The disciples would have remained crushed and defeated men. Even had they continued to remember Jesus as their beloved teacher, His crucifixion would have forever silenced any hopes of His being the Messiah. The cross would have remained the sad and shameful end to His career. *The origin of Christianity therefore hinges on the belief of the early disciples that God had raised Jesus from the dead....*
>
> Now the question becomes: What caused that belief? As R. H. Fuller says, even the most skeptical critic must

presuppose some mysterious X to get the movement going. But what was that X? ... Clearly, it would not be the result of Christian influences, for at that time there was no Christianity. ...

But neither can belief in the resurrection be explained as a result of Jewish influences. ... The Jewish conception of resurrection differed in two important, fundamental respects from Jesus' resurrection.

In Jewish thought the resurrection *always* (1) occurred after the end of the world, not within history, and (2) concerned all the people, not just an isolated individual. In contradistinction to this, Jesus' resurrection was both within history and of one person. ... The disciples, therefore, confronted with Jesus' crucifixion and death, would only have looked forward to the resurrection at the final day and would probably have carefully kept their master's tomb as a shrine, where His bones could reside until the resurrection.[7]

In other words, the disciples' belief in the resurrection of Christ cannot be explained as a result of either Christian belief or Jewish teaching. There is simply no way to explain the origin of such a belief concerning Christ's resurrection apart from the fact that it happened.

This is why secular historians who study the events surrounding the origin of the Church are mystified if they reject the resurrection. The task of the historian is to adequately account for events that occur. No one doubts the Church exists, but the historian cannot adequately account for it apart from *Jesus being alive.* The problem for the secularist who discounts the resurrection is that:

The mysterious X is still missing. According to C. F. D. Moule of Cambridge University, here is a belief nothing in terms of previous historical influences can account for. He points out that we have a situation in which a large number of people held firmly to this belief, which cannot be explained in terms of the Old Testament or the Pharisees, and that these people held onto this belief until the Jews finally threw them out of the synagogue.

According to Professor Moule, the origin of this belief must have been the fact that Jesus really did rise from the dead: "If the coming into existence of the Nazarenes, a phenomenon undeniably attested by the New Testament, rips a great hole in history, a hole of the size and shape of the resurrection, what does the secular historian propose to stop it up with?... The birth and rapid rise of the Christian Church... *remain an unsolved enigma for any historian who refuses to take seriously the only explanation offered by the Church itself.*"

The resurrection of Jesus is therefore the best explanation for the origin of the Christian faith.[8]

Given the disciples' initial skepticism and lack of understanding, given the inability of all history to adequately explain the existence of the Christian Church apart from the actual resurrection of Christ, how do we account for churches on every street corner of the country and throughout most of the entire planet?

Can we really believe that the mental frame of mind of the disciples prior to the resurrection appearances was sufficient to "invent" the Church? Could the unbelieving and skeptical disciples have proclaimed a resurrection when they never expected it in the first place? As Dr. Norval Geldenhuys observes:

It is historically and psychologically impossible that the followers of Jesus, who at His crucifixion were so completely despondent and perplexed, would within a few weeks thereafter enter the world (as they did) with such unheard-of joy, power and devotion, if it had not been for the fact that He had risen from the dead, had appeared to them, and had proved that His claims to be the Son of God were genuine.[9]

Further, every book of the New Testament is based upon the conviction that Christ rose from the dead. If He never did, why were those twenty-seven books written in the first place? And why would the apostles face the hostility and persecution of the Jewish leaders by attempting to found a new movement based on the teachings of a condemned criminal? Why would they continue to follow and speak about a man who was obviously a fraud or worse, in a man who made predictions about His own resurrection from the dead that never came true?

Finally, on what basis would the apostles proclaim this same dead person—who did not resurrect—as God, when their entire religious training had taught them, "Hear, O Israel, the Lord our God is one Lord"? In other words, what would cause devout Jews to widely preach blasphemies that went against the entire grain of their personal religious convictions, unless it were the resurrection?

In light of this, examine the testimony of skeptics who have converted to the Christian faith on the basis of the evidence.

The Testimony of the Skeptics

Is the evidence for the resurrection sufficiently compelling to persuade even convinced skeptics?

Saul. A devout Pharisee named Saul was born in Tarsus. Here he was exposed to the most advanced philosophical learning of his day. He had great command of the Greek language and considerable expertise in argument and logic. At age 14 he was sent to study under one of the greatest Jewish rabbis of the period, Gamaliel (Acts 22:3) (probably the grandson of Hillel).

As a Hebrew zealot and Pharisee who "was advancing in Judaism beyond many of my contemporaries...being more extremely zealous for [his] ancestral traditions" (Galatians 1:14), Saul was not so much intending to disprove Christianity as he was attempting to destroy it (Galatians 1:13). But there is no doubt he was a skeptic both of Jesus and the claims of Christians for the resurrection. He persecuted many Christians "to the death," and literally laid waste to the Church: "And I persecuted this Way to the death, binding and putting both men and women into prisons, as also the high priest and all the council of the elders can testify (Acts 22:4-5a, cf., 8:1,3; 9:1-2,13; 22:19-20; 26:9-11).

But something changed Saul so radically the world has never quite gotten over it. Even the early Christians, after suffering such persecutions at his hand, could not believe it: "[After his conversion] Paul immediately began to proclaim Jesus in the synagogues, saying, 'He is the Son of God.' And all those hearing him continued to be amazed, and were saying, 'Is this not he who in Jerusalem destroyed those who called on this name, and who had come here for the purpose of bringing them bound before the chief priests?'" (Acts 9:19-23).

What was it that converted the greatest enemy of the Church, Saul, into its greatest defender? It was no less than a direct appearance by the risen Christ Himself—for Saul, nothing else would have sufficed. In his own words, he records the experience of meeting the resurrected Christ and how it changed his life forever in Acts chapter 26. He later confessed, "Have I not seen Jesus our Lord?" (1 Corinthians 9:1, see Acts 22:4-21; Galatians 1:11-24; 1 Corinthians 15:1-19).

Yet few people are aware of the impact that this once committed enemy of Christianity has had upon the world's history because of his experiencing the resurrected Jesus. Paul's three missionary journeys and lifelong evangelism and church planting helped to change the Roman Empire and even the destiny of Western civilization. Writing in *Chamber's Encyclopædia,* Archibald MacBride, professor at the University of Aberdeen, asserts of Paul: "Besides his achievements . . . the achievements of Alexander and Napoleon pale into insignificance."[10]

Athanagoras. Consider another former skeptic, Athanagoras. He was a second-century scholar, brilliant apologist, and the first head of the eminent School of Alexandria. He originally intended to write against the faith, being "occupied with searching the Scriptures for arguments against Christianity." Instead, the evidence he discovered resulted in his conversion.[11]

Augustine. Augustine of Hippo (354-430 A.D.) was also raised in a pagan environment. At the age of 12 he was sent by his parents to the advanced schools in Madaura, a center of pagan culture and learning. He later studied and taught rhetoric in Carthage. He mastered the Latin classics, was deeply influenced by Plato, Neoplatonism, and Manicheanism, and was for a period a skeptic of religion. But after careful reading of the Bible and hearing the sermons of Bishop Ambrose while in Milan, he was converted to the Christian faith and became the greatest Father of the Western Church. His two most famous works are *Confessions* and the *City of God;* but he also wrote apologetic texts such as *Contra Academicos* (Against the Academics), a critique of the academic skeptics of his day.[12]

The next 14 centuries contain thousands of additional testimonies of converted skeptics.

George Lyttleton and Gilbert West. In the mid-eighteenth century Lord George Lyttleton (a member of Parliament and Commissioner of the Treasury) and Gilbert West, Esquire, went to Oxford. There they were determined to attack the very basis of Christianity. Lyttleton set out to prove that Saul of Tarsus was never really converted to Christianity, and West intended to demonstrate that Jesus never really rose from the dead. Each had planned to do a painstaking job, taking a year to establish their case. But as they proceeded, they eventually concluded that Christianity was true. Both became Christians.

West eventually wrote *Observations on the History and Evidences of the Resurrection of Jesus Christ* (1747). George Lyttleton wrote a lengthy text titled *The Conversion of St. Paul* (1749). Their correspondence back and forth, showing their surprise at the quality of the evidence, can be found in any university microfilm library. West became totally convinced of the truth of the resurrection, and Lyttleton of the genuine conversion of Saint Paul on the basis of it. For example, Lyttleton wrote to West in 1761, "Sir, in a late conversation we had together upon the subject of the Christian religion, I told you that besides all the proofs of it which may be drawn from the prophecies of the Old Testament, from the necessary connection it has with the whole system of the Jewish religion, from the miracles of Christ, and from the evidence given of his reflection by all the other apostles, I thought the conversion and apostleship of Saint Paul alone, duly considered, was of itself a demonstration sufficient to prove Christianity a divine revelation."[13]

Frank Morison. In our own century, the conversion of skeptics and doubters has continued. In the 1930s a rationalistic English journalist named Frank Morison attempted to discover the "real" Jesus Christ. He was convinced that Christ's "history rested upon very insecure foundations," largely because of the influence of the rationalistic higher criticism so prevalent in his day.[14] Further, he was dogmatically opposed to the miraculous elements in the Gospels. But he was nevertheless fascinated by the person of Jesus, who was to him "an almost legendary figure of purity and noble manhood."[15]

Morison decided to take the crucial "last phase" in the life of Christ and "to strip it of its overgrowth of primitive beliefs and dogmatic suppositions, and to see this supremely great Person as he really was. . . . It seemed to me that if I could come at the truth *why* this man died a cruel death at the hands of the Roman Power, how he himself regarded the matter, and especially how he behaved under the test, I should be very near to the true solution of the problem."[16]

But the book that Morison ended up writing was not the one he intended to. He came to see the truth of the Gospels and proceeded to write one of the most able defenses of the resurrection of Christ in our time, *Who Moved the Stone?*

Cyril Joad. Dr. Cyril E. M. Joad, head of the Philosophy Department at the University of London, once believed that Jesus was only a man. For many years, he was an antagonist toward Christianity. But near the end of his life he came to believe that the only solution for mankind was "found in the cross of Jesus Christ." He also became a zealous disciple.[17]

Giovanni Papine. Giovanni Papine was one of the foremost Italian intellects of his period, an atheist and vocal enemy of the church and self-appointed debunker of religion. But he became converted to faith in Christ and in 1921 penned his *Life of Christ*, stunning most of his friends and admirers.[18]

C. S. Lewis. The Cambridge scholar C. S. Lewis, a former atheist, was converted to Christianity on the basis of the evidence, according to his text *Surprised by Joy.* He recalls, "I thought I had the Christians 'placed' and disposed of forever." But, "A young man who wishes to remain a sound atheist cannot be too careful of his reading. There are traps everywhere—'Bibles laid open, millions of surprises,' as Herbert says, 'Fine nets and stratagems.' God is, if I may say it, very unscrupulous."[19]

But C. S. Lewis became a Christian because the evidence was compelling and he could not escape it. Even against his will he was "brought in kicking, struggling, resentful, and darting [my] eyes in every direction for a chance of escape." The God "whom

I so earnestly desired not to meet" became his Lord and Savior.[20] His book on Christian evidences, *Mere Christianity*, is considered a classic and has been responsible for converting thousands to the faith, among them the keen legal mind of former skeptic and Watergate figure Charles Colson, author of *Born Again.*

Josh McDowell. As a pre-law student, Josh McDowell was also a skeptic of Christianity and believed that every Christian had two minds: one was lost while the other was out looking for it. Eventually challenged to intellectually investigate the Christian truth claims and thinking it a farce, he accepted the challenge and "as a result, I found historical facts and evidence about Jesus Christ that I never knew existed."[21] He eventually wrote a number of important texts in defense of Christianity, among them *Evidence That Demands a Verdict, More Evidence That Demands a Verdict* (a critique of higher critical theories), *More Than a Carpenter,* and *Daniel in the Lion's Den.*

Gary Habermas. Dr. Gary Habermas was raised in a Christian home, but began to question his faith. He concluded that while the resurrection might be believed, he personally doubted it and was skeptical that any evidence for it was really convincing. After critical examination, it was the evidence that brought him around to the conclusion that the resurrection *was* an established fact of history.[22] He proceeded to write four important books in defense of the resurrection: *Ancient Evidence for the Life of Jesus; The Resurrection of Jesus: A Rational Inquiry; The Resurrection of Jesus: An Apologetic;* and *Did Jesus Rise from the Dead?: The Resurrection Debate.*

John Warwick Montgomery. As a brilliant philosophy student at Cornell University, John Warwick Montgomery was a convinced skeptic when it came to Christianity. But he, too, was challenged to investigate the evidence for Christianity. As a result, he became converted. He recalls, "I went to university as a 'garden-variety' 20th century pagan. And as a result of being *forced*, for intellectual integrity's sake, to check out this evidence, I finally came around."[23] He confessed that had it not been for a committed undergraduate student who continued to challenge him to *really* examine the evidence, he would never have believed: "I thank God that he cared enough to do the reading to become a good apologist because if I hadn't had someone like that I don't know if I would have become a Christian."[24]

Montgomery went on to graduate from Cornell University with distinction in philosophy, Phi Beta Kappa. Then he earned his Ph.D. from the University of Chicago, a second doctorate in theology from the University of Strasbourg, France, plus seven additional graduate degrees in theology, law, library science, and other fields. He has written more than 130 scholarly journal articles, plus 40 books, many of them defending the Christian faith against skeptical views. He has held numerous prestigious appointments, is a founding member of the World Association of Law Professors, a member of the American Society of International Law, and is honored in *Who's Who in America, Who's Who in American Law, The Directory of American Scholars, International Scholars Directory, Who's Who in France, Who's Who in Europe,* and *Who's Who in the World.* There are many individuals with the kind of background, temperament, and philosophical premises as Dr. Montgomery, but they simply do not believe in Christianity apart from sufficient evidence.

Malcolm Muggeridge. Among great literary writers, few can match the brilliance of famed author Malcolm Muggeridge. He too was once a skeptic of Christianity, but near the end of his life he became fully convinced of the truth of the resurrection of Christ, writing a book acclaimed by critics, *Jesus: The Man Who Lives* (1975). In it, Muggeridge wrote, "The coming of Jesus into the world is the most stupendous event in human history . . ." and "What is unique about Jesus is that, on the testimony and in the experience of innumerable people, of all sorts and conditions, of all races and nationalities from the simplest and most primitive to the most sophisticated and cultivated, he remains alive." Muggeridge concludes, "That the resurrection happened . . . seems to me indubitably true" and "either Jesus never was or he still is. . . . with the utmost certainty, I assert *he still is.*"[25]

William Ramsay. The famous scholar and archæologist, Sir William Ramsay, was educated at Oxford and a professor at both Oxford and Cambridge. He received gold medals from Pope Leo XII, the University of Pennsylvania, the Royal Geographical Society, and the Royal Scottish Geographical Society, and was knighted in 1906. He was once a skeptic of Christianity and he was convinced that the Bible was fraudulent.

> He had spent years deliberately preparing himself for the announced task of heading an exploration expedition into Asia Minor and Palestine, the home of the Bible, where he would "dig up the evidence" that the Book was the product of ambitious monks, and not the book from heaven it claimed to be. He regarded the weakest spot in the whole New Testament to be the story of Paul's travels. These had never been thoroughly investigated by one on the spot.... Equipped as no other man had been, he went to the home of the Bible. Here he spent fifteen years literally "digging for the evidence". Then in 1896 he published a large volume on *Saint Paul the Traveler and the Roman Citizen.*

> The book caused a furor of dismay among the skeptics of the world. Its attitude was utterly unexpected, because it was contrary to the announced intention of the author years before.... for twenty years more, book after book from the same author came from the press, each filled with additional evidence of the exact, minute truthfulness of the whole New Testament as tested by the spade on the spot. The evidence was so overwhelming that many infidels announced their repudiation of their former unbelief and accepted Christianity. And these books have stood the test of time, not one having been refuted, nor have I found even any attempt to refute them.[26]

Ramsay's own archæological findings convinced him of the reliability of the Bible and the truth of what it taught. In his *The Bearing of Recent Discovery on the Trustworthiness of the New Testament* and other books, he shows why he came to conclude that "Luke's history is unsurpassed in respect of its trustworthiness" and that "Luke is a historian of the first rank.... In short, this author should be placed along with the very greatest of historians."[27]

John Scott. One of the greatest classical scholars of our century, the outstanding authority on Homer, Dr. John A. Scott, professor of Greek at Northwestern University for some 40 years, at one time president of the American Philosophical Association as well as president of the Classical Association of the Midwest and

South, wrote a book at the age of seventy, concluding a lifetime of ripened convictions: *We Would See Jesus.* He, too, was convinced that Luke was an accurate historian: "Luke was not only a doctor and historian, but he was one of the world's greatest men of letters. He wrote the clearest and the best Greek written in that century."[28]

Here we have two of the greatest intellects of recent time (Ramsay and Scott), among many that could be cited, vouching for the historical accuracy and integrity of the Apostle Luke, who wrote not only the Gospel of Luke, but the Book of Acts as well. In the latter book he claimed that the resurrection of Christ had been established "by many convincing proofs" (Acts 1:3). It is only by means of such *convincing* proofs that skeptics such as these individuals could have ever been converted in the first place. Indeed, *the entire history of Christianity involves the conversion of skeptics to Christian faith.*

Unfortunately, however, there are also plenty of scholars who have the evidence laid out clearly before them and still do not believe. For example, Michael Grant, a Fellow of Trinity College, Cambridge, professor of humanity at Edinburgh University, and president and vice chancellor of the Queens University, Belfast, holds doctorates from Cambridge, Dublin, and Belfast and is the author of numerous books, among them *The Twelve Caesars* and *The Army of the Caesars.* In his book *Jesus: An Historian's Review of the Gospels,* he fully admits, "But if we apply the same sort of criteria that we would apply to any other ancient literary sources, then the evidence is firm and plausible enough to necessitate the conclusion that the tomb was indeed found empty."[29]

He proceeds to show how the subsequent events of Christian history astonish the historian, "For by conquering the Roman Empire in the fourth century A.D., Christianity had conquered the entire Western World, for century after century that lay ahead. In a triumph that has been hailed by its advocates as miraculous, and must be regarded by historians, too, as one of the *most astonishing phenomena in the history of the world,* the despised, reviled Galilean became the Lord of countless millions of people over the course of the 1900 years and more between his age and ours."[30]

But he does not believe in the resurrection: "Who had taken the body? There is no way of knowing. . . . at all events, it was gone."[31] Perhaps if Dr. Grant had been both a historian *and* a lawyer, he might have better understood the reason for, in his words, "the most astonishing phenomena in the history of the world." In our next chapter, we will examine what some of the finest legal minds in history and today have concluded concerning the evidence for the resurrection of Jesus and the truth of Christianity. Obviously, if Christianity is true, it makes all the difference in the world whether we personally accept it or not. But Dr. Grant's attitude is a common one, apparently based primarily on a distrust of miracles.

History and the Miraculous

Perhaps the average person's skepticism toward the resurrection is also largely the result, not of some legitimate basis for such skepticism, but of a pervading bias against the idea of the supernatural. From grade school on, Americans have been indoctrinated in a secular mind-set that makes the idea of Christ's resurrection from the dead seem strangely implausible. Thus, when the teaching of Christ's resurrection is presented to the average person, it passes through a secular "grid" that immediately places it into the category of "religion"—that is, superstition or myth, and those are anything but personally relevant. But does the fact that the New Testament is a religious writing, with miraculous events recorded, automatically disqualify it as reliable historical reporting? In other words, does the merely religious demand the absence of objective, verifiable history? Again, this idea is common to many secular and religious commentators who relegate everything religious to the category of myth—by definition outside the realm of genuine history.

But superstition would seem to be on the part of the unbeliever. Such ideas are frequently adopted in order to support a personal bias and escape what is for such individuals an uncomfortable feeling over the idea of supernatural events within history.

If the resurrection is unbelievable to some men because it is a miracle, it is also undeniable. Only an *a priori* bias can attempt to discount it. As James I. Packer points out, "A steady flow of books in this century has shown over and over again that you cannot reasonably deny Jesus' resurrection on *a posteriori* grounds—that is, by maintaining that another explanation of the evidence fits better. Denial of the resurrection can be made to seem reasonable only on *a priori* grounds—that is, by assuming, as rationalist-positivist historians do assume, that only parallel cases, real or imagined, within the system constitute explanation, and by ruling out in advance creative acts of God in his world."[32]

But *a priori* approaches are also indefensible. Supernatural and natural events are not innately or necessarily fundamentally opposed categories. For example, if God has chosen to act within history, then any miraculous events are part of history and just as real as nonmiraculous events. Indeed, books such as C. S. Lewis' *Miracles* and Colin Brown's *Miracles and the Critical Mind* present extremely convincing data for the acceptance of miracles when the evidence warrants it.

History is simply a record of events that happened. An alleged supernatural event in history cannot be properly distinguished from an alleged nonsupernatural event in history in that both are equally historical—that is, observable, nonrepeatable, and subject to the same truth tests of impartial study. By their nature, miracles are rare, nonrepeatable, and observable by men. But this is also true of many nonsupernatural events, such as the signing of the Declaration of Independence. Miraculous events retain the same kind of "subsequent history" as nonmiraculous events. For example, consider a man born blind from birth who by a miracle of healing, is given his sight. This is witnessed by many others (John, chapter 9). This testimony constitutes a "living proof" to the miracle, just as Nazi survivors constitute a "living proof" testimony to the barbarism of Hitler's Germany. Further, in both cases there is undeniable physical proof. Indeed, their primary source value, eyewitness testimony, when committed to writing, has equal historical legitimacy.

A true historian, with all the available means at his disposal, must seek first to determine what, in fact, did occur, not that which could never occur merely because it is ruled out beforehand. In other words, no historian worth his salt can logically reject eyewitness testimony or documentary evidence solely because it involves the miraculous. If, under careful scrutiny, the testimony remains trustworthy or if the documents citing miracles prove reliable, then the miracles must be accepted in spite of their uniqueness.

To conclude, then, that the Gospels are merely "religious" and as such lacking in objective historical content begs the question. It must first be determined if the Gospels are or are not reliable history. If they are, if the writers exercised pains in accurate reporting, then there is no legitimate reason to deny the existence of the miraculous.

A final important point must be noted. If the teachings of Scripture are in error in secular areas, such as science and history, where they can be tested, then we have no guarantee they are not in error in religious teachings—matters of theology such as salvation, Christ's deity, and so on. As Dr. Gleason L. Archer, Jr., professor of Old Testament and Semitic Studies, Trinity Evangelical Divinity School, observes, ". . . if the biblical record can be proved fallible in areas of fact that can be verified, then it is hardly to be trusted in areas where it cannot be tested. As a witness for God, the Bible would be discredited as untrustworthy. What solid truth it may contain would be left as a matter of mere conjecture, subject to the intuition or canons of likelihood of each individual. . . . One opinion is as good as another. All things are possible, but nothing is certain if indeed the Bible contains mistakes or errors of any kind."[33]

No one should be expected to believe the Bible on grounds of hearsay, blind faith, or any other undocumented or irrational basis. To cite an illustration:

> If the attorney can trap the opposing witness into statements that contradict what he has said previously or furnish evidence that in his own community the man has a reputation for untruthfulness, then the jury may be led to doubt the accuracy of the witness's testimony that bears directly on the case itself. This is true even though such untruthfulness relates to other matters having no relationship to the present litigation. While the witness on the stand may indeed be giving a true report on this particular case, the

judge and jury have no way of being sure. Therefore, they are logically compelled to discount this man's testimony.

The same is true of holy scripture. If the statements it contains concerning matters of history and science can be proven [false] by extrabiblical records, by ancient documents recovered through archæological digs, or by the established facts of modern science... then there is grave doubt as to its trustworthiness in matters of religion.[34]

In conclusion, if the Bible's testimony to the resurrection is believed, it should be believed only because the evidence warrants it. Our next three chapters will prove that the evidence warrants it.

Chapter 6

Resurrection on Trial

In chapter 5, we indicated that the historic evidence for the resurrection of Christ was sufficient to convert even skeptics. But is the evidence so good it could stand cross examination in a modern court of law? Here, we will examine what leading lawyers have concluded about the evidence for Christ's resurrection.

Our purpose is to cite sufficient documentation and examples to prove that even those expertly trained to evaluate and sift evidence declare that Christ's resurrection would stand under legal cross examination. To prove our point, we have cited by name more than three dozen well-respected lawyers from past and present.

In Acts 1:3, the physician Luke tells us that Jesus Christ was resurrected from the dead by "many infallible proofs." The Greek *en pollois tekmariois* is an expression which is defined in the lexicons as "decisive proof" and indicates the strongest type of legal evidence.[1]

Does the Evidence for the Resurrection Stand Cross Examination in a Modern Court of Law?

Lawyers, as noted, are expertly trained to deal with evidence. Skeptics can, if they wish, maintain that only the weak-minded would believe in the literal, physical resurrection of Christ, but perhaps this only reveals their own weak-mindedness when it comes to taking the evidence at face value.

Lawyers are not weak-minded. Hundreds of lawyers are represented by The National Christian Legal Society, The O.W. Coburn School of Law, The Rutherford Institute, Lawyers Christian Fellowship, Simon Greenleaf University, Regent University School of Law, and other Christian law organizations, schools, and societies. Among their number are some of the most respected lawyers in the country, men who have graduated from our leading law schools and gone on to prominence in the world of law. The law schools of Cornell, Harvard, Yale, Boston, New York University, University of the Southern California, Georgetown, University of Michigan, Northwestern, Hastings College of Law at U.C. Berkeley, Loyola, and many others are all represented.[2] Among the Board of Reference or distinguished lectureships given at Dr. Weldon's alma mater, Simon Greenleaf University, we could cite Samuel Ericsson, J.D., Harvard Law School; Renatus J. Chytil, formerly a lecturer at Cornell and an expert on Czechoslovakian law; Dr. John W. Brabner-Smith, Dean Emeritus of the International School of Law, Washington, D.C.; and Richard Colby, J.D., Yale Law School, with Twentieth Century Fox.[3] All are Christians who accept the resurrection of Christ as a historic fact. The truth of the resurrection can be determined by the very reasoning used in law to determine questions of fact. (This procedure is also true for establishing the historic reliability and accuracy of the New Testament documents.)

Lord Darling, a former lord chief justice in England, asserts: "In its favor as a living truth there exists such overwhelming evidence, positive and negative, factual and circumstantial, that no intelligent jury in the world could fail to bring in a verdict that the resurrection story is true."[4]

John Singleton Copley (Lord Lyndhurst, 1772–1863) is recognized as one of the greatest legal minds in British history. He was solicitor general of the British government, attorney general of Great Britain, three times the high chancellor of England and elected high steward of the University of Cambridge. He challenges, "I know pretty well what evidence is; and I tell you, such evidence as that for the resurrection has never broken down yet."[5]

Hugo Grotius was a noted "jurist and scholar whose works are of fundamental importance in international law," according to the *Encyclopædia Britannica.* He wrote Latin elegies at the age of eight and entered Leiden University at 11. Considered "the father of international law," he wrote *The Truth of the Christian Religion* (1627) in which he legally defended the historic fact of the resurrection.[6]

J. N. D. Anderson, in the words of Armand Nicholi of the Harvard Medical School (*Christianity Today,* March 29, 1968), is a scholar of international repute eminently qualified to deal with the subject of evidence. He is one of the world's leading authorities on Muslim law, dean of the Faculty of Law at the University of London, chairman of the Department of Oriental Law at the School of Oriental and African Studies, and director of the Institute of Advanced Legal Studies at the University of London.[7] In Anderson's text, *Christianity: The Witness of History,* he supplies the standard evidences for the resurrection and asks, "How, then, can the fact of the resurrection be denied?"[8] Anderson further emphasizes, "Lastly, it can be asserted with confidence that men and women disbelieve the Easter story not because of the evidence but in spite of it."[9]

Sir Edward Clark, K.C., observes, "As a lawyer, I have made a prolonged study of the evidences for the events of the first Easter day. To me the evidence is conclusive, and over and over again in the High Court I have secured the verdict on evidence not nearly so compelling. Inference follows on evidence, and a truthful witness is always artless and disdains effect. The gospel evidence for the resurrection is of this class, and as a lawyer I accept it unreservedly as a testimony of truthful men to facts they were able to substantiate."[10]

Irwin H. Linton was a Washington, D.C. lawyer who argued cases before the U.S. Supreme Court. In *A Lawyer Examines the Bible,* he challenges his fellow lawyers "by every acid test known to the law... to examine the case for the Bible just as they would any important matter submitted to their professional attention by a client..."[11] He believes that the evidence for Christianity is "overwhelming" and that at least "three independent and converging lines of proof," each of which "is conclusive in itself," establish the truth of the Christian faith.[12] Linton observed that "the logical, historical...proofs of...Christianity are so indisputable that I have found them to arrest the surprised attention of just about every man to whom I have presented them...."[13] He further argues the resurrection "is not only so established that the greatest lawyers have declared it to be the best proved fact of all history, but it is so supported that it is difficult to conceive of any method or line of proof that it lacks which would make [it] more certain."[14] And that, even among lawyers, "he who does not accept wholeheartedly the evangelical, conservative belief in Christ and the Scriptures has never read, has forgotten, or never been able to weigh—and certainly is utterly unable to refute—the irresistible force of the cumulative evidence upon which such faith rests..."[15]

He concluded the claims of Christian faith are so well established by such a variety of independent and converging proofs that "it has been said again and again by great lawyers that they cannot but be regarded as proved under the strictest rules of evidence used in the highest American and English courts."[16]

Simon Greenleaf was the Royal Professor of Law at Harvard and author of the classic three-volume text, *A Treatise on the Law of Evidence* (1842), which, according to Dr. Wilbur Smith, "is still considered the greatest single authority on evidence in the entire literature on legal procedure."[17] Greenleaf himself is considered one of the greatest authorities on common-law evidence in Western history. The *London Law Journal* wrote of him in 1874, "It is no mean honor to America that her schools of jurisprudence have produced two of the finest writers and best esteemed legal authorities in this century—the great and good man, Judge Story, and his eminent and worthy associate Professor Greenleaf. Upon the existing law of evidence (by Greenleaf) more light has shown from the New World than from all the lawyers who adorn the courts of Europe."[18]

Further:

> Dr. Simon Greenleaf was one of the greatest legal minds we have had in this country. He was the famous Royal Professor of Law at Harvard University, and succeeded Justice

Joseph Story as the Dane Professor of Law in the same university.

H. W. H. Knotts in the Dictionary of American Biography says of him: "To the efforts of Story and Greenleaf is ascribed the rise of the Harvard Law School to its eminent position among the legal schools of the United States." ...

Greenleaf concluded that the resurrection of Christ was one of the best supported events in history, according to the laws of legal evidence administered in courts of justice.[19]

In his book *Testimony of the Evangelists Examined by the Rules of Evidence Administered in Courts of Justice,* Greenleaf writes: "All that Christianity asks of men ... is, that they would be consistent with themselves; that they would treat its evidences as they treat the evidence of other things; and that they would try and judge its actors and witnesses, as they deal with their fellow men, when testifying to human affairs and actions, in human tribunals. Let the witnesses [to the resurrection] be compared with themselves, with each other, and with surrounding facts and circumstances; and let their testimony be sifted, as if it were given in a court of justice, on the side of the adverse party, the witness being subjected to a rigorous cross-examination. The result, it is confidently believed, will be an undoubting conviction of their integrity, ability and truth."[20]

Lord Caldecote, lord chief justice of England, observed that an "overwhelming case for the resurrection could be made merely as a matter of strict evidence"[21] and that "His resurrection has led me as often as I have tried to examine the evidence to believe it as a fact beyond dispute...."[22]

Thomas Sherlock's *Trial of the Witnesses of the Resurrection of Jesus Christ* places the resurrection in a legally argued forum and in the words of lawyer Irwin Linton, "will give anyone so reading it the comfortable assurance that he knows the utmost that can be said against the proof of the central fact of our faith and also how utterly every such attack can be met and answered."[23] At the end of the legal battle one understands why, "The jury returned a verdict in favor of the testimony establishing the fact of Christ's resurrection."[24]

But any lawyer familiar with the evidence could do the same today either for themselves or an impartial jury. Although admissibility rules vary by state and no lawyer can guarantee the decision of any jury (no matter how persuasive the evidence), an abundance of lawyers will testify today that the resurrection would stand in the vast majority of law courts. The following statements were received in written form from the individuals cited as a result of phone conversations held on March 26-28, 1990 or January 10, 1995. John Whitehead is founder of the Rutherford Institute and one of the leading constitutional attorneys in America. He asserts, "The evidence for the resurrection, if competently presented, would likely be affirmed in a modern law court."

Larry Donahue is an experienced trial attorney in Los Angeles. He has 20 years' experience with courtroom law trials. He also teaches courses on legal evidence at Simon Greenleaf University in Anaheim, California, as well as a lengthy course subjecting the biblical eyewitnesses to legal cross examination titled, "The Resurrection on Trial." He states: "I am convinced that in a civil lawsuit in nearly any courtroom today there is more than sufficient admissible direct and circumstantial evidence that a jury could be persuaded to a preponderance burden of proof that the physical bodily resurrection of Christ did occur."

Richard F. Duncan holds a national reputation as a legal scholar whose area of specialty is constitutional law. He graduated from Cornell Law School (where he wrote for the *Law Review*) and practiced corporate law at White and Case, a major Wall Street law firm. He has spent eleven years teaching at such law schools as Notre Dame and New York University and is a tenured professor at the University of Nebraska. Mr. Duncan has written briefs at the Supreme Court level and is the author of a standard text on commercial law widely used by attorneys practicing under the Uniform Commercial Code, *The Law in Practice of Secure Transaction* (Law Journal Seminars Press, 1987). He observes, "The resurrection of Jesus Christ, the central fact of world history, withstands rational analysis precisely because the evidence is so persuasive.... I am convinced this verdict would stand in nearly any modern court of law."

A. Eric Johnston is currently a member of the law firm of Seier, Johnston, and Trippe in Birmingham, Alabama. He practices in the areas of constitutional law, federal statutory law, and litigation in the federal and state courts on trial and appellate levels. He is a member of the American Bar Association, was the 1988 Republican nominee for place four on the Alabama Supreme Court, and has been listed as one of the Outstanding Young Men of America and in *Who's Who in American Law*. He states, "In a civil court, if the evidence were properly presented, I believe this would be sufficient for a jury to find that Christ did rise from the dead."

Donovan Campbell, Jr., is a graduate of Princeton University and the University of Texas, where he was editor of the *Texas Law Review*. He was admitted to the Texas Bar in 1975; the U.S. Tax Court in 1976; the U.S. Court of Claims in 1977; and the U.S. Court of Appeals for the Fifth Circuit in 1978. He has had wide experience in the field of law and litigation. He states, "If the evidence for the resurrection were competently presented to a normal jury in a civil court of law at the current time, then a verdict establishing the fact of the resurrection should be obtained."

Larry L. Crain, a graduate of Vanderbilt University, a general partner in the law firm of Ames, Southworth, and Crain in Brentwood, Tennessee, a member of the U.S. Supreme Court Bar, the Federal Bar Association, the American Trial Lawyers Association, and who has argued before the Supreme Court, told us that he agrees in principle with the statements we have cited.

Wendell R. Byrd is an Atlanta attorney and graduate of Yale Law School. As a student, he was the first ever to exempt the freshman year at Vanderbilt University, where he graduated summa cum laude; he also received Yale's prize for one of the best two student publications. He is a member of the most prestigious legal organization, The American Law Institute, has published in the *Yale Law Journal, Harvard Journal of Law and Public Policy*, and has argued before the U.S. Supreme Court. He is listed in *Who's Who in the World, Who's Who in the South and South-west,* and *Who's Who Among Emerging Leaders in America.* He asserts: "In a civil trial I believe the evidence is sufficient that a modern jury should bring in a positive verdict that the resurrection of Christ did happen."

William Burns Lawless is a retired justice of the New York Supreme Court and former dean of Notre Dame Law School. He asserts, "When Professor Simon Greenleaf of Harvard Law School published his distinguished treatise on the Law of Evidence in 1842, he analyzed the resurrection accounts in the Gospels. Under the rules of evidence then he concluded a Court would admit these accounts and consider their contents reliable. In my opinion that conclusion is as valid in 1995 as it was in 1842."

In *Leading Lawyers Look at the Resurrection,* many other examples are given. For example: Sir Lionell Luckhoo is listed in the *Guiness Book of Records* as the world's "most successful lawyer," with 245 successive murder acquittals. He was knighted twice by the queen of England and appointed high commissioner for Guyana. He declares, "I have spent more than forty-two years as a defense trial lawyer appearing in many parts of the world . . . I say unequivocally the evidence for the resurrection of Jesus Christ is so overwhelming that it compels acceptance by proof which leaves absolutely no doubt."[25]

Dale Foreman, a graduate of the Harvard Law School and lawyer in Washington state, writes in *Crucify Him: A Lawyer Looks at the Trial of Jesus,* "These facts [the trial, crucifixion, and death of Christ], I believe, are clear and proven beyond a reasonable doubt. . . . The teachings of Jesus have changed the world. In 2000 years not a day has gone by when the influence of this itinerate teacher from Nazareth has not been felt. As a trial lawyer, I am trained to be rational, skeptical and critical, I believe it improbable that any fraud or false Messiah could have made such a profound impression for good. The most reasonable conclusion, and the most satisfying, is that Jesus was indeed the Son of God, that He was who He claimed to be and that He did come back to life."[26]

Val Grieve, senior partner in a Manchester, England, law firm, writes in *Your Verdict on the Empty Tomb of Jesus,* "Ever since I became a Christian, I have carefully examined the evidence for the resurrection.... I claim that logic must point in the direction of His resurrection on an actual day and date in our history..."[27]

Francis Lamb, a Wisconsin lawyer, is the author of *Miracle and Science,* which tests the credibility of biblical miracles through legal examination. He asserts, "Tested by the standards or ordeals of jural science by which questions of fact are ascertained and demonstrated in the contested questions of right between man and man in courts of justice, *the resurrection of Jesus stands as a demonstrated fact.*"[28]

Stephen D. Williams, a lawyer from Detroit, Michigan, and author of *The Bible in Court or Truth Vs. Error* wrote, "We have been asked many times if the proof of the resurrection of Jesus was as complete and convincing from a legal standpoint, as that afforded by the record of other events in his life narrated in the Gospel. To this question, we must answer: yes. The proof is to be found in the same record, supplied by the same witnesses..."[29]

In addition, we may refer to Sir Leslie Herron, chief justice of NSW Australia, Frank J. Powell, the outstanding English magistrate and author of the scholarly *The Trial of Jesus Christ,* and also Mr. Clarrie Briese, a distinguished Australian lawyer, awarded a Churchill Fellowship, graduate of Cambridge University, and chief magistrate of NSW [New South Wales] and author of *Witnesses to the Resurrection—Credible or Not?*[30]

But such citations could be multiplied indefinitely. We have not mentioned the eminent Lord Chancellor Hailsham, the current lord chancellor of England and Wales,[31] or Lord Diplock,[32] or Joseph J. Darlington, the only lawyer in the nation's capital to whom a public monument has been erected, whom former president and chief justice of the U.S. Supreme Court William Howard Taft said was one of the three or four greatest lawyers in the nation's history.[33] We have not mentioned Sir Matthew Hale, the great lord chancellor under Oliver Cromwell, John Seldon, Sir Robert Anderson, former head of Scotland Yard, knighted by Queen Victoria for his utmost skill in exposing "the mazes of falsehood...discovering truth and separating it from error," Daniel Webster, Lord Erskine, or many others.[34]

But it is not merely in the field of law that we find committed believers in Christ's resurrection—eminent philosophers, historians, scientists, physicians, theologians, and experts in literature and comparative religion can be cited in abundance, proving that the resurrection of Christ must be seriously considered by any thinking person.[35]

For example, societies of Christian believers exist for most scholarly categories—law, science, history, philosophy, literature, and the like. Collectively they include thousands of members among whom are some of the most erudite minds of our time. Yet all of them believe in the physical resurrection of Christ *because* they find the evidence convincing. For example, among philosophers we could cite Basil Mitchell, for many years the Nolloth Professor of the Christian Religion at Oxford University and author of *The Justification of Religious Belief*. Alvin Plantinga of Notre Dame has taught at Yale, Harvard, UCLA, Boston University, and University of Chicago, and has been president of the American Philosophical Association and the Society of Christian Philosophers. Richard Swineburn of Oxford University is widely known as one of the premier rational defenders of Christian faith in the twentieth century and is author of *The Coherence of Theism, Faith and Reason*. Mortimer J. Adler has held professorships at Columbia University and the University of Chicago, is director of the *Institute for Philosophical Research*, and, as noted, is chairman of the board of editors of the *Encyclopædia Britannica*, architect of *The Great Books of the Western World* and its *Syntopicon*, and author of more than 50 books including *Truth in Religion, Ten Philosophical Mistakes*, and *How to Think About God*.[36] Hundreds of other distinguished names could also be added from other scholarly disciplines. Men of intellectual caliber as this simply do not believe in the resurrection apart from rational, convincing evidence.

Of course, the more severe the consequences for rejecting a worldview, if it is true, the less we should take chances. The chance that Christianity is true is at least 99 percent, but even if it were only 10 percent, we should accept it because of the possibility of facing God in judgment if wrong. Among all the religions in the world, Christianity is the most trustworthy of all. In other words, the evidence truly *is* clear enough for one to select Christianity over the truth claims of any other religion. Indeed, as the Apostle Luke tells us in Acts 17:31, God "has fixed a day in which He will judge the world in righteousness through a Man whom He has appointed, having furnished *proof* to all men by raising Him from the dead."

In conclusion, we have shown that both those who were committed skeptics and those who are expertly trained to sift evidence have declared, on the basis of the evidence, that the resurrection of Jesus Christ is a historic fact. But that doesn't mean our job is over. Historically, critics have proposed a number of theories to explain the resurrection on other grounds, and these must at least be briefly addressed. However, what we find is that, collectively, these alternate theories do not decrease our faith in the resurrection, they increase it considerably as we discover that, in 2,000 years, only the Christian interpretation of the empty tomb warrants our acceptance.

Chapter 7

Alternate Theories
to the Resurrection

Ever since the time of Jesus (Matthew 28:11-15), critics have been attempting to explain the empty tomb on naturalistic grounds. They assume that Jesus' body remained dead. In two thousand years of history many different theories have been proposed, but "not one of these theories has ever met with general acceptance, even among radical critics and rationalists."[1] The following list is representative of these theories.[2] After a brief discussion, we offer two summary charts and then a more in-depth critique of one popular alternate theory in order to illustrate the inadequacies of skeptical alternate theories generally.

How Credible Are They?

The Swoon Theory

This theory claims that Jesus never died on the cross but merely "swooned." After his crucifixion (which incidentally included a spear thrust into the heart) Jesus was taken down from the cross, wrapped in seventy-five pounds of linen and spices, and placed in a tomb. Yet somehow he revived. After three days without food or water, Jesus unwrapped himself (even though his arms had been wrapped against his body and the spice-soaked linens were probably somewhat dried and hardened by this point), moved the one-to-two-ton stone from

111

the grave entrance, and walked some distance on mutilated feet to find his disciples so that he could falsely proclaim himself to be the resurrected Messiah and conqueror of death. And, the disciples believed him! The Gospel resurrection accounts, however, leave little doubt that he did die on the cross.

The Passover Plot Theory

A version of the swoon theory, this theory asserts that Jesus plotted to fake his death to give the appearance that he arose from the dead. He conspired with Judas to betray him to the Jewish authorities, and with Joseph of Arimathea to see to it that he was given a strong potion on the cross which would put him in "a deathlike trance." Appearing as dead to the Roman authorities, Jesus was to be taken off the cross and laid in a tomb, where he would revive after a short time, and then reappear as "resurrected" to his disciples. According to this entirely unbelievable line of thinking, the unexpected spear thrust led to his unforeseen death. Joseph had him buried in an unknown tomb. The disciples, however, came upon the intended place of burial, found the prearranged grave clothes and falsely concluded from this that he was alive. This theory makes Christ a fraud and the disciples near idiots. Moreover, if Christ was dead, how does one account for the many documented resurrection appearances?

The Stolen or Moved Body Theory

This theory proposes that the disciples had stolen or moved the body to make it appear that Jesus had been resurrected. This would again make the disciples frauds. Moreover, such an act would have been unthinkable to them for several reasons: (1) they never *expected* Jesus to rise from the dead; (2) *all* of them would not have willingly remained silent about this lie in view of the likelihood that they would be killed for adhering to it; nor (3) would they have made God responsible for such a deception. Other versions of the theory propose that the Jews, Romans, or Joseph of Arimathea moved the body, for reasons hardly more compelling. If the authorities had Christ's body, why didn't they drag it out and put an end to the Christian religion at the very start?

The Hallucination/Vision Theory

The hallucination theory asserts that all who had purportedly seen the resurrected Jesus—the twelve disciples, the women, James (Jesus' brother), the crowd of five hundred people—were strange visionaries or mentally ill. They hallucinated the risen Jesus through neurotic or psychotic visions. But this theory is wrong, because all of the known characteristics of hallucination are entirely absent from the Gospel accounts of the encounter of Jesus' followers with the risen Christ.

More generally, the vision theory claims that the resurrected Jesus appeared to his followers through visions in the mind. This theory does not fit the accounts: for example, what of doubting Thomas, who needed physical confirmation, and the crowd of five hundred who simultaneously saw the risen Lord? What of Jesus Himself, who actively encouraged the disciples to touch Him physically to prove to them His resurrection (Luke 24:39; John, ch. 21)?

The Telegram/Telegraph Theory

This theory claims that the spiritually ascended Jesus telegraphed images of himself from heaven to the minds of his followers on earth. These images were so graphic that his followers mistakenly thought that they had physically seen the resurrected Jesus in their midst. There is one major problem with this theory: What about the empty tomb?

The Mistaken Identity Theory

This theory states that the twelve disciples, who virtually lived with Jesus for three years and never expected him to rise from the dead, sometime after Christ's death came to the conclusion that he would come back to life. They then misidentified a complete stranger as the risen Jesus. But surely they would have quickly recognized their error when conversing with the stranger or at least seeing him close up.

The Wrong Tomb/Grave Was Not Visited Theory

This theory proposes that although Jesus' followers saw where his body was buried, three days later they could not locate the tomb. Subsequently they went to the wrong grave, which was empty, and incorrectly assumed from this that Jesus had been resurrected. There were, however, no resurrection appearances. The disciples concluded that Jesus had risen solely on the basis of an empty tomb—a tomb which they were not certain was the correct one in the first place! This theory, however, places an exceedingly low intelligence quotient on the disciples, one greatly at odds with their depiction in the four Gospels.

The Seance Theory

This theory asserts that Jesus was "raised" in the same manner that a spirit is "raised" in a seance through ectoplasmic manifestation. It claims this despite the fact that it makes Jesus' followers participants in a seance, a practice their own Scriptures sternly prohibit (cf., e.g., Deuteronomy 18:9-12). It also makes them out to be either liars or deluded for believing that something as ephemeral as an ectoplasmic manifestation was the same thing as a literal, physical resurrection appearance.

The Annihilation Theory

This theory claims that Jesus' body inexplicably disintegrated into nothingness. It has received no support.

The "Jesus Never Existed" and "Resurrection as Legend" Theories

The first theory proposes that Jesus was a fraudulent invention of the disciples, a legend. It too has no support. But a variation of this theory has held more sway and so we shall discuss it in more detail. It asserts that the followers of Jesus derived the resurrection story from similar stories of contemporary Greco-Roman mystery cults, and sees the figure Jesus as a historical person but the resurrection as strictly legendary. The dissimilarity, however, between the mystery cults of the first century and early Christianity is far too great; moreover, the early Church consistently opposed such assimilation.

Anyone who takes the time to compare these theories to the four Gospel resurrection accounts quickly discovers that they are highly inferior explanations, grossly conflicting at many points with each other and more importantly with the biblical evidence itself. The fundamental problem for the critic is that he has yet to propose a theory that *reasonably* accounts for all the historical data to the satisfaction of believer and skeptic alike (cf. chapter 8).

No Other Options

Since the time of Christ, *no attempt* to offer conclusive proof against the bodily resurrection has succeeded. This in itself is very significant. Every alternate theory is more difficult to believe than the belief that Jesus physically rose from the dead, a conviction shared by all four Gospel writers and all New Testament teaching on this point. And, as we documented in our book on the resurrection, this conviction is most compelling. Summary statements by some leading scholars who have carefully examined the alternate theories is telling in this regard:

James Orr: "None of these theories can stand calm examination ... The objections are but small dust of the balance compared with the strength of the evidence for the fact."[3]

James F. Babcock: "These and other chimerical explanations which have been proposed through the centuries do even less justice to the evidence than [does] the straightforward historical interpretation itself."[4]

George Hanson: "The simple faith of the Christian who believes in the resurrection is nothing compared to the credulity of the skeptic who will accept the wildest and most improbable romances rather than admit the plain witness of historical certainties. The difficulties of belief may be great; the absurdities of unbelief are greater."[5]

Wilbur M. Smith: "Of the several attempts to explain rationalistically the empty tomb ... it need only be said that none is inherently credible or has commanded general respect."[6]

William Lane Craig: "We have seen that the history of the debate over the resurrection of Jesus has produced several dead ends in the attempt to explain away the evidence of the resurrection. The conspiracy theory, the apparent death theory, the wrong tomb theory, and their variations have all proved inadequate as plausible alternative explanations for the resurrection."[7]

John Warwick Montgomery: "The 'swoon theory' is typical of all such arguments: they are infinitely more improbable than the resurrection itself, and they fly squarely in the face of the documentary evidence."[8]

Bernard Ramm: "It has become evident that if certain minimal historical facts be granted, the logic of the believer in the resurrection is impossible to parry. For this reason practically all of the older efforts to explain away the resurrection by recourse to the swoon theory, wrong-grave theory, telegraph theory, stolen body theory, etc., are beside the point, abortive; therefore we will not spend any time rehashing these theories so ably refuted in the other good evangelical literature."[9]

John Lilly: "All of these attacks have been triumphantly repulsed, their futility demonstrated. The field of biblical criticism resembles a vast graveyard filled with the skeletons of discarded theories devised by highly imaginative skeptics.... One might think that so many repeated failures...would lead the opposition to abandon their efforts, but not so. They continue unabated, and men are still wracking their brains, working their imaginations overtime, and parading a vast amount of erudition and ingenuity in their, to us, futile attempts to destroy the impregnable rock of historical evidence on which the Christian faith in the resurrection stands proud and unshaken."[10]

That so many millions of people today continue to believe that the resurrection took place, after nearly two-thousand years of critical scrutiny by some of the world's most brilliant minds, is really rather remarkable if it never happened. Modern skeptics face the same problems that skeptics at the time of Jesus faced: the empty tomb and the resurrection appearances. No one then could disprove the empty tomb or explain away the resurrection appearances, and no one today can do it. As Wilbur Smith asserts, "The closest, most critical examination of these narratives throughout the ages never has destroyed and never can destroy their powerful testimony to the truth that Christ did rise from the dead on the third day, and was seen by many."[11]

To maintain, in the first century, that the resurrection never happened would almost be the modern equivalent of maintaining that men have never traveled to the moon; too much evidence exists for a reasonable person to deny the event. Most critics deny the resurrection because of an antisupernatural bias against miracles, not because of inferior evidence.

As Wilbur Smith asserts, both the empty grave and the resurrection appearances provide "a mass of evidence that can never be destroyed with any of the laws of literary criticism or of logic known to man. They have, consequently, stood the fiercest opposition, investigation, and criticism of at least eighteen successive centuries."[12] Indeed, it is hard to know which is the more amazing, the alternate theories themselves or the fact that they continue to be put forth by otherwise intelligent men. As the apostle Peter confesses: "We did *not* follow cleverly devised tales when we made known to you the power and coming of our Lord Jesus Christ, but we were eyewitnesses of his majesty" (2 Peter 1:16).

It is not just that these theories are improbable, it is that they are, in the end, impossible. Not only is there no literary or historical evidence for their support, the historical facts themselves refute any and every critical theory ever proposed. These facts are accepted by the majority of scholars, Christian or skeptical:

1. Jesus died by crucifixion.

2. Jesus was buried in an easily accessible public tomb.

3. The death of Christ caused His followers to lose all hope in His Messianic claims.

4. The tomb was empty.

5. The disciples had genuine experiences, which they were convinced were literal appearances of the risen Christ.

6. The disciples were *radically transformed* from skeptics and doubters to bold proclaimers of Christ's resurrection.

7. Eleven of the twelve apostles suffered martyrs' deaths for their convictions.

8. The resurrection message was absolutely central to the early preaching of the Church.

9. The resurrection message was central to the entire New Testament.

10. The resurrection was first proclaimed in the very environment most hostile to it, Jerusalem. Even there, those motivated to disprove the resurrection could not do so.

11. The Church exists only because of the disciples' conviction that the resurrection occurred.

12. The Sabbath Day was changed to Sunday.

13. James, Paul, and many other skeptics were convinced on the basis of empirical historical evidence.

Finally, the deathblow to these critical theories is that collectively each of them refutes something of the others until nothing is left. In other words, theory A, in proposing theory B, discredits theory C, and so on. They all collapse for the simple reason that although each critical theory rejects part of the Gospel testimony, each also accepts and independently establishes the truth of another part of the Gospel testimony. The accepted evidence of one theory refutes the substance of some of the others. Taken together, all the critical theories of the nineteenth and twentieth centuries establish *both* the reliability of the New Testament as well as the unreliability of the alternate critical theories themselves. As Dr. Gary Habermas observes, "One interesting illustration of this failure of the naturalistic theories is that they were disproved by the nineteenth-century older liberals themselves, [the very ones] by whom these theories were popularized. These scholars refuted each other's theories, leaving no viable naturalistic hypotheses. . . . Although nineteenth-century liberals decimated each other's views individually, twentieth-century critical scholars have generally rejected naturalistic theories as a whole, judging that they are incapable of explaining the known data. . . . That even such critical scholars have rejected these naturalistic theories is a significant epitaph for the failure of these views."[13]

In the end, facts will always win because facts, unlike mere opinion, cannot be changed or disproved. The twentieth-century theories proposed to explain away the resurrection are no better and suffer the same fate as their nineteenth-century counterparts.

Theologically, the severest criticism of these theories is that they make God responsible for a lie. The undisputed teaching of the New Testament is that God raised Jesus bodily from the dead. But according to these theories, Jesus' body never left the tomb. Yet, for the twelve disciples, all of whom were Jewish, to make God responsible for a work He *clearly* did not do would have been unthinkable.

What is just as unthinkable is that the resurrection was somehow derived from ancient pagan religions.

Christianity, the Resurrection of Christ, and the Mystery Religions

Many university and college courses on Christianity or comparative religion express the view that Christianity is merely a variation of a more ancient religious theme. They teach that Christian faith developed from or was influenced by the ancient pagan mystery religions of Rome, Greece, and Egypt. Therefore, the conclusion of such courses is that Christian faith is not unique as it claims, but at best an imitation faith, claiming to be something it really is not. Professors draw numerous "parallels" between the motifs of "dying and rising," "savior"-gods, and then, observing the centrality of the death and resurrection of Jesus Christ in Christian faith, assert that Christianity was merely a later form of such pagan religions.

In the last hundred years, numerous books have been written that attempt to defend this idea. Among these are J.M. Robertson's *Pagan Christs*[16] and Kersey Graves' *The World's Sixteen Crucified Saviors or Christianity Before Christ.*[17] This idea has also formed one line of argumentation for the larger theme that Jesus never existed as in G. A. Wells' *Did Jesus Exist?*[18] and more recently this concept has been popularized by the late mythologist Joseph Campbell in *The Power of Myth, The Masks of God,* and other books meant to, at least in part, discredit Christianity.

What were the mystery cults? Allegedly, the teachings of the mystery religions were revealed by the Egyptian god Thoth.

They were eclectic religious cults that stressed nature religion, oaths of secrecy, brotherhood, and spiritual quest. They offered rites of initiation that were associated with or dedicated to various gods and goddesses of the ancient world. In fact, these rites often inculcated contact, or "union," with the "gods" (spirits). Participants hoped to attain knowledge, power, and immortality from their worship and contact with these gods. In essence, the mystery religions were part and parcel of the world of the occult in ancient Europe and Asia. They were idolatrous, opposed Christian teachings, and not infrequently engaged in gross or immoral practices.[19]

Nevertheless, it was the theme of alleged dying and rising savior-gods that initially sparked the interest of some scholars and many skeptics as to whether or not Christianity was a derivative of the mysteries. For example, if there were religious cults in Palestine at the time of Christ who believed in a mythological central figure who periodically died and came back to life in harmony with certain agricultural or fertility cycles, it could be argued that Christianity was merely the offshoot of such a religion and that its distinctive theological teachings were later inventions. Hence the appeal of such an idea to skeptics of Christianity.

If true, Christianity would have been only a variation of an earlier pagan religious worldview, a religion that later evolved its distinctive theological doctrines about Jesus Christ being the unique incarnation of God and savior of men. In fact, in this scenario, the biblical Jesus need never even have existed. The mysteries were, after all, based on mythical gods. Hence, some critics (not historians) argue that Jesus was only an invented figure patterned after the life cycles of mythological gods such as Attis, Cybele, Osiris, Mithra, Adonis, Eleusis, Thrace, Dionysus, and the like.

One consequence of interpreting Christianity as an embellished mystery religion is the conclusion that Christian faith per se is the invention of men, not a revelation from God. In the end, virtually all the unique teachings of New Testament theology, including the distinctive doctrines on Jesus Christ, God, man, sin, salvation, and so on, are viewed as mere religious innovation after the fact. For example, concerning Jesus Christ, this would mean His incarnation and virgin birth, miracles and teachings, atonement for sin, physical resurrection from the dead, and promised return are not historical facts, but later revisions of pagan stories. In essence, the cardinal teachings of orthodox Christianity become lies and falsehoods.

But is it Christianity that is the invention and deception, or is such a theory itself the invention and deception of atheists and skeptics merely to discredit Christianity? If we examine the manner in which this concept is utilized, not to mention the fact that not a shred of evidence exists in support, one can begin to see where the real invention lies. One illustration is atheist John Allegro's text, *The Sacred Mushroom and the Cross*. Allegro is a lecturer in Old Testament and Inter-Testamental Studies at the University of Manchester. He weaves the origin of Christianity into pagan religious sects, rituals, secret eulogies, and the hallucinogenic properties of a particular mushroom. Thus, "The death and resurrection story of Jesus follows the traditional patterns of fertility mythology, as has long been recognized."[20] Logically then, for Allegro, the New Testament is a "hoax" because the "validity of the whole New Testament story is immediately undermined."[21] Not surprisingly, he claims it is foolish for Christians to maintain their religion is a unique revelation from God.[22] As a result, Allegro's closing paragraph gives the reader the "assurance" that "we no longer need to view the Bible through the mists of piety."[23]

The truth is that Allegro's views are credible only to skeptics who already wish to find "evidence" to support their skepticism. Dr. J. N. D. Anderson is an authority on comparative religion, a professor of Oriental Laws, and director of the Institute of Advanced Legal Studies at the University of London. He observes that Allegro's book "has been dismissed by fifteen experts in Semitic languages and related fields . . . as 'not based on any philological or other evidence that they can regard as scholarly'—and has met with scathing criticism in review after review."[24] Yet today it continues to be used in college courses on Christianity.

Unfortunately for skeptics, when Allegro's theory—or that involving any other mystery tradition—is objectively examined and compared with Christianity, only superficial similarities remain because Christianity and the mystery religions are as distinct as night and day.[25] Even secular scholars have rejected this idea of Christianity borrowing from the ancient mysteries. The well respected Sir Edward Evans-Pritchard writes in *Theories of Primitive Religion* that, "The evidence for this theory . . . is negligible."[26] Negligible is defined in the *Webster's New World Dictionary* as that which "can be neglected or disregarded because small, unimportant, trifling."

In fact, the gods of the mysteries do not even resurrect; at best they are only resuscitated within the context of a gross mythology. Samuel N. Kramer's thorough work showed that the alleged resurrection of Tammuz (a fertility god of Mesopotamia) was based on "nothing but inference and surmise, guess and conjecture."[27] Pierre Lambrechts maintains that in the case of the alleged resurrection of Adonis no evidence exists, either in the early texts or the pictorial representations. The texts which refer to a resurrection are quite late, from the second to the fourth centuries A.D.[28] He reveals that for Attis there is no suggestion that he was a resurrected god until after 150 A.D.[29] In the case of Adonis, there is a lapse of at least 700 years.[30] If borrowing occurred, it seems clear which way it went.

The cult of Isis and Osiris ends with Osiris becoming lord of the underworld while Isis regathers his dismembered body from the Nile River and subsequently magically restores it. E. A. Wallace Budge, who Dr. Wilbur Smith asserts is "one of the greatest authorities of our century on ancient religions,"[31] has this to say about the cult of Osiris: "There is nothing in the texts which justify the assumption that Osiris knew he would rise from the dead, and that he would become king and judge of the dead, or that Egyptians believed that Osiris died on their behalf and rose again in order that they might also rise from the dead."[32] Smith also observes French scholar Andre Boulanger's observation that, "The idea that the god dies and rises again to lead his worshippers to eternal life does not exist in any Hellenic mystery religion."[33]

It would appear then, that the real mythology is not in the origin of Christianity but in the minds of skeptics who are confusing such beliefs with the historical person and work of Jesus of Nazareth. (This is especially evident when one considers the immoral lives and deeds of the pagan deities since these are entirely disharmonious with the life and deeds of Jesus Christ.)

Indeed, as noted, scholars long ago refuted the idea that Christianity is related to the mysteries. Consider just a few of the great differences between Christian belief and the mystery cults that makes the claim of identity look foolish:

> As for the motif of a dying and rising savior-god, which has so often been compared with the unique event which gave birth to Christianity, Metzger points out that the formal resemblance between them must not be allowed to obscure the great differences in content. In all the Mysteries which tell of a dying god, he dies "by compulsion and not by choice, sometimes in bitterness and despair, never in a self-giving love." There is a positive gulf between this and the Christ who asserted that no man could take his life from him but that he laid it down of his own will (John 10:17; Matthew 26:53); the Johannine pictures of the cross as the place where Jesus was "glorified"; and the Christian celebration of the Passion as a victory over Satan, sin and death. Similarly, there is all the difference in the world between the rising or re-birth of a deity which symbolizes the coming of spring (and the re-awakening of nature) and the resurrection "on the third day" of an historical person.[34]

Former atheist and Cambridge and Oxford scholar C.S. Lewis emphasizes that the biblical concept of God in both Old and New Testaments is in no way compatible with the nature gods of the mysteries. "On the other hand, Jahweh is clearly *not* a Nature-God. He does not die and come to life each year as a true corn-king should . . . He is not the soul of Nature nor any part of Nature. He inhabits eternity; he dwells in the high and holy place; heaven is his throne, not his vehicle, earth is his footstool, not his vesture. One day he will dismantle both and make a new heaven and earth. He is not to be identified even with the 'divine spark' in man. He is 'God and not man.' His thoughts are not our thoughts. . . . "[35]

In fact, Lewis had previously recorded that upon his first serious reading of the New Testament, he was "chilled and puzzled by the almost total absence of such ideas in the Christian documents."[36] In other words, he was familiar with the theories suggesting resemblance between Christianity and the mysteries, expected to find them, and was shocked to discover their absence.

E. O. James concludes, "There is *no valid comparison* between the synoptic story of Jesus of Nazareth and the mythological accounts of the mystery divinities of Eleusis, Thrace, Phrygia or Egypt.... Similarly, the belief in the resurrection of Christ is poles removed from the resuscitation of Osiris, Dionysus or Attis in an annual ritual based on primitive conceptions of mummifications, and the renewal of the new life in the spring."[37]

No less an authority than the late comparative religion scholar Mircea Eliade points out that not only is the idea of Christian borrowing from the mysteries wrong, but that any borrowing probably first began on the part of the mysteries:

> In 1958, one year before Campbell started publishing his fanciful theories in the *Masks of God* volumes, Mircea Eliade published in *Patterns of Initiation* a series of lectures he had given at the University of Chicago in the fall of 1956. In one of those lectures, Eliade said recent research did not support the theories that the origin of Christianity was influenced by pagan mystery cults. "There is no reason to suppose that primitive Christianity was influenced by the Hellenistic mysteries," said Eliade. In fact, the reverse may actually be true:
>
>> The renaissance of the mysteries in the first centuries of our era may well be related to the rise and spread of Christianity.... certain mysteries may well have reinterpreted their ancient rites in the light of the new religious values contributed by Christianity.
>
> Eliade added that it was only much later, when Christianity had to compete with the renaissance of the mystery cults, that Christians began to borrow from the religious symbols of these cults. They did this in order to help them explain their religion to others (not to modify it), thereby hoping to win converts.[38]

Further, and probably most damaging, there is simply *no* evidence that the mystery religions exerted any influence in Palestine in the first three decades of the first century. If so, where did the material originate to make Christianity a mystery religion? In fact, one wonders why such parallels would be suggested at all.[39] The manuscripts we possess prove that the teachings of Jesus and Paul are those given in the New Testament; sufficient time never existed for the disciples to be influenced by the mysteries even if they were open to the idea, which they weren't. When the influence of the mysteries did reach Palestine, principally through gnosticism, the early church did not accept it but renounced it vigorously as trafficking in pagan myths. The complete lack of resulting syncretism is difficult to explain if Christianity was ultimately a derivative of such paganism.

To illustrate, Mythraism was a chief adversary of Christianity, having a large following in the Roman army by 200 A.D.[40] The *Encyclopædia Britannica* comments, "One of the last of the Oriental Mystery cults to reach the West, Mythraism, was also one of the most rigorous, and in the final death struggle of paganism it emerged as a chief rival and opponent of Christianity."[41] But from the earliest moment, the resistance of the Christian Church to all such mystical cults was absolute. One authority on comparative religion, Dr. Robert Speer, author of *The Finality of Jesus Christ*, observes that:

> No Christian teacher of the first two centuries conceived the Christian gospel as a gospel to be bracketed in a fellowship with Stoicism and Neoplatonism, or Christ as a savior to be named with Mythra, or the Lord Jesus to be named with Lord Serapis or Lord Dionysus. The early church named One Name, and One Name Alone (see Romans 5:15, 17, 19) . . . and it steadfastly resisted every heresy from gnosticism onward which imperiled the New Testament view of the personality and primacy of Christ. . . . Against every assault of gnosticism and . . . against almost every conceivable objection to Christianity which the modern mind of our time has raised, the Christian thought of the first two centuries stood its ground utterly and unyieldingly.[42]

Indeed, Christianity waged intellectual warfare, without compromise, against the mystery religions and their varied moral and theological deficiencies. That such deficiencies were indeed varied can be seen in the following accounts describing the Cybelene, Egyptian, Persian, and Dionysian mysteries. No wonder the church so resolutely opposed them!

> In the wild orgies of worship associated with that [cybelene] mystery religion, some devotees voluntarily wounded themselves and, becoming intoxicated with the view of blood [cf. 1 Kings 18:28], with which they sprinkled their altars, they believed they were uniting themselves with their divinity. Others sacrificed their virility to the gods.

> St. Augustine wrote that, as a young man, he "took pleasure in the shameful games which were celebrated in honor of the gods and goddesses," including Cybele. On the day consecrated to her purification, "here were sung before her couch productions so obscene and filthy for the ear . . . so impure, that not even the mother of the foulmouthed players themselves could have formed one of the audience."

> During the ceremonial rites dedicated to the Great Mother, a young man stood beneath a platform upon which a steer was slaughtered and showered himself with the animal's blood. After the blood bath, the gore-covered mystic offered himself to the veneration of the crowd. The ceremony was known as the taurobolia . . .

> The Egyptian goddess Isis was honored especially by "women with whom love was a profession". . . . The morals of the cult of Isis and Osiris were viewed by the Roman community at large as very loose, and the mystery surrounding it excited the worst suspicions.

> Persia introduced dualism as a fundamental principle of religion, and deified the evil principle. It was taught that both evil and the supreme deity must be worshiped. . . . The Persian Mazdeans brought the dimension of magic to their rites and made their "mysteries" a reversed religion with a liturgy focused on the infernal powers. "There was no miracle the experienced magician might not expect to perform with the aid of demons. . . . Hence the number of

impious practices performed in the dark, practices the horror of which is equaled only by their absurdity: preparing beverages that disturbed the senses and impaired the intellect; mixing subtle poisons extracted from demonic plants and corpses already in the state of putridity; immolating children in order to read the future in their quivering entrails or to conjure up ghosts.... "[43]

And:

The initiation ceremonies usually mimed death and resurrection. This was done in the most extravagant manner. In some ceremonies, candidates were buried or shut up in a sarcophagus; they were even symbolically deprived of their entrails and mummified (an animal's belly with entrails was prepared for ceremony). Alternately, the candidates were symbolically drowned or decapitated. In imitation of the Orphic myth of Dionysis Zagreus, a rite held in which the heart of a victim, supposedly a human child, was roasted and distributed among the participants to be eaten.... In the Dionysus and Isis mysteries, the initiation was sometimes accomplished by a "sacred marriage," a sacral copulation.[44]

Again, if Christianity were really simply a derivation of such mystery religions, why did it so staunchly oppose them? The only explanation is that no such similarity existed because Christianity always was what it always claimed—a unique revelation from God.

We may conclude our topic by noting the research of Dr. Ronald H. Nash, head of the Department of Philosophy and Religion at Western Kentucky University and director of its graduate studies in philosophy and religion, and author of a number of books including *Ideas of History, Christian Faith and Historical Understanding, Faith and Reason,* and *The Case for Biblical Christianity.* In *Christianity & the Hellenistic World,* he offers a devastating critique of this theory.

In evaluating the alleged borrowing concerning Christ's death and resurrection, Dr. Nash points out that the death of Jesus is distinct from the deaths of the pagan gods in at least half a dozen different ways. For example, none of the dying and rising "savior-gods" ever died for someone else, and they never claimed to die for sin. The concept of the incarnate Son of God dying a propitiatory, substitutionary atonement for man is a doctrine that is wholly unique to Christianity. In addition, biblically, Jesus died one time for all sin, whereas the pagan gods were often vegetation deities who mimicked the annual cycles of nature in their repeated deaths and resuscitations. Further, Jesus died in space-time history, whereas the pagan deities were simply myths. Finally, Jesus died voluntarily and His death was a victory, not a defeat, both of which stand in contrast to concepts found in the pagan cults.[45] In essence, regardless of the major biblical doctrine we are referring to, whether it be the nature of God, the incarnation, redemption, the resurrection, or the new birth, none of these reveals any dependence whatsoever upon the mystery religions.

Dr. Nash thus refers to the "serious errors" made by those who propose the alleged parallels[46] and remarks, "The tide of scholarly opinion has turned dramatically against attempts to make early Christianity dependent on the so-called dying and rising gods of Hellenistic paganism."[47]

Yet one need only take a course in comparative religion or the origin of Christianity at your local college or university to see how frequently this grotesque caricature continues to be taught as "historical fact." It's almost as bad as the documentary hypothesis of the Pentateuch, which also lives on, despite a similar entombment.*

In conclusion, Nash summarizes eight of the most serious weaknesses in the critics' claim that Christianity was derived from the mysteries. First, similarity does not prove dependence. The fact of some similarities between Christianity and the mysteries no more proves Christianity was derived from them than similarities between dogs and cats proves dogs derived from cats. Second, even the alleged similarities "are either greatly exaggerated or invented." Third, "the chronology is all wrong" because the basic beliefs of Christianity were in existence in the

---

* Critics also maintain that the Apostle Paul borrowed his ideas from the mystery religions, but Nash shows how weak this argument is. In fact, this idea was refuted 70 years ago in J. Gresham Machen's *The Origin of Paul's Religion* and more recently by the Korean scholar Seyoon Kim in *The Origin of Paul's Gospel.*

first century, while the full development of the mystery religions did not happen until the second century. Historically, it is unlikely that any significant encounter took place between Christianity and the pagan mystery religions until the third Century. Fourth, as a devout Jew, the Apostle Paul would never have considered borrowing his teachings from pagan religion. There is not the slightest hint of pagan beliefs in his writings. Fifth, as a monotheistic religion with a coherent body of doctrine, Christianity could hardly have borrowed from a polytheistic and doctrinally contradictory paganism. Sixth, first century Christianity was an exclusivistic faith, not a syncretistic one, which it would have become had borrowing been significant. Seventh, Christianity is demonstrably grounded in the actual events of history, not myths. Eighth, if any borrowing did occur, it was the other way around. In other words, as Christianity grew in influence and expanded in the second and third centuries, the pagan systems, recognizing this threat, would be likely to borrow elements of Christianity to capitalize upon its success. For example, the pagan rite of bathing in bull's blood (taurobolium) initially held its spiritual efficacy at 20 years. But once in competition with Christianity, the cult of Cybele, recognizing that Christians were promised eternal life by faith in Jesus, raised the efficacy of their rite "from 20 years to eternity."[48]

The best way for students or other inquirers to refute the idea of any collusion between Christianity and the mystery cults is simply to study the mystery religions and compare them carefully with the teachings of the New Testament. It is indeed regrettable that so many professors on our college and university campuses have failed to do this before they wrongly instructed their students that Christianity was only an offshoot of ancient paganism.

To date, we have seen that the evidence for the resurrection is persuasive enough to convince skeptics and lawyers and that no alternate theory is credible. All that remains is to test the evidence in public debate forum.

Chapter 8

Did He Rise?
The Resurrection Debates

In the last two decades, more than a thousand debate forums have been held between skeptics and evangelical Christian scholars, especially in the areas of creation versus evolution, the historical evidence for the resurrection, and the existence of God. Through organizations such as *The John Ankerberg Show*, *Probe International* in Dallas, Texas, the *Institute for Creation Research* in Santee, California, and others, scholars have vigorously contended against atheists, agnostics, skeptics, and virtually any and every critic of Christianity. Almost invariably, it seems, Christian scholars win these debates. Given the nature and importance of the subject matter, these deliberations prove beyond any doubt that only a person's prejudice or ignorance would cause him to think the Christian position is intellectually lacking. This chapter will examine two such debates concerning the resurrection of Christ.

Habermas vs. Flew

In February 1985, a scholarly forum was held titled, "Christianity Challenges the University: An International Conference of Theists and Atheists" in Dallas. Participants on the Christian side included philosopher Dr. Gary R. Habermas, and on the skeptical side Antony G.N. Flew, a leading intellectual philosopher and atheist. Dr. Flew has been a visiting professor at 12 universities around the world and has taught at the University of Oxford, the University of Reading in England, and the University of Aberdeen. After this particular series of debates, an invitation was extended to Dr. Flew to debate "The Historicity of the Resurrection: Did Jesus Rise from the Dead?" The invitation was extended to Flew by the philosophy faculty of Liberty University in Lynchburg, Virginia.

The debate was held on May 2, 1985, at Liberty University, before an audience of 3,000 people. Drs. Habermas and Flew were the primary debaters, with participation by W. David Beck, Ph.D. in Philosophy, Boston University, and Terry L. Miethe, who holds Ph.D.s in both philosophy and social ethics and is dean of the Oxford Study Center, Oxford, England, professor of philosophy at Liberty University, and adjunct professor at Wycliffe Hall, Oxford.

Respondents to the debate included three of the world's leading theologians: Wolfhart Pannenberg, who some consider the world's most prominent living systematic theologian, Charles Hartshorne, Ph.D., Harvard University, the noted process theologian, and James I. Packer, D.Phil. from the University of Oxford, a leading evangelical theologian.

Organizers of the debate put together two panels of experts in their respective areas of speciality to render a verdict on the debate. The first panel comprised five philosophers who were instructed to judge the debate *content* and to render a verdict concerning the winner. The second panel comprised five professional debate judges who were told to evaluate the *argumentation* techniques of the debaters. All ten judges serve on the faculties of American universities and colleges such as the University of Virginia, James Madison University, the University of Pittsburgh, and other prestigious institutions.

What were the results of this two-day debate on the historicity of the resurrection? The decision of the judges was as follows:

The panel of five philosophers who judged *content* cast four votes for Habermas, none for Flew, and one draw. One of these philosophers commented, "I was surprised (shocked might be a more accurate word) to see how weak Flew's own approach was. I expected—if not a new and powerful argument—at least a distinctly new twist to some old arguments. . . . Since the case against the resurrection was no stronger than that presented by Antony Flew, I would think it was time I began to take the resurrection seriously. My conclusion is that Flew lost the debate and the case for the resurrection won."[1]

The panel of professional debate judges voted in favor of Habermas three to two concerning *argumentation* technique. One of the judges noted: "I am of the position that the affirmative speaker [Habermas] has a very significant burden of proof in order to establish his claims. The various historical sources convinced me to adopt the arguments of the affirmative speaker. Dr. Flew, on the other hand, failed, particularly in the rebuttal. In the head-to-head session, to introduce significant supporters of his position, Dr. Habermas placed a heavy burden on Dr. Flew to refute very specific issues. As the rebuttals progressed, I felt that Dr. Flew tried to skirt the charges given him."[2]

Another professional debate judge observed: "I conclude that the historical evidence, though flawed, is strong enough to lead reasonable minds to conclude that Christ did indeed rise from the dead. Habermas has already won the debate. . . . Habermas does end up providing 'highly probable evidence' for the historicity of the resurrection 'with no plausible naturalistic evidence against it.' Habermas, therefore, in my opinion, wins the debate."[3]

The overall decision of both panels, judging both *content* and *argumentation* technique, was a seven to two decision, with one draw, "in favor of the historicity of the resurrection as argued by Habermas."[4] Even some later reviews by skeptics in secular publications agreed that Habermas won the debate, or at least that Flew's critique against the resurrection was inadequate.[5]

The conclusions of the scholarly respondents to the debate were also noteworthy. Wolfhart Pannenberg, again, one of the world's best known theologians, concluded:

> Therefore the historical solidity of the Christian witness [to the resurrection] poses a considerable challenge to the conception of reality that is taken for granted by modern secular history. There are good and even superior reasons to claiming that the resurrection of Jesus was a historical event, and consequently the risen Lord himself is a living reality. And yet there is the innumerably repeated experience that

in this world the dead do not rise again. As long as this is the case, the Christian affirmation of Jesus' resurrection will remain a debated issue, in spite of all sound historical argument as to its historicity. Although Christians should never lose their nerve in this matter, but insist on the historicity of Jesus' resurrection as long as the evidence warrants such a claim, they should also not be surprised that only in the kingdom to come, when the dead rise again, will the opposition to their claim vanish.[6]

American philosopher Dr. Charles Hartshorne concluded, "I can neither explain away the evidences to which Habermas appeals, nor can I simply agree with Flew's or Hume's positions," noting "my metaphysical bias is against resurrections."[7]

Dr. James I. Packer declared:

The case for the historical reality of Jesus' bodily resurrection could be made even stronger than Professor Habermas makes it—which, in all conscience, must surely be strong enough already for most people!—by dwelling with more emphasis on the sheer impossibility of accounting for the triumphant emergence of Christianity in Jerusalem, a faith based on acknowledging Jesus as crucified Messiah and risen Lord, without the supposition that his tomb was found mysteriously empty. If the authorities could have produced Jesus' corpse, they would have exploded the resurrection faith for good; the fact that it was not exploded indicates that they did not produce the corpse, and their failure to produce it...shows that they could not produce it. The idea that those who constantly risk their freedom and their lives proclaiming the resurrection faith had in fact stolen the body, and therefore knew all along that their preaching was not true, is unbelievable. One of the tasks of history writing is to identify the causes of events, and one of the marks of good historians is that they show themselves aware of what constitutes a cause, or set of causes, commensurate with what actually happened. What happened here is that Christianity actually started with the resurrection. This is the great fact (too great, apparently, for Flew even to notice) by which the adequacy of any view about Jesus' rising must finally be judged. Claims to have seen Jesus after his death could not have started such a faith had Jesus' corpse been available for inspection. . . . [8]

What is also significant in this debate is that Dr. Flew was directly challenged to answer the positive evidence presented for the resurrection, yet he failed to do so. For example, the concluding affirmative statement of Habermas was: "I would respectfully challenge Dr. Flew to answer evidence for the resurrection, namely, the failure of the naturalistic theories, the positive evidences for this event, the core facts accepted by virtually all scholars, [etc.]. . . . Dr. Flew, please *directly* address the evidence for the resurrection in your rebuttal."[9] As the debate switched to Dr. Flew in the first portion of the rebuttal period, his first words were, "Well, yes, let's try to do it."[10] Unfortunately, he never did.

In Habermas' rebuttal he made a specific point of this: "Let me say in closing that I've been attempting to get Dr. Flew to deal directly with the evidence for Jesus' resurrection. I don't think he has done so. All he's said so far is that we can't tell what happened. Please notice, he's not dealt with the four kinds of evidence I've presented. I believe he has generally sidestepped them, yet in one of his essays on miracles, he admits my point when he asserts that 'our only way of determining the capacities and incapacities of nature is to study what does in fact occur.' I agree with you, Dr. Flew; we need to look at nature and see what does in fact occur. I've given you four sets of arguments for the resurrection, and you haven't addressed yourself to the evidence."[11]

Montgomery vs. Naland

Consider a second example of a modern debate on the resurrection. In 1990 lawyer, philosopher, and theologian Dr. John Warwick Montgomery debated Central American diplomat and agnostic John K. Naland on national television on *The John Ankerberg Show*. This debate concerned the topic: "Did the resurrection of Christ happen, and do the Gospel narratives conflict with one another?"

In a debate of this nature, one would expect that both debaters would refrain from subjective conjecture and confine their discussion to objectively verifiable data. The approach of

Mr. Naland is characteristic of the approach of the critic in general. In his debate with Dr. Montgomery, Naland's discussion was dominated by unfounded and subjective premises. Naland's first undemonstrated assumption was that the resurrection events described by the disciples were not objective history but, rather, internal subjective visions and that this explains why they allegedly conflict with one another. In other words, if the accounts were actual historical reporting, they would probably not conflict, at least not so much. Thus, Naland stated: "I believe the problem was that the events that we are talking about were events that were internal, that people in dreams or—and this is my opinion . . . flat out, my opinion—that people in dreams or on dusty roads or whatever *thought* they experienced the risen Jesus. And that *because* these were not actual physical events . . . [the reports conflict]."[12]

Another unfounded premise of Naland was that the eyewitness accounts were not good enough. Naland held that they must conform to his particular sense of evidential and historical propriety. Thus, Naland took a subjective approach to what he would or would not accept in the Gospel accounts. Event "A" recorded by author "B" is acceptable, but Event "C" recorded by author "B" is unacceptable. This "pick and choose" approach to the resurrection narratives is, again, entirely subjective. Not once did Naland demonstrate any legitimate, objective basis for such preferences. For example, concerning Matthew's account of the Roman guard, Naland simply states, "I don't accept Matthew's description. So I see no evidence for the guard."[13] When Naland asks why God didn't choose witnesses that would give material that "makes sense," he specifically means "makes sense to him." Dr. Montgomery's response was appropriate: "And because God Almighty doesn't do what *you* expect Him to do, therefore, you say, 'I don't have to take these events seriously.' What you ought to be doing is this. You ought to be asking yourself, 'What kind of historical evidence do I require when I handle the general events of human history?' "[14]

Further,

> And what you've done is continually to question this material because it doesn't read the way you'd like. It doesn't

contain all the events that you would like to have recorded. It has what you regard as redundancy. All of this, Mr. Naland, simply says that if you had written this stuff you would have written it differently. And heavens! If *I* had written it, I would have written it differently. But that's not the test of facticity or the test of truth. The universe doesn't happen . . . doesn't have to parallel our writing style or our approach, it just has to represent fact. And eyewitnesses are the key to that.[15]

Naland, for example, bases his rejection of Matthew's account of the guard solely on two factors: (1) Matthew is the only one who mentions the guard and (2) various (already disproved) conjectures concerning the late date and authorship of the Gospels. Obviously, neither factor gives sufficient basis for rejecting Matthew's account. In fact, it is Naland's own approach to the Scriptures that is problematic, not, as he claims, the resurrection narratives. For example, he believes that "Mark is the first and the most honest [reporter]."[16] But then he specifically rejects what Mark says about the resurrection even though he believes that Mark is the most honest of all the disciples.

One wonders upon what logical basis Naland can accept all four Gospel writers' statements on certain historical points as factual, but reject the same writers' accounts of the resurrection as unfactual? When confronted with this question as to why he would accept the historical accuracy of the writers at one point but not concerning the resurrection, he responded with, "That's a very good question . . . "![17] The only basis upon which he could give an answer was subjective preferences.

A final premise of Mr. Naland was that the evidence for Christ's resurrection is not compelling but sufficient only to convince someone already convinced.[18] Naland ignores the fact that for 2,000 years it has been many of those who were *not* already convinced, that is, the skeptics, who have examined the evidence and as a result, become Christians. Dr. Montgomery is himself a prime example. He referred to himself as "the most reluctant convert you'd ever come across"—but he became one solely because of the evidence.[19] In fact, the evidence *is* compelling.

It goes without saying that the burden of proof rests with the one who makes the claim. Mr. Naland claimed the four Gospel accounts contradicted each other to such a degree they could not be trusted: "I believe we would not be here tonight if we only had one Gospel. I think because we have four, we have a problem, because the four are saying different things. If there was only one, there would be no problem. But since there are four and they're saying different things, then I think that's what we need to address, because if one says 'A' and one says 'B' and one says 'C,' they can either all be wrong, one can be right, but they can't all be right. So I hope we get to that."[20]

In an article in the spring 1988 *Free Inquiry*, "The First Easter: The Evidence for the Resurrection Evaluated," Naland also made the following claims concerning discrepancies in the narratives:

> These geographical and chronological contradictions make it impossible to combine the testimony of these ancient authors into a coherent account. For example, if we accepted Luke as being historically accurate, we would have to reject completely the competing accounts in Mark, Matthew, and John 21 as well as partially reject the claims of John and the Marcan Appendix. Similarly, to accept Matthew would necessitate the rejection of Luke, John, and the Marcan Appendix—and so on through the other permutations. We are faced, in other words, with the question of how to explain this extraordinary divergence of New Testament testimony concerning the most important event in human history.
>
> In an effort to explain this divergence, we must first be clear as to what exactly is being contradicted. The ancient sources do not disagree about *what* happened (that the disciples experienced the risen Jesus) but only about *where*, *when*, *how*, and *to whom* it happened. Granted, this is a significant "only." And it raises the possibility that the contradictions are the result not of the honest recounting of differing memories but of the *invention* of narrative details to fill in for unknown historical facts.[21]

Yet, neither in the debate nor in his article did Naland ever supply any evidence that some material was invented, ever demonstrate a single error or prove a genuine contradiction. As Dr. Montgomery pointed out, Mr. Naland apparently did not understand what a logical contradiction was.[22] The response of Montgomery to Mr. Naland's basic approach was that, "We mustn't drag red herrings across the landscape."[23] In essence, Naland, like Dr. Flew, never dealt with the basic issue: the *real* evidence for the resurrection of Jesus Christ.

Part 2

Creation

The Most Unique Phenomenon of Existence

Chapter 9

False Assumptions Concerning Evolution

I have often thought how little I should like to prove organic evolution in a court of law.
—E. White, presidential address
to the Linnean Society, 1966

Most modern scientists are in general agreement that evolutionary theory is an established fact of science and cannot logically be questioned as a view of origins. However, what one concludes about human origins is one of the most crucial points for deciding a whole range of other issues, whether positively or negatively, from the nature of man and the purpose of life to the relevance of morality and religion to the future of humanity. Is man only the end product of the impersonal forces of matter, time, and chance with all this implies, or the purposeful creation of a good and loving God with all this implies? Given the tremendous influence of evolutionary theory in the last 100 years, the answer has already been given to most people.

The Influence of Evolution

In the history of mankind, few theories have had the impact that evolution has. The famous evolutionary zoologist Ernst Mayr of Harvard University observed in 1972 that evolution was coming to be regarded as "perhaps the most fundamental of all intellectual revolutions in the history of mankind."[1] The definitive modern biography by James Moore, *Darwin: The Life of a Tormented Evolutionist,* points out that Darwin, "More than any modern thinker—even Freud or Marx ... has transformed the way we see ourselves on the planet."[2] Wendell R. Bird is a prominent Atlanta attorney and Yale Law School graduate who argued the major creationist case on the issue of creation/evolution before the U.S. Supreme Court. In his impressive criticism of evolutionary theory, *The Origin of Species Revisited: The Theories of Evolution and of Abrupt Appearance*, he observes of *The Origin of Species*, "That single volume has had a massive influence not only on the sciences, which increasingly are built on evolutionary assumptions, but on the humanities, theology, and government."[3]

In his *Mankind Evolving*, eminent geneticist Theodosius Dobzhansky points out that the publication of Darwin's book in 1859 "marked a turning point in the intellectual history of mankind" and "ushered in a new understanding of man and his place in the universe."[4] He reflects that even a hundred years after Darwin " ... the idea of evolution is becoming an integral part of man's image of himself. The idea has percolated to much wider circles than biologists or even scientists; understood or misunderstood, it is a part of mass culture."[5]

Molecular biologist Michael Denton also points out the dramatic influence of this dominant theory, even in disciplines outside the natural sciences:

> The twentieth century would be incomprehensible without the Darwinian revolution. The social and political currents which have swept the world in the past eighty years would have been impossible without its intellectual sanction. ... The influence of evolutionary theory on fields far removed from biology is one of the most spectacular examples in history of how a highly speculative idea for which there is no really hard scientific evidence can come to fashion the thinking of a whole society and dominate the outlook of an age.

> Today it is perhaps the Darwinian view of nature more than any other that is responsible for the agnostic and skeptical outlook of the twentieth century ... [It is] a theory that literally changed the world. ... "[6]

But if evolution has permeated practically the entire fabric of contemporary culture and provides the basis for modern man's worldview and thus his subsequent actions, who can argue that this theory is unimportant? Indeed, it is how an individual views his origin, his ultimate beginning, that to a great extent conditions his worldview, the decisions he makes, and even his general lifestyle. As the philosopher Francis Schaeffer once noted, people usually live more consistently with their own presuppositions than even they themselves may realize.[7]

One only need examine the twentieth century and take note of the impact of evolutionary materialism to see that "evolutionary theory does indeed dominate modern thought in virtually every field—every discipline of study, every level of education, and every area of practice."[8]

However, if it turns out that evolution is wrong, then everything it has impacted may have been affected in a prejudicial or even harmful way. Since we have discussed this topic elsewhere, we will only briefly elaborate on it later in this chapter.[9] What we will do is show why none of the harmful, indeed, often tragic consequences of this theory were ever necessary in the first place.

In the material that follows, we will offer some of the reasons why evolution is widely accepted, why we believe evolutionary theory is wrong, and why we believe it should no longer be accepted by thinking people, at least by those who do not allow their personal materialistic philosophies to color their interpretations of scientific data. Following we offer six false assumptions relating to belief in evolution.[10]

False Assumption 1: Scientists accept evolution because it is a proven fact of science that cannot logically be denied.

There exist many popular misunderstandings concerning the nature of science. Philosopher of science Dr. J. P. Moreland notes some of these misconceptions and observes that "scientists today, in contrast to their counterparts in earlier generations, are often ill-equipped to define science, since such a project is philosophical in nature."[11] In fact, Moreland cites several standard definitions of science given in such texts as *College Physics, Biological Science,* and *Webster's New Collegiate Dictionary,* as well as judge William R. Overton's definition of science in the decision against creationism in the famous creation science trial in Little

Rock, Arkansas, December 1981. He observes that none of these definitions of science is adequate.[12]

It is not our purpose here to discuss the problems involved in the definition of science.[13] We do need to know that the interaction of science and philosophy is a complex one and that there is no universally accepted, clear-cut definition of what science is. We are on safer ground if we define science in a general way, noting the scientific method. For our purposes, the *Oxford American Dictionary* (1982) definition of science is adequate: "A branch of study which is considered either with a connected body of *demonstrated truths* or with *observed facts* systematically classified and more or less colligated and brought under *general laws,* and which includes *trustworthy methods* for the discovery of *new truth* within its own domain" (emphasis added). Scientific work involves things like observation, formulating a hypothesis, experimental testing to repeat observations, predictability, control, and data collection.

> One applies the scientific method by first of all observing and recording certain natural phenomena. He then formulates a generalization (scientific hypothesis) based upon his observations. In turn, this generalization allows him to make predictions. He then tests his hypothesis by conducting experiments to determine if the predicted result will obtain. If his predictions prove true, then he will consider his hypothesis verified. Through continual confirmation of the predictions [e.g., by himself and other parties] the hypothesis will become a theory, and the theory, with time and tests, will graduate to the status of a [scientific] law.[14]

The scientific method may be diagrammed as shown in the chart on the following page.[15] What this definition of science and description of the scientific method will indicate is that, while scientists who study nature utilize the scientific method, evolutionary theory *itself* is not ultimately scientific because evolution has few, if any, "demonstrated truths" or "observed facts." Microevolution or strictly limited change within species can be demonstrated, but this has nothing to do with evolution as commonly understood. After citing evolutionists who confess that evolution is not scientifically provable, Dr. Randy L. Wysong

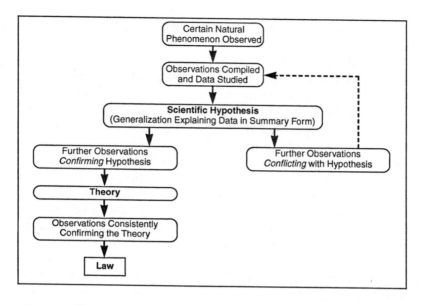

observes, "... evolution is not a formulation of the true scientific method. They [scientists] realize [that, in effect] evolution means the initial formation of unknown organisms from unknown chemicals produced in an atmosphere or ocean of unknown composition under unknown conditions, which organisms have then climbed an unknown evolutionary ladder by an unknown process leaving unknown evidence."[16]

In other words, to the extent that the findings of science *hinge* upon demonstrated truths and observed facts, evolutionary theory has little to do with the findings of science. Evolution is more properly considered a naturalistic philosophy or worldview that seeks to explain the origin of life materialistically. As the late A. E. Wilder-Smith, who held three earned doctorates in science, observed, "As Kerkut has shown [in his *The Implications of Evolution*], NeoDarwinian thought teaches seven main postulates. Not one of these seven theses can be proved or even tested experimentally. If they are not supported by experimental evidence, the whole theory can scarcely be considered to be a *scientific* one. If the seven main postulates of NeoDarwinism are experimentally untestable, then NeoDarwinism must be considered to be a philosophy rather than a science, for science is concerned solely with experimentally testable evidence.[17]

Dr. Willem J. Ouweneel, research associate in Developmental Genetics, Ultrech, Netherlands, with the Faculty of Mathematics and Natural Sciences, points out in his article *The Scientific Character of the Evolution Doctrine*, "It is becoming increasingly apparent that evolutionism is not even a good scientific theory."[18] He argues that evolution should not be considered a scientific fact, theory, hypothesis, or postulate. For example, concerning the latter, evolutionary theory is not strictly properly designated a *scientific* postulate because this must: (a) be in accordance with the principal laws of mathematics and natural science; (b) not be more complicated than necessary for the explanation of observed phenomena; (c) give rise to conclusions which can be controlled by further experimental observations and testing; (d) conform to the general data of science; (e) alternate hypotheses must be shown to be wrong or less acceptable; and (f) finally, the reliability of a scientific conception is inversely proportional to the number of unproved postulates on which it is founded. Evolution fails all criteria for categorization as a scientific postulate.

This is why Dr. Ouweneel concludes that evolution is actually a *materialistic* postulate rather than a credible scientific theory.[19] But one would never know this from reading the scientific literature, literature that constantly assures the world that evolution is a scientific fact.

The principal reason evolution "must" be a scientific fact is because of the materialistic bias that pervades the scientific world—a bias which, in the end, is really unnecessary and in ways even harmful to the cause of science.[20]

Regardless, evolution continues to be set forth as an *established* fact by the scientific community. Pierre-Paul Grasse, the renowned French zoologist and past president of the French Academy of Sciences, states in his *Evolution of Living Organisms:* "Zoologists and botanists are nearly unanimous in considering evolution *as a fact* and not a hypothesis. I agree with this position and base it primarily on documents provided by paleontology, i.e., the [fossil] history of the living world."[21] Theodosius

Dobzhansky, who, according to another leading evolutionist, Steven J. Gould of Harvard, is "the greatest evolutionist of our century,"[22] asserts in his award-winning text, *Mankind Evolving*, "the *proofs of evolution* are now a matter of elementary biology.... In Lamark's and Darwin's times evolution was a hypothesis; in our day it is *proven*."[23] World famous scientist George Gaylord Simpson, distinguished professor of vertebrate paleontology at the Museum of Comparative Zoology at Harvard emphasizes in *The Meaning of Evolution*, "*Ample proof* has been repeatedly presented and is available to anyone who really wants to know the truth.... In the present study the *factual truth* of organic evolution is taken as *established*..."[24] The late Carl Sagan was a distinguished Cornell University astronomer and Pulitzer Prize-winning author. He is perhaps best known as the host and cowriter of the *Cosmos* television series seen in 60 countries by approximately 3 percent of all people on earth; the hard-cover edition of *Cosmos* was on the *New York Times* best-seller list for 70 weeks and may be the best-selling science book in the English language in the twentieth century. In this book, Sagan simply states, "Evolution is *a fact*, not a theory."[25] The eminent anthropologist Konrad Lorenz observed in *Intellectual Digest*, "It is *not* a theory, but an *irrefutable historical fact*, that the living world— since its origin—has evolved from 'below' to 'above.' "[26] Rene Dubos, one of the country's leading ecologists, stated in *American Scientist*, "Most enlightened persons now accept as a *fact* that everything in the cosmos—from heavenly bodies to human beings—has developed and continues to develop through evolutionary processes."[27] Noted geneticist Richard Goldschmidt of the University of California once stated in *American Scientist*, "Evolution of the animal and plant world is considered by all those entitled to judgment *to be a fact* for which no further proof is needed."[28]

Another prominent evolutionist, Sir Julian Huxley, claimed in his famous keynote address at the Darwin Centennial held in 1959 at the University of Chicago, "The first point to make about Darwin's theory is that it is *no longer* a theory, *but a fact*. No serious scientists would deny the fact that evolution has occurred, just as he would not deny the fact that the earth goes around the sun."[29]

On the other hand, creationists and other nonevolutionary scientists argue that evolution cannot logically be considered factual apart from any real evidence: "All the hard data in the life sciences show that evolution is not occurring today, all the real data in the earth sciences show it did not occur in the past, and all the genuine data in the physical sciences show it is not possible at all. Nevertheless, evolution is almost universally accepted as a fact in all the natural sciences."[30]

Consider the comments of the late Canadian scholar, Arthur C. Custance, Ph.D. in Anthropology and author of the seminal ten-volume *The Doorway Papers.* He was a member of the Canadian Physiological Society, a fellow of the Royal Anthropological Institute, and a member of the New York Academy of Sciences. In *Evolution: An Irrational Faith,* he observes, "virtually all the fundamentals of the orthodox evolutionary faith have shown themselves to be either of extremely doubtful validity or simply contrary to fact. So basic are these erroneous [evolutionary] assumptions that the whole theory is now largely maintained *in spite of* rather than *because of* the evidence. As a consequence, for the great majority of students and for that large ill-defined group, 'the public,' it has ceased to be a subject of debate. Because it is both incapable of proof and yet may not be questioned, it is virtually untouched by data which challenge it in any way. It has become in the strictest sense *irrational.* Information or concepts which challenge the theory are almost never given a fair hearing."[31]

In fact, in the opinion of this erudite scholar, "Evolutionary philosophy has indeed become *a state of mind,* one might almost say a kind of mental prison rather than a scientific attitude. To equate one particular interpretation of the data with *the data itself* is evidence of mental confusion. The theory of evolution . . . is detrimental to ordinary intelligence and warps judgment."[32]

He concludes, "In short, the premises of evolutionary theory are about as invalid as they could possibly be. If evolutionary theory was strictly scientific, it should have been abandoned long ago. But because it is more philosophy than science, it is not susceptible to the self-correcting mechanisms that govern all other branches of scientific enquiry."[33]

Why Scientists Can Be Wrong

The history of science reveals many instances where the majority of scientists have been convinced as to a particular theory and yet been wrong. Further, when it comes to the discussion of the creation/evolution issue, many scientists today simply seem to be closed-minded. Why? Because modern science is committed to the ideology of evolution, and any time a philosophical commitment to a particular ideology exists, there will probably be a reluctance to consider alternate viewpoints. Yet consider again the comments of Dr. A. E. Wilder-Smith, the deliverer of the Huxley Memorial Lecture at the Oxford Union, Oxford University, February 14, 1986: "May not a future generation well ask how any scientist, in full possession of his intellectual faculties and with adequate knowledge of information theory could ever execute the feat of cognitive acrobatics necessary to sincerely believe that a (supremely complex) machine system of information, storage and retrieval, servicing millions of cells, diagnosing defects and then repairing them in a teleonomic Von Newman machine manner, arose in randomness—the antipole of information?"[34] In other words, "How could any scientist in possession of the modern facts we now have logically continue to exercise faith in naturalistic evolution?" As molecular biologist Michael Denton observes of the created order of living things, "To common sense it does indeed appear absurd to propose that chance could have thrown together devices of such complexity and ingenuity that they appear to represent the very epitome of perfection."[35]

Nevertheless, there are many reasons explaining why scientists who accept evolution can be wrong. Among them we mention four.

A. A false belief can be accepted by mistakenly assuming there are no legitimate scientific theories to replace it.

Dr. Wilder-Smith observes that when the modern scientific establishment adheres to evolutionary belief, it is "certainly not because experimental evidence encourages the establishment to do so."[36] He explains that a commitment to materialism is the problem. Thus, "There exists at present no other *purely scientific* alternative which postulates a purely scientific *materialistic* basis for biogenesis and biology. To repeat, there is at present no *purely scientific alternative to Darwin.* Creationism, being religious, is of little use to the materialistic thought of today. It is simply an irrelevant subject worthy only of ridicule. Scientists whose upbringing and education are Darwinian and therefore naturalistic, have for this reason no real alternative to Darwinism. Here we have perhaps one of the main reasons for the victory of Darwinism even today, even though the accumulating evidence of science is steadily against the theory."[37]

But what if there is a legitimate scientific option to evolution which is not materialistic? For example, as we will discuss later, Yale Law School graduate Wendell R. Bird fully documents that the theory of "abrupt appearance" is entirely scientific—and also that such a theory was capable of being advanced scientifically by scientists of an earlier era. Further, he shows that creation itself is not *necessarily* religious; it too can be fully scientific.[38] The discussion in J. P. Moreland, ed., *The Creation Hypothesis* (IVP, 1994) reveals that theistic science is anything but an oxymoron and merits real consideration among scientists. In fact, unless we arbitrarily, or by default, allow scientific naturalism to provide the rules of the game convenient to its own worldview, the concept of theistic science *must* be considered a valid competing hypothesis to the current naturalistic paradigm. The question of whether or not scientific naturalism can be challenged is long past, and the issue of a scientific theory of creationism is already settled.

B. A false theory can be accepted because scientific facts can be misinterpreted or unnaturally forced to fit a dominant theory.

The facts of the natural world are in the possession of every scientist, whether creationist or evolutionist. The issue in debate is the interpretation of those facts, whether it concerns the fossil record, origin-of-life experiments, or phylogenetic similarities.

Yet scientific facts may not only *seem* to fit a false theory, but scientific facts themselves may become irrelevant because of the intrinsic appeal of a particular paradigm whose own preservation becomes paramount:

> Yet no matter how convincing such disproofs [of evolution] might appear, no matter how contradictory and unreal much of the Darwinian framework might now seem to anyone not committed to its defense, as philosophers of science like Thomas Kuhn and Paul Feyerabend have pointed out, it is impossible to falsify theories *by reference to the facts* or indeed by any sort of rational or empirical argument. The history of science amply testifies to what Kuhn has termed 'the priority of the paradigm' and provides many fascinating examples of the *extraordinary lengths* to which members of the scientific community will go to defend a theory just as long as it holds sufficient intrinsic appeal.[39]

In other words, once scientists are trained to interpret data in a particular manner, they rarely question the relevance of their interpretations. The perceptual grid of scientific naturalism forces data to be interpreted in very specific ways that may not be correct. Worse, scientific data *must* be made to fit the prevailing dominant theory. (Thomas Kuhn pointed this out in *The Structure of Scientific Revolutions*.)

For example, the geocentric theory of the sun orbiting the earth dominated science for several hundred years. Although a heliocentric alternative was considered as early as the Greek astronomers, the geocentric theory was, by the late middle ages, "a self-evident truth, the one and only sacred and unalterable picture of cosmological reality."[40] But, as with all false theories, there were innumerable facts that got in the way. The response of scientists was to invent "explanations" to account for the irregularities. As more and more explanations were required to deal with more and more problems presented by undeniable facts, by the early sixteenth century the entire Ptolemaic system had become "a monstrosity" of fantastically involved explanations and counter-explanations.[41] Nevertheless, "so ingrained was the idea that the earth was the center of the universe that hardly *anyone*, even those astronomers who were well aware of the growing unreality of the whole system, *ever bothered to consider an alternative theory.*"[42]

The eighteenth-century concept of phlogiston is also instructive. The theory of phlogiston "assumed that all combustible bodies, including metals, contained a common material, phlogiston, which escaped on combustion but could be readily transferred from one body to another."[43] Scientific experiments with zinc and phosphorus appeared to prove the phlogiston theory.[44] The concept was fully accepted for a hundred years and debated for another hundred years before it was finally disproven. But in fact, "The theory was a total misrepresentation of reality. Phlogiston did not even exist, and yet its existence was firmly believed and the theory adhered to rigidly for nearly 100 years throughout the 18th century."[45]

As was true for the geocentric theory, awkward facts were cunningly assimilated, explained away, or ignored. It was the false theory *itself* that determined how science dealt with facts. The facts themselves had to bow to the truth of phlogiston. Thus, as time progressed and more discoveries were made that made it increasingly difficult to believe in phlogiston, the theory was not rejected but "was modified by the insertion of more and more unwarranted and *ad hoc* assumptions about the nature of phlogiston."[46]

In his *Origins of Modern Science,* Professor H. Butterfield observes how the phlogiston theory actually led to scientists being intellectually incapacitated to deal with the evidence: "... the last two decades of the 18th century give one of the most spectacular proofs in history of the fact that able men who had the truth under their very noses, and possessed all the ingredients for the solution of the problem—the very men who had actually made the strategic discoveries—were incapacitated by the phlogiston theory from realizing the implications of their own work."[47]

In a similar fashion Denton comments, "It is not hard to find inversions of common sense in modern evolutionary thought which are strikingly reminiscent of the mental gymnastics of the phlogiston chemists or the medieval astronomers. The Darwinist, instead of questioning the orthodox framework as common sense would seem to dictate, attempts of justifying his position by *ad hoc* proposals, ... which to the skeptic are self-apparent rationalizations to neutralize what is, on the face of it, hostile evidence."[48]

Thus, the great many intractable scientific problems with modern evolutionary belief do *not* constitute a disproof of Darwinian claims but rather situations that require adjustment to the belief in order that the belief be preserved at all costs.

C. A false belief can be accepted because scientists assume the belief to be true only because of broad general support among scientists.

In the case of evolution, no one questions the basic idea because everyone accepts the basic idea: "The fact that every journal, academic debate and popular discussion assumes the truth of Darwinian theory tends to reinforce its credibility enormously. This is bound to be so because, as sociologists of knowledge are at pains to point out, it is by conversation in the broadest sense of the word that our views and conceptions of reality are maintained and therefore the plausibility of any theory or world view is largely dependent upon the social support it receives rather than its empirical content or rational consistency. Thus all the pervasive affirmation of the validity of Darwinian theory has had the inevitable effect of raising its status to an impregnable axiom which could not even conceivably be wrong."[49]

Hence the constant refrain that evolution is an "undisputed scientific fact." As Richard Dawkins asserts in *The Selfish Gene:* "The theory is about as much in doubt as the earth goes around the sun."[50] Once the scientific community elevates a theory, in this case evolution, to a self-evident truth, defending it becomes irrelevant and there is "no longer any point in having to establish its validity by reference to empirical facts."[51] Further, all disagreement with the current view becomes irrational by definition. As P. Feyerabend argues in his article "Problems of Empiricism" in *Beyond the Edge of Certainty:* "The myth is therefore of no objective relevance, it continues to exist solely as the result of the effort of the community of believers and of their leaders, be these now priests or Nobel Prize winners. Its 'success' is entirely manmade."[52]

D. A false belief can be accepted by scientists because they prefer its philosophical implications.

For example, there are many materialistic scientists who are also atheists and therefore more than happy to accept the atheistic implications of naturalistic evolution. Here, as we indicate following, the very purpose of evolution is to explain things without recourse to God. Again, scientists are only human, and if the unregenerate bent of the human heart underscores the attempt to escape God, then naturalistic evolution is certainly an appealing idea. If there is no God, there are no necessary moral standards and one may happily discover justification for any conceivable belief or lifestyle.

Many modern scientists have pointed out with seeming satisfaction that, given evolution, there is no need to even consider God. This tends to make one suspect that some of these scientists may have ulterior motives for wanting evolution to be true.[53] For example, in his *Heredity, Race and Society*, Theodosius Dobzhansky observes, "Most people, however, greeted the scientific proof of this view [i.e., evolution] as a great *liberation from spiritual bondage*, and saw in it the promise of a better future."[54] As noted novelist Aldous Huxley, grandson of "Darwin's bulldog," Thomas Henry Huxley, once confessed in his *Ends and Means*: "I had motives for not wanting the world to have a meaning; consequently I assumed that it had none, and was able without any difficulty to find satisfying reasons for this assumption. Most ignorance is invincible ignorance. We don't know because we don't want to know." Huxley also noted, "The philosopher who finds no meaning in the world is not concerned exclusively with a problem in pure metaphysics; he is also concerned to prove that there is no valid reason why he personally should not do as he wants to do, or why his friends should not seize political power and govern in the way they find most advantageous to themselves. . . . For myself, as, no doubt, for most of my contemporaries, the philosophy of meaninglessness was essentially an instrument of liberation."[55] Huxley proceeds to identify this liberation as being political, economic, and sexual and, no doubt, like many other modern materialists, found evolutionary belief quite satisfying.

False Assumption 2: Scientists are always objective when they do their research and publicly express their belief in evolution.

To the contrary, scientists are people and people are often not objective and neutral. Scientists, of course, work harder at being objective because of the limits and goals of the scientific disciplines, but this doesn't mean personal preferences or ideologies never get in the way of their research. Unfortunately, the scientific community has its share of ambition, suppression of truth, prejudice, plagiarism, and manipulation of data. This is illustrated by Tel Aviv Medical School's professor of Urology Alexander Kohn in his *False Prophets: Fraud and Error in Science and Medicine* (1986), by Broad and Wade's *Betrayers of the Truth: Fraud and Deceit in the Halls of Science* (1982), and other books and articles.

For example, that many scientists have biases against scientific creationism can be seen through contemporary examples. When one of the greatest thinkers and scholars of modern times, Mortimer J. Adler of the University of Chicago, referred to evolution as a "popular myth," the well-known materialist and critic Martin Gardner actually included him in his study of quacks and frauds in *Fads and Fallacies in the Name of Science.*[56] Philosopher and historian Dr. Rousas Rushdoony was entirely correct when he observed of evolution, "To question the myth or to request proof is to be pillared as a modern heretic and fool."[57]

Consider the case of Dr. A. E. Wilder-Smith. As noted, Smith earned three doctorates in the field of science; his noteworthy academic career spanned more than 40 years, including the publication of more than 100 scientific papers and more than 40 books that have been published in 17 languages. Before discussing his own case, he illustrates with two others where eminent scientists have been silenced because they dared question evolutionary belief:

> Over and above this, the situation is such today that any scientist expressing doubts about evolutionary theory is rapidly silenced. Sir Fred Hoyle, the famous astronomer, was well on his way to being nominated for the Nobel Prize. However, after the appearance of his books expressing

mathematically based doubts as to Darwinism, he was rapidly eliminated. His books were negatively reviewed and no more was heard about his Nobel Prize. The case of the halo dating methods developed by Robert V. Gentry tell a similar story. Gentry gave good evidence that the earth's age, when measured by the radiation halo method using polonium, might not be so great as had been thought when measured by more conventional methods. A postulate of this type would have robbed Darwinism of its main weapon, namely long time periods. Gentry lost his research grants and job at one sweep.

It is by such methods, often bordering on psychoterror, that the latter day phlogiston theory (Neodarwinism) still manages to imprint itself in pretty well all scientific publications today. I myself gave the Huxley Memorial Lecture at the Oxford Union, Oxford University, on February 14, 1986. My theses were well received even by my opponents in the debate following the lecture. But I have been to date unable to persuade any reputable scientific journal to publish the manuscript. The comment is uniformly that the text does not fit their scheme of publications.

I recently (December 1986) received an enquiry from the Radcliffe Science Library, Oxford, asking if I had ever really held the Huxley Memorial Lecture on February 14, 1986. No records of my having held the lecture as part of the Oxford Union debate could be found in any library nor was the substance of this debate ever officially recorded. No national newspapers, radio or TV station breathed a word about it. So total is the current censorship on any *effective* criticism of NeoDarwinian science and on any genuine alternative.[58]

Dr. Jerry Bergman and others have documented that there are *thousands* of cases of discrimination against creationists—of competent science teachers being fired merely because they taught a "two model approach" to origins; of highly qualified science professors being denied tenure because of their refusal to declare their faith in evolution; of students' doctoral dissertations in science rejected simply because they supported creation;

of students being expelled from class for challenging the idea that evolution is a fact.[59]

Prominent lawyer Wendell R. Byrd, author of *The Origin of Species Revisited* observes that "most of higher education is dogmatic and irrationally committed to affirm evolution and to suppress creation science, not on the basis of the scientific evidence but in disregard of that evidence."[60] He correctly refers to the "intolerance," "hysteria," and "unfairness" of the evolutionary establishment and to the "intolerable denials of tenure, denials of promotion, denials of contract renewals, denials of earned degrees, denials of admission into graduate programs, and other discrimination against that minority that disagrees with the prevailing dogmaticism and dares affirm creation science. From my research for published articles in the *Yale Law Journal* and *Harvard Journal of Law and Public Policy,* and from my legal work in First Amendment litigation, it is my professional judgment that the cases of discrimination reported [by Bergman] are a very tiny fraction of the general pattern and practice of discrimination against creationists and creation science at both the college and university level and the secondary and elementary school level."[61]

In doing research for his book, *The Criterion,* Dr. Bergman interviewed more than 100 creationists who had at least a master's degree in science, the majority with a Ph.D. degree—among them Nobel Prize winners and those with multiple doctorates in science. "Nevertheless, all, without exception, reported that they had experienced some discrimination. Some cases were tragic in the extent, blatancy and consequences of the discrimination."[62] For example, "over 12 percent of those interviewed stated that they had received death threats, highly emotional non-verbal feedback or irrational verbalizations against them," and "creationists have never won a single employment discrimination court case." Further, "Many persons who were denied degrees or lost jobs were forced to move to another community and start over. Many creationists publish under pseudonyms; others are extremely careful to hide their beliefs while earning their degree and come out of the closet only after they have the degree in hand or have earned tenure."[63]

One department supervisor stated, "You creationists are Stone Age Neanderthals, and if I had my way I would fire every one of you."[64] One creationist had a Ph.D. in biology from Harvard University, and he had actively been seeking a teaching position for 12 years. One employer told him: "Frankly, I don't like holy people, fundamentalists, especially Baptists, Church of Christ types, Pentecostals or other seventeenth century retrogressives. If we find out we hired one, especially if they start talking to the other research scientists about their beliefs, I terminate them within the month. Usually they leave without much of a protest. And I've never had one bring suit even though firing on religious grounds is illegal, and I know that it is."[65]

Consider other illustrations of religious bigotry from the evolutionary establishment:[66]

- Dr. Bergman states that several of his colleagues told him that if they discovered one of their students was a conservative Christian, they would fail him or her. One professor said, "I don't think this kind of people should get degrees and I'm going to do what I can to stop them." Bergman observes that "some professors are openly advocating failing creationists" and he cites examples.

- A professor of biology at a large state university was denied tenure admittedly because of his creationist views, although he had more publications in scientific journals than any other member of his department (well over 100), many of them in the most prestigious journals in his field. When the university that granted his Ph.D. in biology learned he was an active creationist, they assembled a committee to rescind his degree six *years* after it was issued!

- A Michigan science teacher was fired shortly after he donated several boxes of books on creationism to the school library. A "South Dakota Outstanding Teacher of the Year" recipient was also fired because he was teaching creationism in class.

- Dr. David A. Warriner received his B.S. in chemistry from Tulane University, his Ph.D. from Cornell University, and was close to a second Ph.D. He was invited to join the Natural Science Department at Michigan State University *as* a creationist. After four years his department head suggested tenure but the dean of the department claimed he had "damaged the image of science" for the university and was dismissed. He has been unable to find a teaching position at any other university.

- A creationist working on his Ph.D. in zoology at a major university, with almost straight A's, expressed serious reservations about evolution to his dissertation committee. He was required to take four more courses in evolutionary biology before they would permit him to graduate. After the courses were completed, his dissertation committee asked whether he now "believed in evolution." When he replied he was "more firmly convinced of the validity of creationism than ever before," the dissertation committee broke their agreement and refused to grant his degree.

- A researcher at a Cancer Research Center who had earned an excellent reputation for his six years' work was forced to resign once his creationist views became known.

- Chandra Wickramasinghe of the University College in Cardiff, Wales, and coworker with Fred Hoyle, one of the world's best-known living astronomers, allegedly received death threats merely for speaking out in favor of a two-model teaching position.

Jim Melnick's study in the *Newsletter on Intellectual Freedom,* May 1982, observed that "significant creationist literature has been self-censored from nearly every major secular university library in America."[67]

The hypocrisy in all this seems evident enough. The evolutionary establishment demands freedom of expression for itself but refuses this to its opposition. As Dr. Thomas Dwight of Harvard observed, "The tyranny in the matter of evolution is overwhelming to a degree of which the outsider has no idea."[68] In our colleges and universities today, the Christian faith can be ridiculed all day long, Marxism can be espoused, the Constitution criticized, marriage degraded, and homosexuality encouraged, but the theory of evolution is somehow sacrosanct. Chicago University's Professor Paul Shoray observed, "There is no cause so completely immune from criticism today as evolution."[69]

Even the head of the science department at an Ivy League university tore out an article in *Systematic Zoology* because it was critical of natural selection. When confronted he said, "Well of course I don't believe in censorship in any form, but I just couldn't bear the idea of my students reading that article."[70]

False Assumption 3: Evolution is compatible with belief in God.

Mortimer J. Adler is one of the great modern thinkers. He is author of such interesting books as *Ten Philosophical Mistakes, Truth in Religion,* and *How to Think About God,* chairman for the Board of Editors for the *Encyclopædia Britannica,* and architect and editor-in-chief for the 54-volume *The Great Books of the Western World* library. This set contains the writings of the most influential and greatest intellects and thinkers in Western history—from Aristotle to Shakespeare.

In Volume 1 of *The Great Ideas: A Syntopicon of Great Books of the Western World,* Adler points out the crucial importance of the issue of God's existence to the greatest thinkers of the Western world. With the exception of only certain mathematicians and physicists, "all the authors of the great books are represented. . . . In sheer quantity of references, as well as in variety, this is the largest chapter. The reason is obvious. *More consequences for thought and action follow from the affirmation or denial of God than from answering any other basic question.*"[71] Ideas matter; they matter tremendously, especially when ideas impact belief in God. The consequences for individual behavior and the quality of life in society generally hang in the balance.

And here is where we see perhaps the greatest consequence of evolutionary theory—its denial of God and the unfortunate results that have flowed outward into society from this denial. We saw in False Assumption 1 that evolution was not a true scientific theory but a materialistic postulate that seeks to explain life naturalistically. In light of this, to think that evolution has no theological or social consequences is naive. As leading evolutionist Sir Julian Huxley once noted, "Darwinism removed the whole idea of God as the Creator of organisms from the sphere of rational discussion."[72]

Dr. Colin Brown received his doctorate degree for research done in nineteenth-century theology. Concerning the impact of evolution on Christianity, he confesses, "By far the most potent single factor to undermine popular belief in the existence of God in modern times is the evolutionary theory of Charles Darwin."[73]

Religion authority Dr. Huston Smith observes, "One reason education undoes belief [in God] is its teaching of evolution; Darwin's own drift from orthodoxy to agnosticism was symptomatic. Martin Lings is probably right in saying that 'more cases of loss of religious faith are to be traced to the theory of evolution ... than to anything else.'"[74]

British scientist John Randall points out, "There can be little doubt that the rise of Darwinism played an important part in undermining Victorian religious beliefs."[75]

J.W. Burrow concedes that perhaps more than any other work, Darwin's book shook man's belief in "the immediate providential superintendence of human affairs."[76]

Newman Watts, a London journalist, observed, "In compiling my book, *Britain Without God*, I had to read a great deal of anti-religious literature. Two things impressed me. One was the tremendous amount of this literature available, and the other was the fact that every attack on the Christian faith made today has, as its basis, the doctrine of evolution."[77]

What is doubly unfortunate in all this is the extent to which even Christian philosophers and scientists have accepted the idea of scientific naturalism and the implications that flow from it in science, philosophy, and theology. It is hardly surprising, then, that Christian students can graduate from even conservative Christian schools and end up confused. Regrettably, the overall consequences of Christians accepting this unnecessary and unconvincing philosophy have been disastrous. This is so, not only for the credibility of Christian faith in the eyes of the secular world, but for the credibility of biblical authority and the convictions of personal faith among Christians themselves.

As a testimony to the religious impact of scientific naturalism among secularists, consider the well thought out conclusions of the famous Humanist Manifesto II, which were based squarely on naturalistic evolution: "Free thought, atheism, agnosticism, skepticism, deism, rationalism, ethical culture, and liberal religion all claim to be heir to the humanist tradition. We find insufficient evidence for belief in the existence of a supernatural; it is either meaningless or irrelevant to the question of the survival and fulfillment of the human race. As nontheists, we begin with humans, not God, nature, not deity. We can discover no divine purpose or providence for the human species. No deity will save us; we must save ourselves. Promises of immortal salvation or fear of eternal damnation are both illusory and harmful. Rather, science affirms that the human species is an emergence from natural evolutionary forces. There is no credible evidence that life survives the death of the body. We affirm that moral values derive their source from human experience. Ethics is autonomous and situational, needing no theological or ideological sanction. The right to birth control, abortion, and divorce should be recognized. The many varieties of sexual exploration should not in themselves be considered 'evil.' "[78]

In light of this, it should not surprise us to find a logical relationship between naturalistic evolution and philosophical or practical atheism; indeed, this is made evident throughout atheist literature.[79] In *The American Atheist*, Richard Bozarth argues as follows: ". . . Evolution destroys utterly and finally the very reason Jesus' earthly life was supposedly made necessary. Destroy Adam and Eve and the original sin, and in the rubble, you will find the sorry remains of the son of god. If Jesus was not the redeemer . . . and this is what evolution means, then Christianity is nothing."[80] The same individual observed earlier, "We need only insure that our schools teach only secular knowledge. If we could achieve this, God would indeed be shortly due for a funeral service."[81]

The only problem is that without God, man is the one who dies, quite literally. As Dr. Ravi Zacharias observes: "Conveniently forgotten by those antagonistic to spiritual issues are the far more devastating consequences that have entailed when antitheism is wedded to political theory and social engineering. There is nothing in history to match the dire ends to which humanity can be led by following a political and social philosophy that consciously and absolutely excludes God."[82] And,

> One of the great blind spots of a philosophy that attempts to disavow God is its unwillingness to look into the face of the monster it has begotten and own up to being its creator. It is here that living without God meets its first insurmountable obstacle, the inability to escape the infinite reach of a moral law. Across scores of campuses in our world I have seen outraged students or faculty members waiting with predatorial glee to pounce upon religion, eager to make the oft-repeated but ill-understood charge: What about the thousands who have been killed in the name of religion?
>
> This emotion-laden question is not nearly as troublesome to answer if the questioner first explains all the killing that has resulted from those who have lived without God, such as Hitler, Stalin, Mussolini, Mao, et al. . . . why is there not an equal enthusiasm to distribute blame for violence engendered by some of the irreligious? But the rub goes even deeper than that. The attackers of religion have forgotten that these large-scale slaughters at the hands of anti-theists were the logical outworking of their God-denying philosophy. Contrastingly, the violence spawned by those who killed in the name of Christ would never have been sanctioned by the Christ of the Scriptures. Those who kill in the name of God were clearly self-serving politicizers of religion, an amalgam Christ ever resisted in His life and teaching. Their means and their message were in contradiction to the gospel. Atheism, on the other hand, provides the logical basis for an autonomist, domineering will, expelling morality. . . . The Russian novelist Fyodor Dostoevski repeatedly wrote of the hell that is let loose when man comes adrift from his Creator's moorings and himself becomes god—he understood the consequences. Now, as proof positive, we witness our culture as a whole in a mindless drift toward lawlessness—we live with the inexorable result of autonomies in collision. [Zacharias cites Hitler, "I freed Germany from the stupid and degrading fallacies of conscience

and morality. . . . I want young people capable of violence—
imperious, relentless and cruel."][83]

Evolution and the Bible

Many Christians, including scientists who are Christians,
believe that evolution and belief in the God of the Bible, are
entirely compatible. We disagree. Clearly, evolution has negatively influenced the interpretation of the Bible through the
many theories proposed in an attempt to harmonize the theory
of evolution with biblical teaching.

One such theory is called "theistic evolution." This is the idea
that God supposedly used the gradual process of evolution to
create all life, including man. Another idea is the "Day Age"
theory, wherein the days of Genesis 1 become vast geological
ages, usually in which to insert evolution. A third teaching is the
"Gap" theory, which assumes a major chronological gap between
verses 2 and 3 of Genesis 1 wherein the billions of years of evolutionary progress are inserted. Thus, all these ideas accept the
fact of evolution by allowing billions of years for it to occur. A
fourth theory is called "progressive creation," which accepts
long periods of evolution interspersed by creative bursts of
divine activity to sustain the process.

We have studied each of these theories in detail and believe
that they all have fatal biblical flaws, especially insofar as they are
employed to accept evolution.[84] Attempts at accommodation
fail because *evolutionary belief and biblical teaching are only compatible at the expense of biblical authority.* As *The Encyclopædia of Philosophy* points out, "It hardly needs saying that Darwinism is
incompatible with any literal construction put on either the Old
Testament or the New Testament."[85]

Perhaps if we show why evolution and biblical teaching are
incompatible, then we can see that theories that attempt to harmonize them, however well intentioned, are doing a disservice.
For example, if evolution is true, Moses was certainly in error
when he wrote the creation account of Genesis. Thus, in order
to "accommodate" evolution, harmonizing theories usually
impose a figurative or nonliteral interpretation on Genesis chapters one and two. But more than a dozen other biblical books

also interpret Genesis literally. They, too, are implicated with error for falsely interpreting the book of Genesis.[86]

It is always a mistake to interpret Scripture in light of dubious theories, scientific or otherwise. Properly interpreted, Scripture will never conflict with any fact of science simply because God is its author. After all, God not only inspired Scripture, He made the creation itself.

Nevertheless, consider a few examples of how these theories raise more problems than they solve.

Genesis 1-2: God created the entire universe, its flora, fauna, and our first parents, in six literal days. Lexical, grammatical, contextual, and hermeneutical considerations simply do not reasonably permit the "days" *of Genesis 1* to be vast periods of geologic ages, as indicated, for example, by the commentaries on Genesis 1 of such Old Testament scholars as Keil, Delitszch, Leupold, and Young[87] (See Exodus 20:8-11; 31:17).

Genesis 1:27: God created man and woman directly on the sixth day of creation. But if evolution is true, God created men and women indirectly after billions of years.

Genesis 1:31: God pronounced everything He created, including man, "very good." But if evolution is true, God pronounced millions of years of *human* sin and death, "very good" (cf. Romans 6:23; 1 Corinthians 15:26).

Psalm 148:5: Creation is by instantaneous divine fiat, not millions of years of gradual evolution (cf. Genesis 1:3,11,14,20,24).

Matthew 19:4-5: Jesus taught that God made man and woman *"at the beginning."* This is an indisputable reference to Adam and Eve in the Garden of Eden. But if evolution is true, men and women would have appeared extremely late on the evolutionary time scale, not "at the beginning" (cf. Genesis 1:1; 2 Peter 3:4). Was Jesus in error?

Romans 5:12-14; 1 Corinthians 15:21-22: Sin and death entered through Adam, twice stated to be the "first man." But if evolution is true, men, sin, and death had also existed for hundreds of thousands of years prior to Adam (cf., Romans 6:23). Was the Apostle Paul in error?

Jesus Himself accepted divine creation (Mark 13:19), Adam, Eve, and Abel (Matthew 19:4-5; Luke 11:50-51), and Noah's

Flood (Matthew 24:37-9; Luke 17:26-7). For Christians, at least, His authority is supreme. The bottom line is this: If evolution is true, the Bible, literally interpreted, cannot be true and therefore cannot be considered reliable, let alone the Word of God. Conversely, if the Bible is God's Word, then it is evolution that cannot be true.

Yet, in spite of the harmful effects of evolutionary thinking as to personal belief in God, biblical interpretation, and the terrible effects in the modern era, it is new discoveries about the creation itself that are almost forcing modern scientists to reconsider God. Indeed, as a medical doctor and computer specialist point out, "For centuries scientific rationalists have maintained that believing in a Supreme Being or Creator God is akin to committing intellectual suicide. However, the twentieth century has supplied an abundance of scientific discoveries which point to a transcendent Creator who ordered and energized the universe. This evidence is so powerful that numerous prominent scientists have begun to speak openly about the existence of just such a Being." Further, "In this twentieth-century age of skepticism it is indeed ironic to discover that more evidence has accumulated for the existence of a transcendent Creator in this century than any time in the last 1,900 years."[88]

Consider three examples. Astronomer Hugh Ross served as a postdoctoral fellow at the California Institute of Technology for five years in the field of radio astronomy. He points out,

> Theistic science postulates that the universe was created by a personal God a finite time ago and that it was intelligently designed with the arrival of human life in mind. Are these two propositions reasonable in light of evidence from astronomy? They are, in fact, the theme of dozens of books and papers produced by world-renowned astronomers in the late 1980s and early 1990s. . . .
>
> Astronomers have discovered that the characteristics of the universe, of our galaxy and of our solar system are so finely tuned to support life that the only reasonable explanation for this is the forethought of a personal, intelligent Creator. . . .

[In fact] The more astronomers learn about the origin and development of the universe, the more evidence they accumulate for the existence of God, and for the God of the Bible in particular.[89]

Kurt P. Wise received his Ph.D. in paleontology from Harvard University. After examining the evidence for evolution in the fossil record he concludes, "A Hypothesis of [a] divine Designer . . . is much more successful at explaining the major features of life than is macroevolutionary theory."[90]

The text *Cosmos, Bios, Theos*, produced by sixty world-class scientists, including twenty-four Nobel Prize winners, summarizes the logical conclusion for open-minded scientists as they face the incredible complexity and design of the universe they live in. Coeditor and Yale University physicist Henry Margenau, author of *The Miracle of Existence*, reasons that there "is only one convincing answer" to explain the intricate complexity and laws of the universe—creation by an omniscient, omnipotent God.[91]

The reason is obvious: "No scientific theory, it seems, can bridge the gulf between absolute nothingness and a full-fledged universe. . . ."[92]

Contrast Between the Materialistic and Judeo-Christian Worldviews

	Materialistic	*Christian View*
Ultimate Reality	Ultimate reality is impersonal matter. No God exists.	Ultimate reality is an infinite, personal, loving God.
Universe	The universe was created by chance events without ultimate purpose.	The universe was lovingly created by God for specific purposes.
Man	Man is the product of impersonal time plus chance plus matter. As a result, no man has eternal value or dignity nor any meaning other than that which is subjectively derived.	Man was created by God in His image and is loved by Him. Because of this, all men are endowed with eternal value and dignity. Their value is not derived ultimately from themselves, but from a source transcending themselves, God Himself.
Morality	Morality is defined by every individual according to his own views and interests. Morality is ultimately relative because every person is the final authority for his own views.	Morality is defined by God and immutable because it is inherently based on God's immutable character.
Afterlife	The afterlife brings eternal annihilation (personal extinction) for everyone.	The afterlife involves either eternal life with God (personal immortality) or eternal separation from Him (personal judgment).

Chapter 10

More False Assumptions
of Evolution

In our last chapter, we examined why evolution cannot logically be considered a scientific fact, that scientists are not always objective in their use of data, and that belief in evolution was not compatible with belief in the biblical God. In this chapter, we will consider three more false assumptions that surround evolutionary belief.

False Assumption 4: The fossil record offers genuine scientific evidence that evolution is true.

What about all the alleged evidences for evolution? It is generally admitted that the fossil record contains the most cogent evidence for the evolutionary hypothesis. So, if we discover this evidence to be nonexistent, then perhaps the other alleged evidences don't exist either. (In fact, they don't.[1])

The fossil record is continually heralded as "proof" of evolution and conceded to offer the primary scientific evidence that evolution has really occurred. As the eminent French biologist and zoologist Pierre-P. Grassé correctly points out:

> Zoologists and botanists are nearly unanimous in considering evolution as a fact and not a hypothesis. I agree with this position and base it primarily on documents provided by paleontology, i.e., the [fossil] history of the living world. . . .

Naturalists must remember that the process of evolution is revealed only through fossil forms. A knowledge of paleontology is, therefore, a prerequisite; only paleontology can provide them with *the evidence of evolution* and reveal its course or mechanisms. Neither the examination or present beings, nor imagination, nor theories can serve as a substitute for paleontological documents. If they ignore them, biologists, the philosophers of nature, indulge in numerous commentaries and can only come up with hypotheses. This is why we constantly have recourse to paleontology, the *only true science* of evolution. ... The true course of evolution is and can *only be revealed* by paleontology.[2]

Thomas Huxley also realized the importance of this issue when he wrote, "*If* it could be shown that this fact [gaps between widely distinct groups] had always existed, the fact would be *fatal* to the doctrine of evolution."[3]

The problem here is how evolutionary theory can ever be *demonstrated* when it necessarily postulates immense periods of time. It can't. Here, biologist Theodosius Dobzhansky criticizes creationists for asking evolutionists to do the impossible, that is, provide real evidence for the occurrence of evolution. But to our way of thinking, he only points out why the theory of evolution should not be accepted as a proven *scientific* fact, as no scientist has ever lived long enough to observe the evolution of major life forms.

These evolutionary happenings are unique, unrepeatable, and irreversible. It is as impossible to turn a land vertebrate into a fish as it is to effect the reverse transformation. The applicability of the experimental method to the study of such unique historical processes *is severely restricted before all else by the time intervals involved, which far exceed the lifetime of any human experimenter.* And yet, it is just such *impossibility* that is demanded by anti-evolutionists when they ask for "proofs" of evolution which they would magnanimously accept as satisfactory.[4]

To the contrary, if scientists cannot observe evolution as ever having taken place, how can they categorically state evolution is a *fact* of science? They attempt to do so by pointing to the fossil record. They believe it provides the critical evidence for evolution by preserving the record of the past that demonstrates gradual evolutionary change has occurred between the lower and higher life forms.

But even Darwin was concerned about the fossil record. In thinking the geologic record incomplete, Darwin himself confessed the following: ". . . [Since] innumerable transitional forms must have existed, why do we not find them imbedded in countless numbers in the crust of the earth? [and] Why is not *every* geological formation and *every* stratum *full* of such intermediate links? Geology assuredly does not reveal any such finely graduated organic chain; and this perhaps is the most *obvious* and *gravest objection* which can be urged against my theory."[5]

Again, Darwin asked, ". . . why if species have descended from other species by insensibly fine gradations, do we not *everywhere* see innumerable transitional forms?" And, ". . . the number of intermediate and transitional links, between all living and extinct species *must* have been *inconceivably great*."[6]

No Evidence at All

But 140 years later, it has become clear that the fossil record does not confirm Darwin's hope that future research would fill in the unexpected and extensive gaps in the fossil record. This is conceded by many leading evolutionary scientists as the following citations demonstrate. Noted paleontologist Stephen Jay Gould of Harvard points out, "The fossil record with its abrupt transitions offers *no support* for gradual change. . . . All paleontologists know that the fossil record contains *precious little* in the way of intermediate forms; transitions between major groups are characteristically abrupt."[7]

With an estimated 250 million or ¼ *billion* catalogued fossils of some 250,000 fossil species, the problem does certainly not appear to be one of an imperfect record. Many scientists have conceded that the fossil data are sufficiently complete to provide an accurate portrait of the geologic record.[8] University of Chicago professor of geology David Raup also points out the following: "Well, we are now about 120 years after Darwin and the knowledge of the fossil records has been greatly expanded. We now have a quarter of a million fossil species but the situation hasn't changed much. The record of evolution is still surprisingly jerky and, ironically, we have even fewer examples of evolutionary transition than we had in Darwin's time. . . . "[9]

Again, the truth is that the fossil record is composed *entirely* of gaps, not evidence of evolutionary transitions. The claimed transitions, of which there are very few, can all be rationally challenged. This means there isn't even a *single* proven evolutionary transition that exists anywhere in the fossil record. Evolutionary scientists themselves agree that the fossil record is comprised almost entirely of gaps. How, then can it logically offer scientific evidence of evolution? Prior to Dr. Gould's time, Dr. George Gaylord Simpson was one of the world's best-known evolutionists. He was professor of vertebrate paleontology, also at Harvard University, until his retirement. In his book, *The Major Features of Evolution*, he admitted, ". . . it remains true, as every paleontologist knows, that *most* new species, genera, and families and that nearly all new categories above the level of families appear in the record suddenly and are not led up to by known, gradual, completely continuous transitional sequences."[10]

Perhaps this explains why Dr. Austin Clark, once curator of paleontology at the Smithsonian Institute in Washington, D.C., wrote in 1928, "Thus so far as concerns the major groups of animals, the creationists seem to have the better of the argument."[11] But this remains true today. In his *Biology, Zoology and Genetics*, Thompson agrees when he writes, "Rather than supporting evolution, the breaks in the known fossil record support *the creation* of major groups with the possibility of some limited variation within each group."[12]

In "The Nature of the Fossil" record, Dr. Derek Ager also points out what every informed scientist knows, that "if we examine the fossil record in detail, whether at the level of orders or of species, we find—over and over again—not gradual evolution, but the sudden explosion of one group at the expense of another."[13]

Simpson thinks that the fossil record is almost complete for the larger terrestrial forms of North America and yet, "The regular absence of transitional forms is an almost universal phenomenon" among all orders of all classes of animals and analogous categories of plants.[14]

If so, it is not surprising to hear Professor E. J. H. Corner of the Botany Department of Cambridge University say that, although he believes there is evidence for evolution in other fields, "... I still think that, to the unprejudiced, the fossil record of plants is in favor of special creation.... Can you imagine how an orchid, a duck weed, and a palm have come from the same ancestry, and have we any evidence for this assumption? The evolutionist must be prepared with an answer, but I think that most would break down before an inquisition."[15]

Indeed, if, in the words of several evolutionary scientists, the fossil record "fails to contain a single example of a significant transition,"[16] then we are correct in concluding that paleontological histories of the plants and animals simply do not exist. Ichthyologist Dr. Donn Rosen, curator of fish at the American Museum of Natural History in New York, noted that evolution has been "unable to provide scientific data about the origin, diversity and similarity of the two million species that inhabit the earth and the estimated eight million others that once thrived."[17] This complaint has thus been registered for almost every species of plants, animals, insects, birds, and fish known to man.[18]

For example, the authority Johansen observes, "Modern gorillas, orangutans, and chimpanzees spring *out of nowhere*, as it were. They are here today; they have no yesterday."[19] Concerning the evolution of reptiles, University of California paleontologist R. A. Stirton points out, "There is no direct proof from the fossil record..."[20] Boston University biologist Paul B. Weiss comments, "The first and most important steps of animal evolution remain even more obscure than those of plant evolution."[21]

Dr. Pierre-P. Grassé is considered an outstanding scientist of France and the dean of French zoologists. In his *Evolution of Living Organisms* he declares, "We are in the dark concerning the origin of insects."[22] The authority on lungfishes, E. White, reflects, "Whatever ideas authorities may have on the subject, the lungfish, like every other major group of fish that I know, have their origins firmly based on nothing."[23]

Colin Patterson is the senior paleontologist at the British Museum of Natural History in London and author of the museum's general text on evolution. Yet he wrote in a letter to Luther D. Sunderland, April 10, 1979, "I fully agree with your comments on the lack of direct illustration of evolutionary transitions in my book. If I knew of any, fossil or living, I would certainly have included them. . . . I will lay it on the line—there is not one such fossil for which one could make a watertight argument."[24]

As Robert Barnes, in his book *Invertebrate Beginnings*, has confessed: "The fossil record tells us almost nothing about the evolutionary origin of phyla and classes. Intermediate forms are non-existent, undiscovered, or not recognized."[25] Thus, Earl L. Core, then chairman of the Department of Biology at West Virginia University, comments, "We do not actually know the phylogenetic history of any group of plants and animals, since it lies in the indecipherable past."[26]

In *Principles of Paleontology*, Dr. David Raup, who was previously the curator of geology at the Field Museum of Natural History in Chicago, and is now professor of geology at the University of Chicago, has also noted the following concerning the mysterious origins of higher plant and animal forms, "Unfortunately, the origins of most higher categories are shrouded in mystery: commonly new higher categories appear abruptly in the fossil record without evidence of transitional forms."[27]

Dr. Steven M. Stanley is professor of paleobiology at Johns Hopkins University. He was a recipient of the Schuchert award of the Paleontological Society and has also been awarded a Guggenheim Fellowship. He openly admits, "The known fossil record *fails* to document a single example of phyletic [gradual] evolution accomplishing a major morphologic transition and hence offers no evidence that the gradualistic model can be valid."[28]

Thus, the remark of Stephen J. Gould on Darwin's dilemma remains valid: "New species almost always appeared suddenly in the fossil record with no intermediate links to ancestors in older rocks of the same region."[29] Dr. Gould even concedes the lack of fossil evidence is the "trade secret" of paleontology, "The extreme rarity of transitional forms in the fossil record persists as the trade secret of paleontology. The evolutionary trees that adorn our textbooks have data only at the tips and nodes of their branches; the rest is inference, however reasonable, not the evidence of fossils. . . . Most species exhibit no directional change during their tenure on earth. . . . In any local area, a species does not arise gradually by the steady transformation of its ancestors; it appears all at once and 'fully formed.' "[30]

All this is why creationist scientists feel justified in doubting that the fossil record provides any genuine evidence for evolution. For example, Dr. Kurt Wise, cited earlier, received his Ph.D. in paleontology from Harvard University. His essay in J. P. Moreland, ed., *The Creation Hypothesis,* shows that the alleged evidences for evolution in the areas of similarity, the fossil record, fossil order, suboptimal improvisations, nested hierarchy of forms, vestigil organs, so-called embryological recapitulation, biogeography, and so on, are either poorly or not at all explained by evolution or better explained by creation.

Yet interested readers may wonder if evolutionary scientists have developed any new theories to explain the embarrassing lack of transitional forms in the fossil record. Perhaps it was a statement by Darwin concerning the abrupt appearance of many higher plant and animal forms that has recently sparked a new evolutionary theory. For example, Darwin observed: "Nothing is more extraordinary in the history of the Vegetable Kingdom, as it seems to me, than *the apparently very sudden or abrupt development of the higher plants.*"[31] Again, he felt this absence of plant and animal transitions was "the gravest objection" that could be raised against his theory.[32] So what new evolutionary theory has been created to fit the lack of transitional evidence in the fossil record and to explain the "abrupt appearance" of living things that no one can deny the fossil record does display?

Niles Eldredge and Stephen J. Gould tentatively proposed the following theory to account for the record as it exists. They suggest that the major gaps should be viewed as real phenomena of nature, an inevitable result of the mechanism of evolution itself. They see evolution taking place in major creative episodes, occurring at different times and places, interspaced with long periods of stability. They call their theory "punctuated equilibrium," also known as evolutionary saltationism. In part, this theory returns us to geneticist Richard Goldschmidt's "hopeful monsters" theory, which in Stanley's words, "engender[s] such visions as the first bird hatching from a reptile egg."[33]

Gould explains how this idea works in *The Panda's Thumb*, although elsewhere he acknowledges that he and Eldredge do not hold to the exclusive validity of this concept. Nevertheless, they feel their theory is not inconsistent with the Darwinian model and that it helps to explain the gaps in the fossil record, which they believe does adequately express evolutionary history: "Thus, the fossil record is a faithful rendering of what evolutionary theory predicts, not a pitiful vestige of a once bountiful tale. Eldredge and I refer to this scheme as the model of punctuated equilibria. Lineages change little during most of their history, but events of rapid speciation occasionally punctuate this tranquility."[34] Realize that, in part, Gould's concept is an admission that Darwin's theory of gradual evolution is not correct. Gould's theory of "punctuated equilibrium," which assumes the higher categories of plants and animals "suddenly" appeared "fully" formed in the fossil record, is, perhaps in a fashion, not much different from those who believe God created life forms instantaneously.

The fossil evidence is so poor that even the accomplished Swedish botanist and geneticist, Nils Heribert-Nilsson made the following confession and offered an amazing alternate theory. After 40 years of attempting to find evidence for the theory of evolution, he concluded that the task was impossible and that the theory was even "a serious obstruction to biological research." In his 1,200 page magnum opus, *Synthetic Speciation*, he declared the theory "ought to be entirely abandoned," in part because it "obstructs—as has been repeatedly shown—the attainment of consistent results, even from uniform experimental material. For everything must ultimately be forced to fit this speculative theory. An exact biology cannot, therefore, be built up."[35]

After noting "a close inspection discovers an empirical impossibility to be inherent in the idea of evolution,"[36] he went even further than Gould, stating his conviction that geologic periods having incredible spurts of biogeneration produced billions of biosyntheses simultaneously. Gametes and other necessary cells and biocatalytic substances literally appeared spontaneously and led "immediately" to their fully formed end product such as orchids, elephants, and eagles! Listen to his own explanations of why he made such a daring conclusion. It was because the empirical *evidence* forced him to it:

> As I have pointed out, there is no discussion among biologists today whether an evolution has taken place or not. The discussion concerns the how, the causation of evolution. No definite answer has been given to this question.
>
> It then becomes necessary to ask: Has there really been an evolution? Are the proofs of its occurrence tenable?
>
> After a detailed and comprehensive review of the facts we have been forced to give the answer: No! *Neither a recent nor a palaeohistorical evolution can be empirically demonstrated.*
>
> If this is the case, all discussions and problems concerning the causation of an evolution lose all interest. Lamarckism or mutationism, monophyletic or polyphyletic, continuity or discontinuity—the roads of the evolution are not problems any more. It is rather futile to discuss the digestion or the brain functions of a ghost.
>
> When we have arrived at this standpoint, the evolutionist has the obvious right to ask: What has caused the fundamental differentiation in the world of organisms, the immeasurable variation among animals and plants? That it exists is a fact: you owe us an explanation!
>
> We turn to empirical facts to obtain the answer. They tell us that during the geological history of the earth gigantic revolutions have occurred which at the same time mean *tabula rasa* catastrophes for a whole world of organisms but also the origin of a completely new one. The new one is structurally completely different from the old one. There are no other transitions than hypothetical ones. This origination of biota, which from a geological point of view is sudden as a flaring up I have called emication.

> During palaeobiological times whole new worlds of biota
> have been repeatedly synthesized.
>
> I will be asked: Do you seriously want to make such a state-
> ment? Do you not see that the consequences of such a
> theory are more than daring, that they would be *nearly
> insane?* Do you really mean to say that an orchid or an ele-
> phant should have been *instantaneously created out of non-
> living materia?*
>
> Yes, I do.[37]

Here we see an illustration of what was discussed earlier.
Rather than abandon a bad theory entirely, even more absurd
theories are proposed so as to maintain one's materialistic ideology. Regardless, another scientist who supports Gould's new
theory of evolution is Steven M. Stanley, who wrote the following
in the preface of his book *The New Evolutionary Timetable: Fossils,
Genes, and the Origin of Species,* "The [fossil] record now reveals
that species typically survive for a hundred thousand generations, or even a million or more, without evolving very much. We
seem *forced to conclude* that most evolution takes place rapidly,
when species come into being by the evolutionary divergence of
small populations from parent species. After their origins, most
species undergo little evolution before becoming extinct."[38]

But what do other scientists think about replacing Darwin's
theory of "gradualism" with Stephen J. Gould's "punctuated
equilibrium"? In essence, not much. For example, Ernest Mayr
says the "hopeful monsters" theory "is equivalent to believing in
miracles."[39] And he's correct.

Denton succinctly explains the problems faced by this
approach:

> While [Niles] Eldredge and [Stephen Jay] Gould's model
> is a perfectly reasonable explanation of the gaps between
> species (and, in my view, correct), it is doubtful if it can be
> extended to explain the larger systematic gaps. The gaps
> which separate species: dog/fox, rat/mouse, etc., are
> utterly trivial compared with, say, that between a primitive
> terrestrial mammal and a whale or a primitive terrestrial
> reptile and an Ichthyosaur; and even these relatively major
> discontinuities are trivial alongside those which divide

major phyla such as molluscs and arthropods. Such major discontinuities simply could not, unless we are to believe *in miracles*, have been crossed in geologically short periods of time through one or two transitional species occupying restricted geographical areas. Surely, such transitions must have involved long lineages including many collateral lines of hundreds or probably thousands of transitional species.... To suggest that the hundreds, thousands or possibly even millions of transitional species which must have existed in the interval between vastly dissimilar types were all unsuccessful species occupying isolated areas and having very small population numbers is *verging on the incredible*![40]

In other words, if evolution is to be considered a true scientific fact, it must be able to explain the origin of developed life forms by recourse to proven methods of evolutionary change. Can it do so? It would seem that most scientists who have examined this subject critically are honest enough to say no, even though they continue to believe in evolution. The problems of natural selection, mutation, and newer theories attempting to explain *how* evolution occurs are, put simply, too expansive to be resolved by current knowledge.[41] Indeed, some scientists have confessed there is little hope that any conceivable breakthrough in this area will *ever* be forthcoming.[42]

But if it has now been suggested that certain theories relative to evolution require a belief in miracles, is this also true for evolutionary belief generally?

False Assumption 5: Matter alone can explain the origin of life and the complexity of the universe. (Therefore, there is no need to postulate belief in a Creator God.)

The idea that everything has come from nothing is a bit hard to swallow, even for many scientists. Reflecting Darwin's own concerns, leading evolutionists such as Ernst Mayr have conceded that the idea that systems such as the eye, feather, or instinct could evolve and be improved by random mutations, represents "a considerable strain on one's credulity."[43] Darwin himself confessed, "I remember well when the thought of the eye made me cold all over ... [Now] The sight of a feather in a Peacock's tail, whenever I gaze at it, makes me sick."[44] Dr.

Denton also refers to the idea that evolution could occur by purely random processes—and yet produce the complexity of living organisms about us—as "simply an affront to reason."[45]

A Miracle Either Way

As modern science increasingly uncovers the indescribable complexity of the living world and simultaneously fails to explain the nature of abiogenesis (that life can originate from non-life), the miraculous nature of all theories of origins seem to be made more apparent. As we will see, in many ways, the term "miracle" is no longer properly restricted to only creationist belief. Nobel Prize-winning biochemist Dr. Francis Crick commented, "An honest man, armed with all the knowledge available to us now, could only state that in some sense, the origin of life appears at the moment to be almost a miracle, so many are the conditions which would have had to have been satisfied to get it going."[46]

Hoyle's research partner, Chandra Wickramasinghe, also noted, "Contrary to the popular notion that only creationism relies on the supernatural, evolutionism must as well, since the probabilities of random formation of life are so tiny as to require a 'miracle' for spontaneous generation tantamount to a theological argument."[47] In recent years many noted scientists have declared of the origin of life, "the whole process is miraculous" as the earlier mentioned text, *Cosmos, Bios, Theos,* illustrates. Let's briefly look deeper into this idea that belief in evolution is essentially a belief in miracles.

Mark Eastman, M.D., and Chuck Missler point out that when you boil down all the materialistic arguments for the origin of the universe, there are really just two alternatives:

1) that matter is infinitely old, i.e., eternal. Or

2) that matter appeared out of nothing at a finite point in the past.

They point out, "There is no third option."

These authors proceed to cite evidence to show that matter cannot be eternal, including evidence from physics, such as proton decay and evidence from the first and second laws of thermodynamics which "provide some of the strongest evidence for a finite universe."[48]

Everyone agrees that matter does exist, so we have to explain its existence somehow. If matter cannot be infinitely old—and the scientific evidence is so strong at this point as to make this conclusion inevitable—then our only option is that matter appeared in the universe out of nothing at a finite point in the past. Of course, if we begin with the "Big Bang" and an extremely small amount of dense matter, which some dub the "cosmic egg," the problem is not resolved. The origin of the "cosmic egg" is a matter of intense debate as well it should be. Where did such an egg originate? Did it exist forever? If not, where did it come from? Either it existed forever or it appeared

"I THINK YOU SHOULD BE MORE EXPLICIT HERE IN STEP TWO."

out of nothing at a finite point in the past. Such a belief is not only unscientific and irrational, it is an impossibility, as we will see later. Materialistically, there is no explanation, nor will there be. And regardless, doesn't it require a rather long stretch of the imagination to think that something so infinitely small could produce a universe as large as ours? How could a "pinpoint" of extremely dense matter produce the billions and trillions of suns and galaxies in our universe, let alone life? And what were the mechanisms that caused the big bang itself? No one knows.

What is perhaps even more amazing is that we have accepted this infinitely implausible scenario for the origin of the universe over an infinitely more probable one—creation by an infinite God.

In the creation/evolution debate, what must be recognized is that whether you begin with a materialistic or a divine origin for the universe, *both* are miracles. As Eastman and Missler state:

> The creationist's model begins with an infinitely intelligent, omnipotent, transcendent Creator who used intelligent design, expertise or know-how to create everything from the sub-atomic particles to giant redwood trees. Was it a miracle? Absolutely!

> The atheist's [i.e., materialistic] model begins with an even more impressive miracle—the appearance of all matter in the universe from nothing, by no one, and for no reason. A supernatural event. A miracle! However, the atheist does not believe in the outside or transcendent "First Cause" we call God. Therefore, the atheist has no "natural explanation" nor "supernatural explanation" for the origin of space-time and matter. Consequently the atheistic scenario on the origin of the universe leaves us hanging in a totally dissatisfying position. He begins his model for the universe with a supernatural event. This supernatural event, however, is accomplished without a supernatural agent to perform it.[49]

Many religions, especially Eastern religions, believe in the idea of an infinite, eternal universe. Unfortunately, this has serious implications for their doctrine of God. If the universe is infinite and eternal, then by definition there can be nothing else. As a result, even God becomes imminent within the universe, an occupant of it rather than an infinite, transcendent being beyond it. "Therefore, God could not dwell in eternity. He could not exist before time and space began. And because God is confined to the universe, He is subject to its laws. Therefore, God becomes either a product of the universe or the universe itself."[50]

It's beyond the scope of this book to discuss the problems of a solely imminent, pantheistic God, however, they are anything but small as seen in the religious, social, and moral consequences in those cultures that espouse pantheism. If there is now virtual proof that the universe is not infinite and that it has not existed eternally, then the logical conclusion is that pantheism is an impossibility insofar as it would equate God with an infinite, eternal universe.

Nevertheless, books such as Robert Jastrow's *God and the Astronomers*, Henry Margenau and Roy Varghese, eds., *Cosmos, Bios, and Theos*, and many others are proof that even materialistic scientists are now being forced to consider God and religious ideas concerning the origin of the universe.

This is exactly what Romans 1:20 teaches—that the creation itself provides evidence that is clearly seen and understood concerning God's existence. Thus: "The evidence for a finite, decaying, and finely-tuned universe has led many to conclude that there must be a Mind behind it all. Remarkably, many of these men are professed atheists who have been forced by the weight of 20th-century discoveries in astronomy and physics to concede the existence of an intelligent Designer behind the creation of the universe."[51]

For example, Paul Davies was once a leader for the atheistic, materialistic worldview. He now asserts of the universe, "[There] is for me powerful evidence that there is something going on behind it all. . . . It seems as though somebody has fine-tuned nature's numbers to make the Universe. . . . The impression of design is overwhelming." Further, the laws of physics themselves seem "to be the product of exceedingly ingenious design."[52]

Astronomer George Greenstein observed, "As we survey all the evidence, the thought instantly arises that some supernatural agency—or, rather Agency—must be involved. Is it possible that suddenly, without intending to, we have stumbled upon scientific proof of the existence of a Supreme Being? Was it God who stepped in and so providentially crafted the cosmos for our benefit?"[53]

Theoretical physicists Tony Rothman acknowledges, "When confronted with the order and beauty of the universe and the strange coincidences of nature, it's very tempting to take the leap of faith from science into religion. I am sure many physicists want to. I only wish they would admit it."[54]

In 1992, physicist and Nobel Laureat Arno Penzias noted, "Astronomy leads us to a unique event, a universe which was created out of nothing, one with the very delicate balance needed to provide exactly the conditions required to permit life, and one which has an underlying (one might say 'supernatural') plan."[55]

Statements like this could be multiplied many times over. They prove beyond a doubt that the best science by some of the most brilliant scientific minds leads us back, not to dead matter, but to a living God. At the very least, we may accept the following statement without qualification:

> In the case of the origin of the universe and life on earth, as we have seen, there are only two possible explanations— chance or design. In each case a balanced examination of twentieth-century scientific evidence has led a number of world authorities to conclude that appealing to chance is akin to faith in supernatural miracles! In effect, to believe that the universe "just happened," the skeptic must place as much faith in arbitrary and purposeless laws of physics and chance chemistry as the Christian does in the God of the Bible.[56]

But it is not the case that the materialist and the theist are actually exerting *equal* amounts of faith. To the contrary, the materialist's faith is far greater. Let's examine some of the evidence for this.

Probability and Faith

The esteemed late Carl Sagan and other prominent scientists have estimated the chance of man evolving at roughly 1 chance in $10^{2,000,000,000}$.[57] This is a figure with two billion zeros after it and could be written out in about 5,000 books of this size. According to what is termed "Borel's Single Law of Chance," this is no chance at all. Indeed, this number is so infinitely small it is not even conceivable. So, for argument's sake, let's take an infinitely more favorable view toward the chance that evolution might occur. What if the chances are only 1 in 10^{1000}, the figure that a prestigious symposium of evolutionary scientists used computers to arrive at? Even this figure involved only a mechanism necessary to abiogenesis and not the evolution of actual primitive life. Regardless, this figure is also infinitely above Borel's Single Law of Chance—one chance in 10^{50}—beyond which, put simply, events never occur.[58] Not even one chance remains.

Thus, in *Algorithms and the Neo-Darwinian Theory of Evolution*, Marcel P. Schutzenberger of the University of Paris calculated the probability of evolution based on mutation and natural selection. With many other noted scientists, he also concluded that it was "not conceivable" because the probability of a chance process accomplishing this is zero: " . . . there is *no chance* ($<10^{1000}$) to see this mechanism appear spontaneously and, if it did, *even less* for it to remain. . . . Thus, to conclude, we believe there is a *considerable gap* in the neo-Darwinian Theory of evolution, and we believe this gap to be of such a nature that it *cannot be bridged within the current conception of biology.*"[59]

Evolutionary scientists have called just 1 chance in 10^{15} "a virtual impossibility."[60] So, how can they believe in something that has infinitely less than 1 chance in 10^{1000}? After all, how small is one chance in 10^{1000}? It is very small—1 chance in 10^{12} is only one chance in a trillion.

We can also gauge the size of 1 in 10^{1000} (a figure with a thousand zeros) by considering the sample figure 10^{171}. How large is this figure? First, consider that the number of *atoms* in the period at the end of this sentence is approximately 3,000 trillion. Now, in 10^{171} years an amoeba could actually transport *all the atoms, one at a time,* in six hundred thousand, trillion, trillion, trillion, trillion, *universes,* each universe the size of ours, from one end of the universe to the other (assuming a distance of 30 *billion* light years) going at the dismally slow traveling speed of *1 inch* every *15 billion years.*[61] Yet this figure of one chance in 10^{171}, quite literally, cannot even scratch the surface of one chance in 10^{1000}—the "chance" that a certain mechanism necessary to the beginning of life might supposedly evolve. Again, who can believe in something whose odds are 1 "chance" in 10^{1000} to 1 "chance" in $10^{2,000,000,000}$ or even far beyond this? Yale University physicist Harold Morowitz once calculated the odds of a single bacteria reassembling its components after being superheated to break down its chemicals into their basic building blocks at 1 chance in $10^{100,000,000,000}$.[62] In fact, the dimensions of the entire known universe can be packed full by 10^{50} planets—but the odds of probability theory indicate that not on a single planet would evolution have ever occurred.[63]

Who can rationally believe in something whose odds are one chance in $10^{1,000}$, let alone the much more plausible figure of one chance in $10^{100,000,000,000}$? Please note that in exponential notation, every time we add a single number in the exponent we multiply the number itself by a factor of *ten*. Thus, one chance in 10^{171} is *ten times* smaller than one chance in 10^{172}. One chance in 10^{171} is one *million times* smaller than one chance in 10^{177}. And one chance in 10^{183} is *one trillion* times smaller than one chance in 10^{171}. So where do you think we end up with odds like one chance in $10^{100,000,000,000}$?

This kind of probability "progression into absurdity" is the very reason Borel devised his Single Law of Chance—to show that beyond a certain point some things will *never* happen. For example, what are the odds that elephants will ever evolve into helicopters? There are none, no matter how much time we allow for the event to occur.

So what kind of logic deduces that the infinitely more complex things in nature resulted from *chance* when all the *facts* and *evidence* we possess concerning every *single* man-made object in existence around the world says these much simpler objects had to result from intelligence, plan, and design? If the "simple" objects *demand* intelligence, how do the infinitely more complex objects arise by *chance*?

So true scientists require a great deal of faith to believe in evolution, but should their faith be considered a rational faith or an irrational faith? Again, there are really only two options concerning our existence: naturalism or supernaturalism—and both require a belief in miracles. If miracles must be accepted either way, one would think that science would go with the theory having the most evidence in its support—scientific creationism.

Placed into a more practical setting, if a horse had only one chance in 10^{1000} of placing first, how much money would a scientist bet on it? Would he or she bet even a dollar? If not, should anyone gamble their convictions about reality and personal destiny on the basis of one chance in $10^{100,000,000,000}$?

If, in ultimate terms, there are only two possible answers to the question of origins, then the disproving of one logically proves the other. If A or B are the only possible explanations of an event, and A is disproved, only B can be considered the cause. If the chances of evolution occurring are one in $10^{100,000,000,000}$, then the chance of creation occurring would have to be its opposite: 99.9 (followed by one hundred billion more 9s). Evolutionist George Wald of Harvard has stated that a 99.995 percent probability is "almost inevitable."[64] Then what of 99.99 percent, plus one hundred billion more 9s?—the chance that creation has occurred?

Thus, it is not surprising to hear famous astronomer Sir Fred Hoyle concede that, the chance that higher life forms might have emerged through evolutionary processes is comparable with the chance that a "tornado sweeping through a junk yard might assemble a Boeing 747 from the material therein."[65] As he ponders the magnificence of the world about him, even the outstanding French biochemist and Nobel Prize winner Jacques Monod admits in his *Chance and Necessity:* "One may well find oneself beginning to doubt again whether all this could conceivably be the product of an enormous lottery presided over by natural selection, blindly picking the rare winners from among numbers drawn at utter random.... [Nevertheless although] the miracle [of life] stands 'explained'; it does not strike us as any less miraculous. As Francois Mauriac wrote, 'What this professor says is far more incredible than what we poor Christians believe.' "[66]

Not surprisingly, some evolutionists are frank enough to admit that special creation actually is the better theory, either in whole or part.[67] Unfortunately, it seems that most scientists assume evolution has been proven in other fields and that their field of specialty is the only one with difficulties. In fact, every field is fraught with difficulties and those who recognize this are more open to considering creation.

Writing in the *Physics Bulletin* for May 1980, H. S. Lipson at the University of Manchester Institute of Science and Technology and a Fellow of the Royal Society confesses the following: "I have always been slightly suspicious of the theory of evolution because of its ability to account for *any* property of living beings (the long neck of the giraffe, for example). I have therefore tried to see whether biological discoveries over the last 30 years or so fit in with Darwin's theory. I do not think that they do." He further concedes, "In the last 30 years we have learned a great deal about life processes (still a minute part of what there is to know!) and it seems to me to be only fair to see how the theory of evolution accommodates the new evidence. This is what we should demand of a purely physical theory. To my mind, the theory does not stand up at all. I shall take only one example—breathing." And he proceeds to show how one cannot account for breathing on evolutionary assumptions. After further discussion, he asks, "How has living matter originated?" and concludes: "I think, however, that we must go further than this and admit that the *only* acceptable explanation is *creation*. I know that this is anathema to physicists, as indeed it is to me, but we must not reject a theory that we do not like if the experimental evidence supports it."[68] It is refreshing indeed to read such words.

In his *Biology, Zoology, and Genetics: Evolution Model Versus Creation Model 2*, Dr. A. Thompson observes, "Rather than supporting evolution, the breaks in the known fossil record support the creation of major groups with the possibility of some limited variation within each group."[69]

Dr. Austin Clark, the curator of paleontology at the Smithsonian Institution observed in the *Quarterly Review of Biology:* "Thus so far as concerns the major groups of animals, the creationists seem to have the better of the argument."[70]

In the area of comparative biochemistry, Bird observes, "This comparative unrelatedness argument is an affirmative evidence for the theory of abrupt appearance, as not just Denton and Sermonti but Zihlman and Lowenstein acknowledge in reference to the comparative biochemistry evidence, saying that 'this constitutes a kind of "special creation" hypothesis.' "[71] Even such eminent scientists as Sir Fred Hoyle and Chandra Wickramasinghe, his research partner, in discussing the "theory that life was assembled by an [higher] intelligence" state, "Indeed, such a theory is so *obvious* that one wonders why it is not widely accepted as being self evident. The reasons are psychological rather than scientific."[72]

Indeed they are. But before we proceed to our next and final assumption, let us examine our current assumption from a different angle.

The Myth of Chance

In *Not a Chance: The Myth of Chance in Modern Science & Cosmology*, theologian and apologist R.C. Sproul points out that mythology was not only practiced by premodern cultures, it occurs in every culture and has even intruded significantly into the realm of science, such as in the "spontaneous generation" theory of evolution, that claims all life arose from dead matter solely by chance. He shows that the concept of chance—something happening totally without cause—is *impossible*. The *Macmillan Dictionary for Students* (1984) defines impossible as, "not capable of coming into being or occurring" and "not acceptable as truth." And yet modern science argues that the universe and all life in it arose solely by chance. In the words of Nobelist Jacques Monod, "... chance *alone* is at the source of every innovation, of all creation in the biosphere. Pure chance, absolutely free but blind, [is] at the very root of the stupendous edifice of evolution ... "[73]

Sproul argues persuasively that, for science and philosophy to continue in fruitful fashion, the modern penchant for chance must be abandoned once and for all. If not, the stakes are not insignificant—the very possibility of doing science lies in the balance. Essentially, when logic and empirical data are neglected or neutralized in the doing of science, then "mythology is free to run wild."[74]

In effect, modern sciences' assigning the origin of the universe and all life in it to pure, random chance does an incalculable disservice to science because it "reduces scientific investigation not only to chaos but to sheer absurdity. Half of the scientific method is left impaled on the horns of chance. The classical scientific method consists of the marriage of induction and deduction, of the empirical and the rational. Attributing instrumental causal power to chance vitiates deduction and the rational. It is manifest irrationality, which is not only bad philosophy but horrible science as well. Perhaps the attributing of instrumental power to chance is the most serious error made in modern science and cosmology. . . . if left unchallenged and uncorrected, [it] will lead science into nonsense. . . . Magic and logic are not compatible bedfellows. Once something is thought to come from nothing, something has to give. What gives is logic."[75]

Chance can explain nothing because chance itself is nothing: "Chance has no power to do anything. It is cosmically, totally, consummately impotent. . . . It has no power because it has no being."[76] One of the most inviolate and oldest laws of science is *Ex nihilo nihil fit*—"Out of nothing, nothing comes." When scientists ascribe absolute power to nothing, it is doing myths. Here, chance is the "magic wand to make not only rabbits but entire universes appear out of nothing."[77]

To illustrate, the Nobel Laureate and Harvard professor Dr. George Wald once stated concerning the evolution of life, "One only has to concede the magnitude of the task to concede the possibility of the spontaneous generation of a living organism is impossible. Yet here we are—as a result, I believe, of spontaneous generation." However, Wald went on to say that in terms of originating life, the impossible really isn't impossible after all: "Time is in fact the hero of the plot. The time with which we have to deal is of the order of 2 billion years. What we regard as impossible on the basis of human experience is meaningless. Given so much time, the 'impossible' becomes possible, the possible probable, and the probable virtually certain. One only has to wait: time itself performs the miracles."[78]

Time, of course, is not the hero and cannot perform miracles. To argue otherwise violates Borel's Single Law of Chance. Borel's law, in effect, states that time has no power to perform that which is impossible according to the laws of probability. Regardless, how did the universe exist *forever* and then do in time what it had not done *forever* (i.e., create life)? Sproul comments,

> Here is magic with a vengeance. Not only does the impossible become possible; it reaches the acme of certainty—with time serving as the Grand Master Magician.
>
> In a world where a miracle-working God is deemed an anachronism, he is replaced by an even greater miracle-worker: time or chance. I say these twin miracle workers are greater than God because they produce the same result with so much less, indeed infinitely less, to work with.
>
> God is conceived as a self-existent, eternal being who possess inextricably the power of being. Such power is a sufficient cause for creation. Time and chance have no being, and consequently no power. Yet they are able to be so effective as to render God an anachronism. At least with God we

have a potential miracle-worker. With chance we have
nothing with which to work the miracle. Chance offers us
a rabbit without a hat and—what's even more astonishing—
without a magician.[79]

Further, to argue as modern science does that the universe
"exploded into being" billions of years ago would seem to
require a belief that the universe exploded from *nonbeing* into
being. Since science has proven that matter cannot be eternal,
this phrase, presumably, must be taken literally. But to do so
requires more faith in magic, not science, and is in effect a faith
in self-creation, which, as Sproul shows, is something logically
impossible. Thus:

> we can hardly resist the inference that that which exploded,
> since it was not yet in being, was nonbeing, or nothing.
> This we call self-creation by another name. This is so absurd
> that, upon reflection, it seems to be downright silly. It is so
> evidently contradictory and illogical that it must represent
> a straw-man argument. No sober scientist would really go so
> far as to suggest such a self-contradictory theory, would
> they? Unfortunately, they would and they do. This raises
> questions about the soberness of the scientists involved.
> But generally these are not silly people who make such silly
> statements. Far from it. They number some of the most
> well-credentialed and erudite scholars in the world, who
> make a prophet out of Aristotle when he said that in the
> minds of the brightest men often reside the corner of a
> fool. In other words, brilliant people are capable of making
> the most foolish errors. That is understandable, given our
> frailties as mortals. What is not so understandable are the
> ardent attempts people make to justify such foolishness.[80]

Of course, there is much more going on here than poor
science. In Romans 1:18-25 we are told that the unregenerate
deliberately suppress the truth of God as Creator. Here the
truth is suppressed by the rejection of the laws of science such
as the law of causality, the law of noncontradiction, and the law
of biogenesis, that life arises only from life. That the *rejection* of
scientific principles, laws, and reasoning should be so force-
fully employed in defense of what is inherently irrational and
impossible (the creation of the universe from nothing), is

surely a commentary on the condition of modern origins science.

However, because God has created us as rational creatures, it may even be argued that sin against reason is a sin against God. Scientists should know better. And, generally, in their rational moments they do. They know the universe didn't arise from literally nothing. The suppression of truth is to try and make it seem as if it did. Most scientists, it seems, prefer to disguise their belief in magic by making the idea of chance origins appear scientific and rational. Why? *Because they do not personally like the consequences of having to seriously consider the implications of a Creator God.*

But in the end, a Creator God is our only logically *possible* explanation for origins. How do we know this? In order to answer this question, we must first make one assumption that is crucial to almost everything else. Dr. Sproul has pointed out the necessity of not only assuming the validity of the laws of logic but the necessity of adhering to them. Without this, even science is impossible and must end up teaching nonsense, as it does now in the area of origins.

Put another way, "How do we know that the real is rational? We don't. What we do know is that if it isn't rational, we have no possible way of knowing anything about reality. That the real is rational is an assumption. It is the classical assumption of science. Again, it is a *necessary* assumption for science to be possible. If the assumption is valid and reality is rational and intelligible, then the falsifying power of logic can play a major role in scientific inquiry."[81]

If we reject the laws of logic, we reject everything and all knowledge becomes impossible. But if we accept the laws of logic, as we must, then this leaves us only *one* valid option for explaining the origin of the universe: creation by God.

Only Four Options

As Sproul points out, there are really only four options to consider for the origin of the universe: (1) that the universe is an illusion—it does not exist; (2) that it is self-created; (3) that it is self-existent and eternal by itself; and (4) that it was created by something self-existent. He further argues that there are no other options: "Are there are options I've overlooked? I've puzzled over this for decades and sought the counsel of philosophers, theologians, and scientists, and I have been unable to locate any other theoretical options that cannot be subsumed under these four options."[82] For example, the idea of spontaneous generation inherent to naturalistic evolution is the same as option 3, self-creation; philosopher Bertrand Russell's concept of an infinite regress, an infinite series of finite causes, is simply a camouflaged form of self-creation disguised to infinity.

Dr. Sproul proceeds to show that the first three options concerning the origin of the universe *must* logically be eliminated as rational options.

Option 1 must be eliminated for two reasons. First, if the universe is an illusion, the illusion must somehow be accounted for. If it's a false illusion then it isn't an illusion; if it's a "true" illusion then someone or something must be existing to have the illusion. If this is the case then that which is having the illusion must either be self-created, self-existent, or caused by something ultimately self-existent, again, everything is not an illusion.

The second reason for eliminating option 1 is that if we assume the illusion is absolute (that nothing exists), including that which is having the illusion, then there is no question of origins even to answer because literally nothing exists. But if something exists, then whatever exists must either be self-created, self-existent, or created by something that is self-existent.

The problem with option 2, self-creation, is that "it is formally false. It is contradictory and logically impossible."[83] In essence, self-creation requires the existence of something before it exists: "For something to come from nothing it must, in effect, create itself. Self-creation is a logical and rational impossibility. . . . For something to create itself it must be *before* it is. This is impossible. It is impossible for solids, liquids, and gases. It is impossible for atoms, and subatomic particles. It is impossible for light and heat. It is impossible for God. Nothing anywhere, anytime, can create itself."[84] Sproul points out that an entity can be self-existent and not violate logic but it can't be self-created. Again, when scientists claim that 15 to 20 billion years ago "the universe exploded into being" what are they really saying? If it exploded from nonbeing into being then what exploded?

Sproul summarizes his reasoning this way: first, chance is not an entity. Second, nonentities are powerless because they have no being. Third, to argue that something is caused by chance attributes instrumental power to nothing. Fourth, something caused by nothing is self-created. Fifth, the idea of self-creation is irrational and violates the law of noncontradiction. Sixth, to retain a theory of self-creation requires the rejection of logic and rationality.[85] While the concept of self-creation can be believed, it cannot be argued rationally. It is as rationally inconceivable as a round square or a four-sided triangle.[86]

The problem with option 3, that the universe is self-existent and eternal, is that the discoveries of modern science force us to reject it, as we have already discussed. Again, how did the universe exist *forever* and then do in time what it had not done *forever*? Are all parts of the cosmos self-existent and eternal or only some parts? If we say all parts, that includes ourselves and every single man-made item that exists. But we know these *cannot* be self-existent and eternal. Cars, watches, chairs, and all people were brought into existence at some point in time. If we say some parts of the material cosmos are self-existent and that they created other parts, we have essentially transferred the attributes of a transcendent God to the self-existent, eternal parts of the universe and thereby rejected our own assumption of materialism. Besides, it simply is not rational to argue that matter created life. All the laws of science, logic, and common sense show that life does not originate from nonlife.

Finally, if there were ever a "time" when nothing existed, what would exist now? Clearly, nothing would exist—unless we argue something can come from nothing—which means more magic, which places us back at self-creation, a logical impossibility. So if anything exists now, then *something* is self-existent, and it must either be God or matter. If it *can't* be matter, and it *can't*, then it must be God.[87]

Sproul continues to point out that the remaining concept of a self-existent reality: God is not only logically possible, but is logically *necessary:*

> There must be a self-existent being of some sort some-
> where, or nothing would or could exist. A self-existent
> being is both logically and ontologically necessary....We
> have labored the *logical* necessity of such being. Yet it is
> also necessary ontologically. An ontologically necessary
> being is a being who cannot not be. It is proven by the law
> of the impossibility of the contrary. A self-existent being, by
> his very nature must be eternal. It has no antecedent cause,
> else it would not be self-existent. It would be contingent.[88]

After logically demonstrating option 4 as the only reasonable option available in the realm of the debate over origins, Sproul also shows that the classic arguments by Kant and Hume against the cosmological argument are invalid.

In sum, based upon the law of noncontradiction and its extension, the law of causality, he has demonstrated that we have no other *rational* option than option 4, that the universe was *created* by something that is self-existent—God.[89] But it is also a necessary and practical conclusion that this God be personal, not impersonal. "Can there be an impersonal cause of personality ultimately?"[90] No. Of course, many people today prefer the idea that God is impersonal, whether we have the Brahman of Hinduism, some other form of pantheism, or the essentially illogical "deification" of matter as in naturalistic evolution. (Again, if the universe is created, then pantheism is impossible for this would mean God was created.)

The reason for this preference for impersonality is evident. If God is impersonal, we are off the hook and accountable to no one. The concept of an impersonal origin is attractive because it allows us to think we escape moral responsibility to a personal God. We can live as we wish and do what we want. Biblically, of course, and often practically, this is the ultimate exercise in self-delusion.

Sproul concludes by stating, "Chance as a real force is a myth. It has no basis in reality and no place in scientific inquiry. For science and philosophy to continue the advance in knowledge, chance must be demythologized once and for all."[91]

If the results of a recent Gallup poll reported on a CNN "factoid" are correct, only 9 percent of Americans believe that life on earth arose by chance anyway. This would seem to imply that most Americans are better informed about origins than most scientists. Of course, most Americans also believe in evolution; they simply believe God used the evolutionary processes to create life. The reasoning is that, if life exists, it is much more reasonable to think it came from God than from nothing, regardless of the process. At this point, unfortunately, most Americans have also bought into the second level of modern scientific myth-making, the garnering of scientific data in such a manner as to make evolution *seem* possible. In other words, if chance is rejected, and we assume God used the process of evolution to create life, then all the "evidence" scientists *claim* for evolution "must" be valid. Biblically, however, it is impossible that God could have used the process of evolution and this explains why its claimed evidences are found to be nonexistent.

In conclusion, once we have God onboard, it is simply a matter of logically employing Christian evidences to prove that the Christian God is the one true self-existent being. Indeed, what other rational, comprehensive, convincing worldviews do we have as options? Apart from Christianity, there are none. For example, Eastern religions are philosophically self-refuting and nihilistic; modern materialism/secularism/atheism/humanism is bankrupt philosophically, morally, and in most other ways, as demonstrated by a number of modern philosophers and theologians.[92] Polytheism, deism, pantheism, and other worldviews are also inadequate or logically deficient.[93] Only Christianity survives the tests of logic, rationality, and empirical, historical verification as a comprehensive worldview.

False Assumption 6: Scientific creationism is only a religion and has no scientific merit.

When considering the issue of the nature of creationism it must be remembered that the real problem is not with a scientific formulation of the creation concept, but with materialism and its inherent limitations. These not only wrongly restrict creation solely to the religious sphere, they also tend to skewer the interpretation of scientific data. The *bon mot* that evolution is "1/10 bad science and 9/10 bad philosophy" has more truth to it than many scientists are willing to concede. For example, in *Darwin and His Critics*, philosophy professor David L. Hull of the

University of Wisconsin points out that evolutionary theory has been criticized philosophically from the beginning: "The leading philosophers contemporary with Darwin, John Herschel, William Whewell, and John Stuart Mill, were equally adamant in their conviction that the *Origin of Species* was just one mass of conjecture. Darwin had proved nothing! From a philosophical point of view, evolutionary theory was sorely deficient. Even today, both Darwin's original efforts and more recent reformulations are *repeatedly found philosophically objectionable*. Evolutionary theory seems capable of offending almost everyone."[94]

The reason that evolutionary belief is deficient philosophically is because it attempts to address the issue of origins on the basis of an inadequate approach. The issue is argued exclusively at the level of naturalism, while it is forgotten that theology itself is a legitimate discipline of knowledge that should also be considered in the debate on origins. Why? Because approaching the issue of origins only materialistically leaves too many major problems for explaining the data—data that everyone agrees is there. Thus, meaning or interpretation that is assigned on the premise of materialism alone will be deficient because the data is incapable of organizing itself adequately solely on this basis. This is why many scientists are currently unhappy with the nature of the case for evolution.

What is needed is a more objective discussion of the issue of origins at the worldview level. This is really what is occurring in both creationist and evolutionist camps anyway, whether or not this is recognized.

The components of science itself—classification, theory, experiment, conclusion—reflect a framework of concepts that transcend scientific data. All attempts to explain or interpret data are to some degree impositions on the data. So are attempts to disprove or disallow alternate explanations. In other words, because the data of science does not automatically organize itself, interpretive structures, which themselves transcend the data, must be imposed upon it. Again, the question is whether or not a solely materialistic structure is adequate.

We think that an approach that attempts to look at the data without a bias against larger theological implications is more productive. And there is nothing unscientific about this. The worldview of theism is just as adequate an explanatory framework for the scientific data as is the world view of naturalism. For example, the data from science (e.g., thermodynamics, astronomy) clearly indicate a point of origin for the universe. Thus, despite the dogma of eternal matter, "all the observable data" produced by astronomy indicate the universe was created at a point in time.[95] The data from science also confirm a high degree of complexity *throughout* the history of life and such complexity requires explanations which not only include but also transverse natural processes alone. In addition, the data from science reveal an incredibly high degree of fine-tuning or balance within the structure of the universe at all levels. This also calls for an explanation that transcends natural processes and invokes the need for a supernatural Creator.

In other words, a compelling case from philosophy, logic, and science itself suggests that natural laws alone are woefully insufficient to account for the existence of the universe and the complexity of life that inhabits it. This becomes especially true when we consider the distinctive character of man, such as his abstract reasoning powers, moral sensibility, complex personality, and spiritual nature. Humans are so far removed from the level of the animals that we simply cannot account for them on the basis of purely natural processes.*

The value of science is undeniable as a *part* of the larger picture explaining the world, but it cannot explain the entirety of that picture. But theism, in terms of its ability to explain a much larger range of data, as well as the integration of data in other disciplines, actually offers a more coherent "big picture." Thus, when creation is affirmed in the context of theism, it meets the criteria of good science: it is testable, unified, and fruitful in a heuristic sense.

Thus, creation science cannot simply be dismissed, as it often is, as a religion in disguise, designed to underhandedly put Genesis back into the school system. Although creationism is certainly a religious philosophy, it can also be a scientific doctrine,

---

*See, for example, Mortimer Adler, *The Difference of Man and the Difference It Makes.*

not just dogma. This is something attested to by many noted scientists and experts on the nature of the relationship between science and religion. For example, the volumes by Bird, Moreland (ed.), Geisler and Anderson, and Morris and Parker are only some of those demonstrating that creationism can be scientific.[96]

Dean H. Kenyon, Ph.D., professor of biology and coordinator of the general biology program at San Francisco State University, wrote the foreword to Morris and Parker's *What Is Creation Science?* Dr. Kenyon is one of America's leading nonevolutionary scientists and has a Ph.D. in biophysics from Stanford University.[97] A former evolutionist and coauthor of *Biochemical Predestination*, a standard work on the evolutionary origin of life, Kenyon now believes that the current situation where most consider creation science simply a religion in disguise "is regrettable and exhibits a degree of close-mindedness quite alien to the spirit of true scientific inquiry."[98] Kenyon is only one prominent scientist who has "extensively reviewed the scientific case for creation" and finds it legitimate.[99]

For example, in presenting the scientific evidence for the theory termed "abrupt appearance" (which incorporates relevant data from paleontology, morphology, information content, probability, genetics, comparative discontinuity, and so on), Bird observes, "These lines of evidence are affirmative in the sense that if true, they support the theory of abrupt appearance. They are not negative in the sense of merely identifying weaknesses of evolution.... The theory of abrupt appearance is scientific. It consists of the empirical evidence and scientific interpretation that is the content of this chapter. The theory of abrupt appearance also satisfies the various definitions of science.... Its many testable and falsifiable claims are summarized in sections 10.3 (a) and 10.4 (a)."[100]

Dr. Wilder-Smith also presents a scientific alternative to Neo-Darwinism in his *A Basis for a New Biology* and *The Scientific Alternative to Neo-Darwinian Evolutionary Theory: Information Sources and Structures.*[101] The scientific case for creation is also ably marshalled by leading scientists in J. P. Moreland's (ed.), *The Creation Hypothesis* (InterVarsity, 1994). For example, consider what one leading evolutionist said of this volume. Dr. Arthur N. Shapiro is with the Center for Population Biology at the University of California, Davis. Although an atheist writing in *Creation/Evolution,* a journal with certainly no love lost for creationists or creationism, he nevertheless closes his review in the following words:

> I can see *Science* in the year 2000 running a major feature article on the spread of theistic science as a parallel scientific culture. I can see interviews with the leading figures in history and philosophy of science about how and why this happened. For the moment, the authors of *The Creation Hypothesis* are realistically defensive. They know their way of looking at the world will not be generally accepted and that they will be restricted for a while to their own journals. They also know that they will be under intense pressure to demonstrate respectability by weeding out crackpots, kooks and purveyors of young-earth snake oil. If they are successful, the day will come when the editorial board of *Science* will convene in emergency session to decide what to do about a paper which is of the highest quality and utterly unexceptionable, of great and broad interest, *and* which proceeds from the prior assumption of intelligent design. For a preview of that crisis, you *should* read this book. Of course, if you are smug enough to think "theistic science" is an oxymoron, you won't.

He also noted, "In reasonably objective fashion the chapters...demonstrate how regularly we have prematurely proclaimed victory on each and every front. A certain humility on our part seems called for. At the least, we should be candid in admitting that if we consider material solutions to these problems inevitable, that is a matter of faith on our part. We can point with great pride to tremendous advances in the past, but we of all people should know the limitations of inductive generalization."[102] Dr. Shapiro is correct that faith is a necessary component of naturalism.

In his survey of the alleged evidence for evolution, Randy L. Wysong, D.V.M., an instructor in human anatomy and physiology, points out that belief in evolution requires faith:

Evolution requires plenty of faith: a faith in L-proteins [left-handed molecules] that defy chance formation; a faith in the formation of DNA codes which if generated spontaneously would spell only pandemonium; a faith in a primitive environment that in reality would fiendishly devour any chemical precursors to life; a faith in experiments [on the origin of life] that prove nothing but the need for intelligence in the beginning; a faith in a primitive ocean that would not thicken but would only hopelessly dilute chemicals; a faith in natural laws including the laws of thermodynamics and biogenesis that actually deny the possibility for the spontaneous generation of life; a faith in future scientific revelations that when realized always seem to present more dilemmas to the evolutionists; faith in probabilities that treasonously tell two stories—one denying evolution, the other confirming the creator; faith in transformations that remain fixed; faith in mutations and natural selection that add to a double negative for evolution; faith in fossils that embarrassingly show fixity through time, regular absence from transitional forms and striking testimony to a world-wide water deluge; a faith in time which proves only to promote degradation in the absence of mind; and faith in reductionism that ends up reducing the materialist arguments to zero and enforcing the need to invoke a supernatural creator.

The evolutionary religion is consistently inconsistent. Scientists rely upon the rational order of the universe to make accomplishments, yet the evolutionist tells us the rational universe had an irrational beginning from nothing. Due to lack of understanding about mechanisms and structure, science cannot even create a simple twig. Yet the evolutionary religion speaks with bold dogmaticism about the origin of life.[103]

If scientific creationism is really religion masquerading as science, and evolutionary theory alone is true science, which alone should be taught in science classes, why is it that literally thousands of scientists worldwide have abandoned evolution as a scientific theory and become *scientific* creationists? For so many reputable scientists to accept creationism as legitimately scientific means that evolutionists who claim it is only religion must be wrong.

Further, evolutionists have often claimed that no qualified scientist having academic Ph.D.'s from accredited institutions believes in creation. But those who argue in this manner are also wrong. Collectively, thousands of creationists have Ph.D.'s in all the sciences, some from the most prestigious universities in America and Europe. They have held honors, positions, and appointments that are equal to the best of their evolutionary colleagues. There are also thousands of non-creationist scientists who reject evolutionary theory, some of whom have also admitted that creationism can be scientific.

As one indication of the scientific nature of creation, consider the chart comparing the predictions of creation and evolution with the scientific data:

Predictions and Data for Creation/Evolution

Predictions	*Data*
c. Eternal omnipotent Creator e. Eternal matter	Universe began; matter degrades; life highly ordered
c. Natural laws and character of matter unchanging e. Matter and laws evolve	Laws constant; matter constant; no new laws
c. Trend toward degradation e. Trend toward order	Second law of thermodynamics
c. Creation of life the only possibility e. Spontaneous generation probable	Biochemical improbabilities
c. Life unique e. Life-matter continuum	Life-matter gap; biochemicals formed naturally from nonlife
c. No current creation e. Continual creation	First law of thermodynamics
c. Life eternal e. Life began	Law of biogenesis

—Continued—

Predictions and Data for Creation/Evolution

Predictions	*Data*
c. Basic categories of life unrelated e. All life related	Law of biogenesis; reversion to type; fossil gaps; heterogeneity; similarities
c. World catastrophe e. Uniformity	Fossils; sedimentary strata; frozen muck; present uniformity
c. Organs always complete e. Gradual evolution of organs	Organs always fully developed; Natural selection culls
c. Mutations harmful e. Mutations can improve	Mutations vitiate; laws of information science
c. Language, art and civilization sudden e. Civilization gradual	Archæology and anthropology show civilization sudden
c. Man unique e. Man an animal	Man-animal similarities, also gap: art, language, religion
c. Design manifest e. Naturalism	Life complex and highly ordered; Natural syntheses[104]

This chart indicates that the scientific facts support the theory of creation far better than they support evolution. Finally, if creationism is really only a religion, why do evolutionists consistently lose their *scientific* debates to creationists?[105]

Perhaps all this helps explain why polls indicate most people favor the idea of schools teaching the theory of creation in addition to the theory of evolution. This includes the vast majority of the national public (more than 85 percent), two-thirds of lawyers nationally (who also find it constitutional), most university presidents at secular universities, and two-thirds of public school board members. One poll indicated even 42 percent of public school biology teachers now apparently favor the theory of creation over the theory of evolution.[106] Yet how few schools actually allow their teachers the option of a two model approach?

Perhaps our discussion to date helps explain why so many evolutionists are increasingly on the defensive. Those philosophically and psychologically committed to materialism, to the exclusion of all else, can hardly be expected to be happy with the current state of evidence for evolution—let alone be happy with the increasing acceptance of creationism.

Part 3

The Bible

The Most Unique Book on Earth

Chapter 11

Biblical Prophecy—Part One

Someone once said, "We should all be concerned about our future because we will have to spend the rest of our lives there."

In the movie version of H.G. Wells' *Time Machine*, "George" (Rod Taylor) began an incredible journey that would transport him far into the future. If you watched that intriguing motion picture, perhaps you remember being captivated. As this intrepid adventurer sat in his time machine, he could literally view time passing by—the hours rolled into days, the days into years, the years into decades, and the decades into centuries and millennia. Because he was able to leap into the distant future, he could actually behold the "destiny" of humanity.

Perhaps some things we find impossible to fathom, let alone achieve, really are possible under different circumstances. For example, who would deny that God—if He chose—could transport people into the future and reveal to them what would happen? Jesus Himself once commented in a different context, "With man this is impossible, but not with God; all things are possible with God" (Mark 10:27, cf. Luke 1:37).

Perhaps the truth about "time travel" may be just as startling as in H. G. Wells' novel. Perhaps a select few in history actually have been "transported into the future" so to speak—and lived to tell about it. In essence, this is just what God did with several biblical prophets and apostles. Ezekiel, Daniel, the Apostle John, and others were each shown events that would take place in the future or at the end of the world. Impossible? The only question is whether the evidence for such a claim is convincing.

211

The writings of these prophets were "consistently oriented around predictive themes.... the prophets 'regarded the foretelling of the future as of the essence of their function.' "[1]

For H. G. Wells, humanity's future was both terrifying and hopeful. This is also the future of mankind seen by the biblical prophets. And this future may have more relevance to us than we think.

Who would deny that the future affects us all? Which man or woman alive would ever say his or her future was unimportant? This is why millions of people turn to astrologers and other diviners or fortune tellers, because they think such people can accurately predict their future or their destiny. Unfortunately, as we documented in our *Encyclopedia of New Age Beliefs* (Harvest House, 1996), such divinatory methods are not only unreliable, they are consequential.

On the other hand, the ancient Hebrew prophets made startling predictions about the future, predictions that should amaze anyone. Most of these predictions have already come true, and there is every reason to believe that all their prophecies will sooner or later be fulfilled.

Any brief study of comparative religion reveals that the religious world today offers men and women many different gods to whom they may give their allegiance. But which god should they choose when all the gods contradict one another? And what about the vast majority of gods who are aloof, capricious, amoral, or actually evil? Isn't there a truly good and loving God somewhere?

The Purpose of Prophecy: To Prove Who the True God Is

Many people today think that all religions are equally true and that it is somehow wrong to say there is only *one* true God. Jesus however, declared that not only was there only one true God, but that this God could be known personally. He stated, "Now this is eternal life: that they may know you, *the only true* God, and Jesus Christ whom you have sent" (John 17:3). How can a person know Jesus was right? One way is by the study of prophecy. A central purpose of biblical prophecy is to show men and women who the one true God is "so that all the people of the earth may know that the Lord is God and that there is no other" (1 Kings 8:60; cf. verses 1-59).

God Himself challenges people, including the "gods" they trust, to compare His predictions with all others. He teaches that His knowledge of the future is proof that *He alone is the Lord.* No one else has consistently told of things to come and *also* had them come true exactly as forecast (See Isaiah 41:20-29). Thus, God informs us that He has many witnesses to His predictions, and He emphasizes again and again that His prophecies of the future prove that He alone is God. Thus, ". . . the fact of predictive prophecy brings, first of all, glory to God; for each prediction testifies to its Author's wisdom and sovereignty over the future. As Isaiah spoke forth to the Israelites of his day, 'Who hath declared it from the beginning, that we may say, He is right, . . . Predictions point up His powers, as contrasted with those of any conceivable rivals . . . When Joshua spoke out in faith and foretold the miracle of the cutting off of the waters of the Jordan (Josh. 3:13), he assured his people, 'Hereby ye shall know that the living God is among you' (v. 10); and to this end the prediction itself contributed, just as did the subsequent miracle."[2]

Because the numerous false prophets of history (and their "gods") cannot produce convincing evidence for their claimed powers of prediction, God even mocks them: "All the nations gather together and the peoples assemble. Which of them foretold this and proclaimed to us the former things? Let them bring in their witnesses to prove they [the false prophets and their gods] were right, so that others may hear and say, 'It is true.' [However] 'You are my witnesses,' declares the Lord. . . . 'So that you may know and believe me and understand that I am he. Before me no god was formed, nor will there be one after me. I, even I, am the Lord, and apart from me there is no savior. . . . You are my witnesses,' declares the Lord, 'that I am God. . . . I am the Lord, who has made all things . . . who *foils* the signs of false prophets and *makes fools of diviners,* who overthrows the learning of the wise and turns it into *nonsense, who carries out the words of his servants and fulfills the predictions of his messengers....'"* (Isaiah 43:9-12, 44:24-26, emphasis added). And why has God done all this?

> ... so that people may *see and know,* may *consider and understand,* that the hand of *the Lord* has done this... "Present your case," says the Lord. "Set forth your arguments.... Bring in your idols to tell us what is going to happen.... Or declare to us the things to come, tell us what the future holds, so we may know that you are gods.... But you are less than nothing.... Who told of this from the beginning, so we could know, or beforehand, so we could say, 'He was right'? No one told of this, no one foretold it, no one heard any words from you. *I was the first to tell [you]."* (Isaiah 41:20-24, 26, 27, emphasis added)

God actually challenges us to put Him to the test so that even the skeptics and stubborn-hearted will have no excuse for rejecting His predictions. "I foretold the former things long ago, my mouth announced them and I made them known; then suddenly I acted, and they came to pass. For I knew how stubborn you were; the sinews of your neck were iron, your forehead was bronze. Therefore, I told you these things long ago; *before they happened I announced them to you* so that you could not say, 'My idols did them';... You have heard these things; look at them all. Will you not admit them? From now on I will tell you of new things, of hidden things unknown to you.... You have not heard of them before today. So you cannot say, 'Yes, I knew of them'" (Isaiah 48:3-7).

Totally accurate prediction of the future is the domain of the Bible exclusively—and one of the great proofs of its divine origin. This is one reason God emphatically warns men to not presumptuously speak of the future in *His* name; to do so is to bring dishonor to God when the prophecy fails, and therefore to lead people to *not* trust in Him. In the Old Testament the penalties for doing so were severe: "But a prophet who presumes to speak in my name anything I have not commanded him to say, or a prophet who speaks in the name of other gods, must be put to death" (Deuteronomy 18:20).

Thus, when the people wondered how to discern whether God was the author of a prophetic message or not, He clearly told them: "You may say to yourselves, 'How can we know when a message has *not* been spoken by the Lord?' If what a prophet proclaims in the name of Lord does *not* take place or come true, that is a message the Lord has *not* spoken. That prophet has spoken presumptuously. Do not be afraid of him" (Deuteronomy 18:21-22, emphasis added).

God further warns that He Himself will be against anyone who falsely pretends to be one of His prophets: "Their visions are false and their divinations a lie. They say, 'The Lord declares,' when the Lord has not sent them; yet they expect their words to be fulfilled.... Therefore this is what the Sovereign Lord says: Because of your false words and lying visions, I am against you, declares the Sovereign Lord" (Ezekiel 13:6, 8).

But God also tells us it is possible that a false prophet can, on occasion, accurately predict the future or perform a miracle. These are counterfeit or demonic miracles that originate from the supernatural world of lying spirits. In these cases God instructs: "If a prophet, or one who foretells by dreams, appears among you and announces to you a miraculous sign or wonder, and if the sign or wonder of which he has spoken *takes place*, and he says, 'Let us follow other gods' (gods you have not known) 'and let us worship them,' you must not listen to the words of that prophet or dreamer.... That prophet or dreamer must be put to death, because he preached rebellion against the Lord your God..." (Deuteronomy 13:1-3, 5, emphasis added).

All this proves that God does claim in the Bible that He accurately predicts the future. His predictions are to be judged on the basis of their accuracy, and He emphasizes that His accuracy will be nothing less than 100 percent for He is a "God who does not lie" (Titus 1:2)—indeed this is impossible for Him (Hebrews 6:18; cf., 1 John 2:21). Therefore, God tells us the prophet is "recognized as one truly sent by the Lord *only* if his prediction comes true" (Jeremiah 28:9, emphasis added) because "whatever I say will be fulfilled, declares the sovereign Lord" (Ezekiel 12:28).

The Importance of Prophecy

Anyone who seriously studies biblical prophecy will quickly discover three things that prove its importance. First, the subject of prophecy is not something rare or occasional to the pages of Scripture. There are more than 600 direct references in the Bible to "prophecy" and "prophets." As we discuss in our next chapter, approximately 27 percent(!) of the entire Bible contains prophetic material, most of which has already come true and some which remain to be fulfilled. Only four of the 66 books of the Bible are without prophecy—Ruth, the Song of Solomon, Philemon, and 3 John.[3] Even the shortest book of the Bible mentions prophecy (Jude 14, 17-18). Thus: ". . . out of the OT's 23,210 verses, 6,641 contain predictive material, or 28½ percent. Out of the NT's 7,914 verses, 1,711 contain predictive material, or 21½ percent. So for the entire Bible's 31,124 verses, 8,352 contain predictive material, or 27 percent of the whole."[4] Of these, more than 1,800 verses (including 318 in the New Testament) deal with the Second Coming of Christ.[5] If this means anything, it means that the physical return of Jesus Christ to the earth has the same chance of being fulfilled as all of the other prophecies God has given—a 100-percent probability.

The second thing we learn as we study Bible prophecy is that this is a serious matter because God Himself encourages its study. The Apostle Peter tells us that we "will do well to pay attention to it" because biblical prophecy is not the words of men, nor the interpretations of men, but the words and interpretation of God Himself:

> And we have the word of the prophets made more certain, and you will do well to pay attention to it, as to a light shining in a dark place . . . Above all, you must understand that no prophecy of Scripture came about by the prophet's own interpretation. For prophecy never had its origin in the will of man, but men spoke from God as they were carried along by the Holy Spirit. (2 Peter 1:19-21)

The Apostle Paul taught, "*All* Scripture is God-breathed and is useful for teaching, rebuking, correcting and training in righteousness, so that the man of God may be thoroughly equipped for every good work" (2 Timothy 3:16). If *all* Scripture is inspired by God and useful, then this must also refer to all prophecy, for it, too, is Scripture. God Himself, therefore, teaches that the study of prophecy is useful for teaching, for training in righteousness, and, in fact, for much more.

Third, prophecy is important because our Lord Jesus Christ, in Matthew chapter 24, encouraged the study of prophecy. On one particular occasion when Jesus was speaking of future events, He was asked a question by His disciples: "Tell us, when will this happen, and what will be the sign of your coming and of the end of the age?" (Matthew 24:3). Jesus' answer clearly reveals what He thinks about the topic of prophecy. Did Christ inform them the issue was irrelevant? Did He say the subject dealt with predictions so obscure that they were useless? Did He report that there were so many commentators who disagreed over the issue that a discussion of it was futile? No, He answered their question directly and in detail, supplying a great deal of information about future events, including those that would immediately precede His personal, physical return to the earth from heaven (Matthew 24).

To realize how much importance Jesus placed on prophetic material, one only need read some of His statements in Mark 13: "Watch out that no one deceives you....The end is still to come....You must be on your guard....So be on your guard; I have told you everything ahead of time....When you see these things happening, you know that it [my return] is near, right at the door....Be on guard! Be alert!....Therefore keep watch.... What I say to you, I say to everyone: Watch!" (Mark 13:5,7,9,23, 29,33,35,37).

In fact, Jesus never chided His disciples for seeking to be informed on prophecy, but He did scold them for ignoring it: "How foolish you are, and how slow of heart to believe all that the prophets have spoken!" (Luke 24:25). In addition, Jesus taught that Old Testament predictions concerning Himself were of special importance. He said, "This is what I told you while I was still with you: Everything must be fulfilled that is written about me in the Law of Moses, the Prophets and the Psalms" (Luke 24:44, cf. v. 27; Matthew 5:17; John 5:39). Here and elsewhere, Jesus taught that the entire Hebrew Bible was about Him—that 39 separate books written by 30 different authors over a period of 1,000 years, from 1500 to 400 B.C., predicted the events of His life in particular detail.

Thus, prophecy is important because the entire Bible is Christological: "Jesus Christ remains the heart of prophecy."[6] In a fascinating study, *Christ: The Theme of the Bible*, Dr. Norman Geisler concludes that Christ is present in *all* 66 books of the Bible, even though 39 were written before He was even born! Thus Christ fulfills literally dozens of Old Testament types, prefigurements, and prophecies, from the Priesthoods and Tabernacle to Levitical feasts and offerings, from Messianic principles and pictures, even to the complex structural architecture of the Bible itself.[7] Throughout its pages, "Christ is seen as the implicit or underlying theme of all of Scripture."[8] How could this logically be possible if God were not its author?

Is Christ the Theme of the Bible?

Dr. Geisler documents that Christ is the theme of both testaments of the Bible as well as each of the eight major sections of Scripture. Further, Christocentric themes are found in each one of the sixty-six books of the Bible. As a sample, he lists the following:

Old Testament	
THEME	SCRIPTURE
Christ is the Seed of the Woman	Genesis 3:15
He is the Passover Lamb	Exodus 12:3f.
The Atoning Sacrifice	Leviticus 17:11
The Smitten Rock	Numbers 20:8,11
The Faithful Prophet	Deuteronomy 18:18
Christ is the Captain of the Lord's Host	Joshua 5:15
The Divine Deliverer	Judges 2:18
The Kinsman Redeemer	Ruth 3:12
Christ is anticipated as the Anointed One	1 Samuel 2:10
The Son of David	2 Samuel 7:14
Christ may be viewed as the coming King (1 and 2 Kings) and in 1 and 2 Chronicles as the Builder of the Temple	1 Chronicles 28:20

Christ as the Restorer of the Temple	Ezra 6:14, 15
The Restorer of the Nation	Nehemiah 6:15
The Preserver of the Nation	Esther 4:14
Christ is also seen as the Living Redeemer	Job 19:25
As the Praise of Israel	Psalm 150:6
The Wisdom of God.	Proverb 8:22, 23
The Great Teacher	Ecclesiastes 12:11
The Fairest of Ten Thousand	Song of Solomon 5:10
Christ is the Suffering Servant	Isaiah 53:11
The Maker of the New Covenant	Jeremiah 31:31
The Man of Sorrows	Lamentations 3:28-30
The Glory of God	Ezekiel 43:2
The Coming Messiah	Daniel 9:25
The Lover of the Unfaithful	Hosea 3:1
The Hope of Israel	Joel 3:16
The Husbandman	Amos 9:13
The Savior	Obadiah 21
The Resurrected One	Jonah 2:10
The Ruler in Israel	Micah 5:2
The Avenger	Nahum 2:1
The Holy God	Habakkuk 1:13
The King of Israel	Zephaniah 3:15
The Desire of Nations	Haggai 2:7
The Righteous Branch	Zechariah 3:8
And the Sun of Righteousness	Malachi 4:2

New Testament

The King of the Jews	Matthew 2:2
The Servant of the Lord	Mark 10:45
The Son of Man	Luke 19:10
The Son of God	John 1:1
Christ is the Ascended Lord	Acts 1:10
The Believer's Righteousness	Romans 1:17
Sanctification	1 Corinthians 1:30
Sufficiency	2 Corinthians 12:9

Liberty	Galatians 2:4
He is revealed as the Exalted Head of the Church	Ephesians 1:22
The Christian's Joy	Philippians 1:26
The Fullness of Deity	Colossians 2:9
Christ is the believer's Comfort	1 Thessalonians 4:16, 17
Christ is the believer's Glory	2 Thessalonians 1:12
He is seen as the Christian's Preserver	1 Timothy 4:10
The Christian's Rewarder	2 Timothy 4:8
The Christian's Blessed Hope	Titus 2:13
The Christian's Substitute	Philemon 17
He is also High Priest	Hebrews 4:15
The Giver of Wisdom	James 1:5
The Rock	1 Peter 2:6
Precious Promise	2 Peter 1:4
John presents Christ as the Life	1 John
Christ as the Truth	2 John
Christ as the Way	3 John
Christ as the Advocate	Jude
King of Kings and Lord of Lords	Revelation 19:16

It is literally true that the Bible is all about Christ.[9]

Probability Considerations and Messianic Prophecy

In light of our discussion, let us take just one aspect of Bible prophecy—Messianic prophecy—and apply the laws of probability to this subject just as we did earlier to evolutionary theory.

Anyone can make predictions. Having them fulfilled is another story entirely. The more statements you make about the future and the greater the detail, the better the chances proportionately, even exponentially, that you will be proven wrong. For example, think how difficult it would be for someone to predict the exact city in which the birth of a future U.S. president would take place 500 years from now. But that's what the prophet Micah did with the birthplace of the Messiah *700 years before He was born* (Micah 5:2).

How difficult do you think it would be to indicate the precise kind of death that a new, unknown religious leader would experience a thousand years from today? Could you invent and predict today a new method of execution not currently known, one that won't even be invented for hundreds of years? That's what David did in 1000 B.C. when he wrote Psalm 22. Or, how difficult would it be to predict the specific date of the appearance of some great future leader hundreds of years in advance? But that's what the prophet Daniel did 530 years before Christ (Daniel 9:24-27).[10]

On the other hand, if you created 50 specific prophecies about some man in the future you will never meet, how difficult do you think it would be for that man to fulfill all 50 of your predictions? How hard would it be for him if 25 of your predictions were about what *other* people would do to him and were completely beyond his control?

For example, how could someone "arrange" to be born in a specific family (Genesis 12:2-3; 17:1, 5-7; 22:18 with Matthew chapter 1 and Galatians 3:15-16)? How does someone "arrange" in advance to have his parents give birth to him in a specified city, which is not their own (Micah 5:2 with Matthew 2:5-6; Luke 2:1-7)? How does one "arrange" to be virgin born (Isaiah 7:14; Luke 1:26-35; Matthew 1:18-24)? How does one plan to be considered a prophet "like Moses" (Deuteronomy 18:15 with John 1:45; 5:46; 6:14; 7:40; Acts 3:17-26; 7:37)? How does someone orchestrate (a) his own death, including being put to death by the strange method of crucifixion, (b) being put to death, not alone, but with company, specifically two criminals, and (c) then arrange to have his executioners gamble for his clothes during the execution (Psalm 22; Isaiah 53 with Matthew 27:31-38)?

And how could someone organize to have God inform and send the proper messenger to go before him (Malachi 3:1 with Matthew 11:10)? How does one arrange to be betrayed for a specific amount of money, 30 pieces of silver (Zechariah 11:13 with Matthew 27:3-10)? How does one plan in advance that his executioners will carry out their regular practice of breaking the legs of the two victims on either side of him, but not his own (Psalm 34:20 with John 19:33)? Finally, how does a pretender to being the Messiah arrange to be God (Isaiah 9:6; Zechariah 12:10 with John 1:1; 10:30; 14:6), and how could he possibly escape from a grave and appear to people after he has been killed (Psalm 22; Isaiah 53:9, 11 with Luke chapter 24; 1 Corinthians 15:3-8)?

It might be possible to fake one or two of these predictions, but it would be impossible for any man to arrange and fulfill *all* these predictions (and many others) in advance. If it can be proved that such prophecies were given of the Messiah hundreds of years in advance, and one man fulfilled *all* of them, then that man would logically have to be the predicted Messiah of the Old Testament.

A Sampling of Jesus' Fulfillment of Messianic Prophecies

1. He will be born of a virgin (Isaiah 7:14; see Matthew 1:23)

2. He would live in Nazareth of Galilee (Isaiah 9:1-2; Matthew 2:23; 4:15)

3. He would occasion the massacre of Bethlehem's children (Jeremiah 31:15; see Matthew 2:18)

4. He would be anointed by the Holy Spirit (Isaiah 11:2; see Matthew 3:16-17)

5. He would be heralded by the Lord's special messenger, John the Baptist (Isaiah 40:3; Malachi 3:1; see Matthew 3:1-2)

6. His mission would include the Gentiles (Isaiah 42:1-3, 6; see Matthew 12:18-21). But He would be rejected by the Jews, His own people (Psalm 118:22; see 1 Peter 2:7)

7. His ministry would include miracles (Isaiah 35:2-6; 61:1-2; see Matthew 9:35; Luke 4:16-21)

8. He would be the Shepherd struck with the sword, resulting in the sheep being scattered (Zechariah 13:7; see Matthew 26:31, 56; Mark 14:27, 49-50)

9. He would be betrayed by a friend for 30 pieces of silver (Zechariah 11:12-13; see Matthew 27:9-10)

10. He would die a humiliating death (Psalm 22; Isaiah 53) including:

11. Rejection (Isaiah 53:3; John 1:10-122; 7:5, 48)

12. Silence before His accusers (Isaiah 53:7; Matthew 27:12-19)

13. Being mocked (Psalm 22:7-8; Matthew 27:31)

14. Piercing His hands and feet (Psalm 22:16; Luke 23:33)

15. Being crucified with thieves (Isaiah 53:12; Matthew 27:38)

16. Praying for His persecutors (Isaiah 53:12; Luke 23:43)

17. Piercing His side (Zechariah 12:10; John 19:34)

18. Buried in a rich man's tomb (Isaiah 53:9; Matthew 27:57-60)

19. Casting lots for His garments (Psalm 22:18; John 19:23-24)

20. He would be given vinegar and gall to drink (Psalm 69:21; see Matthew 27:34)

21. He would rise from the dead (Psalm 16:10; Mark 16:6; Acts 2:31)

22. He would be hated without a cause (Psalm 69:4; Isaiah 49:7; John 7:48; John 15:25)

23. He would be rejected by the rulers (Psalm 118:22; Matthew 21:42; John 7:48)

24. He would asend into heaven (Psalm 68:18; Acts 1:9)

25. He would sit down at God's right hand (Psalm 110:1; Hebrews 1:3) and in the future He will be presented with dominion over all peoples, nations, and men of every language (Daniel 7:13-14; see Revelation 11:15)

(Adapted from Norman Geisler, Ron Brooks, *When Skeptics Ask: A Handbook of Christian Evidences* [Wheaton, IL: Victor Books, 1990], pp. 114-15)

The prophecies in this chart are only a few of those we could list. Smith discusses 73; Payne more than 125; and Edersheim more than 400.[11] All these prophecies refer only to Christ's first coming. God gave a great number of prophecies about the Messiah for at least two reasons: to make identifying the Messiah obvious, and to make an impostor's task impossible.

To illustrate, consider the following account adapted from a true story on how governments use prearranged identification signs to identify their covert agents. Soviet double agent "Condor" was a World War II traitor. He gave atomic secrets to the Russians, then fled to Mexico after the war. His conspirators arranged to help him by planning a meeting with the secretary of the Russian ambassador in Mexico City. Proper identification for both parties became vital.

"Condor" was to identify himself with six prearranged signs. These instructions had been given to both the secretary and "Condor" so there would be no possibility of making a mistake. They were: (1) Once in Mexico City, the Russian spy was to write a note to the secretary, signing his name as "I. Jackson." After three days (2) he was to go to the Plaza de Colon in Mexico City and (3) stand before the statue of Columbus, (4) with his middle finger placed in a guide book. In addition, (5) when he was approached, he was to say it was a magnificent statue and that he was from Oklahoma. (6) The secretary was to then give him his passport.

The six prearranged signs worked. Why? With six identifying characteristics it was impossible for the secretary not to identify "Condor" as the proper agent.

If that is true, think how impossible it would be not to identify the Messiah if he had been given not just six, but scores of major specific prophecies and hundreds of minor, more general prophecies. In fact, according to the great Oxford scholar, Alfred Edersheim, there are some 456 identifying characteristics of the Messiah. Edersheim was author of the definitive 1500 page *The Life and Times of Jesus the Messiah.* In appendix nine, he has all the prophecies listed and yet asserts the list is still incomplete. First, he writes of the organic *unity* of the Old Testament and the Jewish Messiah to show that these prophecies form a unit. Note carefully what he says:

> The most important point here is to keep in mind the organic *unity* of the Old Testament. Its predictions are not isolated, but features of one grand prophetic picture; its ritual and institutions parts of one great system; its history, not loosely connected events, but an organic development tending towards a definite end. . . . The Messiah and His history are not presented in the Old Testament as something separate from, or superadded to, Israel. The history, the institutions, and the predictions of Israel run up into Him. . . . This organic unity of Israel and the Messiah explains how events, institutions, and predictions, which initially were purely Israelitish, could with truth be

regarded as finding their full accomplishment in the Messiah. From this point of view the whole Old Testament becomes the perspective in which the figure of the Messiah stands out. And perhaps the most valuable element in Rabbinic commentation on Messianic times is that in which, as so frequently, it is explained, that all the miracles and deliverances of Israel's past would be re-enacted, only in a much wider manner, in the days of the Messiah. Thus the whole past was symbolic, and typical of the future—the Old Testament the glass, through which the universal blessings of the latter days were seen. It is in this sense that we would understand the two sayings of the Talmud: "All the prophets prophesied only of the days of the Messiah," and "The world was created only for the Messiah."[12]

Second, Edersheim discusses the specific number of predictive passages, "In accordance with all this, the ancient Synagogue found references to the Messiah in many more passages of the Old Testament than those verbal predictions, to which we generally appeal; and the latter formed (as in the New Testament) a proportionately small and secondary, element in the conception of the Messianic era. This is fully borne out by a detailed analysis of those passages in the Old Testament to which the ancient Synagogue referred as Messianic. Their number amounts to upward of 456 (75 from the Pentateuch, 243 from the Prophets, and 138 from the Hagiographa), and their Messianic application is supported by more than 558 references to the most ancient Rabbinic writings."[13]

Significantly, Edersheim proceeds to observe that, "a careful perusal of their [the Rabbi's] Scripture quotations shows that the main postulates of the New Testament concerning the Messiah [i.e., that Jesus Christ is the Jewish Messiah] are fully supported by Rabbinic statements."[14] Obviously, if six identifying characteristics can identify a key double agent, then 456 can certainly identify the true Messiah!

Now, if we assume 456 prophecies are fulfilled in one person, what does the science of probability tell us about this? In brief, it says, if accurate predictions were made about a future Messiah and fulfilled years later by one person, this is not only proof that one individual is the Messiah, but further, proof that there is a

God, and specifically, that this one true God is the God of the Christian Bible.

Here is why: the science of probability attempts to determine the chance that a given event will occur. The value and accuracy of the science of probability has been established beyond doubt. For example, probability statistics are the foundation on which all kinds of insurance rates are fixed. Professor emeritus of science at Westmont College, Dr. Peter Stoner, has calculated the probability of one man fulfilling the major prophecies made concerning the Messiah. The estimates were worked out by twelve different classes of 600 college students.

The students carefully weighed all the factors, discussed each prophecy at length, and examined the various circumstances that might indicate that men had conspired together to fulfill a particular prophecy. They made their estimates conservative enough so that there was finally unanimous agreement even among the most skeptical students.

But then Professor Stoner took their estimates and made them even more conservative. He also encouraged other skeptics or scientists to make their own estimates to see if his conclusions were more than fair. Finally, he submitted his figures for review to a Committee of the American Scientific Affiliation. Upon examination, they verified that his calculations were dependable and accurate in regard to the scientific material presented.[15]

For example, concerning Micah 5:2, where it states the Messiah would be born in Bethlehem Ephrathah, Stoner and his students determined the average population of Bethlehem from the time of Micah to the present; then they divided it by the average population of the earth during the same period. They concluded that the chance of one man being born in Bethlehem was one in 2.8×10^5—or rounded, one in 300,000.

After examining only *eight* different prophecies, they conservatively estimated that the chance of one man fulfilling all eight prophecies was one in 10^{17}.

To illustrate how large the number 10^{17} is (a figure with 17 zeros), Stoner gave the following illustration. Imagine covering the entire state of Texas with silver dollars to a level of two feet deep. The total number of silver dollars needed to cover the whole state would be 10^{17}. Now, choose just one of those silver dollars, mark it and drop it from an airplane. Then thoroughly stir all the silver dollars all over the state. When that has been done, blindfold one man, tell him he can travel wherever he wishes in the state of Texas. At some point he must stop, reach down into the two feet of silver dollars, and try to pull up that one specific silver dollar that has been marked. Now, the chance of his finding that one silver dollar in the state of Texas would be the chance the prophets had for eight of their prophecies coming true in any one man in the future.

In practical terms, is there anyone who would fail to invest in a financial venture if the chance of failure were only one in 10^{17}? This is the kind of sure investment we are offered by God for belief in His Messiah.

Professor Stoner concluded: "The fulfillment of these eight prophecies alone proves that God inspired the writing of those prophecies to a definiteness which lacks only one chance in 10^{17} of being absolute."[16] Another way of saying this is that any person who minimizes or ignores the significance of the biblical identifying signs concerning the Messiah would be foolish.

But, of course, there are many more than eight prophecies. In another calculation Stoner used 48 prophecies (even though he could perhaps have used 456) and arrived at the extremely conservative estimate that the probability of 48 prophecies being fulfilled in one person is 10^{157}.[17]

How large is the number one in 10^{157}? As noted earlier, 10^{157} contains 157 zeros! Let us once again try to illustrate the size of this number, this time using electrons instead of silver dollars.

Electrons are very small objects, smaller than atoms. It would take 2.5 times 10^{15} of them, laid side by side, just to make one inch. Even if we counted four electrons every second, and counted day and night, it would still take us *19 million years* just to count a line of electrons one-inch long.

Assuming you have some idea of the number of electrons we are talking about, imagine marking just *one* of those electrons in that huge number. Stir them all up, then appoint one person to travel in a rocket ship for as long as he wants, anywhere he wants to go. Tell him to stop anytime he chooses, take a high-powered microscope, and search for that one marked electron in that segment of space. What do you think would be his chances for success? It would be one in 10^{157}.

But how many electrons are we dealing with in 10^{157} electrons? Imagine building a solid ball of electrons that would extend in all directions from the earth a length of 6 billion light years. The distance in miles of just *one* light year is 6.4 trillion miles. That would be a big ball! But not big enough to measure 10^{157} electrons.

In order to do that, you must take that big ball of electrons reaching the length of 6 billion light years long in all directions and multiply it by 6×10^{28}! How big is that? It's the length of the space required to store trillions and trillions and trillions of the same gigantic balls and more. In fact, the space required to store all of these balls combined together would just start to "scratch the surface" of the number of electrons we would need to really accurately speak about 10^{157}.

Remember, this number represents the chance of only 48 prophecies coming true in one person. It illustrates why it is absolutely impossible for anyone to have fulfilled all these Messianic prophecies solely by chance. Using Borel's Single Law of Chance, the odds of someone meeting those 48 prophecies are so small it's impossible to think they will ever occur.[18]

Then what of 456 prophecies? The probability of someone fulfilling them by chance is infinitesimal. All this is proof that there must be a God who supernaturally gave this information to point to the promised Messiah. He alone is the one true God!

Just as probability considerations completely rule out a naturalistic cause for the origin of life, they also reveal who the one true God is. As the Bible tells us in John 3:16, "For God so loved the world that he gave his one and only Son, that whoever believes in him shall not perish but have eternal life."

Chapter 12

Biblical Prophecy—Part Two

*"There is only one real inevitability: It is necessary
that the Scripture be fulfilled."*[1]

Perhaps the most definitive text on biblical prophecy yet
written is Dr. J. Barton Payne's *Encyclopedia of Biblical Prophecy.* It
carefully excludes Scriptures which "do *not* appear to constitute
valid forecasts of the future,"[2] and proceeds to cite every verse
of prophecy in the Bible. It identifies 8,352 predictive verses in
the Bible, including 1,817 total predictions and 737 separate
matters predicted.

The Statistics of Scripture

Consider the number of prophecies in some of the following
biblical books:[3]

	Number of Predictions	Number of Predictive Verses	Total Verses	Percentage of Predictive Verses
Genesis	77	212	1533	14
Exodus	69	487	1213	40
Numbers	50	458	1288	36
Deuteronomy	58	344	959	36
2 Kings	50	144	719	20
Psalms	59	242	2526	10
Isaiah	111	754	1292	59
Jeremiah	90	812	1364	60
Ezekiel	66	821	1273	65
Daniel	58	161	357	45
Hosea	28	111	197	56
Joel	25	50	73	68
Amos	26	85	146	58

	Number of Predictions	Number of Predictive Verses	Total Verses	Percentage of Predictive Verses
Obadiah	10	17	21	81
Micah	40	73	105	70
Zechariah	78	144	211	69
Zephaniah	20	47	53	89
Matthew	81	278	1067	26
Mark	50	125	661	19
Luke	75	250	1146	22
Acts	63	125	1003	13
Romans	29	91	433	21
Hebrews	52	137	303	45
Revelation	56	256	404	63

Payne's text contains 14 tables, 4 statistical appendices, 5 complete indices, and a discussion of all 8,352 predictive verses in the Bible. In the Old Testament, Ezekiel (821), Jeremiah (812), and Isaiah (754) alone contain 2,387 verses of predictive material; Zephaniah is 89 percent predictive, Obadiah 81 percent, Nahum 74 percent and Zechariah 69 percent predictive. In all, Isaiah contains 111 separate predictions; Jeremiah 90; Zechariah 78 and Genesis 77.[4] In the New Testament, we find that Matthew (278), Revelation (256) and Luke (250) alone contain almost 800 verses of predictive material. Twenty-nine separate books of the Bible predict Christ's Second Coming, and Payne cites more than 125 separate specific prophecies in the Old Testament about Christ's first coming, in effect proving they were prophetic and showing their fulfillment in Christ and no other person.[5]

Not everyone accepts these prophecies. Critics contend that while the Bible makes predictions, most are after the fact or never came true. Skeptics believe the Bible does not predict the future because they assume it was written merely by men and that predicting the future is impossible by definition. What this anti-supernatural bias fails to adequately consider is that the universe is quite larger than their personal philosophies and that if an omniscient God exists, knowledge of the future *is* possible by definition. The only issue should be whether the evidence warrants the conclusion.

Of course, modern astrologers, psychics, and other prognosticators also claim they can accurately predict the future, but when pressed fail miserably.[6] On the other hand, the Bible is consistently accurate in its prediction of future events. Proof of this is detailed throughout many scholarly commentaries on individual biblical books,[7] and in popular compilations such as John Urquhart's *Wonders of Prophecy*, Josh McDowell's *Evidence That Demands a Verdict* and *Prophecy—Fact or Fiction?: Daniel in the Critic's Den*, Merrill Unger's *Great Neglected Prophecies*, and J. W. Bradbury's (ed.) *The Sure Word of Prophecy*; Alfred Edersheim's *Prophecy and History in Relation to the Messiah*, Willis Beecher's *The Prophets and the Promise*, Sir Robert Anderson's *The Coming Prince*, and Dr. Arthur Custance's *Hidden Things of God's Revelation*.

In this chapter we will cite sufficient examples to show that from the beginning the Bible accurately predicts the future. Consider that even the first book of the Bible, written 3,500 years ago, contains startling predictions:

> Genesis 49, for example, miraculously forecasts certain aspects of the settlement in Canaan made by the twelve tribes that were to descend from Jacob's sons. Moses, moreover, comes prior to Israel's entrance into Canaan and could therefore have had no natural knowledge of the modes of settlement.... Predictions begin to appear in Genesis from its very start: eight occur in the first three chapters, even before mankind's expulsion from Eden.... Predictions are involved in 212 out of the book's 1,533 verses, which amounts to some 14 percent of the whole. Yet these embrace 77 distinct prophecies, more than for any other narrative portion of the OT. It exceeds the sum even for most of the overtly prophetic books of the Bible, e.g., the 66 of Ezekiel or the 56 of Revelation; and it is surpassed in count only by the major prophecies of Isaiah and Jeremiah, the detailed apocalyptic of Zechariah, and, in the NT, by the total of 81 prophecies that appear in the Gospel of Matthew.[8]

Dr. Payne makes the following comment upon the book of Daniel: "The last and shortest of the four Major Prophets is Daniel. It is also the one that contains the smallest percentage of predictive material: its 58 separate forecasts involve but 162 out of the book's 357 verses, or a modest 45 percent. Chapter 7, together with its parallel in chapter 2, constitutes Scripture's most sweeping panorama of what was then future world history; and Daniel's predictions form one of the Bible's outstanding blocks of apocalyptic literature—along with Zechariah and Revelation. His writing, as a result, exhibits the highest proportion of symbolic prophecy to be found within the word of God, engaging slightly more than two-thirds of this book's prophetic content, even though Daniel's total number of symbolical predictions (20) is exceeded by Revelation's 24."[9] For critics to maintain the Bible does not accurately predict the future is nonsense. The words are there for everyone to see. Sound critical scholarship has proven beyond a doubt the time of these prophecies, so no one can convincingly argue they were made after the fact.

One of the strongest objective evidences of the divine inspiration of the Bible is the testimony of fulfilled prophecy. In world literature, the Bible is unique in this respect. At best, other religions' scriptures contain a small number of vague predictions, or their predictions fail, but nothing anywhere is comparable to the large number of detailed prophecies in Scripture.

Categories of Prophecy

The Bible contains various categories of prophecy, among them (1) Messianic, (2) geopolitical, and (3) eschatological.

A. Messianic

Having discussed this in the previous chapter, we will briefly note the following additional information here. Considered by itself, Messianic prophecy alone is proof that the Bible is the Word of God. How else could many of the 39 separate books in the Old Testament written by more than 30 different authors over a period of a thousand years all describe in detail the life and death of One Person, narrated in four separate biographies hundreds of years into the future?[10] As we indicated in the last chapter, many Old Testament typologies and foreshadowings of Christ are impossible to explain unless God Himself is their author. Why? As Dr. Arthur Pink explains:

> Of the many typical persons in the Old Testament who pre-figure the Lord Jesus Christ, the striking, the accurate, and the manifold lights, in which each exhibits Him is truly remarkable.... That an authentic *history* should supply a series of personages in different ages, whose characters, offices, and histories, should exactly correspond with those of Another who did not appear upon earth until centuries later, can only be accounted for on the supposition of Divine appointment. When we consider the utter dissimi-larity of these typical persons to one another; when we note they had little or nothing in common with each other; when we remember that each of them represents some peculiar feature in a composite Antitype; we discover that we have a literary phenomenon which is truly remarkable. Abel, Isaac, Joseph, Moses, Samson, David, Solomon (and all the others) are each deficient when viewed separately; but when looked at in conjunction they form an harmo-nious whole, and give us a complete representation of our Lord's miraculous birth, His peerless character, His life's mission, His sacrificial death, His triumphant resurrection, His ascension to heaven, and His millennial reign. Who could have invented such characters? How remarkable that the earliest history in the world, extending from the cre-ation and reaching to the last of the prophets—written by various hands [through] a period of fifteen centuries—should from start to finish concentrate in a single point, and that point the person and work of the blessed Redeemer! Verily, such a Book *must have been written by God*—no other conclusion is possible. Beneath the histor-ical we discern the spiritual: behind the incidental we behold the typical: underneath the human biographies we see the form of Christ, and in these things we discover on every page of the Old Testament the "watermark" of heaven.[11]

B. Geopolitical Prophecies

The Bible also contains numerous geopolitical prophecies. For example, Isaiah, Jeremiah, Ezekiel, Daniel, and others all predicted "future events in vivid detail, including the rise and fall of every major world empire which left its mark on the Middle East."[12] Nothing unusual here, either.

Only those who have studied the tenuous and mercurial nature of geopolitical power and its historical vagaries can appreciate the miraculous nature of these prophecies. For example, the prophet Daniel foresaw the rise of the Medo-Persian, Greek, and Roman empires hundreds of years before events unfolded that led to the establishment of those empires.

C. Eschatological Prophecy

The Bible further contains eschatological prophecies in great detail. Using the term in a restrictive sense, these involve predictions dealing with the events immediately preceding the miraculous physical return of Jesus Christ to the earth. They are found scattered throughout the Old Testament prophetical books in nonchronological order and are clarified in general chronological order and great detail in the book of Revelation.

One particularly noteworthy study on this subject is by Dr. Arnold G. Fruchtenbaum. He has degrees in Hebrew, Greek, Old Testament studies, and Semitics, and has studied and conducted research at the American Institute of Holy Land Studies, The Hebrew University of Jerusalem, The Jewish Theological Seminary in New York, Dallas Theological Seminary, and New York University. In his detailed investigation, *The Footsteps of the Messiah*, he presents the results of a six-year research program (including two years in Israel) examining the chronology of prophetic events leading up to the Second Coming. No one who will read this book can easily deny that these prophecies are exact and detailed.[13]

The Important Relationship
of Past to Future Prophecies

But if we grant fulfilled prophecy in the *past,* why do we assume that the Bible's prophecies of the *future* can also be trusted? How can we know they are accurate predictions if they have not *yet* been fulfilled? First, we can know that all these prophecies are accurate and will be fulfilled because they are given by God Himself. "All Scripture is inspired by God..." (2 Timothy 3:16) and "Prophecy never had its origin in the will of men, but men spoke from God as they were carried along by the Holy Spirit" (2 Peter 1:21). Further, God emphasizes that He "cannot lie" (Titus 1:2) because—due to His holy and righteous character—by His very nature "it is impossible for God to lie" (Hebrews 6:18, cf. Numbers 23:19). God Himself promises us, "*Whatever I say will be fulfilled,* declares the Sovereign Lord" (Ezekiel 12:28). As we saw earlier, in Deuteronomy 13:1-11 and 18:21-22, God promises 100 percent reliability in His predictions of the future. In fact, in ancient Israel, the one who prophesied falsely in God's name and led people to worship other gods was to be put to death. This illustrates how seriously God views prophecy in His name.

With God Himself promising that His word will come true with 100 percent certainty, one can hardly receive more trustworthy assurance. But two things must be kept in mind. First, the problem is not one of trusting the prophecies, it is one of accurately interpreting them, and this can require great care and caution. One must be careful to not teach something that Scripture does not teach: "For Mickelsen admonishes: 'Read nothing into prophecy that is not there. It is just as dangerous to put more on the map than God put there as it is to remove any part of that which he did unfold.'"[14] A good general rule is adhering to what is clear and refusing to authoritatively interpret what is currently unclear. If there is more than enough information that is clear, then there is little necessity to speculate on that which isn't.

A second issue is that, although many of these prophecies have not yet been realized, we can know they are to be *literally* fulfilled rather than symbolically or allegorically fulfilled. All prophecy that *has* been fulfilled has been fulfilled in a literal manner. Literal fulfillment in the past implies literal fulfillment in the future. If the Bible has accurately predicted the future in the past and if its confirmed accuracy is 100 percent, then there is no reason to doubt that it can predict events that are still future with that same degree of accuracy.

Fulfilled Predictions

As noted, the existence of supernatural prophecy in the Bible cannot be denied except on the basis of an anti-supernatural bias. Supernatural prediction is only impossible when predefined as such—and this is, unfortunately, precisely the assumption that critics make. "There is no question that if miracles are either physically or morally impossible, then prediction is impossible; and those passages which have been accounted predictive, must be explained away as being vague, as applying only to something in the writer's lifetime, or on some other hypothesis."[15] Thus, rather than fairly examining the evidence, the critics ignore it or explain it away because they assume predictive prophecy is impossible to begin with. But they are wrong. There are sufficient examples to prove them wrong and demonstrate genuine fulfilled prediction in the Bible.

Josiah in the Book of Kings

1 Kings 13:2 predicts King Josiah by name and lineage 300 years before he was ever born;[16] Josiah was a contemporary of Pharoah Neco, King of Egypt (610–595), 2 Kings 23:29: "This is what the Lord says: A son named Josiah will be born to the house of David." God also predicts that this king will destroy the altar at Bethel after sacrificing the evil prophets and burning their bones upon it. All this happened exactly as God prophesied—300 years later (see 2 Kings 23:15-19).

Bethlehem in the Book of Micah

Another example is the prophet Micah, who predicted by name the very term and region of the birthplace of the Messiah, Jesus, 700 years in advance.[17] He is also predicted to be eternal and the ruler of Israel. "But as for you, Bethlehem Ephrathah

[Ephrathah is the region in which Bethlehem was located], too little to be among the clans of Judah, from you One will go forth for Me to be ruler in Israel. His goings forth are from long ago, from the days of eternity" (Micah 5:2). Everyone who has read the Gospels knows that Jesus was born in Bethlehem, that He claimed to be the Messiah and eternal God (John 4:26; 8:58), and that Matthew, under divine inspiration, declared Jesus' birth to be the fulfillment of the prophecy in Micah (Matthew 2:1-6).

The Babylonian Captivity in the Book of Isaiah

No one can logically deny that the internal and external evidence in the book of Isaiah clearly proves Isaiah was written approximately 700–680 B.C.[18] In other words, the book of Isaiah was indisputably in existence 100 years *before* the Babylonian captivity of the Jews, which began in 605 B.C. Yet in Isaiah 39:5-7, we find the Babylonian captivity itself predicted:

"Then Isaiah said to Hezekiah, 'Hear the word of the Lord Almighty: The time will surely come when everything in your palace, and all that your fathers have stored up until this day, will be carried off to Babylon. Nothing will be left, says the Lord. And some of your descendants, your own flesh and blood who will be born to you, will be taken away, and they will become eunuchs in the palace of the King of Babylon'" (see Daniel 1:1-3).

Indeed, the Assyrian (722–721 B.C.) captivity is hinted at as early as Deuteronomy 28:49-50, 64-65 [written in 1,500 B.C.]: "...Then the Lord will scatter you among all nations, from one end of the earth to the other. There you will worship other gods—gods of wood and stone, which neither you nor your fathers have known. Among those nations you will find no repose, no resting place for the sole of your foot."

But Isaiah also contains specific predictions *against* Babylon (Isaiah 3:19-22; 14:23; cf. Jeremiah 51:36, 43, etc.). The invincible Babylon was to be devastated by the Medes (Isaiah 13:17-22). It was to become like Sodom and Gomorrah and never to be inhabited again. Tents would not be placed there by Arabs, sheep folds would not be present, and desert creatures would infest the ruins. Stones would not be removed for other construction projects, the ancient city would not be frequently visited, and it would be covered with swamps of water. One hundred fifty years after Isaiah's amazing prediction, the Medes and Persians besieged the walls of Babylon—considered an impossible military feat. In the exact manner predicted by Isaiah (and Jeremiah 25:11-14 and chapters 51–52), Babylon was conquered. The prophet Daniel himself recorded the specific night of the fall of Babylon: "That very night Belshazzar, king of the Babylonians, was slain, and Darius the Mede took over the kingdom, at the age of sixty-two" (Daniel 5:30-31).[19]

In his *Evidence That Demands a Verdict,* Josh McDowell discusses how these specific predictions against Babylon were fulfilled. The probability that these items could be fulfilled by chance alone is about one in five billion.[20]

King Cyrus in Isaiah

Isaiah also predicted a very important Persian king by name 120 years before he was born. The prophet predicts King Cyrus as the one who would permit the Jews to return to their land after the Babylonian captivity (Isaiah 44:24-45:6; cf. Ezra 1:1-11). Again, the reason God does this is so man will understand and know that He alone is the one true God:

> I am the Lord who . . . fulfills the predictions of his messengers, who says of Jerusalem, "It shall be inhabited," of the towns of Judah, "They shall be built," and of their ruins, "I will restore them" . . . [and] who says of Cyrus, "He is my shepherd and will accomplish all that I please;" he will say of Jerusalem, "Let it be rebuilt," and of the temple, "Let its foundations be laid."
>
> This is what the Lord says to His anointed, to Cyrus, whose right hand I take hold of to subdue nations before him. . . . So that you may know that I am the Lord, the God of Israel, who summons you by name. For the sake of Jacob my servant, of Israel my chosen, *I summon you by name* and bestow on you a title of honor, though you do not acknowledge me. I am the Lord, and there is no other; apart from me there is no God. I will strengthen you, though you have not

acknowledged me, *so that from the rising of the sun to the place of its setting men may know there is none besides me. I am the Lord, and there is no other.* (Isaiah 44:24-28; 45:1, 3-6, emphasis added)

Ezra records the fulfillment of this prophecy in chapter 1 of his book, referring to related prophecies in Jeremiah 25:11-12; 29:10-14: "In the first year of Cyrus king of Persia, in order to fulfill the word of the Lord spoken by Jeremiah, the Lord moved the heart of Cyrus king of Persia to make a proclamation throughout his realm and put it in writing: 'This is what Cyrus king of Persia says:...Let [them] go up to Jerusalem in Judah and build the temple of the Lord, the God of Israel, the God who is in Jerusalem...'" (Ezra 1:1-3).

What is the probability that Isaiah could predict, 120–150 years in advance, not only the name of a specific future king but also give wholly unexpected details concerning that king's actions toward the people of Israel? Even skeptics will admit that specific predicting of the future is a miracle. Perhaps skeptics should reconsider their skepticism. To determine whether a miracle, such as predictive prophecy, has occurred, one only need impartially investigate the evidence.

For example, everyone admits that the founder of the Persian empire, Cyrus, reigned over the Persians from 559–530 B.C., and that he conquered Babylon in October of 539 B.C. All acknowledge that Cyrus' decree for the Jews to return to their homeland was issued in March, 538 B.C., five months after his capture of Babylon (see Isaiah 41:2, 25; 44:28–45:6, 13; 46:11; Ezra 1:1-11). Thus, Isaiah predicts 150 years before it occurred the return to the Holy Land—and the one who issued the decree is named 120 years before he is even born!

Isaiah further predicts the nature and death of the person of the Jewish Messiah, including His virgin birth, deity, and manner of death by crucifixion (Isaiah 7:14; 9:6; 53:1-12). This was done 700 years before Jesus Christ, the Jewish Messiah, was even born.

Future Kingdoms in the Book of Daniel

Consider another incredible case of the Bible predicting the future. The internal and external evidence virtually demands a sixth century (530) B.C. composition for the book of Daniel. Yet the prophet Daniel (Matthew 24:15) predicts the Medo-Persian, Greek, and Roman Empires in such detail that anti-supernaturalists are forced, against all the evidence, to date the book at 165 B.C., implying it is essentially a forgery.

Moreover, anyone who studies Daniel, chapters 2, 7, and 8, as well as chapter 11:1-35, in light of subsequent Medo-Persian, Greek, and Roman history, including the dynasties of the Egyptians and the Syrians (the Ptolemies and Seleucids), cannot fail to be amazed. The NIV text notes, which are based on the accumulated scholarship of more than 100 authorities, observe:

> The widely held view that the book of Daniel is largely fictional rests mainly on the modern philosophical assumption that long-range predictive prophecy is impossible. Therefore all fulfilled predictions in Daniel, it is claimed, had to have been composed no earlier than the Maccabean period (2nd Century B.C.), after the fulfillments had taken place. But objective evidence excludes this hypothesis on several counts:
>
> 1. To avoid fulfillment of long-range predictive prophecy in the book, the adherence of the late-date view usually maintained that the four empires of chs. 2 and 7 are Babylon, Media, Persia and Greece. But in the mind of the author, "The Medes and Persians" (528) together constituted the second in the series of four kingdoms (2:36-43). Thus, it becomes clear that the four empires are the Babylonian, Medo-Persian, Greek and Roman....
>
> 2. The language itself argues for a date earlier than the second century. Linguistic evidence from the Dead Sea Scrolls (which furnish authentic examples of Hebrew and Aramaic writing from the 2nd century B.C.... demonstrates that the Hebrew and Aramaic chapters of Daniel must have been composed centuries earlier. Furthermore, as recently demonstrated, the Persian and Greek words in Daniel do not require a late date....
>
> 3. Several of the fulfillments of prophecies in Daniel could not have taken place by the second century anyway, so

the prophetic element cannot be dismissed. The symbolism connected with the fourth kingdom makes it unmistakably predictive of the Roman empire (see 2:33; 7:7-9, 19), which did not take control of Syro-Palestine until 63 B.C. Also, the prophecy concerning the coming of "the Anointed One the ruler," 483 years after "the issuing of the decree to restore and rebuild Jerusalem" (9:25), works out to the time of Jesus' ministry.

Objective evidence, therefore, appears to exclude the late-date hypothesis and indicates that there is insufficient reason to deny Daniel's authorship.[21]

Thus, in Daniel, chapters 2 and 7, no one can logically deny the Bible has accurately predicted future world military powers such as the Medo-Persians, Alexander's Greece, and the Roman Empire. Indeed, "[The great Jewish historian] Josephus adds that the [Jewish] priests showed Alexander the prophecies in Daniel concerning a Greek conquering the Persian Empire. This pleased Alexander, and he treated the Jews with kindness."[22]

But there is a more relevant point here for us personally. If Daniel so easily predicted the military and political lineups in the succeeding centuries of his own period, then he and other biblical prophets can be expected to just as easily have predicted the military and geopolitical lineup immediately preceding the return of Christ Himself.[23] (And it looks as if we may indeed be approaching the Second Coming.)[24]

Consider the comments of Dr. Gleason Archer concerning the evidence for Daniel's predictive prophecy. Dr. Archer is a scholar who received his Ph.D. in comparative literature from Harvard University and has spent 30 years teaching on the graduate seminary level in the field of biblical criticism. He has received training in Latin, Greek, French, and German, and in seminary majored in Hebrew, Aramaic, and Arabic. In all, he reads 15 different languages.[25] Dr. Archer reveals of Daniel:

... The linguistic evidence from Qumran makes the rationalistic explanation for Daniel no longer tenable [i.e., that it was written 165 B.C.]. It is difficult to see how any scholar can defend this view and maintain intellectual respectabil-

> ity.... The symbolism of Chapter 7 and Chapter 8 points unmistakably to the identification of the second kingdom as Medo-Persian and the third as Greek.... For this amazing pattern of prediction and fulfillment, there can be no successful answer on the part of the critics who espouse the Maccabean date hypothesis [165 B.C.]. There is no evading the conclusion that the prophecies of the Book of Daniel were inspired by the same God who later fulfilled them, or who will fulfill them in the last days, which are destined to close our present era with the final great conflict of Armageddon and second coming of our Lord Jesus Christ.[26]

Of course, the same conclusion of Daniel's prophetic accuracy was reached many decades ago by the famed Princeton scholar, Robert Dick Wilson. Dr. Wilson was at home in 45 different languages and dialects, and challenged any person living to set forth an argument that he could not personally refute that would undermine the integrity and accuracy of the prophetic text of Daniel or indeed any book of the Old Testament.[27] Scholars such as Robert Dick Wilson,[28] K.A. Kitchen,[29] Charles Boutflower[30] and others[31] have demolished critical arguments against Daniel's predictions. The historical, archæological, and linguistic evidences all support Daniel's prophecies.

How can anyone account for these startling predictions if the Bible is only written by men who were guessing? Cyrus is predicted 120 years beforehand, Josiah 300 years, Bethlehem 700, and the Medo-Persian, Greek, and Roman empires up to 500 years before they existed. Anyone who takes the time to sit down and attempt to calculate specific future events, persons, and political alliances and kingdoms will discover the impossibility of the task. For example, the late Canadian scholar Dr. Arthur Custance observes that most people have never really considered the difficulty of the task faced by the biblical prophets if they were *not* subject to divine inspiration:

> Human history is not repetitive. Like culture, it is cumulative. Experience grows, not only in the individual, but in societies and nations, so that no situation can ever be exactly repeated a second time. Consequently there is

always something unpredictable, because a new element is added with every consecutive moment of unfolding.

Although it may appear a simple matter to predict what will happen a few years from now in some particular context, in actual fact it becomes more and more impossible as one tries to be more and more explicit. Generalizations are easy, and their fulfillment can be claimed when events bear any semblance at all to the prediction. But the mind somehow refuses to create any exact picture of the future. It sounds simple, yet the difficulty can be verified experimentally by anybody who is willing to make the attempt to put down on a piece of paper some striking event that he is prepared to state will happen on his own street or in his own home one year from the present—excluding natural events. If the one-year limit is too restricting, try ten years. If this won't work, enlarge your horizon to include your city, not just your street; or, if you like, take the world. I believe this simple test will demonstrate to any honest mind the sheer impossibility of predicting history in any specific detail unless one falls back upon making pretty safe assumptions about events linked directly to situations of which one is able to make reasonable "extensions."

And he concludes, "Biblical prophecies are not this, and the distinction is of fundamental importance."[32]

Further, one appreciates these prophecies all the more when one realizes they were often entirely unexpected possibilities when they were first given. For example, Isaiah predicted the Babylonian captivity when Babylon was a somewhat obscure power and gave no indication of its future greatness. One may as well make a similar prediction for Nicaragua today. No one would risk one's reputation by making such unexpected predictions. However, the biblical prophets did make such predictions because God told them what would happen. And by the time of Jeremiah, Babylon had become a great world power. But, at this time, no evidence whatever existed that Babylon would be destroyed. To the contrary, the Babylonian empire was considered invincible. However, Jeremiah said Babylon would soon be destroyed because of the manner in which she treated Israel (Jeremiah 50–51). Ezekiel, too, confirmed this prediction and also declared, quite out of harmony with expectation, that the city of Tyre would be destroyed, giving extremely specific prophecies—all of which, as we will see, were exactly fulfilled (Ezekiel chapters 26–28).[33]

Tyre in the Book of Ezekiel

In Ezekiel chapters 25–32, the prophet makes specific prophecies against the Mediterranean nations of Ammon, Moab, Edom, Philistia, Tyre, and Egypt. As one reads the prophecies, one wonders how Ezekiel could, on his own, possibly have known all this, for again his prophecies were literally fulfilled.

Consider the prophecy against Tyre:

> ... Therefore this is what the Sovereign Lord says: I am against you, O Tyre, and I will bring many nations against you, like the sea casting up its waves. They will destroy the walls of Tyre and pull down her towers; I will scrape away her rubble and make her a bare rock. Out of the sea she will become a place to spread fishnets, for I have spoken, declares the Sovereign Lord. She will become plunder for the nations, and her settlements on the mainland will be ravaged by the sword. Then they will know that I am the Lord.

> For this is what the Sovereign Lord says: From the north I am going to bring against Tyre Nebuchadnezzar king of Babylon, king of kings, with horses and chariots, with horsemen and a great army.... His horses will be so many that they will cover you with dust. Your walls will tremble at the noise of the war horses, wagons and chariots when he enters your gates as men enter a city whose walls have been broken through. The hoofs of his horses will trample all your streets; he will kill your people with the sword, and your strong pillars will fall to the ground. They will plunder your wealth and loot your merchandise; they will break down your walls and demolish your fine houses and throw your stones, timber and rubble into the sea.... I will make you a bare rock, and you will become a place to spread fishnets. You will never be rebuilt, for I the Lord have spoken, declares the Sovereign Lord....

> Then they will take up a lament concerning you and say to you: "How you are destroyed, O city of renown, peopled by men of the

sea! You were a power on the seas, you and your citizens; you put your terror on all who lived there. Now the coastlands tremble on the day of your fall; the islands in the sea are terrified at your collapse."

This is what the Sovereign Lord says: When I make you a desolate city, like cities no longer inhabited, and when I bring the ocean depths over you and its vast waters cover you, then I will bring you down with those who go down to the pit, to the people of long ago. I will make you dwell in the earth below, as in ancient ruins, with those who go down to the pit, and you will not return to take your place in the land of the living. I will bring you to a horrible end and you will be no more. You will be sought, but you will never again be found, declares the Sovereign Lord. (Ezekiel 26:3-21).

Robert W. Manweiler has a Ph.D. in physics from Cornell University and is a graduate of respected Westminster Seminary. He points out that critics have no logical reason to deny that this is a genuine prophecy concerning Nebuchadnezzar, who first attacked Tyre in the time of Ezekiel, and also of Alexander the Great and his further destruction of Tyre 200 years in the future. "In particular, chapter 26, the prophecy against Tyre, is regarded by critics as truly authentic and written in the sixth century as claimed. . . . centuries of scholarship have found no good reason to date the book later than the time of Ezekiel. Instead it has been regarded as a remarkably historical book. And chapter 26 is in a privileged category in this privileged book. We can say with confidence that the prophecy of chapter 26 was written long before Alexander began his career."

Further, he points out that the prophecy against Tyre is not only detailed, but unusual for what could be expected, and that it contains "many elements which surpass the best that human ability could foretell." Finally, he shows that the historical data proving the accuracy of the prophecy comes from secular historical records, not from Christians or Jews: "[The] historical records narrating events fulfilling these prophecies are detailed and well-documented, particularly with respect to the most unusual statements. These narratives are in full agreement with the prophecies, and they were not written by Christians, Jews or Muslims who might be suspected of trying to make Ezekiel look good. . . . The Bible believer, then, is not blindly trusting anyone who *claims* to have had a revelation. He or she is accepting Scripture on the basis of strong verification that it comes from One who knows, the God who controls history."[34]

In Ezekiel chapter 26, a number of things are stated: that Nebuchadnezzar would destroy the city of Tyre; that many nations would be against Tyre; that Tyre would become bare like the top of a flat rock; that fishermen would spread nets over the site; that the debris of Tyre would be thrown into the water, and that it would never be rebuilt. As Dr. Custance, McDowell, and others have pointed out by citing various historical sources, all these predictions were literally fulfilled, principally by Nebuchadnezzar first, and later by Alexander the Great.[35]

Tyre was both an island city and a coastal colony of Sidon, and corresponds to modern Sur (not what is called modern Tyre). The *coastal* city of Tyre was attacked by Nebuchadnezzar and destroyed, thus fulfilling part of the prophecy. Some 200 years later, Alexander the Great fulfilled the remaining prophecy in an amazing manner. He built a causeway out to the island city that remained and subsequently destroyed the *island* of Tyre as well. Who could possibly have predicted such an unlikely series of events?

Consider these facts: the island fortifications were not insignificant. There was a 150 foot high wall facing the shore, harbors on the northern and southern end and various other fortifications. The population of mainland Tyre was over 40,000, and it stretched for more than 20 miles along the shore. Tyre traded with nearly every country in the known world (Ezekiel 27) and Ezekiel 28 discusses the great wealth and pomp of Ethbaal III, the King of Tyre. In Jeremiah 27, God had warned the surrounding nations to submit to Nebuchadnezzar. Sidon did, Tyre did not. Nebuchadnezzar besieged Tyre for 13 years (Josephus, *Contra Appion* I. XXI). Slowly, using ships, the coastal inhabitants moved all their belongings and treasures out to the island. Nebuchadnezzar soon destroyed the mainland city of Tyre, but received no spoils. For this 13-year seige by Nebuchadnezzar,

God gave Egypt to Babylon as spoils, in judgment against Egypt's sins (Ezekiel 29:2-13, 18-20).

Nevertheless, for 240 years the island of Tyre continued its trade while the mainland lay in ruins. It seemed unexpected that, given its fortification, Tyre would be attacked again and that the prophecies of Ezekiel would yet be fulfilled. Who would have expected that Alexander the Great would arise to conquer the greatest empire the world had yet known, or that he would be forced to reckon with the "insignificant" coastal island of Tyre? Before the time of Alexander, critics could have cited the prophecy as an illustration of "biblical error," or as evidence that the Bible was not divinely inspired. Yet, after 240 years, this prophecy was to be precisely fulfilled.

During this time, Alexander, the King of Macedonia who was educated by Aristotle, was beginning his unparalleled lightning-like conquest of the Middle East. After conquering the mighty Persians, he proceeded down the coast of Palestine until he reached Tyre in 333 B.C. Strategically, he was unwilling to continue down to Egypt while such a fortified city, containing such a powerful fleet of ships, was at his rear. He knew he had to first conquer Tyre before proceeding southward, and this comprises one of the most dramatic sieges in military history. Thus, with ulterior motives, he requested from city officials permission to worship their deity, Hercules, within the city walls. The plan was to bring in enough soldiers to capture the city. Not unexpectedly, his request was refused. But now, even more determined to take the city, he at once set about entering its gates by the only means available to him—the construction of a causeway across the ocean.

Alexander's soldiers were ordered to throw into the sea the very rubble and remains of Nebuchadnezzar's conquests some 200 years earlier. This was a vast undertaking, and it was necessary to use everything they could find. According to the second-century Greek historian and governor of Cappadocia, Arrian, in *History of Alexander and Indicia* (II, 18-20, T. E. Page [ed.] Harvard University Press, 1954), the project went well at first.[36] But the farther out the soldiers went, both the depth of the water and the harassment by the soldiers of Tyre increased.

It is hard to comprehend the difficulties faced by Alexander. For example, from the high walls the defenders of the city could do considerable damage, particularly since Alexander's men were clothed for work, not war. Occasional raids were also staged against the Greek troops, which greatly hindered their progress. This literally forced them to build two tall towers directly on the causeway for protection. The citizens of Tyre countered with a full-scale raid—even using fire ships to start the towers burning. After routing the Greeks, they then swarmed over the causeway and destroyed whatever they could.[37] There were other difficulties. At one point, a great storm washed away part of the causeway. Nevertheless, Alexander remained determined to conquer Tyre. He organized a flotilla of ships from several conquered nations, including 80 ships from Sidon, Aradus, and Byblus, 10 from Rhodes, 10 from Lycia, and 120 from Cyprus.[38] With this superior naval force, Alexander was able to finally finish the causeway. As Ezekiel predicted, many nations made Tyre their plunder. Thus, it was only after seven full months of immense toil, in which literally the very dust of the old city was scraped from the shore and cast into the sea, that Tyre was conquered—and Alexander's army finally marched across a *200-foot wide* causeway into the island city. This occurred in 332 B.C.

The statistics are grim. Eight thousand Tyrians were killed in battle, an additional two thousand men of military age were crucified around the city; thirty thousand women and children were sold as slaves. Even today, as fishermen spread their nets on the shore—in literal fulfillment of prophecy—the remains of Alexander's causeway can still be seen! Yet: "How unlikely it all was! What kind of human foresight would have enabled a man to foresee that a thriving city stretching for twenty miles along the shore, of which seven miles were densely populated and built up with large buildings, would one day be desolated and then laid in the midst of the sea, even its very dust? But it all came to pass."[39]

The prophecy also predicts the city would never be rebuilt, and for 2,500 years this city has not been rebuilt. This is in spite of the fact that cities are almost always rebuilt when they reside in favorable locations. By all canons of expectation, Tyre, which is strategically located on the coast, is a location which should have been rebuilt. For example, few things are more important to a city than fresh water. At the mainland city are fresh water springs, which flow at the rate of 10 million gallons per day, enough water for even a larger modern city. For 2,500 years Tyre has remained an excellent site for a city, but it has never been rebuilt. Why? The best explanation is biblical prophecy. God declared it would not be rebuilt: "I will make you a bare rock and you will become a place to spread fishnets. You will never be rebuilt, for I the Lord have spoken . . ." (Ezekiel 26:14, cf., 27:36; 28:19).

How do we explain that old mainland Tyre has never been rebuilt? Today only a small town on the island (which became a peninsula from Alexander's causeway), remains. "This fact is in remarkable harmony with Ezekiel's prophecy."[40]

Tyre in the Book of Joel

The prophet Joel, writing in the ninth century B.C., also made startling predictions, including to the city of Tyre (Joel 3:4-8):

> Now what have you against me, O Tyre and Sidon and all you regions of Philistia? Are you repaying me for something I have done? If you are paying me back, I will swiftly and speedily return on your own heads what you have done. For you took my silver and my gold and carried off my finest treasures to your temples. You sold the people of Judah and Jerusalem to the Greeks, that you might send them far from their homeland.

> See, I am going to rouse them out of the places to which you sold them, and I will return on your own heads what you have done. I will sell your sons and daughters to the people of Judah, and they will sell them to the Sabeans, a nation far away. The Lord has spoken.

We can see from history that these predictions were also fulfilled. Tyre, the senior Phoenician merchant city, had sold the Israelites as slaves (Amos 1:9). The Greeks traded with the Phoenicians (present day Lebanon) as early as 800 B.C., and Philistia had frequently attacked Israel (Judges 13:1; 1 Samuel

5:1; Ezekiel 25:15-17). But what happened was exactly what God predicted. He brought on these nations' own heads what they had done to Israel. As noted, Tyre was besieged by the Babylonians in 586 and conquered by the Greeks under Alexander the Great in 332. When Alexander marched his army down the coastline, he decimated Tyre, Sidon, and Phoenicia in that order. Thousands of citizens of Tyre were killed or sold into slavery. Sidon was captured by Antiochus III in 345 B.C.[41] and when it was taken by Artaxerxes Ochus, 40,000 people perished.[42] The Jews were free from their captors and parts of Philistia and Phoenicia were brought under Jewish rule.[43] Who would have predicted the above outcome of events? Only the biblical prophets.

Two Captivities of Israel in Deuteronomy, Jeremiah, and Other Books

Equally, if not more startling, are other predictions concerning Israel itself. Consider a prophecy written by Moses in the fifteenth century B.C., in Deuteronomy 28:49-50, 64-65: "The Lord will bring a nation against you from far away, from the ends of the earth, like an eagle swooping down, a nation whose language you will not understand, a fierce-looking nation without respect for the old or pity for the young. . . . Then the Lord will scatter you among all nations, from one end of the earth to the other. There you will worship other gods—gods of wood and stone, which neither you nor your fathers have known. Among those nations you will find no repose, no resting place for the sole of your foot. There the Lord will give you an anxious mind, eyes weary with longing, and a despairing heart."

Notice that the prophecy says that God will bring a nation against Israel from afar, and that the Israelites will not understand the language of the nation and that this nation will be pitiless and brutal. Historically, this was fulfilled during the Assyrian captivity, 722–721 B.C. But in Deuteronomy 28, we also find more than 20 additional prophecies, all of which were fulfilled.

In the eighth century B.C., the prophet Isaiah predicted the Babylonian captivity when he declared, "Then Isaiah said to Hezekiah, 'Hear the word of the Lord Almighty: The time will surely come when everything in your palace, and all that your fathers have stored up until this day, will be carried off to Babylon. Nothing will be left, says the Lord'" (Isaiah 39:5-6). What is significant is that Isaiah mentions the Babylonians by name and yet they were only a minor power in this geographical region during Isaiah's time. But all this and more happened during the Babylonian sieges and captivity in 606–586 B.C.

Consider Jeremiah 25:9, 11: " '. . . I will summon all the peoples of the north and my servant Nebuchadnezzar king of Babylon,' declares the Lord, 'and I will bring them against this land and its inhabitants and against all the surrounding nations. I will completely destroy them and make them an object of horror and scorn, and an everlasting ruin. . . . This whole country will become a desolate wasteland, and these nations will serve the king of Babylon seventy years.' " Here we find Nebuchadnezzar, the king of Babylon himself, prophesied in advance, in addition to the specific time of the captivity, 70 years.

Again, all this happened in history as the prophets predicted. In 606 B.C., Nebuchadnezzar attacked the nation of Israel. In his first campaign, he seized Jehoiakim, the king of Judah. Three years later, when Jehoiakim rebelled against the authority of Nebuchadnezzar who had made him his vassal, Nebuchadnezzar camped against the city of Jerusalem. In 589, the Jews again rebelled against Babylon, and Babylon attacked Judah. After an unrelenting assault, they broke through the walls of Jerusalem and destroyed the city and the temple of God. According to 2 Chronicles 36:17, the Babylonians were extremely vicious. The final siege of Babylon in 587 began the 70-year period spoken of in Jeremiah 29:10, Daniel 9:2, and Jeremiah 27:6-11; 38:17-21.

The Modern Return of Israel in Ezekiel, Jeremiah, and Other Books

Most people do not realize the startling nature of the prophecies in Ezekiel and elsewhere, over 2500 years before they were fulfilled, concerning the fact of the rebirth of the nation of Israel. They are one reason why Marquis D'Argens, when asked by Frederick the Great, "Can you give me one single irrefutable proof of God?" replied, "Yes, your Majesty, the Jews."[44] God had clearly said that He would regather His people to the land of Israel. From 70 A.D., when Titus destroyed Jerusalem, until May 14, 1948, the Jewish people lived disbursed in various locations among the nations of the world. What is an unprecedented fact in history is that during this time, they retained their religious identity and culture! "In virtually every other case, when a people or nation is reduced to a small remnant and disbursed around the world, they lose their cultural identity within just a few generations as they are 'absorbed' into the local population."[45]

No one should be surprised that when David Ben Gurion announced the rebirth of Israel on May 14, 1948, he used the prophecies in the book of Ezekiel as his authority. The prophecies in Ezekiel 37:21-28 and Isaiah 11:11-12 refer to the regathering of Israel from its long dispersion beginning in 70 A.D. It is unlikely Ezekiel 37 is speaking of the Jewish return from Babylon after the 70-year displacement, since the Jews were removed again in 70 A.D. Ezekiel 37:25-27 says the Jews at this time will live in the land forever. Further, Isaiah 11:11-12 specifically identifies the return he speaks of as a *"second"* return, where the people are gathered from the four corners of the earth. Again, this cannot refer to the return from the Babylonian captivity, which was not a second return and would have been limited only to a return from Babylon, not the nations of the world.

What Are the Ancient Prophecies Regarding Israel?

Ezekiel 36:24 (586 B.C.):

For I will take you out of the nations; I will gather you from all the countries and bring you back into your own land.

Ezekiel 37:21 (586 B.C.):

And say to them, "This is what the Sovereign Lord says: I will take the Israelites out of the nations where they have gone. I will gather them from all around and bring them back into their own land."

Ezekiel 39:27-28 (586 B.C.):

> When I have brought them back from the nations and have gathered them from the countries of their enemies, I will show myself holy through them in the sight of many nations. Then they will know that I am the Lord their God, for though I sent them into exile among the nations, I will gather them to their own land, not leaving any behind (see also Ezekiel 36:3-6, 15, 26-30, 35-36; 37:26-27; 38:17-18; 39:21-22, 27-29).

No one can deny that Israel is again a nation after 1900 years of geopolitical nonexistence. It is also evident that this little country is increasingly capturing the attention and concern of the entire world, the beginnings of a fulfillment of biblical prophecy (Zechariah 12:2-3). These prophecies of a national return seem clear enough for anyone living in the twentieth century, after their fulfillment. But consider how difficult it might be for people to accept such prophecies prior to the twentieth century. Such prophecies were not as easy to appreciate for those living in the extremely long period of 1900 years before their fulfillment. How tempting it would be to "spiritualize" such prophecies and ignore their literal meaning.

But God predicted both that the Jews would be scattered throughout the nations and that He would return them to their land. Again, these predictions occurred 2,600 years ago. As Dr. Henry Morris observes, "That a nation could be completely destroyed as an organized entity by an invading army (as Israel was, by the Romans, in 70 A.D.), its people either slaughtered or scattered from one end of the world to the other, its land occupied and ruled by aliens for 1900 years, and yet survived as a distinct nationality, and then finally regain its homeland and be recognized as a viable nation once more by the other nations of the world, seems impossible. Yet it has happened in spite of the impossibilities, and to make it still more amazing, it was predicted to happen many centuries before it happened."[46]

The historical impossibility of a revived nation of Israel was why even some Christians over the centuries concluded that God was through with Israel and that all the promises to Israel would therefore have to be fulfilled spiritually in the Church and not literally to the nation.

Consider Jeremiah 24:9 and Hosea 9:17: "I will make them abhorrent and an offense to all the kingdoms of the earth, a reproach and a byword, an object of ridicule and cursing, wherever I banish them" (Jeremiah 24:9). "My God will reject them because they have not obeyed him; they will be wanderers among the nations" (Hosea 9:17). But God also promised that in spite of their repeated idolatry, "I am with you and will save you, declares the Lord. Though I completely destroy all the nations among which I scatter you, I will not completely destroy you" (Jeremiah 30:11).

The Second Return

Some people claim that the Ezekiel prophecies cited above were already fulfilled in history. Again, how do we know these prophecies do not refer to the Israelites returning after the Babylonian captivity? We can know this for several reasons.

First, when God spoke of the return from Babylon it was identified as such—as a return from Babylon. The Jews returned from Babylon specifically, not from all the nations of the world (Jeremiah 25:9-12; 29:10; Ezra 1:1-8). In other words, the Babylonian return could not involve an international regathering as the prophecies demand. But as we saw, God predicted an international return to Israel of people gathered from geographical areas other than Babylon.

Second, the prophecies reveal details that require they be placed after the Babylonian return and even after 70 A.D. or 1948 A.D. (Ezekiel 36:12-15, 24-38; 37:11-14, 21-28; chapters 38–39). When the Jews returned to Jerusalem under Nehemiah, they were never ruled by the predicted King, nor was their nation united in the manner predicted in Ezekiel 37:21-28.

Third, Isaiah seems to assume either two international returns or two aspects of one international return. A first return, or part of a return, will be in unbelief, which we are now experiencing, and a second return (or its second part) will be in belief, which will occur prior to the Second Coming: "In that day [see verse 15, Revelation 16:12] the Lord will reach out His hand *a second time* to reclaim the remnant that is left of his people from Assyria, from Lower Egypt, from Upper Egypt, from Cush, from Elam, from Babylonia, from Hamath and from the islands of the sea. He will raise a banner for the nations and gather the exiles of Israel; he will assemble the scattered people of Judah from the four quarters of the earth" (Isaiah 11:11-12, emphasis added). Thus, "The regathering spoken of in this passage is the one in faith in preparation for the millennial kingdom. But this regathering in faith is specifically stated to be a second international regathering. The question this raises is: when did the first one occur? It cannot refer to the Babylonian Return as that was hardly international as the text demands. Hence, it is clear that this passage speaks of two international regatherings while emphasizing the second one. The second regathering will be in faith but not the first."[47]

In evaluating the prophecies of Ezekiel 38, Dr. Fruchtenbaum discusses the relevance of the first (or the first part of the) international regathering:

> After 1900 years, 46 invasions, the War of Independence, the land is Jewish again and free from foreign domination. This nation is gathered from many nations and peoples (38:8, 12). The Jews in Israel today come from 80-90 different nations. The continual waste places are now inhabited (38:8, 12). The Israelis today are rebuilding the ancient places and turning them into modern towns and cities. They dwell securely (38:11, 14). This has often been misconstrued as meaning a state of peace. But this is not the meaning of the Hebrew root batach. The nominal form of this root means "security." This is not the security due to a state of peace, but a security due to confidence in their own strength. This, too, is a good description of Israel today. The Israeli army has fought four wars since its founding and won them swiftly each time. Today Israel is secure, confident that her army can repel any invasion from the Arab states. Hence, Israel is dwelling securely. Israel is dwelling in unwalled villages (38:11). This is very descriptive of the present-day kibbutzim in Israel.[48]

In other words, the current regathering of Israel in unbelief is apparently the first part of an extended regathering. A full regathering is promised—one in belief. Faith begins in Israel only after a massive invasion from a northern confederacy, described in Ezekiel 38–39 and then covered in the next nine chapters (40–48).[49] Ezekiel's prophecies are hardly "after the event." The text notes for the NIV introduction to Ezekiel reveal that there is no doubt about when Ezekiel was written: "Since the book of Ezekiel contains more dates . . . than any other OT prophetic book, its prophecies can be dated with considerable precision. In addition, modern scholarship, using archæology (Babylonian Annals on cuneiform tables) and astronomy (accurate dating of eclipses referred to in ancient archives) provides precise modern calendar equivalence. Twelve of the thirteen dates specify times when Ezekiel received a divine message.[50] Thus, Ezekiel's *last* dated prophecy was received in April, 571 B.C. How could Ezekiel have predicted this kind of a regathering of Israel unless God told him so?

Consider another prophecy in Ezekiel, found in chapters 36–39. Ezekiel predicts a major power to the extreme north of Israel that, along with a confederacy of nations, will attack Israel in great hordes. This invading army will be dramatically and supernaturally destroyed by God. The description of this event given makes it clear that it has not yet happened.

In essence, anyone who read these prophecies prior to the mid-twentieth century would find it easy to either think that these were false prophecies or interpret them nonliterally. Why? Because they had clearly not been fulfilled for 1900 years, it was "impossible" for a once dispersed nation to ever become a nation again, and no great northern power existed above ancient Israel.

But since 1948, Israel is a nation again. And with the rise to power of Russia and her former satellite states, six of whom are predominantly Muslim, the prophecy takes on new meaning. A great power does exist to Israel's north.

Thus, many people have learned to treat biblical prophecies with respect, even when it seems unlikely they could be literally fulfilled.

In conclusion, all these prophecies demonstrate that the Bible does accurately predict the future. We have given only a very small sampling of fulfilled prophecies, but anyone who wishes can examine this subject in considerably more detail.[51] What these predictions indicate is that because the Bible already has *demonstrated* accuracy in prediction, there is no basis for assuming that future prophecies will not be just as accurately fulfilled. Because most of these yet-unfulfilled prophecies could easily be fulfilled in our own lifetimes, they should be considered seriously by those of our generation.

Skeptics, who discount the possibility of predictive prophecy, have attempted to late-date all these prophecies, thereby asserting they were written after the fact and making the biblical authors frauds and deceivers. However, all of their attempts have proven futile. The simple fact is that we know who wrote these books and when they were written. Both internal and external criteria show they were written long before the events themselves had been fulfilled. No one can logically deny the Bible contains scores, indeed hundreds, of both general and specific prophecies, and that this makes the Bible unlike any other book that has ever existed.[51]

Chapter 13

Archæology and
the Biblical Record

K. A. Kitchen, Lecturer in Egyptian and Coptic in the School of Archæology and Oriental Studies at the University of Liverpool, was certainly correct when he wrote that the Bible and archæology "remains a theme of unending fascination."[1] Biblical archæology is fascinating both for what it studies (the Bible and ancient remains) and the results (how these fit together in the belief system of Christians).

Human interest in things of the past has existed since there has been history. Indications of "archæological" or antiquities interest goes back into very early times. Nabonidus, king of Babylon, with his co-regent son Belshazzar, was actively involved in archæological research when Babylon fell to the Persians more than 500 years before Christ's birth. Assyrian kings collected tablets from earlier times and Ashur-bani-pal (died 626 B.C.) boasted of his ability to read and understand ancient cuneiform script. Modern involvement with what became known as "biblical archæology" did not become a serious activity until the famous Assyrian palaces began to be excavated in the 1840s, continuing up to present times. The establishment of the nation of Israel led to a great increase in archæological activity in Israel.[2] Since that time there has been somewhat of an explosion of interest in biblical archæology, with numerous scholarly journals and periodicals devoted to the subject.[3] Even marine or underwater archæology is now a scientific discipline.

259

Defining Archæology

How do we define archæology? Archæology has been defined by different writers in slightly different ways. Consider the following definitions, all of which give an idea of what archæology does:

> "Archæology is simply the recovery of man's past by systematically discovering, recording and studying the surviving material remains that he has left behind."[4]

> "Archæology is concerned with the recovery of the remains of ancient civilizations."[5]

> "The study and historical interpretation of *all* the material remains that vanished civilizations have left in the ground."[6]

> "The study of the things men made and did, in order that their whole way of life may be understood."[7]

> "The systematic recovery, analysis, and interpretation of the surviving evidence of human activity."[8]

> "That branch of knowledge which takes cognizance of past civilizations, and investigates their history in all fields, by means of remains of art, architecture, monuments, inscriptions, literature, language, implements, customs, and all other examples which have survived."[9]

In *Archæology, Artifacts and the Bible*, British scholar P. R. S. Morey even wrote, tongue-in-cheek, that "Archæology is the study of durable rubbish."[10] The *New American Standard Open Bible* defines *biblical* archæology as "a study based on the excavation, decipherment and critical evaluation of the records of the past as they affect the Bible" (1978, p. 1257).

There has been much interest in biblical archæology among Christians whose attention to archæology is primarily apologetic; that is, to explore how it confirms the biblical record. In this chapter we will address this theme, explaining why, on the one hand, it is logically impossible for archæology to prove everything true in the Bible while, on the other hand, archæology does provide amazing confirmations of Scripture. Such confirmation is hardly surprising to the one who knows the Bible is the inerrant Word of God, but it has been an unexpected occurrence to those who have believed the Bible is merely the record of fallible men. Such critics had expected archæology would "disprove" Christian claims in many areas. But Kitchen is correct in stating that, as far as orthodox Christianity is concerned, it has nothing to fear from any "soundly-based and fair-minded intellectual inquiry" from archæology or any other field.[11] (As Kitchen observes, anything less than a soundly based and fair-minded investigation is invalid by definition.)

In what way does archæology confirm the biblical record? Primarily by demonstrating that it is trustworthy where it *can* be tested. Obviously, biblical claims cannot be tested everywhere. Archæology cannot be expected to confirm *every* statement of biblical history, geography, or culture because the amount of information archæology has uncovered is still relatively small. Further, dealing as it does with material remains, archæology can hardly prove the spiritual claims of the Bible, since those claims must be established independently by other means. Nor can archæology prove that literally everything in the Bible happened in just the way the Bible says it did. Again, the extensive amount of data necessary for such a confirmation is simply not available and probably never will be.

Consider the comments of Dr. Walter Kaiser, Jr., professor of Semitic languages and Dean of Trinity Evangelical Divinity School, concerning chronological uncertainties in one Old Testament passage: "This solution does not help us with the synchronisms given with Hoshea in 2 Kings 18:1, 9, 10. In fact, Edwin Thiele, that great solver of every other synchronism and chronological fact in the chronologies of the Hebrew kings simply gave up when he came to this one in his doctoral study submitted to the University of Chicago."[12] We use this as an example to show that we do not have solutions to every historical problem. What we do have is the knowledge that there are no final or finally unsolvable problems because the Scriptures are the inerrant Word of God. Future archæological work will continue to prove the Scriptures are trustworthy. The significant point is this: when sufficient factual information becomes known, and is properly interpreted, it always confirms the biblical record. In cases where a discovery initially seems not to confirm the Bible, sufficient factual data is never encountered in order to *disprove* a biblical statement. Given the thousands of minute details in the Bible that archæology has the *opportunity* to disprove, this confirmation of the biblical record is striking. As scientist and Christian apologist Dr. Henry M. Morris points out, "It must be extremely significant that, in view of the great mass of corroborative evidence regarding the biblical history of these periods, there exists today not one unquestionable find of archæology that proves the Bible to be in error at any point."[13]

The importance of archæological data in confirmation of the biblical record is evident when we understand that such material confirmation should also logically lead one to have confidence in its spiritual teachings. Those who believe that the Bible is unreliable in historical matters can hardly be expected to accept its teachings in spiritual matters. A famous cookbook may promise culinary delights that are heavenly, but if the recipe ingredients are wrong, it won't matter. Thus, "Although confirmation of one kind of truth (historical) does not demonstrate the validity of another kind of truth (theological), the veracity of the historical narrative of Scripture lends credence to the theological message. Those who do not accept the historical accuracy of the Bible find it easier to dismiss its theological claims."[14]

The Problems of Archæology

If we examine the nature and problems of archæological investigation, it will become apparent why it is impossible for archæology to prove everything in the Bible and equally apparent why any findings which first seem not to confirm the biblical record are insufficient reason to declare that the Bible contains an error. Because the Bible is independently established to be the divinely inspired and inerrant Word of God on other grounds, archæology cannot logically sit in judgment upon the biblical record whenever an *apparent* discrepancy is encountered. As archæologist Dr. Clifford Wilson points out, because archæology deals with insufficient data and unknown variables, and comprises a human endeavor subject to human failings, "The Bible itself, not archæology, is our absolute." In *The Stones and the Scriptures,* Dr. Edwin Yamauchi observes, "By its very nature archæological evidence is fragmentary, often disconnected, and always with the exception of texts—mute and materialistic. Far more than our need of these materials for an understanding of the Bible is our need of the Bible for an understanding of the materials."[15]

Nevertheless, archæology is a highly important endeavor for shedding light on biblical content. In essence, archæology helps us to understand, appreciate and, at times, properly interpret the Bible. Thus, the major function of biblical archæology is both practical and apologetic, to not only illuminate the text but to confirm the biblical record. Dr. Yamauchi is correct in stating that properly understanding the historical and cultural background of the Bible "has maximal significance for the theologian." He quotes the distinguished excavator of Mari, Andre Parot, who states, "As is well-known, certain currents of theological thought profess towards history an attitude almost of disdain. . . . What matters, we are told, is the Word, and the Word alone. But how are we to understand it without setting it against its proper chronological, historical, and geographical background? How are blunders to be avoided if our interpretation treats a given situation completely *in vacuo* [in a vacuum], and without first attempting to define its exact contours?"[16] As archæologist Joseph P. Free (1910–1974), who did extensive excavations at the city of Dothan for ten years, observed, "In my lifetime I have heard many messages or sermons that could have some point driven home by the effective use of some archæological item."[17] He further points out that archæology "has confirmed countless passages that have been rejected by critics as unhistorical or contradictory to known facts."[18]

Dr. Keith Schoville, author of the comprehensive textbook, *Biblical Archæology in Focus*, discusses the three main factors involved in the process of recovering the story of biblical history: the Bible, archæology, and the archæologist. Further, "each of these has its own peculiarities and limitations that affect the total phenomenon that we call archæological research, including the final results."[19] For example, one limitation of the biblical record involves the inability, in certain cases, to properly interpret a portion of Scripture due to lack of information.

Problems with archæology itself include limitations resulting from the relative newness of the discipline and problems with the sites or excavation methods themselves. A limitation of the archæologist involves the kind of educational background and philosophical or theological presuppositions he or she brings to the interpretation of data.

The first problem with archæological work per se is the relative newness of the discipline. This means that not only are there relatively few actual sites excavated among all known sites, but even when sites are excavated, the process is so painstaking that only a small fraction of a particular site can be examined:

> There are over 5,000 ancient ruins in what is now Israel and Jordan, leaving aside for the moment the sites in the other areas of the ancient world. Most of the Palestinian sites are tells [mounds of city remains], and of these only a few hundred have attracted excavators. Of the excavated sites, only about 30 have been the scenes of major excavations; the remainder have consisted of small-scale soundings, emergency clearances, or salvage operations. It is important to be aware, also, that even the major excavations have left most of their sites untouched. It is apparent, then, that almost 98 percent of the major ruins of Palestine remain untouched by an expedition. In other words, in comparison to the minuscule amount that has been recovered, a massive amount of data remains untouched, despite nearly a century of excavations.[20]

As another example, "The Iraq Department of Antiquities has records of over 6,500 tells (mounds of buried cities) in the country; well over 6,000 of them have not yet been excavated at all."[21]

Archæology is, of course, about digging, and many ancient sites are buried far beneath the ground making access to them very difficult. Indeed, "only a minute area of an entire site can ever be dug, especially if explored to any great depth. Thus, ancient Ashdod comprised about 70 acres of lower city area and about 20 acres of Acropolis, some 90 acres in all—but only one and one-half acres of this surface (less than two percent) has been excavated....While surface-potshurds from the slopes of a mound can give valuable indications of the periods during which a former ancient town was inhabited, only full-scale excavation can reveal the total occupation-history. But as even 'full-scale' excavations rarely touch more than a fraction of a site . . . important features can still be missed by accident. If levels of a particular period occur in only one part of a site—a part not dug—then the archæologist's 'record' will appear to show a gap in the town's history, much as when erosion has taken its toll. If one digs 5 percent of a site, one must expect to miss 95 percent (and 100 percent, if it is the wrong site!)."[22]

Kitchen proceeds to discuss other difficulties of archæological work. Besides gaps in the record caused by erosion, "Decayed mud-brick walls can sometimes barely be distinguished at first from the mud in which they are buried. Styles of pottery sometimes changed only slowly, making precise dating difficult. Foundation-trenches, and storage or rubbish-pits cut from one level down into another can mix up the remains from two or more different levels. An undulating town-site can result in late levels in one part being physically lower down than early levels in another part. These and other pitfalls frequently beset the field archæologist."[23]

Then there is the problem of site-shift:

> The citizens of an ancient town sometimes could no longer live comfortably on the crest of their tall mound; or destruction made a new start desirable; or new prosperity led to expansion beyond the old citadel. In such cases a new town or suburb was built either adjoining the old mound or at some little distance from it. Such a development could occur more than once. . . . For modern investigators, the practical result is that a site appears not to have been lived in at certain periods of history—whereas, in fact, people had simply "moved down the road" and actually lived nearby during the supposedly "missing" periods. Thus, Old Testament Jericho (now Tell es-Sultan) was abandoned from Hellenistic times, and settlement moved to near the springs of Ain-Sultan, onto the site which became modern Jericho (Er-Riha). But in Hellenistic/Roman times, palaces and residential villas were built at a third site nearby (Tulul Abu el-Alaiq). So, today, there are three "Jerichos." Consequent shifts of the ancient name can thus be deceptive.[24]

A situation like this helps one understand the problems associated with identifying the walls dating to the time of the conquest of that city by Joshua and the Israelites."[25] Ancient Jericho (modern Tell es-Sultan) has been the site of more than two dozen ancient cities, each one built and destroyed on top of the other.

There are also problems with the methodologies involved in excavation. When you crack an egg for breakfast you have to live with it—so if you want it "over easy" and not scrambled you have to be careful. Every archæological site is unique, and once part of a site is disturbed, that experiment can never be redone. This underscores why the methodological approach of the archæologist is so important. To illustrate, problems have arisen not only from lack of proper techniques but from the archæologist's own methodological idiosyncrasies. For example, a good number of major excavations were conducted before 1936, prior to the development of the more sophisticated techniques currently employed. As a result, "The results of earlier excavations may be suspect. . . . Megiddo, Jericho, Shechem, Gezer, and the famed Tell el-Hesi are among these sites which have been re-excavated recently in order to clarify the work of the earlier excavations. [Tell el-Hesi, originally incorrectly identified with Lachish, was the 120 foot mound near Gaza where, in 1890, Sir Flinders Petrie introduced the first steps toward stratigraphical excavation. This greatly increased interest in Palestinian excavation in that prior to this time, mounds were usually considered natural formations rather than archæological deposits.] Undoubtedly the final results of other earlier excavations will be reevaluated in the future through similar operations."[26]

Archæologists themselves can sometimes be the source of the problem, either by nature or nurture: "In archæology as in other fields, different individuals do things differently, and if any statement can be made about archæologists generally it is that each one is strongly individualistic. Therefore no self-respecting individual will feel constrained to excavate his site according to an absolute standard that has been imposed upon him by an exterior source."[27] Further, the archæologist is "inevitably a product of his times. The world in which he grew up and in which he functions has left its indelible mark upon him, and it affects not only what he is particularly interested in, in terms of his archæological activities, but also how he understands and interprets what he finds. The general validity of this idea can be recognized by noting that Palestinian archæology has gone through several phases in which the predominant interests of the investigators have undergone gradual modification."[28]

Besides those issues there are also problems associated with recording of the data: "The exact and meticulous recording that is required in modern archæological research is also subject to manifold variations. No two excavations are going to employ, among other things, exactly the same recording forms, and the emphasis upon meticulousness will vary from dig to dig, again because archæology is a distinctly human enterprise and because directors of digs are notoriously individualistic."[29]

To cite an example, the importance of pottery analysis as a key to chronology is still evolving as a method. Thus, "only occasionally are shurds profiled by cutting them with a ceramic saw so that a clean, sharp surface is observed and recorded."[30] And there are additional problems associated with photography, recording of ecological data, and many other important details.[31]

Finally, there is the issue of properly interpreting the data one uncovers. Although some archæologists avoid interpretation and merely present the evidence from their excavations, leaving the interpretative task to other specialists, most archæologists seek to interpret the meaning of their finds in their publications and lectures. Despite the necessity of interpretation, this is one of the most problematic aspects of archæological research, because of the "incomplete and fragmentary nature of the surviving remains and, especially, because of the complexity of the human element, the interpreter. Interpretation has been called an art, with the interpreter as the artist, and as with an artist, the interpreter brings all that he or she is to the task, including his educational background, his experiences in life, his philosophical presuppositions, and in biblical archæology his views about the Bible."[32] Finally, it is crucial to remember that "there are no pieces of evidence that carry their own interpretation. Meaning can only be derived from context. Archæological evidence is dependent on the context of date, place, materials, and style. Most important, how it is understood depends on the interpreter's presuppositions and world view. Therefore, not all interpretations of the evidence will be friendly to Christianity."[33]

The above discussion gives one an idea of the problems inherent to archæological work. However, this should never cause us to conclude that archæology is an unimportant or impossible endeavor. To the contrary, a large number of important discoveries and legitimate conclusions continue to be made from modern archæological work. One only need think of the law code of Hammurabi, king of Babylon, the Egyptian Rosetta Stone and the Behistun inscription, the Mesha Stone, the Amarna Letters from Egypt, the Elephantine papyri, the Hittite clay tablets from Boghazkoy, the religious texts from Ras Shamra in Syria, the Nuzi tablets and the Mari texts, the Dead Sea Scrolls, Nag Hammadi, the fascinating search for Noah's Ark, 600,000 Babylonian clay tablets, 25,000 Ebla fragments (Tell Mardikh), and other magnificent finds. All this and more helps us to understand how truly important archæology is and how great a debt we owe to archæologists for the many sacrifices involved in their painstaking work.

The problems inherent to archæological work mean only that findings must be viewed cautiously and critically until all the data are in. One often hears of the "assured results" of archæological research and yet such assured results often turn out to be fragile. "These limitations indicate the importance of the idea of 'the present level of information.' There must always be an openended quality to archæological research which permits and encourages whatever changes in the understanding of old data the new data may require."[34]

Regardless, what is most satisfying about biblical archæology is that, even with all the problems, archæology has repeatedly confirmed the accuracy of the biblical record. Archæological work has confirmed a great deal of both the Old Testament and the New Testament, and even theological liberals and Bible skeptics are forced to admit this. Archæology has consistently refuted higher critical views of the Bible and corrected claims of alleged errors in Scripture.

Archæology and the Biblical Record

"Nowhere has archæological discovery refuted the Bible as history."
—John Elder, *Prophets, Idols and Diggers*[35]

In considering the Old Testament, archæology has vindicated the biblical record time and again. *The New International Dictionary of Biblical Archæology,* written by a score of experts in various fields, repeatedly shows that biblical history is vindicated. To illustrate, the editor's preface remarks, "Near Eastern archæology has demonstrated the historical and geographical reliability of the Bible in many important areas. By clarifying the objectivity and factual accuracy of biblical authors, archæology also helps correct the view that the Bible is avowedly partisan and subjective. It is now known, for instance, that, along with the Hittites, Hebrew scribes were the *best historians in the entire ancient Near East,* despite contrary propaganda that emerged from Assyria, Egypt, and elsewhere."[36]

John Arthur Thompson was director of the Australian Institute of Archæology in Melbourne and has done archæological fieldwork with the American Schools of Oriental Research. In *The Bible and Archæology* he writes, "Finally, it is perfectly true to say that biblical archæology has done a great deal to correct the impression that was abroad at the close of the last century and in the early part of this century, that biblical history was of doubtful trustworthiness in many places. If one impression stands out more clearly than any other today, it is that on all hands the over-all historicity of the Old Testament tradition is admitted. In this connection the words of W. F. Albright may be quoted: 'There can be no doubt that archæology has confirmed the substantial historicity of Old Testament traditions.'"[37] Geisler and Brooks point out, "In every period of Old Testament history, we find that there is good evidence from archæology that the scriptures are accurate. . . . While many have doubted the accuracy of the Bible, time and continued research have consistently demonstrated that the Word of God is better informed than its critics."[38]

For example, many aspects of Bible books have been confirmed over the views of critics, in particular the books of Moses, Daniel, Ezra, Kings, and Luke in the book of Acts. Daniel, for example, because of its clear supernatural predictions, is dated by critics to the time of the Maccabeans, around 165 B.C., though Daniel himself indicates or implies a sixth century B.C. date at the beginning of every chapter but one. Critics had also doubted the Exile and the return of the Jews referred to in the book of Esther, as well as its official government decrees. And the chronological records of the books of Kings were held to be hopelessly confused, according to the critics. To the contrary, archæologist Dr. Clifford Wilson and others have provided many examples of how archæology has confirmed the accuracy of these books. In his *Rocks, Relics and Biblical Reliability*, Dr. Wilson supplies examples, some of which we quote below:

> There are other evidences of eyewitness recording by Daniel. That he knew Nebuchadnezzar rebuilt Babylon (Daniel 4:30) is a problem by those who argue for a later date for Daniel. This fact of history was recovered by excavation only in modern times, yet Daniel had recorded it correctly. One critic wrote that this was a difficulty, the answer to which "we shall presumably never know".... Linguistic pointers from the Dead Sea Scrolls (e.g., a recent targum of Job) also suggest an early, not a late, date for Daniel.... The overthrow of the nonhistorical view of the Exile and the return of the Jews came with the finding of the famous Cyrus Cylinder.... By this decree [of King Cyrus] the Hebrew people were given leave to rebuild the temple in Jerusalem.... The same can be said about the style of writing in the Book of Ezra, for as Albright says, "If we turn to the Book of Ezra, recent discoveries have indicated the authenticity of its official documents in the most striking way." Albright shows that the language of Ezra had been seriously challenged, but that some of the very words that have been challenged have turned up in Egyptian, Aramaic, and Babylonian cuneiform documents that date to the exact time of Ezra. Albright goes on: "If it were practicable to quote from still unpublished Aramaic documents

from fifth century Egypt, the weight of factual evidence would crush all opposition".... Still another convincing evidence of the genuineness of the Bible records is in *The Mysterious Numbers of the Hebrew Kings* by Edwin R. Thiele. Where once it seemed that the dates of the kings in the divided-kingdom period were inaccurate and vague, he has been able to show remarkable synchronisms.... Once again, an area that many believed was total confusion has been shown to be staggeringly accurate recording, with fine chronological interweaving that cannot be claimed for any other book of ancient history.[39]

The reliability of the New Testament is also confirmed; based on archæological data, "the evidence for its historical reliability [is] overwhelming."[40] In the case of the book of Acts, "It is widely agreed today that in this book [Acts] we can see the hand of a historian of the first rank.... Luke is shown to be a most careful recorder of information, whether it be matters of geography and political boundaries, local customs, titles of local officers, local religious practices, details of local topography, or the disposition of buildings in Greek or Roman, Asian or European towns."[41] A. N. Sherwin-White remarks, "For Acts the confirmation of historicity is overwhelming.... Any attempt to reject its basic historicity must now appear absurd. Roman historians have long taken it for granted."[42]

Consider some examples of Luke's accuracy in historical reporting:

Luke demonstrated a remarkably accurate knowledge of geographical and political ideas. He referred correctly to provinces that were established at that time, as indicated in Acts 15:41; 16:2, 6-8. He identified regions, such as that referred to in Acts 13:49, and various cities, as in Acts 14:6. He demonstrated a clear knowledge of local customs, such as those relating to the speech of the Lycaonians (Acts 14:11), some aspects relating to the foreign woman who was converted at Athens (Acts 17:34), and he even knew that the city of Ephesus was known as "the temple-keeper of Artemis" (Acts 19:35).... he refers to different local officers by their exact titles—the proconsul (deputy) of Cyprus (Acts 13:7), the magistrates at Philippi (Acts 16:20, 35), the politarchs (another word for magistrates) at Thessalonica (Acts 17:6), the proconsul of Achaia (Acts 18:12), and the treasurer of Corinth (Aedile)—which was the title of the man known as Erastus at Corinth (Acts 19:22; Romans 16:23)....

Luke had accurate knowledge about various local events such as the famine in the days of Claudius Caesar (Acts 11:29); he was aware that Zeus and Hermes were worshiped together at Lystra, though this was unknown to modern historians (Acts 14:11, 12). He knew that Diana or Artemis was especially the goddess of the Ephesians (Acts 19:28); and he was able to describe the trade at Ephesus in religious images (Acts 19:26-27).[43]

As Merrill C. Tenney, professor of New Testament, points out about Luke's writings, the Gospel of Luke and the book of Acts, "The two volumes he wrote comprise at least one-fourth of the total canon of the New Testament and provide the only piece of continuous historical writing that covers the period from the birth of Jesus of Nazareth to the establishment of a church in the capitol of the Roman Empire."[44] In other words, the fact that Luke has been established as such a careful writer means that fully one-fourth of the entire New Testament, on the basis of his accuracy alone, bears the same marks of authenticity.

But it is this very same careful historical writer, the physician Luke, who reports that Jesus Christ was resurrected from the dead "by many convincing proofs"—and that he had carefully investigated the evidence for this from the beginning (cf., Luke 1:1-4; Acts 1:1-3). If Luke was so painstakingly accurate in his historical reporting, on what logical basis may we assume he was credulous or inaccurate in his reporting of matters that were far more important, not only to him but to others as well?

Noted biblical scholar and apologist Dr. John Warwick Montgomery summarizes the evidence when he writes, "Modern archæological research has confirmed again and again the reliability of New Testament geography, chronology, and general history."[45] And Dr. Wilson concludes, "Those who know the facts now recognize that the New Testament must be accepted as a remarkably accurate source book..."[46]

In general, if not always in the particulars, the entire Bible, both Old Testament and New Testament, has been strikingly confirmed. Kitchen remarks that after "a fair and full investigation of the total available resources, the verdict is frequently a high measure of agreement between the Bible and the world that is its ancient and original context."[47] Dr. Schoville observes, "Thus far, no historical statement in the Bible has been proven false on the basis of evidence retrieved through archæological research."[48] Thompson concludes his book by stating, "It is very evident that the biblical records have their roots firmly in general world history."[49] Archæologist Joseph Free, chairman of the department of archæology at Wheaton College and later professor of archæology and history at Bemidji State College in Minnesota, concluded his *Archæology and Bible History* with the following words: "I thumbed through the book of Genesis and mentally noted that each of the 50 chapters was either illuminated or confirmed by some archæological discovery—the same would be true for most of the remaining chapters of the Bible, both the Old and New Testaments."[50]

Again, given the large amount of data already uncovered in the last 150 years, this is no insignificant conclusion. There are literally thousands of opportunities for archæological research to indisputably prove the Bible false—and yet it has never done so.

Silencing the Critics

Perhaps more significant, even liberal theologians, secular academics, and critics generally cannot deny that archæology has confirmed the biblical record at many points. Rationalistic detractors of the Bible can attack it all day long, but they cannot dispute archæological facts. Consider the weekly PBS series "Mysteries of the Bible." Despite some shortcomings, such as the theologically liberal experts and non-Christian commentators, this program has offered example after example, week after week, of the archæological reliability of the Bible.

To further illustrate, probably the three greatest American archæologists of the twentieth century each had their liberal training modified by their archæological work. W. F. Albright,

Nelson Glueck, and George Ernest Wright all "received training in the liberal scholarship of the day, which had resulted from the earlier and continuing critical study of the Bible, predominantly by German scholars."[51] Despite their liberal training, it was archæological research that bolstered their confidence in the biblical text:

> Albright said of himself, "I must admit that I tried to be rational and empirical in my approach [but] we all have presuppositions of a philosophical order." The same statement could be applied as easily to Glueck and Wright, for all three were deeply imbued with theological perceptions which infused their work. Albright, the son of a Methodist missionary, came to see that much of German critical thought was established upon a philosophical base that could not be sustained in the light of archæological discoveries. . . . Nelson Glueck was Albright's student. In his own explorations in Trans-Jordan and Negev and in his excavations, Glueck worked with the Bible in hand. He trusted what he called "the remarkable phenomenon of historical memory in the Bible." He was the president of the prestigious Hebrew Union College-Jewish Institute of Religion and an ordained Rabbi. Wright went from the faculty of the McCormick Theological Seminary in Chicago to a position in the Harvard Divinity School which he retained until his death. He, too, was a student of Albright.[52]

Glueck forthrightly declared, "As a matter of fact, however, it may be clearly stated categorically that no archæological discovery has ever controverted a single biblical reference. Scores of archæological findings have been made which confirm in clear outline or exact detail historical statements in the Bible."[53]

In fact, "Much of the credit for this relatively new assessment of the patriarchal tradition must go to the 'Albright school.' Albright himself pointed out years ago that apart from 'a few diehards among older scholars' there is hardly a single biblical historian who is not at least impressed with the rapid accumulation of data supporting the 'substantial historicity' of patriarchal tradition."[54]

And, in fact, this is true not just for the patriarchal tradition but the Bible generally. The earlier statement by assyriologist

A. H. Sayce continues to hold true today: "Time after time the most positive assertions of a skeptical criticism have been disproved by archæological discovery, events and personages that were confidently pronounced to be mythical have been shown to be historical, and the older [i.e., biblical] writers have turned out to have been better acquainted with what they were describing than the modern critic who has flouted them."[55]

Millar Burrows of Yale points out that, "Archæology has in many cases refuted the views of modern critics. It has been shown in a number of instances that these views rest on false assumptions and unreal, artificial schemes of historical development...." And, "The excessive skepticism of many liberal theologians stems not from a careful evaluation of the available data, but from an enormous predisposition against the supernatural."[56]

Many other examples could be given of how firsthand archæological work changed the views of a critic. One of the most prominent is that of Sir William Ramsay, the details of which we cited in chapter 5, pages 91-92.[57]

Ramsay's own archæological findings convinced him of the reliability of the Bible and the truth of what it taught. In his *The Bearing of Recent Discovery on the Trustworthiness of the New Testament* and other books, he shows why he came to conclude that "Luke's history is unsurpassed in respect of its trustworthiness" and that "Luke is a historian of the first rank.... In short, this author should be placed along with the very greatest of historians."[58]

As part of his secular academic duties, Dr. Clifford Wilson was for some years required to research and teach higher critical approaches to the Bible. This gave him a great deal of first-hand exposure and insight to the assumptions and methodologies that go into these approaches. Yet his own archæological research was found to continually refute such skeptical theories, so much so that he finally concluded, "It is the studied conviction of this writer that the Bible is...the ancient world's most reliable history textbook...."[59]

In a personal communication he added the following,

> I was not always the "literalist" I am today. I've always had a
> profound respect for the Bible, but accepted that the use of

poetic forms meant that the record could often be interpreted symbolically where now I take it literally—though of
course there are times when symbolism is clearly utilized.
Thus in later scriptures "Egypt" can be a geographic
country or a symbolic term.

That literalism is especially true in relation to Genesis chapters 1 through 11, often considered allegorical or mythical, where my researches have led me to the conclusion
that this is profound writing, meant to be taken literally.
There was a real Adam, creation that was contemporaneous
for the various life forms as shown in Genesis chapter 1, and
a consistent style of history writing—such as the outlines
given in Genesis 1, then zeroing in on the specifics relating
to mankind in Genesis chapter 2; the history of all the early
peoples in Genesis chapter 10, then the concentration on
Abraham and his descendants from Genesis chapter 11
onwards. Early man, "the birth of the lady of the rib," long-
living men, giants in the earth (animals, birds, and men),
the flood, the tower of Babel—and much more—point to
factual, accurate recording of history in these early chapters
of Genesis.

Over 40 years have passed since I first became profession-
ally involved in biblical archæology and my commitment to
the Bible as the world's greatest history book is firmly settled. As Psalm 119:89 states, "Forever O Lord, your word is
established in heaven."

Indeed, one of the most valuable contributions of modern
archæology has been its refutation of higher critical views toward
Scripture. Consider for example the discovery of the Dead Sea
Scrolls.

J. Randall Price (Ph.D., Middle Eastern Studies) currently
working on a forthcoming apologetic text on biblical
archæology writes, "Those who expected the [Dead Sea] Scrolls
to produce a radical revision of the Bible have been disap-
pointed, for these texts have only verified the reliability and stability of the Old Testament as it appears in our modern
translations."[60]

He further points out how the Daniel fragments of the Dead
Sea Scrolls should require scholars to abandon a Maccabean

date. The same kind of evidence forced scholars to abandon Maccabean dates for Chronicles, Ecclesiastes, and many of the Psalms. But so far, most scholars refuse to do this for Daniel: "Unfortunately, critical scholars have not arrived at a similar conclusion for the book of Daniel, even though the evidence is identical."[61] In fact, according to Old Testament scholar Gerhard Hasel, a date for Daniel in the sixth or fifth century B.C. "has more in its favor today from the point of view of language alone than ever before."[62] The Dead Sea Scrolls also provide significant evidence for the unity and single authorship of the book of Isaiah. Dr. Price concludes, "The discovery of the Dead Sea Scrolls, then, has made a contribution toward confirming the integrity of the biblical text and its own claim to predictive prophecy. Rather than support the recent theories of documentary disunity, the Scrolls have returned scholars to a time when the Bible's internal witness to its own consistency and veracity was fully accepted by its adherents."[63]

The noted classical scholar Professor E. N. Blaiklock once wrote, quite correctly, "Recent archæology has destroyed much nonsense and will destroy more. And I use the word nonsense deliberately, for theories and speculations find currency in biblical scholarship that would not be tolerated for a moment in any other branch of literary or historical criticism."[64] Geisler and Brooks remark, "As for the critical theories which were spawned in the early 1800's but still persist today, they are left without substantiation. The great archæologist William F. Albright says, 'All radical schools in New Testament criticism which have existed in the past or which exist today are pre-archæological, and are therefore, since they were built in Der Luft [in the air], quite antiquated today.' "[65]

Indeed, the biases of modern critical biblical scholarship seems evident to everyone except those doing it. And those with biases to uphold usually don't want to be bothered with troubling little facts. As Kitchen points out:

> Nowhere else in the whole of Ancient Near Eastern history has the literary, religious and historical development of a nation been subjected to such drastic and wholesale reconstructions at such variance with the existing documentary

evidence. The fact that Old Testament scholars are habitu-
ated to these widely known reconstructions, even mentally
conditioned by them, does not alter the basic gravity of the
situation which should not be taken for granted. . . . [citing
Bright] 'The new evidence [i.e., objective Near Eastern
data], far from furnishing a corrective to inherited notions
of the religions of earliest Israel tends to be subsumed
under the familiar developmental pattern'. . . . And the
same applies to other aspects besides history. . . . [66]

Thus, "Biblical studies have long been hindered by the per-
sistence of long-outdated philosophical and literary theories
(especially of nineteenth-century stamp), and by wholly inadequate use of first-hand sources in appreciating the earlier
periods of the Old Testament story in particular."[67] One predominant example is the documentary hypothesis or the "JEDP"
theory of the first five books of the Bible, which we will discuss
in a moment.

The irony, or perhaps *hypocrisy*, of liberal critical scholarship
at this point is illustrated in its two-minded approach to biblical
archæology. On the one hand, any time archæology does not
directly confirm something the Bible teaches, the tendency is to
allege an error in the text. Thus, "any element in the [biblical]
traditions which was not corroborated by archæological evidence has been considered suspect or anachronistic."[68] On the
other hand, liberal critics frequently tend to *avoid* the use of
archæology where it confirms the Bible: "One of the striking
characteristics of the scholars who have approached the Bible
primarily through literary analysis [e.g., the documentary
hypothesis] is the non-use or at best the grudging use they have
made of archæological evidence."[69] For example, "A few scholars
who had accepted the views of higher criticism, such as A. H.
Sayce, revised their positions because of the impact of the early
archæological discoveries, but most higher critics chose not to
make use of the new data."[70]

To cite another example, archæology has discredited the theories of *form criticism*, which holds that the content of the gospels
was largely invented and only written down 100–150 years after
the apostles lived, in the second century A.D.[71] It may surprise no
one that form critics have ignored archæology when it discredits

personal theories that they have held to for emotional as well as academic reasons. But how scholarly are they being? Scholars, presumably, are interested in the truth and will allow the evidence to take them where it will. Yet when it comes to the Bible, it seems there aren't very many real scholars in modern academia.

An illustration involves the *documentary hypothesis*. This theory rejects Mosaic authorship in the fifteenth century B.C., and supposes a much later compilation by a variety of authors who wrote documents termed "J," "E," "D," and "P." This material was later shuffled and reassembled by editors to form the Pentateuch and, allegedly, later writings of the Old Testament also. Yet "even the most ardent advocate of the documentary theory must admit that we have as yet *no single scrap* of external, objective *material* (i.e., tangible) evidence for either the existence or the history of 'J,' 'E,' or any other alleged source-document."[72]

For more than 100 years the Graf-Wellhausen or "documentary" theory has been taught in most seminaries and universities as the "absolute truth" concerning the literary evolution and development of the Old Testament—and yet not a *shred* of evidence exists to support it! Instead, this theory has been thoroughly disproven for decades, even by non-evangelical scholarship, yet it continues to be taught as truth. How's that for illustrating the objectivity of those in the scholarly community supporting this theory? Essentially, liberal biblical scholars are promoting elaborately devised myths in order to reject Mosaic authorship and the divine inspiration of the Old Testament so that they can "uphold" their own personal views of the Bible as a humanly devised document. What could be fairer?

> The theories current in Old Testament studies, however brilliantly conceived and elaborated, were mainly established in a vacuum with little or no reference to the Ancient Near East and initially too often in accordance with *a priori* philosophical and literary principles. It is solely because the data from the Ancient Near East coincide so much better with the existing observable structure of Old Testament history, literature and religion than with the theoretical reconstructions, that we are compelled—as happens in Ancient Oriental studies—to question or even

to abandon such theories regardless of their popularity. Facts not votes determine the truth.[73]

As Dr. Kitchen infers, the documentary hypothesis, since it is disproven, should be abandoned, but perhaps one should not hold one's breath. Anyone who reads even a relatively brief survey of the evidence against the documentary hypothesis, as that given by the noted biblical and linguistic scholar, Gleason L. Archer in his *A Survey of Old Testament Introduction,* will realize how thoroughly liberal Old Testament scholarship has been based in fantasy. For example:

> [Even in the nineteenth century] in America the Princeton Seminary scholars Joseph Addison Alexander and William Henry Green ... subjected the documentarian school to devastating criticism which has never been successfully rebutted by those of liberal persuasion.... How shall we characterize the trend of twentieth-century scholarship and its treatment of Pentateuchal criticism and of the Wellhausen hypothesis?.... Almost every supporting pillar has been shaken and shattered by a generation of scholars who were brought up on the Graf-Wellhausen system and yet have found it inadequate to explain the data of the Pentateuch.... We close with an apt quotation from H. F. Hahn, "This review of activity in the field of Old Testament criticism during the last quarter-century has revealed a chaos of conflicting trends, ending in contradictory results, which create an impression of ineffectiveness in this type of research. The conclusion seems unavoidable that the higher criticism has long since past the age of constructive achievement."[74]

Incidentally, Archer's text, *A Survey of Old Testament Introduction* has many examples of archæological confirmation of Old Testament books; and yet he also points out that an attitude of skeptical prejudice toward the Bible "has persisted, without any logical justification."[75] That the majority of liberal Old Testament scholars allow their personal biases to dictate their research methods and conclusions—merely to support personal views—is no small indictment given the fact that such theories have been discredited for decades.

What one finds through archæological research is that alleged biblical errors have later been shown to be factual truths. What else, then, can one conclude about higher critical scholarship—other than the fact that *it* is the problem, not the Bible? "In the light of past discoveries one may expect that future archæological finds will continue to support the biblical traditions against radical reconstructions."[76]

As we have noted, biblical critics have pointed to all kinds of people, places, and things in the Bible that no archæological evidence could confirm. Skeptics rashly heralded such lack of confirmation as proof of "biblical errors." Consider one more example: "It has become almost a dogma of critical scholarship to insist that Genesis 14, which recounts the battle between Abraham and his allies and the four kings of the East, is unhistorical precisely because the five cities mentioned in the story are never referred to in any ancient literature apart from the Old Testament. The assumption is that unless a person, place or event in early Israel's history can be validated by extrabiblical documentation it must be unhistorical. The fallacy in that method ought to be obvious, for if this principle were applied to all of ancient (and even modern) history virtually nothing could be recovered from the past in the name of history."[77]

In fact, until scholars can manage to keep their biases against the biblical text in check and treat it as they do other ancient documents, probably no amount of extrabiblical supporting evidence will convince them otherwise. And until this occurs, conservatives will be correct in referencing such work more as propaganda than good scholarship.[78] Further, archæologists sometimes admit that their chronology has been wrong and that this is why there has been a lack of supporting evidence for the Scriptures. As noted scholar Dr. John Warwick Montgomery points out, "[American Institute of Holy Land Studies] researcher Thomas Drobena cautioned that where archæology and the Bible seemed to be in tension, the issue is almost always dating, the most shaky area in current archæology and the one at which scientistic *a priori* and circular reasoning often replace solid empirical analysis."[79] There is ongoing debate among scholars as to dates, and even as to the nature of such buildings as the stables or store houses dated now to Ahab's time instead of to Solomon's.

"[David Noel] Freedman, for example, says that 'the reason that the story [of Abraham] has never been located historically is that scholars, all of us, have been looking in the wrong millennium. Briefly put, the account in Genesis 14, and also in chapters 18–19, does not belong to the second millennium B.C., still less to the first millennium B.C., but rather to the third millennium B.C.' "[80] Most conservative scholars, however, have always placed Abraham close to the third millennium B.C., about 1900 B.C.

Nevertheless, as archæological excavations continued in Israel, time and again what was once an "error" was subsequently confirmed as fact. Whether it was the fact of a branch of the Hittites mentioned some 50 times in the Bible (as early as Genesis 10:15), King Sargon (Isaiah 20:1), Darius the Mede (Daniel 6:1),[81] or many others, biblical history was repeatedly upheld:

> Archæological research has established the identity of literally hundreds of places—in Mesopotamia, Persia, ancient Canaan, and Egypt—that are mentioned in the Bible. Furthermore, the discovery of thousands of historical texts in Egypt and Mesopotamia has enabled scholars to work out the historical chronology of the ancient world in considerable detail. Historical synchronisms have been established for dating the accession of Solomon (ca. 961 B.C.), the accession of Jehu, the Israelite king (842/1 B.C.), the fall of Samaria (722/1 B.C.), and the first capture of Jerusalem (March 15/16, 579 B.C.).[82]

Ebla and Politics

But now even cities as ancient as Sodom and Gomorrah, routinely ridiculed by critics as myths, have been found mentioned in extrabiblical literature. The recent finds of the Eblaite Kingdom that existed more than 4,300 years ago in Syria revealed the following: "Sodom and Gomorrah, thought by many to have been more legendary than real, were mentioned in a commercial text, and thus were given firm historical status for the first time in an extrabiblical source."[83] Further, "The tables refer to various sites, including *urusalima* (Jerusalem), Hazor, Lachish, Megiddo, Gaza, Sinai, Joppa, and Haran. The five cities of the plain (Genesis 14:2), including Sodom and Gomorrah, are referred to, and so also is Salim, apparently the city of Melchizedek, who is also referred to in Genesis 14."[84]

This Semitic Eblaite kingdom lasted for about 800 years and at one point was populated by an estimated 260,000 people. The amount of material that has already been uncovered and is expected to be uncovered is massive. "There can be no doubt that this material is some of the most important ever discovered as far as OT studies are concerned."[85]

Unfortunately, political and religious opposition by the principals involved (predominantly Syrians and Muslims) may have caused some very monumental findings to be falsely interpreted or even suppressed because of their religious, cultural, and historical implications for Christians and Jews.

To illustrate, it was first reported that one Eblaite document implied the teaching that the universe was created out of nothing. What theological liberals had held was the "mythical" teaching of a first millennium B.C. *oral* tradition is now found in a third-millennium B.C. *written* text! Our good friend Dr. Clifford Wilson, who was personally present when a team of archæologists and linguists met informally (over a lunch hosted by Professor David Noel Freedman at Ann Arbor) with the discoverer (Matthiae) and translator (Pettinato) of the Ebla tablets, told us, "A creation tablet indicated that one great Being had brought creation into being—especially the heavens, the earth, the moon, and the stars. Once again this written record from Ebla was dramatically earlier than critics had deemed possible for Genesis, which was again proven a greatly superior record."[86] Another source writes, "One cosmological tablet recorded that the heavens, earth, sun, and moon were created in that order, which corresponds exactly to the sequence in Genesis."[87]

The creation tablet discovered at Ebla declares, "Lord of heaven and earth: the earth was not, you created it, the light of day was not, you created it, the morning light you had not [yet] made exist."[88] Significantly, creation is attributed to only one God, and the order is identical to that in Genesis 1:1-5. There is also the inference that creation is ex-nihilo, not remanufacturing something from an eternal primitive substance.

This obviously "confirms" the Genesis account and, to some degree, the religious beliefs and claims of Jews and Christians—and clearly not all Syrians or Muslims are happy about that. In his second printing of *Ebla Tablets: Secrets of a Forgotten City,* Clifford Wilson includes information from Syrian authorities as to the restrictions to be observed in the release of materials from Ebla. The Syrians do not want to be identified as "cousins" of Jews, or to have the Old Testament preferred to the Koran. To them, to confirm the Old Testament record is to confirm the Abrahamic covenant in which Jews, not Arabs, were promised the Holy land.[89]

James D. Muhly is Professor of Ancient Near East History and chairman of the Ancient History Program at the University of Pennsylvania, in addition to being director of excavations at Tel Michal and Tel Gerisa on Israel's Mediterranean coast. He writes in *Biblical Archæology Review,* "It should be added, however, that archæological work at Ebla is inevitably political, in the sense that all archæological research in the Middle East is political. One is working in a highly charged atmosphere, and everything that takes place is in some way connected with politics. Every archæologist must also be a skilled diplomat or he will not survive."[90] Consider the following account:

> Unfortunately, Pettinato who announced the connection between Genesis 14 and the Ebla texts in a public meeting in 1976 (which this author attended), later disclaimed his own conclusions. In a travesty of modern scholarship he has backed away from his original and very dogmatic assertion that Ebla mentioned the cities of the plain. The reason, tragically, is not that the linguistic evidence compels a shift in his thinking but the realities of modern Middle Eastern politics have been brought to bear. The Syrian government, under whose auspices the site of Tell Mardikh [Ebla] has been excavated, has become alarmed at the obvious relationship between Genesis and the Ebla texts. They feel that these materials lend some kind of support to the antiquity of the Hebrew people and possibly to the claims of Israel on certain parts of the Arab world. They therefore threatened

to prevent further work at the site and publishing of the inscriptions unless these damaging Ebla-Genesis connections were disavowed. Because Pettinato wished to continue on the project he apparently acceded to these pressures and relinquished his previously held convictions. Ironically Pettinato has been removed as head epigrapher (decipherer) anyway and has been replaced by Alfonso Archi. But even in a later publication (1981) Pettinato conceded that *si-da-mu* (Sodom) and *sa-ba-i-im* (Zeboiim) might be mentioned in the Ebla inscriptions.[91]

Though the question of five cities of the plain may now be uncertain because of the acrimonious climate surrounding the publication of the tablets, there is persistent support for the attestation of at least Sodom and Zeboiim.... [Regardless] A parallel line of evidence in support of the historicity of the cities of the plain and therefore of the patriarchal stories associated with them has been the exploration and excavation of sites near the Lisan, the peninsula in the southeast part of the Dead Sea.[92]

Further, Muhly points out that the seeming confusion and uncertainty over the tablets at Ebla is nothing new:

What has happened with the Ebla tablets is, unfortunately, exactly what happened with several other major textual discoveries of this century, such as the Ugaritic texts, the Dead Sea scrolls and the Linear B tablets in Mycenaean Greek.... Scholars share the vanities and insecurities common to all humanity. When asked for their opinion by a reporter from the *New York Times*, *Time* magazine or *BAR*, few can resist. The fact that they know nothing about the subject has never hindered most scholars from contributing to the general confusion. With Ebla, I hope we are now past this trial by fire.... Scholars will refuse to go beyond the precise letter of the text. To allay suspicions that changes in interpretation of the finds reflect a refusal to have anything to do with ancient Israel or the world of the Bible, those tablets that supposedly formed the basis for the unfounded claims should be published.[93]

The latest information on Ebla is that, due to the politicization of archæology in Syria, in most cases we are still uncertain whether the Ebla tablets help confirm the early chapters of Genesis. Only time will tell. Regardless, when all the facts are known, history repeatedly tells us that archæological discovery will side with what the Bible already declares: "If even 10 percent of the alleged comparisons should prove to be valid, Ebla will have established itself as a major resource against which all future Old Testament study must be done. It is beyond question that traditional and conservative views of biblical history, especially of the patriarchal period, will continue to be favored by whatever results accrue from ongoing Ebla research."[94]

Examples of Confirmations

As Dr. Yamauchi points out for Scripture generally, "There are a number of striking cases where specific passages have been doubted (it is a rare passage that has not be questioned by some critic) and have been directly confirmed. There are many more items and areas which have afforded a general illumination of biblical backgrounds, making the narratives more credible and understandable."[95] He proceeds to quote the noted scholar D. J. Wiseman, now retired, formerly Professor of Assyriology at the University of London who writes:

> When due allowance has been paid to the increasing number of supposed errors which have been subsequently eliminated by the discovery of archæological evidence, to the many aspects of history indirectly affirmed or in some instances directly confirmed by extra-biblical sources, I would still maintain that the historical facts of the Bible, rightly understood, find agreement in the facts culled from archæology, equally rightly understood, that is, the majority of errors can be ascribed to errors of interpretation by modern scholars and not to substantiated "errors" of fact presented by the biblical historians. This view is further strengthened when it is remembered how many theories and interpretations of Scripture have been checked or corrected by archæological discoveries.[96]

In the chart below, we consider just a few examples of hundreds that could be cited. In all the following examples, and many more, critics doubted what the Bible declared. Allegedly, these places, people, and things were anachronistic, errors, or myths. The "scholarly" conclusion was that the Bible was merely a human document and not very trustworthy. But thanks to archæology, it was the authority of the critics that was silenced, not the authority of the Bible. In contrast to critical views, archæology has proven the historicity and biblical time frame of many biblical events like these.

Archæological Confirmations

1. Abraham and the patriarchs and the city of Ur (Genesis 11:28-31)

2. Mosaic authorship of the Pentateuch

3. The five cities of the plain (Genesis 14:2)

4. Scores of additional biblical cities, e.g.: "Within the past hundred and fifty years however, all of these cities have been uncovered, some receiving additional archæological attention in recent years. The importance of the discoveries is apparent when we realize that the excavation of these cities, and dozens more, has produced material that confirms the Scriptures at point after point." (Free and Vos, 16)

5. The use of straw in brick making (Exodus 15:13-18)

6. The general date and route of the Exodus

7. Sennacherib's failure to capture Jerusalem and his death at the hands of his own sons (2 Kings 19:35-37)

8. Jehoiachin's exile in Babylon (2 Kings 25:27-30)

9. The unconquered status of the cities of Lachish and Azekah (Jeremiah 34:7)

10. Ezekiel's dating of events by the years "of king Jehoiachin's captivity." (Ezekiel 1:1; 8:1ff.)

11. The Psalms of David as a tenth century composition and the book of Daniel as a sixth century B.C. composition (every chapter in Daniel but one clearly states this)

12. Nabonidus and Belshazzar (Daniel 5)

13. The time of Nehemiah's return, and Sanballat and Tobiah as his enemies (Nehemiah 2:1, 10, 19; 4:1-3, 7-8; 6:1ff.)

14. The drachma coin in Nehemiah (Nehemiah 7:70)

15. The census at the time of Christ's birth (Luke 2:1-3)

16. Sergius Paulus, the proconsul of Paphos (Acts 13:6-7)

17. The relationship between Iconium, Lystra, and Derbe (Acts 14:6)

18. The district of Macedonia (Acts 16:12)

19. The magistrates of Philippi (Acts 16:20)

20. Herod's Temple and winter palace (Luke 1:9; Matthew 2:4)

21. The pools of Siloam and Bethesda (John 5:2; 9:7)

22. Peter's house (Matthew 8:14)

23. Jacob's well (John 4:5-6)

24. Artemis' temple, statues, and altar (Acts 19:27-28, 35)

25. The Ephesian theatre and Golden House of Nero (Acts 19:29; 25:10; 1 Peter 2:13)[97]

These examples again prove that "archæological discoveries have shown that these critical charges and countless others are wrong and that the Bible is trustworthy in the very statements that critics have set aside as untrustworthy."[98]

We only wish space were available to continue our discussion of showing how archæology continually confirms Scripture. Indeed by 1958 "over 25,000 sites from the biblical world have been confirmed by some archæological discoveries to date."[99] Forty years later, the list is longer. But let us refer the interested reader to the 17-volume survey, *Archæology—the Bible and Christ* by Dr. Clifford Wilson, which brings together over 5,000 facts relating archæology to the Bible.[100] Dr. Wilson begins volume 17 by stating, "Archæology is highly relevant for Bible studies, consistently demonstrating that the Bible is the world's most accurate history text-book.... This present volume (and each of the other volumes) takes its place in offering significant evidence to show how archæology illustrates, explains and verifies the integrity and authenticity of God's own Word of Truth." He closes by stating, "It is remarkable that where confirmation is possible and has come to light, the Bible stands investigation in ways that are unique in all literature. Its superiority to attack, its capacity to withstand criticism, its amazing facility to be proved right after all, are all staggering by any standards of scholarship. Seemingly assured results 'disproving' the Bible have a habit of backfiring. Over and over again the Bible has been vindicated. That is true from Genesis to Revelation, as we have seen in this book."

In essence, from the perspective of the hope of biblical critics—if that hope was to be proved correct—archæological research has provided vast opportunities to establish their view of the Bible. Their belief was that it merely constituted the error-filled writings of men and was of no particular or lasting spiritual import. Their hopes have consistently been smashed: the Bible has stood up to the investigation of a type that has not been hurled at any other reputable book of history.

We cannot stress this strongly enough: given the thousands of minute details recorded in the Bible, if the Bible *were* only the writings of men, surely archæology would have proven it by now. Modern archæology has thoroughly disproven the *Book of Mormon,* as we indicated in our *Behind the Mask of Mormonism* and as Mormon experts Jerald and Sandra Tanner have detailed in *Archæology and the Book of Mormon.*[101] Modern archæology has also corrected the writings of many other ancient and new texts. But modern archæology has never corrected the Bible beyond legitimate adjustments because of new knowledge, such as translation errors relative to Bible backgrounds and the correct use of titles of Israel's neighbors. How do we account for what must be viewed as a startling fact, apart from the claims of the Bible itself, that indeed, we have in our possession the literal Word of God?

In conclusion, we cannot but end our discussion by reminding ourselves of the spiritual implications of biblical archæology: "The serious investigator has every reason for great confidence in the reliability of both Old and New Testament Scriptures. . . . However, the historical material—seen through archæology to be of remarkable integrity—is penned by the same men who witnessed and recorded the miracles and elaborated on spiritual realities. It is reasonable to believe that they would be as reliable in those areas as they are in the areas now subject to investigation by archæology."[102]

Chapter 14

Biblical Inerrancy:
An Introduction

Men cannot shut their eyes to truth and fact. The Bible itself nowhere makes the claim that it is inerrant. Nor do the creeds of the Church sanction such a theory. Indeed, the theory that the Bible is inerrant is the ghost of modern evangelicalism to frighten children.

—Charles Briggs[1]

I regard the subject of this book, biblical inerrancy, to be the most important theological topic of this age. A great battle rages about it among people called evangelicals. I did not start the battle and wish it were not essential to discuss it. The only way to avoid it would be to remain silent. And silence on this matter would be a grave sin.

—Harold Lindsell,[2] *The Battle for the Bible*

What is your opinion on the authority of the Bible? Do you see it as the literal Word of God which commands our obedience? Or do you view it as the humanly inspired words of great men so that we are pretty much free to pick and choose what we will accept or reject? Or perhaps you see the Bible as something in between, as a combination of divine ideas and human beliefs? In this chapter, we will seek to examine the important subject of biblical inerrancy, the claim that the Bible is without error.

The Importance of Inerrancy

Why do we think biblical inerrancy is such a crucial subject? Because of its implications, the fabric of which is woven throughout this book. The Bible is the most important book in the world because it alone is God's Word. Its influence in history is incalculable. The Bible has literally changed the world. Not just Western history, but all of history.

What People Have Said About the Bible

Ulysses S. Grant—"To the influence of this book we are indebted for all the progress made in true civilization, and to this book we must look as our guide in the future."

Patrick Henry—"There is a Book worth all other books which were ever printed."

Thomas Jefferson—"The studious perusal of the sacred volume will make better citizens, better fathers and better husbands."

Abraham Lincoln—"This great book . . . is the best gift God has given to man . . . "

President Woodrow Wilson—"A man has found himself when he has found his relation to the rest of the universe, and here is the Book in which those relations are set forth."

William Lyon Phelps—"Western civilization is founded upon the Bible; all our ideas, our wisdom, our philosophy, our literature, our art, our ideals come more from the Bible than all other books put together."

John Quincy Adams—"Great is my veneration for the Bible."

Sir William Blackstone—"The Bible has always been regarded as part of the Common Law of England."

Samuel Taylor Coleridge—"For more than a thousand years, the Bible, collectively taken, has gone hand in hand with civilization, science, law—in short, with the moral and intellectual cultivation of the species, always supporting and leading the way."

Charles Dickens—"The New Testament is the best book the world has ever known or will know."

Cecil B. DeMille—"After more than 60 years of almost daily reading of the Bible, I never fail to find it always new and marvelously in tune with the changing needs of every day."

William Gladstone—"The Bible was stamped with speciality of origin, and an immeasurable distance separates it from all competitors."

Johann Wolfgang von Goethe—"The Bible grows more beautiful as we grow in our understanding of it."

Immanuel Kant—"The Bible is the greatest benefit which the human race has ever experienced." "A single line in the Bible has consoled me more than all the books I ever read besides."

Robert E. Lee—"The Bible is a book in comparison with which all others in my eyes are of minor importance . . . "

John Locke—"The Bible is one of the greatest blessings bestowed by God on the children of man."

Jean Jacques Rousseau—"I must confess to you that the majesty of the Scriptures astonishes me. . . . "

Galileo—"I believe that the intention of Holy Writ was to persuade men of the truths necessary to salvation. . . . "

Isaac Newton—"I account the Scriptures of God the most sublime philosophy."

Roger Bacon—"I wish to show that there is one wisdom which is perfect, and that this contained in the Scriptures."

E. S. Bates—"No individual, no Caesar or Napoleon, has had such a part in the world's history as this book."

Henry De Lubac—"The Bible makes an extraordinary impression on the historian. . . . no where else can be found anything in the least like it."

Blanche Mary Kelly—"The most stupendous book, the most sublime literature, even apart from its sacred character, in the history of the world."

I. Friedlander—" . . . the Bible . . . has called into being a system of morality which has become the corner-stone of human civilization."

A. M. Sullivan—"The cynic who ignores, ridicules or denies the Bible, spurning its spiritual rewards and aesthetic excitement, contributes to his own moral anemia."

The Bible claims to be inerrant and Jesus Christ claimed the Bible was inerrant. If the Bible claims inerrancy and this is wrong, then the Bible contains errors and is wrong on a critical subject: its own authority. But then Jesus would also be wrong. Indeed, if the Bible and Jesus were both wrong on this point, they could have been wrong on any point. It seems logical that granting a position of biblical errancy leaves one sinking within a spiritual quagmire. Subjectivism and uncertainty concerning divine revelation can only result in either agnosticism or blind trust on any given Scripture or teaching of Scripture. In other words, if the Bible contains errors, can we be certain we are capable of determining where it speaks truth? If the answer is yes, then on what logical basis is the judgment made?

On the other hand, if a rational defense of inerrancy can be made, then, given the conditions under which it was written, it is exceedingly difficult to reject the thesis that the Bible is the inspired Word of God. The Bible was written in Hebrew and Greek, two extremely different languages (plus some Aramaic), by more than 40 different authors from many walks of life during a vast period of 1,500 years. It was not written by a single author over a period of a few years. The Bible was laboriously hand-copied on perishable materials. It was not typed with a modern computer on high quality reading paper. Over 3,000 years, from 1500 B.C. to 1600 A.D., biblical parchment was frequently subject to the stresses of weather, human neglect, political and military upheavals, and deliberate destruction. It was not protected in a modern climate-controlled library. Given these and other adverse conditions, if the Bible were only written by men, it would *necessarily* contain a good number of errors. But if it is actually errorless, then given the thousands of details in its contents and its specific predictions of the future, such inerrancy cannot reasonably be accounted for *apart* from divine inspiration and preservation.

Biblical Authority

Why do we think it is vital for everyone to investigate the issue of the authority of the Bible? Because of its teachings. Again, the Bible is the single most important book the world has ever known. To be ignorant concerning its claims and contents constitutes an abdication of personal responsibility.

If the Bible *is* the Word of God, then its importance to every person and every culture is obvious. Religious scripture that is obviously a human product, or false or mythic or fraudulent, can hardly command our attention as the inspired Word of God. And, despite what anyone claims and no matter how offensive we are to some for saying it, this is the lot of all non-biblical scripture. So the only question is whether or not this is also the case for the Bible. If the Bible is the inerrant Word of God, and if it authoritatively answers the fundamental questions of life, then who can ignore its message? If the Bible accurately tells us who *God* is, who *we* are, *why* we are here, and what *happens* when we die, there is not a living soul anywhere who could fail to be impressed. If the Bible gives us true absolutes in a world of relatives, there are profound implications. Who wants to live a life of uncertainty when they can actually know the truth?

Indeed, the plague of the modern world is its own relativism—in ethics, law, politics, sexuality, education, psychotherapy, medicine, religion, business, and everything else. If people live only for themselves and do whatever they want—often in disregard of others' welfare—it is because they feel life is meaningless and that nothing finally matters. If there is no final authority in anything, and if when you die you are gone forever, why not live any way you please?

It would be difficult to deny that if people today merely lived by the Ten Commandments, most of our social ills would be solved or greatly reduced. People don't because they do not really believe those words and commandments came from God. And they certainly don't believe that God will hold them personally accountable in the next life for the kind of life they lived here on earth. But what if they are wrong?

In essence, helping people to believe in the Bible and live by its precepts is the single most important issue for our nation's direction and future. It is the one single thing that would solve most of our problems immediately, heal our nation, and prosper us again in every way.

Non-Christians, of course, aren't going to start believing in the Bible through osmosis. It is only through Gospel evangelism by Christians and personal discipleship that this occurs. But with God's blessing, it clearly is possible to reach tens of millions with salvation, and for Christianity to once again start exerting such a cultural influence that even non-Christians will, by choice, live according to generally biblical precepts.

But if only the Church can save our nation from the perilous direction it is headed, then the Church must be fully persuaded as to biblical authority and inerrancy. Unfortunately, many in the Church are no longer sure of their spiritual moorings.

When God's people again honor God and His Word, then He will again honor our nation. In the meantime, as church historian Dr. Harold Lindsell so clearly pointed out in his book by the same title, *The Battle for the Bible* will continue within and without the church. And as always, the victors will be the diligent.

Whatever one's view of the Bible, it stands as written and can be frankly investigated and evaluated by anyone who wishes. We think it is significant that given two thousand years of the most intense scrutiny by critics and skeptics, millions of people in the modern era continue to believe the Bible is the literal inerrant Word of God and argue that it can be rationally defended as such. Can members of any other religious faith in the world logically defend such a claim concerning their own scripture?

As sad (and ironic) as it is, the "battle" over inerrancy lies primarily *within* the Evangelical Church. This is not a result of any defect in the defense of biblical inerrancy, but has occurred for a variety of reasons. Much of it has to do with infection by liberal theology, higher critical methodologies (source, form, and redaction criticism), and the premises of secular culture, not the biblical text itself. The battle lies between those who maintain the complete inerrancy of Scripture and those who limit the inerrancy of Scripture to matters of faith and practice, leaving biblical history, geography, and science open to the possibility of error.

A generation ago, when someone said, "I believe in the inspiration of the Bible," the meaning was generally understood. It meant this person believed the Bible was inerrant. As the doctrine became increasingly questioned, however, the list of descriptive adjectives needed to say the same thing grew longer and longer. Consider the following chart as an illustration:

The Initial Phrase: "I Believe in the Inspiration of the Bible"

Progressive Qualifications on the Term Inspiration *by Liberal, Neo-Orthodox, and Some Evangelical Theologians:*	*Conservative Response and Biblical Support:*
1. The denial that individual words were inspired	1. The belief in *verbal* inspiration (Matthew 4:4; Romans 3:2)
2. The denial that the entire Bible was inspired (limited inspiration)	2. The belief in verbal *plenary* (complete) inspiration (2 Timothy 3:16; 2 Peter 1:21)
3. The denial that inspiration requires infallibility (*fallible* inspiration)	3. The belief in verbal plenary *infallible* inspiration (God doesn't lie; Titus 1:2; cf. Hebrews 6:18)
4. The denial that infallibility equals inerrancy, i.e., to say the Bible is infallible is not to say it is inerrant (the term infallible vs. inerrant)	4. The belief in verbal plenary infallible *inerrant* inspiration (cf. John 17:17)
5. The denial that inerrancy extends to all parts of Scripture (inerrancy only in matters of faith and practice, i.e., limited inspiration again)	5. The belief in verbal plenary infallible inerrant *unlimited* inspiration

If one were to accept the increasing qualifications on the term *inspiration,* one would now have to say "I believe in the verbal, plenary, infallible, inerrant, unlimited, inspiration of the Bible" merely to declare what was clearly understood a generation ago by "I believe in the inspiration of the Bible."

Limited Inerrancy?

These qualifications have failed at every level they have been attempted. This is the case with the most recent "limited inerrancy" view held among some evangelicals, who argue that only this view squares with the facts. They claim, e.g., that the Bible is inerrant in doctrine but not in science. How should we respond? Let's begin by noting with the biblical scholar Dr. Gleason Archer the issue involved and the requirements needed for the full inerrancy position to be established:

> ...a new school of revisionists has risen to prominence, and this school poses a vigorous challenge to biblical inerrancy and yet lays claim to being truly and fully evangelical.... Proponents of this approach invariably argue that they alone are the honest and credible defenders of scriptural authority because the "phenomena of Scripture" include demonstrable errors (in matters of history and science, at least), and therefore full inerrancy cannot be sustained with any kind of intellectual integrity....

> In answer to this claim, it is incumbent on consistent Evangelicals to show two things: (1) the infallible authority of Scripture is rendered logically untenable if the original manuscripts contained any such errors and (2) no specific charge of falsehood or mistake can be successfully maintained in the light of all the relevant data.... In other words, we must first show that the alternative of infallibility without inerrancy is not a viable option at all, for it cannot be maintained without logical self-contradiction. And, second, we must show that every asserted proof of mistake in the original manuscripts of Scripture is without foundation when examined in the light of the established rules of evidence.[3]

As we will seek to show, the "limited inerrancy" position collapses on two fronts. First, nowhere does the Bible make such a distinction; to the contrary, *it assumes full inerrancy*. The "limited inerrancy" view never originated from the claims of Scripture, only from its supposedly fallible contents, an assumption that when examined critically has never proven itself a credible theory, let alone a demonstrable fact. Second, the theological parts of the Bible are inseparable from the non-theological portions. Matters of faith (doctrine) and practice (morality) are intimately tied to matters of science and history. In other words, if we accept errors in the areas of science and history, it is impossible to maintain inerrancy in matters of faith and practice. Consider for a moment how the limited inerrancy position collapses when we evaluate this basic thesis: maintaining inerrancy in matters of doctrine and morality but accepting errors in matters of science and history.

We can illustrate the inseparable relationship between these two areas with two examples: A) in the area of science, with the biblical fact of creation, and B) in the area of history, with the biblical fact of Christ's resurrection. In each case the teaching of Scripture is clear. In the area of science, if we accept errors at one point, what happens to theology at another point? For example, if a literal, supernatural, six-day creation is rejected in favor of something like theistic evolution in deference to the "fact" of the modern scientific theory of evolution, it implicates both Jesus and the Apostle Paul in error. If so, Adam and Eve were not originally created by God as our first parents as Jesus taught (Matthew 19:4-5), and six literal days becomes six hundred million years of slow evolutionary progress necessary for producing man. If so, then Adam was not the first man, death did not arrive through Adam, and further Eve was not created from Adam's side, and therefore the Apostle Paul was in error for teaching these things (Romans 5:12-19; 1 Corinthians 15:42-49; 1 Timothy 2:1-14). If we assume the Bible is in error on the creation account because we choose to believe in the scientifically discredited theory of evolution, it is not just the credibility of the creation account that suffers but everything logically based on it, which is a *great* deal more, as Henry Morris documents in *Biblical Creationism: What Each Book of the Bible Teaches About Creation and the Flood.* If we reject a literal reading of Genesis chapters 1–11, then "The only other honest alternative would seem to be to abandon our professed belief in biblical inspiration and authority altogether."[4] Darwin himself rejected the book of Genesis because of his belief in evolution. But he then found it necessary to reject the entire Old Testament because of its integral relationship to Genesis. And, of course, one cannot logically discard the Old Testament without discarding the New Testament which is based on it.

To give up Genesis, therefore, is to give up Christianity. Regardless, the events of science (creation) and history (the resurrection) are integrally tied to matters of faith and practice as the chart below shows.

Science and History/Faith and Practice

A. Facts Related to the Biblical Creation (Science)

Related Area of Faith/Practice (Theological and Moral)

1. Six literal days (Genesis 1–2:3)

1. The Sabbath observance is based on the literal six-day creation account (Exodus 20:8-11)

2. Adam and Eve as literal persons (Genesis 3)

2. The Divine institution of marriage and prohibition of divorce and homosexuality are dependent on the creation account (Genesis 2:23-24; Matthew 19:4-5) (See our *The Facts on Homosexuality* for the importance of the creation account concerning homosexuality.)

3. Eve was created from Adam's side (Genesis 3:2-22)

3. The role of men and women in marriage and the church is based on the priority of Adam in creation (1 Timothy 2:12-14; Ephesians 5:22-32)

4. Adam as the first created man (Genesis 2:5-7; 1 Corinthians 15:21, 45) and his subsequent fall

4. The imputation of Adam's sin and the entrance of death into the world is based on Adam being the first man (Romans 5:12-19); the fact of our physical resurrection is tied to Adam's fall (1 Corinthians 15:21-22; 42-49)

B. Facts related to the Resurrection of Christ (History)

Related Areas of Faith/Practice

1. The resurrection as space-time history, not religious allegory or myth (1 Corinthians 15:4-8)

1. The resurrection is proof of Christ's Messiahship (Luke 24:44-7), incarnation (Philippians 2:1-10), and of coming divine judgment (Acts 17:31)

2. The resurrection was physical not spiritual (Luke 24:39)

2. The resurrection of our body and the validity of Christian faith are both tied to the physical nature of Christ's resurrection (1 Corinthians 15:12-22; 42-50)

3. Christ resurrected from genuine death (John 19:30-35; Luke 23:46; Mark 15:44-45)	3. Propitiation/justification and salvation in general are based on Christ having truly died (Romans 4:25; 1 Peter 2:24)
4. Christ was raised to eternal life (Romans 6:2-10)	4. Christ's resurrection parallels regeneration to eternal life (John 3:16; 5:24; 6:47); The symbol of baptism commemorates Christ's (and ours) resurrection to new life (Romans 6); the symbol of communion commemorates Christ's death (1 Corinthians 11:23-26; Matthew 26:26-28)

Clearly then, the areas of science and history can be inseparably related to matters of faith and practice. It is therefore logically impossible to maintain the "limited inerrancy" view—that the Bible is *without* error in its doctrinal and moral teaching but *with* error in teachings concerning science and history. If the credibility of Christian doctrine and morality is directly related to the credibility of what the Bible teaches in the areas related to science and history—and the latter aren't credible—then how can the teachings based upon them be considered credible? In other words, to charge one with error is to implicate the other with error. There is no escaping this conclusion.

In addition, note that the resurrection, besides being a historical event, is also a miraculous event and as such related negatively to the domain of science. If materialistic science is the authority by which we judge "scientific error" to be in the Bible, how do we safely preserve the truth of Christian doctrine and yet retain the absolute authority of science? Every major doctrine of Scripture is intimately tied to the supernatural (God, creation, incarnation, virgin birth, Jesus' Messianic role, prophecy, miracles, atonement, salvation, eschatology, and so on). If presuppositional and theoretical scientific naturalism is the authority, then Christianity is clearly false, for miracles are impossible by definition, no God exists, and Jesus was only a man.

Indeed, if there are genuine mistakes or errors in the "earthly" portions of Scripture, those having to do with science and history, which we *can* test, how can we safely assume inerrancy in the more crucial "heavenly" areas, those areas we *can't* test, such as salvation by grace through faith alone? And if the biblical authors wrote carelessly in the important "little" details of history, how can we trust they wrote flawlessly in the crucial matters of salvation? If, as some evangelicals enamored with higher criticism maintain:

- Daniel was written in 165 B.C., not the sixth century B.C., then it is a rank fraud and forgery, and Jesus was certainly in error in calling Daniel a genuine prophet of God (Matthew 24:15).

- If Isaiah had two or three authors, it, too, is a fraud and the Apostle John was in error ascribing authorship to the traditional prophet (John 12:38-41).

- If Genesis chapters 1–3 and the book of Jonah are legends, "didactic fictions," then Jesus was again in error when He upheld them as history and called Jonah a prophet (Matthew 12:39-41).

If the Jews canonized such obviously fraudulent books, what other part of the canon may we trust? And if New Testament authors made such evident errors in "common knowledge," what can we say about the rest of their reporting?

- If Paul did not write most of his letters, who did, and how can we trust the writings of a fraudulent impersonator?

- If, according to redaction theories, Jesus did not say everything attributed to Him by the Gospel writers, which of His teachings do we trust and which do we question? And how do we know which is which? Aren't we back to the hopeless confusion and nonsense of the Jesus Seminar?

- And if, according to "evangelical" redaction theories, the Holy Spirit *inspired* the writers to record sayings of Jesus that He never actually spoke, can we trust anything the Holy Spirit inspired? Would the

Holy Spirit do this and implicate Himself in deception?

Some evangelicals do believe these things, and this is precisely the issue in the inerrancy debate: the reliability and
authority of Scripture. Not unexpectedly, these kinds of destruc-
tive conclusions often arise from the use of so-called "higher criticism" of the Bible.

How do evangelical errantists defend their views? Those who
reject inerrancy often claim they are actively preserving true
evangelicalism. As Lindsell writes of those errantists who work in
Christian institutions that accept inerrancy:

> Many who hold that the Bible is fallible are deeply con-
> vinced that those who think it infallible are wrong. Rightly
> or wrongly, they think they are doing the Christian faith a
> service by staying where they are and working to delete any
> commitment to an infallible Bible from the creeds and con-
> fessions.... They wish to deliver those who believe in it
> from their error. The decision to remain where they are
> and to work for this change is based on the conviction that
> to do so is more important than the ethical dilemma of
> signing statements of faith they do not actually believe.[5]

Others argue the entire issue is blown out of proportion. In
other words, they wonder about the difference between a person
who believes no present translation is 100 percent correct and
an individual who rejects inerrancy but treats the Scripture infallibly in matters of faith and practice. After all, no evangelical
errantist believes the Bible is "full of errors," and some would
probably be reluctant even to claim a single demonstrable error.
Are the two positions all that divergent? What if the errantist, in
good conscience, truly does *not* believe the Bible claims its own
inerrancy? And what if he staunchly defends the inerrancy of
Scripture in matters relating to salvation? What if he simply does
not believe that biblical inerrancy is necessary for God to achieve
all the purposes He intended in revealing His Word? In the end,
what is the difference between an inerrantist, who believes in
something he cannot finally prove (inerrancy can't be proven
without the autographs), and the errantist, who also believes in
something he cannot prove (errors in Scripture)? Do not both

positions result in the same practical end: the infallibility of Scripture for all of God's *intended* purposes, revealing the one true God, His plan of salvation, and everything necessary for the Christian's spiritual health?

To answer that question, we must understand that the issue surrounding inerrancy is not merely the ability of Scripture to accomplish God's purposes, but to establish God's character. All Christians agree God is a God of truth, omnipotent and sovereign. If He did inspire or permit errors in the autographs, there are implications for His character and nature. Further, how can we know where the errors are? In the end, we would not know if God *or* His Word could be trusted. And how can we be truly certain the Scripture will provide all that Christians need for spiritual health if Christians themselves are not certain what parts to believe?

The issue is more important than the "limited inerrantist" supposes. Can a fallible scripture, which demands individual uncertainty over the location of truth, really accomplish the will of God? As Dr. Archer points out, the doctrine of inerrancy and the doctrine of salvation are more closely tied than some Christians think:

> God's written revelation came in inerrant form, free from discrepancies or contradictions, and this inerrancy contributes to its achieving its saving purpose. If there were genuine mistakes of any sort in the original manuscripts, it would mean, obviously, that the Bible contains error along with truth. As such it would become subject to human judgment, just like any other religious document. The validity of such judgment, of course, depends on the judge's own knowledge and wisdom. If he rejects the truth of the scriptural record simply because it seems to him to be unlikely or improbable, then he is in danger of eternal loss. The charge of scriptural self-contradiction or factual error is to be taken quite seriously; it cannot be brushed off as a matter of minor consequence. At stake is the credibility and reliability of the Bible as authentic revelation from God. . . . For this reason there is no such thing as an inconsequential scriptural error. If any part of the Bible can be

proved to be in error, then any other part of it—including the doctrinal, theological parts—may also be in error.[6]

Further, inerrancy has implications for how we treat Scripture. The words of men must be perceived differently than the words of *God*. One we examine critically, one we bow before. If our finite minds must be the rational judge of what is Scripture, where does such a process end? After all, does even the central salvation truth of Scripture seem probable or reasonable? That God became a Man to die on a cross to freely forgive the sin of the world two millennia ago?

On the surface, that idea seems difficult, if not foolish (1 Corinthians 1:23). Indeed, our reasonable minds would not normally accept that proposition. And what about the rationalistic or theological problems inherent in biblical revelation on the Trinity, the hypostatic union, the virgin birth (an absolutely key doctrine for Christology and soteriology), the method of inspiration, the imputation of sin, the means of atonement, or eternal punishment? If we are competent to judge the truth or error of biblical *history* on rationalistic grounds, are we not, then, at least competent to question the legitimacy of biblical *theology* on rationalistic grounds?

The issue is not the practical "closeness" of the two evangelical camps, but the theological implications and demonstrable negative results that flow from a position of errancy. For example, consider the historic Arian controversy of the fourth century where one letter in a word (one "iota," the Greek letter "i") made a crucial difference for subsequent historical theology and accurate Christology. Dr. Harold O. J. Brown illustrates the importance and implications of the matter:

> Is this [inerrancy controversy] not another example of the sort of issue that separated the orthodox, *homoousian* party from the moderate Arian *homiousians* in the fourth century; nothing more than an *iota*? Indeed, the inerrancy controversy is similar to the Arian controversy in that the difference between the positions appears to be small but in reality is of tremendous significance. To have abandoned the Nicene definition of the Son as *homoousios to patri*, of one substance with the Father, for *homoiousios to patri*, of similar substance with the Father, would have undermined

the basic structure of Trinitarian faith with its fundamental confession that the Son *is* God, identical in nature to the Father although distinct in His personhood from Him. In addition, to abandon the term *homoousios* would have been to confess that the whole church, for decades, had been fundamentally mistaken as to the true nature of Jesus the Messiah. The parallel with the inerrancy controversy is this: to abandon the definition "inerrant autographs, virtually inerrant copies" would also be a step of tremendous magnitude; it would undermine the basic structure of Biblical authority with its principle that the Scripture *is* the Word of God. In addition, to abandon the definition would be to confess that the whole church has been mistaken about inerrancy for seventeen and more centuries. It is important to see precisely where the conflict lies in order to understand the crucial significance of the inerrancy debate and of its ultimate outcome for conservative Protestantism, indeed, for Christianity as a whole....

We must frankly acknowledge the apparent practical similarity between our views and those of the opposing party. To see the similarity and not to realize that it is only apparent would be very dangerous, for this reason we must point it out, even though initially it might appear to make our position excessively pedantic and a trifle ridiculous to those whose attention it has not yet caught. No one would mistake the poisonous rattlesnake for a harmless variety, because the rattle proclaims his deadly difference. Unfortunately the even more poisonous coral snake closely resembles harmless snakes and is frequently mistaken for them with grave consequences.[7]

Dr. Brown's point is well taken. The beautiful mountain king snake is harmless; the equally beautiful coral snake is deadly. Both have great surface similarities but the beauty of one is a terrible deception for the unwary. Many things in life that seem innocent or inconsequential are actually anything but.

Inerrancy and Historic Watersheds

The history of Christianity reveals that in every age the Church has dealt with one or more key theological issues that are integrally related to its own health and vitality. Such issues typically developed as a result of the attacks by critics, heretics, or enemies of Christianity and led to greater precision of doctrinal formulation. In the early era of the Church (the first through fourth centuries) key issues that were decided included the extent of the New Testament canon (the 27 books of the N.T. vs. false claimants), the tri-personal nature of the Godhead (three persons versus one person) and the divine nature of the Trinity (the deity of Jesus Christ and the Holy Spirit). In the middle ages (the fifth through fourteenth centuries) the nature of the atonement became a watershed issue. In the Reformation era (the sixteenth through seventeenth centuries) the nature of and the proper place of church tradition were vitally reaffirmed. In the modern era (the eighteenth through twentieth centuries) the question of biblical authority has become the prominent issue.

Although biblical authority had seen the beginnings of challenge in the Renaissance period, skepticism fully blossomed in the era of the Enlightenment, a period that left in its wake a cancerous theological liberalism that wasted the Church from within. As a result, for more than a century, liberals and conservatives have opposed one another over the issue of biblical inspiration and authority. However, not until the 1960's did the issue of inerrancy come to the forefront for conservatives, largely as a result of the increasingly perceived influence of the liberal methodology upon evangelicalism itself. That is, the impact of liberal higher criticism and its hermeneutical presuppositions were increasingly being felt within the ranks of the Church and negatively affecting its view of Scripture.

The debate over inerrancy represents a stand for the absolute authority and trustworthiness of Scripture. Perhaps no single issue is more important to the Christian Church today. How the individual and the Church view the Bible influences how the individual and the Church view almost everything else. And if "everything else" is not viewed biblically, through God's eyes, it can only be viewed humanistically, to one degree or another, through man's eyes. Of all the major issues the Church has decided, this is clearly the watershed issue for our age.

Definition and Explanation of Inerrancy

The doctrine of inerrancy claims:

1. To constitute an absolutely errorless original text.

Inerrancy means that what the Bible teaches is true without a single error in the original manuscripts. Dr. Paul Feinberg defines inerrancy as follows:

> Inerrancy means that when all facts are known, the Scriptures in their original autographs and properly interpreted will be shown to be wholly true in everything that they affirm, whether that has to do with doctrine or morality or with the social, physical, or life sciences.[8]

A more concise definition would be, "What Scripture says, God says—through human agents and without error."[9]

2. To apply equally to all parts of Scripture.

Inerrancy must apply equally to all parts of Scripture as it was originally written. Again, a belief in limited inerrancy demands the impossible—that a fallible exegete become an infallible discerner and interpreter of the "Word of God" within the Scriptures. This only opens the door for confusion and uncertainty, undergirded by either subjectivism or personal bias.

3. To be limited to the proper application of hermeneutics.

Higher critical interpretive methods assume errors in the Bible and have little trouble "finding" them. However, the proper way to interpret the Bible involves a respect for the text as given until proven otherwise. In other words, due attention is given to claims for biblical authority. Also, interpretation must involve an objective and impartial methodology.* The need for such an approach is obvious. If one does not first determine the authority of Scripture and second the *correct meaning* of a text, one is incapable of saying whether or not it is true or false. Here, we must also understand that inerrancy is related to the *intent* of Scripture. For example, when the intent of the writer is to *record*

---

*See W. C. Kaiser Jr., "Legitimate Hermeneutics" in Norman Geisler (ed.), *Inerrancy*, pp. 116-47.

a lie or error by someone, the fact of a lie or error can hardly deny inerrancy, for inerrancy only affirms that what is recorded is recorded accurately. What the Bible *records* must be distinguished from what the Bible approves.

The doctrine of inerrancy does not claim:

1. To be absolutely proven.

The doctrine of inerrancy cannot guarantee the final solution to every alleged problem passage. Given the present limited state of human knowledge, no one can logically expect proof when the means of proof are absent. Proof of inerrancy is thus limited by our present state of knowledge. Nevertheless, such realities in no way deny or disprove inerrancy, especially when the weight of the evidence so strongly supports inerrancy. The fact that so many opportunities exist within the biblical record to disprove inerrancy and yet it remains capable of rational defense after all these years is certainly impressive. The fact that, historically, alleged errors are routinely proven later to be truths when more knowledge becomes available is equally impressive.

2. To refer to manuscript copies or translations.

Copies and translations may be considered inerrant only to the degree they reproduce the originals. For obvious reasons, none of them do this 100 percent. Nevertheless, an accurate translation, based as it is upon a 99+ percent original text, virtually reproduces the originals and the remaining 1 percent is present in the variant readings. Thus we may say without being proven wrong that we have "inerrant originals and virtually inerrant copies."[10]

3. Absolute precision.

Approximations are not errors. To illustrate, no one would argue it was an error to say the following:

- I earned $20,000 last year (it was really $20,200).
- I received my B.A. degree in 1978 (it was June of 1978).

- In Montgomery's book, it states.... (Montgomery is the dominant author and editor).

- What a lovely sunset (the earth's rotation appears as the sun setting).

- Look! There just ain't no free lunch! (breaking the rules of grammar to emphasize a point).

- Steve went to the store (he also stopped by the pool on the way back).

In the interest of improved communication we often use approximations, or are technically incorrect in grammar, number, science, or history. This is also true of the biblical writers: their purpose was to communicate, not to write in technicalities.

Thus, inerrancy does not demand the Bible be written in the technical language or knowledge of modern twentieth-century science, which would certainly keep it a book closed to all but the specialist. Regardless, such scientific precision would still, technically, not make the Bible correct to the last degree. For which centuries' scientific precision do we speak of—first, twentieth, or thirtieth? Also, precision may become so precise as to be awkward or useless. To speak of a setting sun is not error in spite of its scientific imprecision. Jesus called the mustard seed the smallest of all seeds (Matthew 13:32), and this was perfectly true for His hearers; it was the smallest of all the seeds they planted. This author can still remember speaking with a Bible professor concerned because Jesus was "in error on this point." But science has still probably not discovered the smallest of all created seeds. What if Jesus had named *this* still undiscovered seed, or named the smallest seed *currently* known to twentieth-century botany? In either case, it would leave him doubted and misunderstood by His hearers. If Jesus were to name the still undiscovered seed, by what name would He call it? He would be technically inerrant, but considered errant based on His listener's current knowledge.

For similar reasons, inerrancy does not require strict grammatic, semantic, numeric, or historic precision. September 14, 15, or 16 is still, properly, the middle of the month. Inerrancy also does not exclude the use of nonliteral, figurative language (allegory, personification, hyperbole) or various literary genre (apocalyptic, drama, poetry, parable). Indeed, to exclude these would rob Scripture of much of its richness and universal appeal.

Inerrancy does not demand verbatim exactness when the New Testament quotes the Old. A New Testament author has the right to give the basic idea or summarize for purpose of brevity. Only if a New Testament quotation denied or contradicted an Old Testament Scripture would there be an error—but this never occurs.

In a similar fashion, inerrancy does not demand that any given biblical event or account be exhaustively reported. As Dr. Charles Ryrie points out: "[T]he inerrancy of the Bible means simply that the Bible tells the truth. Truth can and does include approximations, free quotations, language of appearances, and different accounts of the same event as long as those do not contradict."[11]

To illustrate, let's say that two police officers are called into a bar to break up a fist fight. Recalling the incident to a friend three weeks later, one of the combatants says, "I would have won that fight, but this cop came in and broke it up." Is his statement an error because he failed to mention the presence of the second policeman? Obviously not. If a newspaper account of the event read: "Two policemen end noted brawl in local bar," and the "other" policeman was actually a woman, is it an error? What if it really was an English pub? Is this an error? Again, no. Would we assume one statement was in error or that the reporter was lying? Of course not, because we could see from the context both statements were true.

In a similar fashion, it is good to remember that looking back at biblical events we do not always have access to the entire context or story, only the summarized reporting. Why should we assume there is an error or contradiction without the information necessary to prove there really is one?

Inspiration and Inerrancy

In the clearest of terms the Bible declares it is the inspired Word of God: "All Scripture is God-breathed [*theopneustos*] . . ."

(2 Timothy 3:16). In what sense is the Bible inspired? Biblical inspiration is verbal (extending to the very words, not just the ideas, of Scripture), plenary (extending equally to every part of Scripture), and what is termed *perspicuous*—sufficiently clear for the average person to understand and be spiritually nourished without recourse to scholarly or technical insight.

Non-biblical theories of inspiration include *verbal dictation*, which undercuts the uniquely human input in recording Scripture, *limited* or *partial inspiration*, which undercuts the authority of Scripture, since we cannot know what is inspired and what is not, and merely *human inspiration*, which undercuts the very concept of revealed Scripture since it is not divine inspiration to begin with. If the Bible is no more than human "religious genius," it could hardly be accorded greater authority than other works of human inspiration or religious genius.

Biblically speaking, the mere fact of verbal, plenary, divine inspiration virtually demands a belief in inerrancy. To separate inspiration from inerrancy is to "separate" God from His attributes.[12] For example, is it credible to believe that a *holy* God who identifies Himself as "the God of truth" would inspire error? Or that an *omnipotent* God would not safeguard His own words from corruption during the process of inspiring human agents? Is it reasonable to believe that a just, merciful, and loving God engages in limited inspiration and then leaves it to His sinful and imperfect children to attempt to discover where the truth is—knowing in advance the hopelessness of the task, and the subjectivity and unbelief it would foster? What would be the point of inspiration?

The only logical option is to maintain that whatever God speaks is truth and only truth, for, as Scripture declares, God "does not lie" (Titus 1:2) because "it is impossible for God to lie" (Hebrews 6:18). As Dr. Lindsell observes, "The very nature of inspiration renders the Bible infallible, which means that it cannot deceive us. It is inerrant in that it is not false, mistaken, or defective.... Inspiration involved infallibility from start to finish. God the Holy Spirit by nature cannot lie or be the author of untruth. If the Scripture is inspired at all it must be infallible. If any part of it is not infallible, then that part cannot be inspired. If inspiration allows for the possibility of error, then inspiration ceases to be inspiration."[13]

Again, if the process of inspiration cannot be trusted, of what value is it? Inspiration has no value, let alone credibility, if "all it does is guarantee us the Bible has in it both truth and error."[14] Defective or deceptive inspiration could certainly be expected in something like New Age channeling and other forms of spiritism, but to ascribe it to an infinitely perfect God is hardly worthy of His perfection.

If we assume the truth of a limited inspiration, or limited inerrancy, shouldn't we begin correcting Scripture accordingly so that its teachings are consistent with the "facts" as we know them? To cite an example of one Scripture that surely would need the following revision, consider 2 Timothy 3:16:

> Most Scripture is partially God-breathed and profitable (usually) for teaching (except where wrong), rebuking (assuming you are certain you have the authority), correcting (when you find the inerrant parts), and training in righteousness (unless it concerns sexist and culturally prejudiced moralizing) so that the man of God may (possibly) be thoroughly equipped for most good works.

If the Bible is merely a humanly inspired document, then it should be treated as such, for it would just as certainly be subject to human correction as it would contain human error. However, if it is truly inspired by God, then it must *not* be assumed errant without sufficient evidence, lest we impugn the character and majesty of the infinite God who so graciously gave it to us. It is after all, *His* word. The notion of an infinite God speaking through men is far, far different than the notion of men speaking by themselves. As E. J. Young states in *Thy Word Is Truth:*

> If the Bible is the Word of God we certainly may not approach it believing that we are capable of subjecting it to the test of our own unaided reason. If we think that we can employ theories and hypotheses which conflict with the express statements of the Bible, we deceive only ourselves, and the reason why we deceive ourselves is that we are thus setting up the human mind above God. . . . Nor in our study, may we advance theories which conflict with what the Bible

itself says. How then must we approach the Bible? There is only one way; it is the way of humility. We are coming unto the message which the Creator of heaven and earth has given. Ours must be the receptive attitude. We are to pattern all our thought upon what God has said. We shall never understand the Bible aright until we accept it for what it claims to be, the infallible Word of the ever-living and true God.[15]

Inspiration guarantees the truth of what is stated, but it does not mean everything inspired is necessarily of equal importance. To cite an obvious example, the theological content of Romans chapters 3-8 is more important to us than the census data of the Israeli tribes recorded in Leviticus chapters 1-4. Both are equally inspired and neither is unimportant (Leviticus was crucial to the Israelis), but both are not equally important for us today spiritually. All Scripture is truth, but some of its truth is more central (for example, the atonement) and some is more peripheral (the number of men slain in a given war):

> ...inspiration means that the record of what is said and done is correct. It does not mean that everything that God did and said is recorded. It does not mean that everything recorded is of equal importance, but every part of it is necessary to the purpose of the record, and no part is unimportant. One part is no more inspired than any other part.[16]

Again, no Scripture is unimportant, however mundane. As any good quality commentary will show, some of the greatest treasures can actually be found in Leviticus, what some consider one of the most "boring" books in the Bible. It should also be remembered that even when a particular Scripture's commandments are not directed to a later generation, such as the Old Testament sacrificial regulations, they will nevertheless still possess special spiritual *significance* to or necessary practical *instruction* for them: "For everything that was written in the past was written to teach us..." (Romans 15:4).[17]

Inerrancy is a genuinely important topic in the Church today and, in light of Church history, it represents one among several truly watershed issues. Thus, the debate that exists should not be surprising. We have shown what biblical inerrancy means and the importance of the relationship of biblical inspiration to the doctrine of inerrancy. In our next chapter, we will cite some of the evidence for inerrancy.

Chapter 15

Biblical Inerrancy:
The Evidence

In this chapter we will examine the strength of inerrancy from the perspective of (1) God's character, (2) the biblical testimony to inerrancy, (3) the historic and prophetic accuracy of the biblical text, (4) the Bible's scientific accuracy, (5) the lack of proven error in the Bible, and (6) the weakness of the alternate position concerning errancy.

1. The Strength of Inerrancy from the Nature of God

Many errantists, that is people who believe the Bible contains errors, do not view inerrancy as a necessary corollary of inspiration; nor do they see any conflict between errancy and the character of God. Pinnock argues, "Although this position [of inerrancy] may seem reasonable at first sight, it is difficult to see how human beings would be capable of drawing such inferences from the fact of inspiration. God uses fallible spokesmen all the time to deliver his word, and it does not follow that the Bible *must* be otherwise. We are simply not in a position by sheer logic to judge how God ought to have given his Word."[1]

We are convinced otherwise. God does indeed use fallible spokesmen to deliver His word, but this hardly requires us to conclude that God permitted errors during the original inspiring of His word. Inerrancy is a necessary corollary given inspiration by a truthful and holy God. Errancy and Biblical inspiration are simply incompatible, and "sheer logic" can judge the issue because of the immutability of God's character. Would we not expect a God of truth to communicate truthfully? And would we not expect an omnipotent God to safeguard the process of inspiration even though it comes through fallible men? What appears to us as unreasonable is for a righteous God to be *able* to inspire error or to *fail to* exercise the power or means needed to preserve an infallible revelation through fallible instruments. Errancy can certainly be imagined from a Brahman or Krishna or Allah, but not from Yahweh. Put succinctly, "Since God could not conceivably be the agent of falsehood, the Bible must be guaranteed free from any error."[2] Otherwise, how could we "handle *accurately* the word of *truth*" (2 Timothy 2:15)? Indeed, can the *Holy* Spirit inspire error; can the Spirit of *Truth* inspire untruth? The issue is not one of *human* fallibility, but of divine righteousness and divine sovereignty. Why would God permit or inspire error when He is obviously capable of preventing His Word from corruption during the process of inspiration? If we accept the idea of errant inspiration, and are therefore incapable of determining where truth and error lie, we are back to listening to that subversive entity in the Garden who said, "Did God *really* say..." (Genesis 3:1).

To impugn God's righteousness is not the only divine attribute one must discard. To argue God was incapable of inerrantly inspiring fallible men is a denial of both His omnipotence and sovereignty. If God was impotent to preserve His inspiration, He is not truly the omnipotent God. If God is not absolutely in control of free human actions, He is not sovereign. And if He is omnipotent and holy, He is neither loving nor merciful if He communicates errantly and leaves His people in an impossible dilemma over what to trust and how to find it. This would seem to suggest more of a divine apathy or even mischievousness rather than divine communication and compassion.

No, we think it is more logical that an omnipotent God of truth and love would inerrantly preserve His revelation than uncaringly permit its corruption and implicate His holy character. As B. B. Warfield once stated: "Revelation is but half revelation unless it be infallibly communicated; it is but half communicated unless it be infallibly recorded."[3]

If God is holy, righteous, and true, what He speaks must also be holy, righteous, and true for God *cannot* deny Himself (Titus 1:2; 2 Timothy 2:13) and further, it is *impossible* for God to lie (Numbers 23:9; Hebrews 6:17-18). If God is true (John 3:33; 17:3; Romans 3:4) then one would assume that which is God-breathed (2 Timothy 3:16) is also true.

Our conclusion must be that Scripture originated from a holy God, thus the doctrine of inerrancy is primarily a *theological* doctrine and secondarily a bibliological one. As Dr. Harold O. J. Brown points out:

> We contend, therefore, that the doctrine of inerrancy is essentially a theological doctrine, pertaining to the character of God, and only secondarily a bibliological one, pertaining to the nature of the Bible. It is doxological in the sense that it is an expression of praise to the God whom we know as the author of Scripture. To affirm inerrancy is to pay a particular kind of honor to certain aspects of God's nature and character, to deny it, or even simply to refuse to affirm it, is to say either that those aspects are less important than Christians have traditionally thought them to be or that they are not displayed in Scripture.[4]

2. The Strength of Inerrancy from the Revelation of God

In this important section we will briefly show the following: the inspired Old Testament teaches inerrancy; Jesus Himself, God's own Son, teaches inerrancy in the Gospels; the rest of the inspired New Testament teaches inerrancy; and in confirmation we will observe that the Church recognized this Biblical attestation and taught inerrancy for eighteen centuries until the rise of rationalism and higher criticism corrupted the Church from within. The burden of proof is upon those who assert the Bible does not teach inerrancy to prove their thesis. This they have not done.

Thus, in this section we will briefly examine the Bible's testimony to its own inspiration and inerrancy.[5]

Clark Pinnock observes that "in every defense of biblical inerrancy it is maintained that the notion is scriptural, that is, a concept taught by Jesus and the apostles . . . [but] we are forced to ask whether it is really scriptural or simply an inference drawn by godly minds."[6] The answer to this question should be decided by every believer on the basis of Scripture and nothing else. God, not man, is the most competent authority on His own revelation. In brief fashion we will cite relevant Scriptures (NASB) under specific categories to show that the Bible does indeed teach inerrancy. The implications of such a conclusion virtually force us to adopt a belief in inerrancy.

God's description of His Word:

A. *The Old Testament*

Eternal

Isaiah 40:8	The grass withers, the flower fades, but the word of our God stands forever.
Psalm 119:89	Forever O Lord, Thy word is settled in heaven.
Psalm 138:2	I will bow down toward Thy holy temple, and give thanks to Thy name for Thy lovingkindness and Thy truth; For Thou has magnified Thy word according to all Thy name.

Perfect and Trustworthy

Proverbs 30:5,6	Every word of God is tested; He is a shield to those who take refuge in Him. Do not add to His words, lest He reprove you, and you be proved a liar.
Psalm 12:6	The words of the Lord are pure words, as silver tried in a furnace on the earth, refined seven times.
Psalm 18:30	As for God, His way is blameless; the word of the Lord is tried; He is a shield to all who take refuge in Him.
Psalm 19:7,9	The law of the Lord is perfect, restoring the soul ... the judgments of the Lord are true, they are righteous altogether.

True

Psalm 119:43,142,151,160	The word of truth ... Thy law is truth ... all Thy commandments are truth ... the sum of Thy word is truth and every one of Thy righteous ordinances is everlasting.

Holy and Righteous

Psalm 105:42
For He remembered His holy word with Abraham His servant.

Psalm 119:123
My eyes fail with longing for Thy salvation and Thy righteous word.

Psalm 119:140
Thy word is very pure, therefore Thy servant loves it.

Good

Jeremiah 33:14
... I will fulfill the good word which I have spoken ...

Vital (and verbal)

Isaiah 59:21
"And as for Me, this is My covenant with them," says the Lord. "My Spirit which is upon you and My words which I have put in your mouth, shall not depart from your mouth, nor from the mouth of your offspring" says the Lord, "from now and forever."

B. *Jesus Christ and the Gospels*

Eternal

Matthew 24:35
Heaven and earth will pass away, but My words shall not pass away.

Trustworthy

Matthew 5:18
For truly I say to you, until heaven and earth pass away, not the smallest letter or stroke shall pass away from the law, until all is accomplished.

John 5:47
But if you do not believe his [Moses'] writings, how will you believe My words?

John 10:35
... the Scripture cannot be broken ...

John 12:49-50
For I did not speak on My own initiative, but the Father Himself who sent Me has given Me commandment, what to say and what to speak, and I know that His commandment is eternal life; therefore the things I speak, I speak just as the Father has told Me.

John 17:8
... the words which Thou gavest Me, I have given them ...

Luke 16:17	But it is easier for heaven and earth to pass away than for one stroke of a letter of the law to fail.

True

John 17:17	Sanctify them in the truth; Thy word is Truth.

Holy

John 7:16	My teaching is not Mine, but His who sent Me (cf 12:49-50).

Vital (and verbal)

Matthew 4:4	But He answered and said, "It is written, 'Man shall not live on bread alone but on every word that proceeds out of the mouth of God.' "

C. The Rest of the New Testament

Eternal

1 Peter 1:25	But the Word of the Lord abides forever and this is the word which was preached to you.

Inspired

2 Timothy 3:16-17	All Scripture is inspired by God and profitable for teaching, for reproof, for correction for training in righteousness, that the man of God may be adequate, equipped for every good work.[7]
2 Peter 1:20-21	... no prophecy [of Scripture] was ever made by an act of human will, but men moved by the Holy Spirit spoke from God.
2 Peter 3:2, 15-16	"...You should remember the words spoken beforehand by the Holy Prophets and the commandment of the Lord and Savior spoken by the apostles... Our beloved brother Paul, according to the wisdom given him, wrote to you... letters, speaking in them of these things, in which are some things hard to understand, which the untaught and unstable distort, as they do *the rest of the Scriptures...*"

Living and Active

Hebrews 4:12	For the word of God is living and active... (cf. Acts 7:38)

1 Peter 1:23	For you have been born again not of seed which is perishable, but imperishable, that is, through the living and abiding word of God.

True

2 Timothy 2:15	Be diligent to present yourself approved to God as a workman who does not need to be ashamed, handling accurately the word of truth.

Not Human

1 Thessalonians 2:13	And for this reason we also constantly thank God that when you received from us the word of God's message, you accepted it not as the word of men, but for what it really is, the word of God which also performs its work in you who believe.
1 Thessalonians 4:8	...he who rejects this [instruction] is not rejecting man, but the God who gives His Holy Spirit to you.

Holy

2 Timothy 3:15	...from childhood you have known the sacred writings...

Vital (and verbal)

Revelation 22:18-19	I testify to everyone who hears the words of the prophecy of this book; if anyone adds to them, God shall add to him the plagues which are written in this book; and if anyone takes away from the words of the prophecy of this book, God shall take away his part from the tree of life and from the holy city which are written in this book.
1 Corinthians 2:12-13	Now we have received, not the spirit of the world, but the Spirit who is from God, that we might know the things freely given to us by God...in those [words] taught by the Spirit.
Romans 3:2	They have been entrusted with the very words (Gk: *logia)* of God.

Collectively taken, these verses teach the doctrine of inerrancy. In fact, we can't see the possibility of any other conclusion. Although a great deal could be said about each of these verses (and there are scores of others), let us simply ask some plain questions of them. Is it proper to call *errant* writings "holy"? How is inspiration *divine* if it merely guarantees the presence of

324	THE BIBLE: THE MOST UNIQUE BOOK ON EARTH

truth and error—is it not then human, and, like every other book, to be treated like every other book? If we answer "no" by appealing to its unique theological content, how do we know such content is true? If God's Word is eternal, are we content with a certain amount of *eternal* error? What did God mean when He called His Word "perfect," "true," "righteous," "good," "trustworthy," and "pure"? Is "perfection" really "imperfection," or truth really error? Is the trustworthy in fact the doubtful, or the pure actually impure? E. J. Young observes,

> God has revealed to us His Word. What are we to think of Him if this Word is glutted with little annoying inaccuracies? Why could not the omnipotent and omniscient God have taken the trouble to give us a Word that was free from error? Was it not a somewhat discourteous thing for Him to have breathed forth from His mouth a message filled with mistakes? Of course, it was discourteous, it was down-right rude and insulting. The present writer finds it difficult to have much respect for such a God. Does He expect us to worship Him? What kind of a God is He if He has given such an untrustworthy Word to mankind? And this brings us to the heart of the matter. The Scriptures claim to be breathed forth from His mouth, if they partake of error, must not He Himself also partake thereof?
>
> He, of course, tells us that His Word is pure. If there are mistakes in that Word, however, we know better; it is not pure. He tells us that His judgments are righteous, but we know better; as a matter of fact, His judgments are mixed with error. He declares that His law is the truth. His law contains the truth, let us grant Him that, but we know that it contains error. If the autographs of Scripture are marred by flecks of mistake, God simply has not told us the truth concerning His Word. To assume that He could breathe forth a Word that contained mistakes is to say, in effect that God Himself can make mistakes. We must maintain that the original of Scripture is infallible for the simple reason that it came to us directly from God Himself.[8]

As the great London preacher Charles Spurgeon once stated, "This is the book untainted by any error, but is pure, unalloyed, perfect truth. Why? Because God wrote it. Ah! Charge God with

error if you please; tell Him that His book is not what it ought
to be...."[9]

The most important criteria for evaluating inerrancy is the
teaching of Jesus, although God's other Words in the Bible are
no less authoritative. But if Jesus Christ is the example for Christians, then one could argue that limited inerrantists should be
ashamed, for they do not maintain the same confidence in Scripture as that of their Lord and Savior. They claim there are errors
and mistakes and contradictions in the text; therefore they do
not trust it when they think they have sufficient reason for
doubt. But did Jesus ever express any doubts about Scripture at
any time in any manner? Is there the slightest indication He did
not trust Scripture fully? Was there even a single reservation
about one Scripture anywhere? Indeed the strength of the case
for Jesus' view of inerrancy can only be seen by a detailed study
of His absolute trust in and use of Scripture[10]—and this is certainly a strong indication of scriptural inerrancy. If it were otherwise, Jesus would have told us that there were errors in
Scripture and corrected them, but even this is unthinkable for
it presumes either errant inspiration or a lack of providential
preservation of the text (cf. John 14:2). For Jesus, what Scripture
said, God said—period. Not once did He say "This Scripture is
in error" and proceed to correct it. John Wenham points out:

> Surely He would have explained clearly a mingling of
> divine truth and human error in Scripture had He thought
> such to exist. The notion that our Lord was fully aware that
> the view of Holy Scripture current in His day was erro-
> neous, and that He deliberately accommodated His
> teaching to the beliefs of his hearers, will not square with
> the facts. His use of the Old Testament seems altogether too
> insistent, positive, and absolute. He unequivocally main-
> tained that "the Scripture cannot be broken" (John 10:35);
> "Not the smallest letter, not the least stroke of a pen, will by
> any means disappear from the Law..." (Matthew 5:18); "It
> is easier for heaven and earth to disappear than for the least
> stroke of a pen to drop out of the Law" (Luke 16:17).[11]

The weight of these three verses mentioned by Wenham is
impressive indeed when we consider them in more detail. In
Matthew 5:17-19, for example,

The "jot" is the smallest letter of the Hebrew alphabet and the "tittle" is the minute horn or projection that distinguishes consonants of similar form from one another. It would be impossible to think of any expression that would bespeak the thought of the meticulous more adequately than precisely this one used here by our Lord. In respect of the meticulous, our English expression "one letter or syllable" is scarcely equivalent. Could anything establish more conclusively the meticulous accuracy, validity, and truth of the law than the language to which Jesus here attaches his own unique formula of asservation?[12]

In John 10:35, we see that . . .

. . . when he says the Scripture cannot be broken, he is surely using the word "Scripture" in its most comprehensive denotation as including all that the Jews of the day recognized as Scripture, to wit, all the canonical books of the Old Testament. It is of the Old Testament without any reservation or exception that he says, it "cannot be broken." . . . He affirms the unbreakableness of the Scripture in its entirety and leaves no room for any such supposition as that of degrees of inspiration and fallibility. Scripture is inviolable. Nothing less than this is the testimony of our Lord. And the crucial nature of such witness is driven home by the fact that it is in answer to the most serious of charges and in the defense of his most stupendous claim that he bears this testimony.[13]

The above two verses establish the particularity of inerrancy ("jot," "tittle") and the extent of inerrancy (all Scripture). As John Murray notes of Jesus' view, "We found it to be nothing less than that of the infallible character and authority of the Old Testament. A higher view of plenary or verbal inspiration we could not expect to find."[14] Theologian Dr. Charles Ryrie also has relevant comments on these two passages.

A jot is the Hebrew letter *yod*, the smallest letter in that alphabet. It looks much like an English apostrophe. The word tittle means a minor stroke and refers to the almost unnoticeable strokes which distinguish certain Hebrew letters from others. For instance, the tittle that differentiates a *d* (*daleth*) from an *r* (*resh*) is a protrusion that in a

normal font of type would not be more than ¹⁄₁₆ of an
inch. Of course the presence or absence of the tittle could
change the spelling of a word and likely change the meaning. The Lord was emphasizing that every letter of every
word is important, and what those words say in sentences
and paragraphs is completely accurate. In fact, they can
be depended on to be fulfilled exactly as spelled out letter
by letter and word by word in all the promises of the Old
Testament. Such a specific statement by our Lord would
have no meaning if the Scripture were subject to errors in
the text.

John 10:33-36 is another passage where the Lord states that
the Scripture cannot be broken. This is an assertion that
the entire Scripture cannot be broken and that the particular words being quoted on that occasion cannot be
broken. This is only possible because the Scripture is true
in each particular and in all its parts.[15]

Finally, concerning Luke 16:17, if it is *easier* for heaven and
earth to pass from existence than for the "least stroke of a pen"
to be lost, can we possibly believe Jesus thought there were
errors in Scripture? John Warwick Montgomery comments on
another statement by Jesus, this time in Matthew 4:4: "Christ tells
us simply, quoting the God of the Old Testament, that 'man
shall not live by bread alone, but by *every word* that proceedeth
out of the mouth of God.' One must therefore consider every
word as significant. Had God 'intended' otherwise, the text
would (by definition) be different from what it is!"[16]

He makes the highly relevant observation, that "the weight
of Christ's testimony to Scripture is so much more powerful
than any alleged contradiction or error in the text or any
combination of them, that the latter must be adjusted to the
former, not the reverse."[17]

Further, in several ways we can see how Jesus, in preauthenti-
cating the New Testament, also assumed its inerrancy, even as He
clearly taught the inerrancy of the Old Testament. In John 17:20,
He confirms His belief that new revelation was forthcoming. In
promising the disciples that the Holy Spirit would teach them all
things and bring to remembrance the things Jesus taught them
(John 14:26, cf., Matthew 24:35) and that the Holy Spirit would

guide them into all the truth (John 16:13), He clearly preauthenticated the inspiration and hence the inerrancy of the New Testament. Again, is it logical to think that Jesus would believe that the Holy Spirit, the Spirit of Truth, would either corrupt His own words or inspire error? How could the incarnate God teach the infallibility of the Old Testament and not know the same condition would apply to the New Testament? Thus Jesus never wrote anything because He knew it was unnecessary: the Holy Spirit would inspire an inerrant Word.

Confirmation in Church History

The Roman Catholic, Protestant, and Eastern Orthodox churches have historically held to an infallible or inerrant Bible. This is an indisputable fact, for the only basis upon which Christianity could logically hold to such a position is scriptural testimony itself. Our only other option is to accept that, on so vital a subject, the Church has been in error all these centuries. If true, it has been in error for some 2000 years, and certainly has not, as Jesus promised, been guided into all the truth. On the other hand, if Scripture so clearly taught errancy, how could the Church have ever taught otherwise?

When errantists maintain that inerrancy has not been the historic position of the Church they are either unacquainted with the data, or they refuse to accept it.[18] As Lindsell states: "There is no evidence to show that errancy was ever a live option in the history of Christendom for eighteen hundred years in every branch of the Christian Church that had not gone off into aberration."[19] Dr. John D. Woodbridge, professor of Church History at Trinity Evangelical Divinity School, is correct when he writes, "The vast majority of Christians from diverse confessional backgrounds until the middle of the 17th century included the teachings of the natural world and history under their definition of inerrancy.... Today's evangelical Christians who propose that the Bible's infallibility extends beyond faith and practice to its teachings about the natural world and history reside squarely in the *central tradition* of the church. Only by a serious misreading of Western history can they be viewed as doctrinally innovative on that point."[20]

In conclusion, either Jesus was correct in His view of Scripture or He was not. If He was not, everything Christian tumbles into the abyss. But, if He was correct in His view of Scripture, the question is, will we follow His lead or will we implicate Him with error in the face of His holy testimony? Would not the Christian rather stand with Christ than against Him?

3. The Strength of Inerrancy from the Historic and Prophetic Accuracy of the Biblical Text

We have been attempting to show that the available data support a belief in inerrancy far more strongly than its opposite. This fact, coupled with the arguments from the nature of God and the teachings of Scripture, make its denial by evangelicals all the more perplexing. For example, note the following brief assessments by men of undoubted scholarship, all of whom argue that the factual reliability of the biblical text itself is evidence of inerrancy:

Harold O. J. Brown

> ... if it were possible to point to undeniable, substantial errors in the present Hebrew and Greek texts of Scripture, it would certainly suggest the presumption that the originals had errors. The fact that it is still possible today to claim the autographs were inerrant is an indication that no one has yet succeeded in showing there is even one substantial, undeniable error or contradiction in our present copies. If such an error could be found, it would wreak havoc within the ranks of the inerrantists.[21]

J. I. Packer

> ... no compelling necessity springs from modern knowledge to conclude that Scripture errs anywhere: possibilities of its statements being all true and harmonious still remain open, and can often be shown to be likelier possibilities than that of their falsity.[22]

Charles Ryrie

> After all, the Bible has proved its reliability in many ways and in many areas, and it is worthy of our trust. Man's knowledge has often proved unreliable and at best it is

limited.... Even though the problems connected with apparent discrepancies, parallel passages, manner of quotation, absence of original autographs, etc., may not yet have been fully solved, neither have they ever been conclusively demonstrated to contain errors.[23]

Nevertheless, in spite of the wealth of confirmation for two thousand years, and even in light of two hundred years of recent skeptical attack, the advice of Dr. J. Barton Payne is still sound:

While evangelicals, however, can and do receive encouragement from the relatively few discrepancies that remain unanswered by today's increased knowledge, it is still important to caution that Christian commitment to Scripture does not depend on their infrequency. It is not as though the discovery of additional problems would thereby alter the basis for the evangelical's belief, namely Christ's authentication of Scripture.[24]

Methodological analysis of inerrancy have been very effectively and successfully argued by Sproul,[25] Montgomery,[26] Feinberg,[27] and others.[28] Our own brief illustration of the methodological approach is as follows.

We have established that inspiration implies inerrancy; indeed sufficient evidence exists to show the Bible is divinely inspired. What are some of the things we would expect to be true for the Bible if it were the inspired and inerrant Word of God? First, it would be accurate in historical, archæological, and scientific matters; thus, no fact of history, science or archæology would contradict it. Second, it would stand the test of time. Its authors would be proven trustworthy over the centuries, and would be shown to have not been deceived or to have lied. Third, the book would be without contradiction or other error and would be unified in terms of its themes in spite of comprising 60 books with 40 authors who would write it over a period of 1,500 years. Fourth, it would claim to be the Word of God, and its origin, transmission, and preservation would be unlike any other book in history. Fifth, it would not be unexpected for it to make accurate predictions about the future, all of which would be fulfilled. Sixth, it would have a unique message. Since there is only one God, its message would be different from all false claims to divine revelation. A seventh element is that it would be logical to expect that those who spoke or wrote the Word of God would have their messages confirmed by miracles. Eighth, its prophecies about the Messiah would all prove true. It would be clearly Christ-centered. Ninth, without question, it would have the impact in people's lives one would expect from a divine message, in terms of its transforming power for individuals and cultures. Tenth, it would not be unexpected for the greatest man who ever lived to have authenticated it as the inerrant Word of God.

These ten factors have been discussed to varying degrees throughout this book. For example, genuine prophecy would probably be the most difficult phenomenon to produce, but also the most evidential for substantiating the Bible's claim to divine inspiration.

Anyone who fairly considers the material we discussed in chapters 11-12 will have a difficult time concluding that the Bible is anything other than the inspired Word of God.[29-32] It is simply impossible to account for books like Zephaniah, Obadiah, and Nahum that are over 70 percent predictive apart from an omniscient God who knows the future. All it takes is one undeniable false prophecy and inerrancy is undermined.

In the same way, a logical defense of inerrancy may be constructed based on historical argument centering on Christ's resurrection. Following the arguments of Montgomery and Sproul,[33] a series of points can be given to show how the resurrection supports inerrancy.

First, on the basis of accepted principles of historic and textual analysis the New Testament documents are shown to be reliable and trustworthy historical documents. That is, they give accurate primary source evidence for the life and death of Jesus Christ. In fact, in 2000 years the New Testament authors have never been proven unethical or dishonest, or to have been the objects of deception.

Second, in the Gospel records, Jesus claimed to be God incarnate (John 5:18; 10:27-33). He exercises innumerable divine prerogatives and rests His claims on His numerous and abundantly testified, historically unparalleled miracles (John

10:37-38) and His forthcoming physical resurrection from the dead (John 10:17-18).

Third, in each Gospel Christ's resurrection is minutely described, and for 2000 years it has been incapable of disproof despite the detailed scholarship of the world's best skeptics. The simple truth is that the historic fact of the resurrection proves His claim to deity.

Fourth, because Jesus is the Son of God, he is an infallible authority. In this role He taught that Scripture originates from God and is inerrant since that which originates from an utterly trustworthy God must be utterly trustworthy itself.

Thus, having established the documentary evidence that the Gospels are reliable primary source material, having shown the literary evidence that these documents declare that Christ claimed to be God incarnate, and having given philosophical-scientific evidence that Christ performed the acts of God on earth, including unique miracles but principally conquering death in a physical resurrection, we have thereby verified Christ's claim to deity. If Jesus is God, what God says is by definition true and therefore His unqualified teaching on the inerrancy of the Scriptures proves the validity of the inerrancy position.

In their segment showing how Jesus confirms the authority of the Old Testament, Dr. Norman Geisler and Ron Brooks indicate in summary fashion what Jesus believed about the Old Testament:

What Jesus Taught About the Old Testament

- Authority—Matthew 22:43

- Reliability—Matthew 26:54

- Finality—Matthew 4:4, 7, 10

- Sufficiency—Luke 16:31

- Indestructibility—Matthew 5:17-18

- Unity—Luke 24:27, 44

- Clarity—Luke 24:27

- Historicity—Matthew 12:40

- Facticity (scientifically)—Matthew 19:2-5

- Inerrancy—Matthew 22:29; John 3:12; 17:17

- Infallibility—John 10:35[34]

Our conclusion is that both the miraculous nature of the Bible itself, which speaks for its inspiration (and hence inerrancy) and the infallible pronouncements of God incarnate on an inerrant Scripture are sufficient reasons to accept the proposition that the Bible is inerrant.

The Uniqueness of the Bible

1. The Bible is the only book in the world that offers objective evidence to be the Word of God. Only the Bible gives real proof of its divine inspiration.

2. The Bible is the only religious Scripture in the world that is inerrant.

3. The Bible is the only ancient book with documented scientific and medical prevision. No other ancient book is ever carefully analyzed along scientific lines, but many books have been written on the theme of the Bible and modern science.

4. The Bible is the only religious Scripture that offers eternal salvation as a free gift entirely by God's grace and mercy.

5. The Bible is the only major ancient religious Scripture whose complete textual preservation is established as virtually autographic.

6. The Bible contains the greatest moral standards of any book.

7. Only the Bible begins with the creation of the universe by divine fiat and contains a continuous, if often brief and interspersed, historical record of mankind from the first man, Adam, to the end of history.

8. Only the Bible contains detailed prophecies about the coming Savior of the world, whose prophecies have proven true in history.

9. Only the Bible has the most realistic view of human nature and the power to convict people of their sin and the ability to change human nature.

10. Only the Bible has unique theological content including its theology proper (the Trinity; God's attributes); soteriology (depravity, imputation, grace, propitiation/atonement, reconciliation, regeneration,

union with Christ, justification, adoption, sanctification, eternal security, election, etc.); Christology (the incarnation; hypostatic union); pneumatology (the Person and Work of the Holy Spirit); eschatology (detailed predictions of the end of history); ecclesiology (the nature of the Church as Christ's bride and in organic union with Him), and so on.

11. Only the Bible offers a realistic and permanent solution to the problem of human sin and evil.

12. Only the Bible has its accuracy confirmed in history by archæology, textual criticism, science, and the like.

13. The internal and historical characteristics of the Bible are unique in its unity and internal consistency despite production over a 1,500-year period by 40-plus authors in three languages on three continents discussing scores of controversial subjects yet having agreement on all issues.

14. The Bible is the most translated, purchased, memorized, and persecuted book in history. For example, it is translated into some 1,700 languages.

15. Only the Bible is fully one-quarter prophetic, that is, containing a total of some 400 pages of predictive material.

16. Only the Bible has withstood 2,000 years of intense scrutiny by critics and not only survived the attacks but prospered and had its credibility strengthened by such criticism. (Voltaire predicted the Bible would be extinct within 100 years; within 50 years Voltaire was extinct and his house was a warehouse for the Bibles of the Geneva Bible Society.)

17. Only the Bible has molded the history of Western civilization more than any other book. The Bible has had more influence in the world than any other book.

18. Only the Bible has a person-specific (Christ-centered) nature for each of its 66 books detailing the person's life in prophecy, type, anti-type, and so on, 400–1,500 years before the person was born.

19. Only the Bible proclaims a resurrection of its central figure proven in history.

20. Only the Bible provides historic proof that the one true God loves mankind.

4. The Strength of Inerrancy from Scientific Prevision

In *The Creator Beyond Time and Space*, Mark Eastman and Chuck Missler provide a number of examples illustrating how, scientifically speaking, the Bible was thousands of years ahead of its time. They note that "It has become fashionable to ridicule the Bible as scientifically inaccurate and outdated. However, as we will see, there are dozens of passages in the Bible which demonstrate tremendous scientific foreknowledge."[35] In fact, the only credible way to explain the existence of these passages is through divine inspiration. These kinds of statements are simply too far beyond the ability of men living two or three thousand years ago to have made accurate guesses.

In fact scientists themselves have been impressed by the scientific accuracy of the Bible. An example is A.E. Wilder-Smith, having multiple doctorates in science, who wrote *The Reliability of the Bible*. Critics who claim the Bible is scientifically errant are wrong: "In the twentieth century it is commonly presumed that the Bible is fraught with scientific inaccuracies and misconceptions. Students are often given the impression that numerous scientific fallacies, including a flat earth and a geocentric universe, are contained within the Bible. However, when the biblical text is carefully examined the reader will quickly discover an uncanny scientific accuracy unparalleled by any document of antiquity. . . . The Bible does not use scientific jargon nor is it a scientific text per se. However, as we will see, the Bible does describe scientific phenomena in common terminology with unmistakable clarity. . . . In virtually all ancient religious documents it is common to find scientifically inaccurate myths about the nature of the universe and the life forms on planet earth. Any cursory review of ancient mythology will readily confirm this statement. However, the Bible is unique because of the conspicuous absence of such myths. In fact, throughout the Bible we find scientifically accurate concepts about the physical universe that were not 'discovered' by modern scientists until very recent times."[36]

As a result, "one of the ways that the Bible authenticates its divine authorship is by revealing an accurate and detailed knowledge of the physical universe. Throughout the Bible's text there are highly specific and accurate statements regarding the laws of physics, the nature of our solar system, planet earth, and its life forms. ... Furthermore, we find that the scientific statements in the Bible are without error or contradiction."[37]

Consider some examples:[38]

> In the beginning you laid the foundations of the earth, and the heavens are the work of your hands. They will perish, but you remain; they will all wear out like a garment. Like clothing you will change them and they will be discarded. (Psalm 102:25-26 NIV)

> Lift up your eyes to the heavens, look at the earth beneath; the heavens will vanish like smoke, the earth will wear out like a garment and its inhabitants die like flies. But my salvation will last forever, my righteousness will never fail. (Isaiah 51:6 NIV)

> Heaven and earth will pass away, but my words will never pass away. (Matthew 24:35 NIV)

Eastman and Missler comment, "It is fascinating to find such accurate scientific descriptions of the universe. Prior to the 20th century, the notion that the universe is 'wearing out' or 'passing away' was foreign to the minds of most scientists and philosophers. Such scientific foreknowledge could not have been derived from observation or intuition. When the Bible was being penned there was no observable evidence that the universe was wearing out. In fact, the consensus of the world's scientists and philosophers was that it *was not* decaying."[39]

Jeremiah 33:22 says that "the host of heaven cannot be numbered." Jeremiah made this statement in the eighth century B.C. when astronomers believed that it was possible to number all the stars. Today we know there are at least 100 billion stars in our galaxy and probably several hundred billion galaxies in the universe. For anyone to number the stars would take trillions and trillions of years.

Some 3,000 years ago, the Psalmist wrote that the sun follows a circular path through the universe, "It rises at one end of the heavens and makes its circuit to the other; nothing is hidden from its heat" (Psalm 19:6). Of course, today we know that the sun does move in a "circuit" at speeds close to 600,000 miles per hour within one of the spiral arms of the Milky Way Galaxy. That galaxy itself is hurling through space at about two million miles per hour.

At the time Job and Isaiah wrote, it was commonly believed that the earth rested upon something, whether an elephant, turtle, or the strong back of Atlas. It was also believed that the earth was flat. Yet in Isaiah 40:22, written in 700 B.C., we read, "He sits enthroned above the circle of the earth, and its people are like grasshoppers. He stretches out the heavens like a canopy, and spreads them out like a tent to live in." The Hebrew *khug*, often translated *circle*, literally means sphere. In Job 26:7 we also read, "He spreads out the northern skies over empty space; he suspends the earth over nothing."

Consider that Isaiah wrote 28 centuries ago and that Job is probably the oldest book in the Bible. When these authors wrote, the common view was that the earth was flat, or resting on the back of an animal or a Greek god. The biblical view must have been startling to read. Again, there is simply no way that the biblical writers could have made educated guesses about this. Indeed, in the *Remarkable Record of Job,* scientist Dr. Henry Morris points out that in Job alone there are some two dozen disclosures of scientific foreknowledge.

In Hebrews 11:3 we read, "By faith we understand that the universe was formed at God's command, so that what is seen was not made out of what was visible." Here the author of the book of Hebrews is accurate when he describes the fact that what we can see—matter—is made of particles that aren't visible in natural light.

In 2 Peter 3:10 we find, "But the day of the Lord will come like a thief. The heavens will disappear with a roar; the elements will be destroyed by fire, and the earth and everything in it will be laid bare." Written 2,000 years ago, when the beliefs concerning the nature of matter were quite crude, isn't it amazing to find descriptions such as these? Second Peter certainly seems to be describing what happens when the nucleus of radioactive elements are split, releasing incredible amounts of energy and radioactivity.

In Psalm 8:8 we read about "the birds of the air, and the fish of the sea, all that swim the *paths* of the seas." But it wasn't until the mid-nineteenth century when Matthew Fontaine Maury, the "father of oceanography," published his discovery that the ocean possesses predictable paths or currents. When Psalm 8 was written, the only seas known to the Hebrews were the Dead Sea, the Sea of Galilee, the Mediterranean, and the Red Sea. These bodies of water did not possess "paths" or significant observable currents. It took Matthew Maury a great deal of time to collect the crude observational data that existed from the fifteenth to the nineteenth century to make his own discovery. And yet the Psalmist wrote of "the paths of the seas."

In Job 36:27 and 28 is the statement, "He draws up the drops of water, which distill as rain to the streams; the clouds pour down their moisture and abundant showers fall on mankind." Here we find an accurate description of the earth's hydrologic cycle. Even during the Middle Ages, the source of rain water was something of a mystery. But in approximately 2,000 B.C. we find Job accurately describing the rain cycle.

We read in Ecclesiastes 1:6-7, "The wind blows to the south and turns to the north; round and round it goes, ever returning on its course. All streams flow into the sea, yet the sea is never full. To the place the streams come from, there they return again." Here, King Solomon, writing 3,000 years ago, speaks of global wind currents and the earth's water cycle. "The phrase, 'the wind blows to the south and turns to the north; round and round it goes, ever returning on its course' is an accurate and astonishing description of the circular flow of air around the earth, called the 'jet stream,' well known to anyone who watches the evening news weather reports."[40]

So far we have briefly looked at aspects of cosmology, physics, oceanography, and the hydrologic cycle. But in other sciences we find similar scientific prevision. In medicine, God had directed Abraham to circumcise newborn males specifically on the eighth day (Genesis 17:12). It wasn't until the twentieth century we discovered that only after eight days of life does vitamin K in the infant's diet permit prothrombin, an important blood clotting factor, to reach its peak. To circumcise on an earlier day, when the clotting mechanism is immature, could result in excessive bleeding. Further, there are many other cultures that circumcise their males on the first, fourth, sixth, seventh, or twentieth days of life. If the Jews had discovered the eighth day merely by trial and error, why didn't other cultures do so? Clearly, Jewish practice was based on obedience to divine revelation. Deuteronomy 23:12-14, Leviticus 17:11, and many other Scriptures reflect hygienic or medical knowledge far in advance of its time.

In his 500-page text, *The Biblical Basis for Modern Science,* Dr. Henry Morris supplies a large number of additional examples of scientific foreknowledge or allusions in the Bible. A sampling is given in his *Many Infallible Proofs:*

Science	Phenomenon or Process	Scripture
Hydrology	Hydrologic Cycle	Ecclesiastes 1:7; Isaiah 55:10
	Evaporation	Psalm 135:7; Jeremiah 10:13
	Condensation Nuclei	Proverbs 8:26
	Condensation	Job 26:8; 37:11,16
	Precipitation	Job 36:27, 28
	Run-off	Job 28:10
	Oceanic Reservoir	Psalm 33:7
	Snow	Job 38:22; Psalm 147:16
	Hydrologic Balance	Isaiah 40:12; Job 28:24-26
Geology	Principle of Isostasy	Isaiah 40:12; Psalm 104:5-9
	Shape of Earth	Isaiah 40:22; Psalm 103:12
	Rotation of Earth	Job 38:12, 14
	Gravitation	Job 26:7; 38:6
	Rock Erosion	Job 14:18, 19
	Glacial Period	Job 38:29, 30
	Uniformitarianism	2 Peter 3:4
Astronomy	Size of Universe	Isaiah 55:9; Job 22:12; Jeremiah 31:37
	Number of Stars	Jeremiah 33:22; Genesis 22:17
	Variety of Stars	1 Corinthians 15:41
	Precision of Orbits	Jeremiah 31:35, 36
Meteorology	Circulation of Atmosphere	Ecclesiastes 1:6
	Protective Effect of Atmosphere	Isaiah 40:22

Science	Phenomenon or Process	Scripture
Meteorology	Oceanic Origin of Rain	Ecclesiastes 1:7
	Relation of Electricity to Rain	Jeremiah 10:13
Biology	Blood Circulation	Leviticus 17:11
	Psychotherapy	Proverbs 16:24; 17:22
	Biogenesis and Stability	Genesis 1:11, 21, 25
	Uniqueness of Man	Genesis 1:26
	Chemical Nature of Flesh	Genesis 1:11, 24-27; 3:19; 1 Peter 1:24, 25
Physics	Mass-Energy Equivalence	Hebrews 1:3; Colossians 1:17
	Source of Energy for Earth	Genesis 1:14, 17; Psalm 19:6
	Atomic Disintegration	2 Peter 3:10
	Radio Waves	Job 38:35[41]

Certainly, for skeptics to successfully argue that the Bible is not the inspired Word of God, they must explain how the Bible contains statements such as these, which were often disharmonious with the accepted knowledge of the time in which they were written—and yet so accurate in light of today's facts of science. In essence: "To argue that the evidences for biblical inspiration are the result of a myriad of lucky guesses requires an enormous measure of faith. Such an assertion requires us to believe that ancient fishermen, tent makers, shepherds, kings and paupers, who were separated by 1,500 years on three different continents, could consistently, and without error, describe the nature of the universe, planet Earth and its life forms, in a way that is fully consistent with twentieth-century science. It requires us to believe that those same men wrote history in advance—all of this *without* the guidance of One with supernatural 'inside information.' "[42]

Indeed, "In the twentieth century, more than any time in history, it can be demonstrated that the Bible is a skillfully designed, integrated message system that evidences supernatural engineering in every detail."[43]

This sampling of historic, prophetic, and scientific information in the Bible is why scholars of impeccable standing have sided with an inerrant Bible.

5. The Strength of Inerrancy from Lack of Proven Error

Those who reject inerrancy believe there are original errors in certain areas of the Bible outside doctrine and morality, usually in science and history. The truth is that no error can be proven in the autographs since we don't have them. In His wisdom God has seen fit not to preserve them. The original God-breathed manuscripts would certainly have become items of worship, and, as with the Koran of Islam, translations would likely have been prohibited as causing a "perverting" of the pure Word of God. This eventually would have kept Scripture from all but those studied in Greek and Hebrew. (As an illustration, consider that in Judges 8:27, "all Israel prostituted themselves by worshipping" the gold image of an ephod or priestly garment. How much more likely, then, that the actual autographs would have become objects of idolatry?)

Regardless, an error can't logically be suggested in the autographs because our copies strongly support inerrancy. Gleason L. Archer was an undergraduate classics major who received training in Latin, Greek, French, and German at Harvard University. At seminary he majored in Hebrew, Aramaic, and Arabic, and in post-graduate study became involved with Akkadian and Syriac, teaching courses on these subjects. He has had a special interest in middle kingdom Egyptian studies and at the Oriental Institute in Chicago did specialized study in Eighteenth Dynasty historical records, as well as studying Coptic and Sumerian. He has also visited the Holy Land where he visited most of the important archæological sites and spent time in Beirut, Lebanon, for a specialized study of modern literary Arabic. He holds a degree from Princeton Theological Seminary and a Ph.D. from Harvard Graduate School. This background enabled him to become expert in the issue of alleged contradictions in Scripture.

Regarding alleged errors in the extant copies of Scripture he says,

> In my opinion this charge can be refuted and its falsity exposed by an objective study done in a consistent, evangelical perspective. . . . I candidly believe I have been confronted with just about all the biblical difficulties under discussion in theological circles today—especially those pertaining to the interpretation and defense of Scripture. . . . As I have dealt with one apparent discrepancy after another and have studied the alleged contradictions between the biblical record and the evidence of linguistics, archæology, or science, my confidence in the trustworthiness of Scripture has been repeatedly verified and strengthened by the discovery that almost every problem in Scripture that has ever been discovered by man, from ancient times until now, has been dealt with in a completely satisfactory manner by the biblical text itself—or else by objective archæological information.[44]

Given the fact that Dr. Archer has done extensive studies in archæology and other areas relative to the biblical text, become fluent in 15 languages, and received full training in legal evidences, this statement can hardly be summarily dismissed.

But there are many similar testimonies by other competent scholars. Dr. Robert Dick Wilson, an Old Testament authority and author of *A Scientific Investigation of the Old Testament* could read the New Testament in nine different languages by the age of 25. In addition, he could repeat from memory a Hebrew translation of the entire New Testament without missing a single syllable, and do the same with large portions of the Old Testament. He proceeded to learn 45 languages and dialects and was also a master of paleography and philology: "I have made it an invariable habit never to accept an objection to a statement of the Old Testament without subjecting it to a most thorough investigation, linguistically and factually" and "I defy any man to make an attack upon the Old Testament on the grounds of evidence that I cannot investigate." His conclusion was that no critic has succeeded in proving an error in the Old Testament.[45]

Theologian, philosopher, and trial attorney John Warwick Montgomery, holding nine graduate degrees in different fields, observes, "I myself have never encountered an alleged contradiction in the Bible which could not be cleared up by the use of the original languages of the Scriptures and/or by the use of accepted principals of literary and historical interpretation."[46]

Rev. John W. Haley examined 900 alleged problems in Scripture, concluding, "I cannot but avow, as the [conclusion] of my investigation, the profound conviction that *every difficulty and discrepancy in the scriptures is... capable of a fair and reasonable solution*."[47] Greek scholar Dr. William Arndt concluded in his own study of alleged contradictions and errors in the Bible, "[W]e may say with full conviction that no instances of this sort occur anywhere in the Scriptures."[48]

Clearly the evidence of the text lies in favor of biblical inerrancy. The apparent discrepancies and errors in the Bible constantly "discovered" and exploited by critics for millennia have been explained and reconciled by conservative scholars for the same length of time. Critics, however, commonly ignore the resolution and continue to present the same old alleged errors and contradictions.

6. The Strength of Inerrancy from the Weakness of the Alternate Position (Limited Inerrancy)

Assuming verbal plenary inspiration and inerrancy restricts us to the evangelical camp. The neoevangelical believes in verbal plenary inspiration but also in limited inerrancy. Perhaps the quandary faced here is best illustrated by R. C. Sproul, who cites a discussion he has had:

> On numerous occasions I have queried several Biblical and theological scholars in the following manner.—"Do you maintain the inerrancy of Scripture?"—"No!"—"Do you believe the Bible to be inspired of God?"—"Yes"—"Do you think God inspires error?"—"No"—"Is all of the Bible inspired by God?"—"Yes"—"Is the Bible errant?"—"No!" "Is it inerrant?"—"No!"—At that point I usually acquire an Excedrin headache.[49]

One problem is in the term "limited inerrancy" itself as Dr. Ryrie observes:

But why say "limited inerrancy"? Why not "limited errancy"? If the Bible has limitations on its inerrancy, then obviously it is errant, though not completely so. So limited inerrancy and limited errancy amount to the same thing.... Limited inerrancy is a much more palatable label than anything that has the word *errancy* in it.... To speak of limited inerrancy seems much more respectable, but it is also more deceitful. Intentional or not, it is a semantic game played to help cover up a dangerously deceptive view. We need to expose limited inerrancy for what it is. If parts of the Bible are not inerrant, then those parts are errant. That is an inescapable conclusion.[50]

Limited inerrancy is simply meaningless, biblically and practically. Biblically it is incorrect to speak of *degrees* of inerrancy or inspiration. Where does the Bible make such a distinction? No Scripture gives us the right to view any Scripture as less than fully inspired and inerrant. It is the same as if I say an invisible, intangible, purple-and-green-dotted giraffe lives in my kitchen when there is not a shred of evidence to support my claim. To maintain the Bible is errant when it does not teach this is like maintaining the Bible teaches Christ is not God when it so clearly affirms His deity. Practically speaking, limited inerrancy leaves us in the same subjective quagmire as "limited inspiration." How limited is the inspiration? How limited is the inerrancy? How much is true and how much is false? *Who* determines where the "limitation" is? And if there are errors, should we not correct them? *How* do we do this? Does this not require divine inspiration on the part of the one making the corrections? Otherwise the only criteria for making corrections is fallible human scholarship. This means, therefore, that outside criteria have become the judge of the Bible. In turn, this means that if such outside criteria are to judge it, such criteria must be truer or more reliable than the Bible. The conclusion is that a noninspired source is given preference over a divinely inspired one.[51] Here, at least, the errantist has more in common with the cultist than evangelicalism. If the errantist position is true, with a potential plethora of subjective factors at work, can we even maintain the Bible is an authority and trustworthy? On the other hand, the true biblical concept of inspiration rescues us from coming to any part of the Scripture and asking, "Can I trust it?"

James Barr's book, *Fundamentalism,* points out another problem of limited inerrantists: the inconsistency of their message. They claim to accept the authority of the Bible, yet believe it contains an undetermined number of errors. Here one is reminded of the dilemma of the Christian theistic evolutionist, whose denials of Scripture are so blatant that even militant atheists cite their works to prove Christians don't *really* believe the teaching of their Bibles. For example, in *Atheism: The Case Against God,* George H. Smith states:

> On occasion, however, even the Christian is forced to acknowledge the supremacy of reason if he is to avoid pushing his beliefs beyond the limits of absurdity. This is where his religion undergoes a rewrite. Previous articles of faith, once disproved, are declared to be non-essential, and those beliefs that cannot be discarded without demolishing Christianity are now interpreted "symbolically" instead of literally.
>
> Through history Christianity has sought to eliminate scientific principles that conflict with Christian faith, and it has not hesitated to employ intimidation and violence in pursuit of this end. When science finally triumphed, Christianity refused to abandon its appeal to faith. Previous conflicts between religion and science were attributed to misunderstandings. Former articles of faith, after they are conclusively refuted, are now viewed as misinterpretations of the "true" faith; and new theories, such as evolution, are incorporated within Christianity.
>
> It is rather amusing that, after years of violent hostilities between religion and scientific discovery, a modern Christian will claim that the Christian faith (properly understood, of course) really supported the new theory all along. Evolution ceased to contradict divine creation only after the evidence for evolution became overwhelming. Now every enlightened theologian can deliver an impressive account of how evolutionary theory actually magnifies the greatness of God.[52]

Perhaps it goes without saying, but when evangelical literature provides *legitimate* ammunition for the enemies of the Church to reject God, something is terribly wrong. Of course, if real Christians do not believe what God declares is true, why should non-Christians even *consider* Him? Barr's book thus shows the inconsistency of those who wish to retain the benefits of Biblical authority and yet are clearly errantists. Some, presumably, do so in hopes of greater scholarly recognition or dialogue with liberals and secularists: "These writers are convinced that greater respect for the Christian faith will be retained in the academic community if Christian scholars demonstrate an openness to evolution and higher criticism."[53] Nevertheless, the same fate meets the limited inerrantists as the theistic evolutionist: ridicule by those who would never accept their dubious modified beliefs anyway and derision for their compromise and inconsistency. Certainly it is not compromise that honors Christ and leads men into His kingdom.

For example, does the following statement make any sense? Jack Harwell, editor of the *Christian Index,* a publication of the Baptist Convention of the State of Georgia stated, "I do believe that the Bible is the Word of God. I do not use the word infallible because the Bible is written by men. . . . I do not believe in the plenary verbal inspiration of the Bible. . . . I do not believe that Adam and Eve were one man and one woman. I believe that the terms Adam and Eve represented mankind and womankind. There are volumes and volumes of Biblical scholarship which document this theory many years back."[54] Yet both Jesus and Paul clearly taught that a literal Adam and Eve were created by God (Matthew 19:4-5; Romans 5:12; 1 Corinthians 15:45). Is this kind of compromise helpful?

When T. C. Smith, president of the liberal Association of Baptist Professors of Religion, says "It is the Bible, not God, that we are questioning,"[55] what does one do? When God declares He exalts His Word according to His Name (Psalm 137:2, cf., Isaiah 42:21), how can the two be separated?

Indeed, the very nature of the limited errantist position is inherently indefensible, as John Murray points out:

Those who thus contend should, however, be aware of the implications of their position. If human fallibility precludes an infallible Scripture, then by resistless logic it must be maintained that we cannot have any Scripture that is infallible and inerrant. All of Scripture comes to us through human instrumentality. If such instrumentality involves fallibility, then such fallibility must attach to the whole of Scripture. For by what warrant can an immunity from error be maintained in the matter of "spiritual content" and not in the matter of historical or scientific fact? Is human fallibility suspended when "spiritual truth" is asserted but not suspended in other less important matters?

Furthermore, if infallibility can attach to the "spiritual truth" enunciated by the Biblical writers, then it is obvious that some extraordinary divine influence must have intervened and become operative so as to prevent human fallibility from leaving its mark upon the truth expressed. If divine influence could thus intrude itself at certain points, why should not this same preserving power exercise itself at every point in the writing of Scripture? Again, surely human fallibility is just as liable to be at work in connection with the enunciation of transcendent truth as it is when it deals with the details of historical occurrence.[56]

The choice is simple. We choose the opinions of errantist brethren and biased critics, or the testimony of God and His Son. We accept the infallibility of the critic or of the Scriptures. Of the one who doubts God's Word, or of the God who testifies to it. Was *Christ* ever in error? If He was, then can He be a sinless Savior or incarnate God?

If God inspired errors concerning the creation, the flood, Joshua's long day, and Jonah's great sea creature, if He deceived us with the false prophecies of a pseudo-Daniel and deutero-trito Isaiah, the alleged sexism of the apostle Paul (or pseudo-Paul), the rank deception of pseudo-Peter, and the cultural accommodations of Jesus—then certainly He may also have erred or deceived us in the matter of our salvation! Who can prove He has not, if the critics claims be true? "What does inspiration mean if it does not involve reliability?"[57] Is an allegedly demonstrable error "profitable"? Again, should 2 Timothy 3:16

be revised to correct its error? What is at stake here is nothing less than the integrity of God. We believe that, indeed, God will "be found true, though every man be found a liar" (Romans 3:4).

If God could and did preserve the Bible from error in matters of theology (faith and practice), why would He *not* do so in non-theological matters of science and history?

A renowned Roman Catholic scholar, Bruce Vawter, claims, "The truth of the Bible has nothing to do one way or the other, pro or contra, with either scientific fact or scientific history."[58] This is nonsense. The truth of the Bible has everything to do with scientific fact and history. It is this kind of argument that the Bible has nothing to do with.

Dr. Gleason Archer gives us a relevant illustration from the legal profession. He clearly shows that claiming the Bible does not err where it cannot be tested is a meaningless claim if it does err where it can be tested.

> There can be no infallibility without inerrancy—even in matters of history and science—and sooner or later the schools or denominations that accept this *via media* slip away from their original evangelical posture and shift into substantial departures from the historic Christian faith. There are some good and solid reasons for this doctrinal decline.
>
> In any court of law, whether in a civil or criminal case, the trustworthiness of a witness on a stand is necessarily an important point at issue if his testimony is to be received. Therefore, the attorney for the opposing side will make every effort in his cross-examination of the witness to demonstrate that he is not a consistently truthful person. If the attorney can trap the opposing witness into statements that contradict what he has said previously or furnish evidence that in his own community the man has a reputation for untruthfulness, then the jury may be led to doubt the accuracy of the witness's testimony that bears directly on the case itself. This is true even though such untruthfulness relates to other matters having no relationship to the present litigation. While the witness on the stand may indeed be giving a true report on this particular case, the judge and

jury have no way of being sure. Therefore, they are logically compelled to discount this man's testimony.

The same is true of Holy Scripture. If the statements it contains concerning matters of history and science can be proven by extrabiblical records, by ancient documents recovered through archæological digs, or by the established facts of modern science to be contrary to the truth, then there is grave doubt as to its trustworthiness in matters of religion. In other words, if the biblical record can be proved fallible in areas of fact that can be verified, then it is hardly to be trusted in areas where it cannot be tested. As a witness for God, the Bible would be discredited as untrustworthy. What solid truth it may contain would be left as a matter of mere conjecture, subject to the intuition or canons of likelihood of each individual. An attitude of sentimental attachment to traditional religion may incline one person to accept nearly all the substantive teachings of Scripture as probably true. But someone else with equal justification may pick and choose whatever teachings in the Bible happen to appeal to him and lay equal claim to legitimacy. One opinion is as good as another. All things are possible, but nothing is certain if indeed the Bible contains mistakes or errors of any kind.[59]

This quotation reminds us of the evangelical adoption of redaction criticism. "Liberal" redaction criticism flatly rejects verbal plenary inspiration; "evangelical" redaction criticism believes the Holy Spirit inspired the Biblical writers to record statements Jesus never said *as if* He said them![60]

To end our discussion, we close by citing Dr. Feinberg:

I have never been able to understand how one can be justified in claiming *absolute* authority for the Scriptures and at the same time deny their inerrancy. This seems to be the height of epistemological nonsense and confusion.

Let me try to illustrate the point. Suppose that I have an Amtrak railroad schedule. In describing its use to you, I tell you that it is filled with numerous errors but that it is *absolutely* authoritative and trustworthy. I think you would be extremely dubious. At least the schedule would have one thing going for it; it declares itself to be subject to change without notice.[61]

Chapter 16

The Historic Reliability of Scripture

There is, I imagine, no body of literature in the world that has been exposed to the stringent analytical study that the four gospels have sustained for the past 200 years. . . . scholars today who treat the gospels as credible historical documents do so in the full light of this analytical study.
—F. F. Bruce

Christians and skeptical non-Christians, including members of other religions like Islam and various religious cults like Mormonism, have different views concerning the credibility of the Gospels and the other New Testament documents. For the Christian, nothing is more vital than the very words of Jesus Himself, who promised, "Heaven and earth will pass away, but my words will never pass away" (Matthew 24:35). Jesus' promise is of no small import. In essence, if His words were not accurately recorded, how can anyone know what He really taught? The truth is, we couldn't know. Further, if the remainder of the New Testament cannot be established to be historically reliable, then little can be known about what true Christianity really is, teaches, or means.

Who is right in this debate—the Christians who claim the Bible is historically accurate or the rationalistic critics who claim otherwise? The latter group usually approach the Bible from a materialistic viewpoint, discounting its supernatural elements, employing higher critical methods, and maintaining it wasn't even written until the late first or early second century. After summarizing the critical and conservative views, in a brief point-by-point format we offer the following analysis designed to show why the New Testament is historically reliable.

The Critical View

The skeptics' argument, characteristically based on the use of higher critical methods such as source, form, and redaction criticism, is often given as follows: by a number of criteria the reliability of the New Testament text may be doubted. This includes its dominant "mythological" (supernatural) character, the fabrication of a fictitious view of Jesus on the basis of erroneous Messianic expectation, the theological embellishments of the Apostle Paul, and finally, the invention of most of the teachings of Christ to suit the spiritual or other needs of the early church and, some argue, the removal of the actual teachings of Christ in later church councils for the purpose of political expediency or theological bias. The Jesus Seminar, for example, widely employs higher critical methods, especially form criticism, to supposedly determine what Jesus actually said. They conclude that less than 18 percent of Jesus' sayings recorded in the New Testament are original. The remainder are inventions by the early church.

Thomas C. Oden provides a common view of Jesus held by most modern critical scholars: "Jesus was an eschatological prophet who proclaimed God's coming kingdom and called his hearers to decide now for or against that kingdom. After he was condemned to death and died, the belief emerged gradually that he had risen. Only after some extended period of time did the remembering community develop the idea that Jesus would return as the Messiah, Son of Man. Eventually this community came to project its eschatological expectation back upon the historical Jesus, inserting in his mouth the eschatological hopes that it had subsequently developed but now deftly had to rearrange so as to make it seem as if Jesus himself had understood himself as Messiah. Only much later did the Hellenistic idea of the God-man, the virgin birth, and incarnation emerge in the minds of the remembering church, who again misremembered Jesus according to its revised eschatological expectation." James W. Sire, who cites the above, remarks, "Oden in the following eight pages shows how and why this 'modern view' is seriously at odds with reason." For example, "How such a vacuous implausible interpretation could have come to be widely accepted is itself perplexing enough. Even harder to understand is the thought that the earliest remem- berers would actually suffer martyrdom for such a flimsy cause. One wonders how those deluded believers of early centuries gained the courage to risk passage into an unknown world to proclaim this message that came from an imagined revolution of a fantasized Mediator. The 'critical' premise itself requires a high degree of gullibility."[1]

The Conservative View

The conservative view takes quite another approach based on historical facts, logic, and common sense. It maintains that, on the basis of accepted bibliographic, internal, and external cri- teria, the New Testament text can be established to be reliable history in spite of the novel and sometimes ingenious specula- tions of critics who, while often familiar with the facts, refuse to accept them due to a preexisting bias. Textually, we have restored more than 99 percent of the autographs, and there is simply no legitimate basis upon which to doubt the credibility and accuracy of the New Testament writers. Further, the methods used by the critics (rationalistic higher critical methods) which claim "assured results" proving the Scripture unreliable have been weighed in the balance of secular schol- arship and been found wanting. Their use in biblical analysis is therefore unjustified. Even in a positive sense relative to the biblical text, the fruit they have born is minuscule while, nega- tively, they are responsible for a tremendous weight of destruc- tion relative to people's confusion over biblical authority and their confidence in the Bible.

In this sense, the critics, who continue to advance discredited theories, conform to the warnings of Chauncey Sanders, asso- ciate professor of military history at The Air University, Maxwell Air Force Base, Montgomery, Alabama. In his *An Introduction to Research in English Literary History,* he warns literary critics to be certain they are also careful to examine the evidence *against* their case: "He must be as careful to collect evidence against his theory as for it. It may go against the grain to be very assiduous in searching for ammunition to destroy one's own case; but it must be remembered that the overlooking of a single detail may be fatal to one's whole argument. Moreover, it is the business of the scholar to seek the truth, and the satisfaction of having found it should be ample recompense for having to give up a cherished but untenable theory."[2]

What allows us to resolve this issue, and logically demonstrate the credibility of the conservative view is the following ten facts:

Fact One: The existence of thousands of Greek and Latin manuscripts, with the papyri and early uncials dating much closer to the originals than for any other ancient literature;

Fact Two: The lack of proven fraud or error on the part of *any* New Testament author;

Fact Three: The writings of reliable Christian resources outside the New Testament;

Fact Four: The existence of a number of Jewish and secular accounts about Jesus;

Fact Five: Detailed archæological data concerning the New Testament;

Fact Six: The existence of many powerful enemies of Jesus and the apostolic church who would have proven fraud or pointed out other problems if they could;

Fact Seven: The presence of living eyewitnesses to the events recorded;

Fact Eight: The positive appraisals by conservative and even some liberal authorities bearing on the issue of the genuineness of traditional authorship and the early date of the New Testament books;

Fact Nine: The consistent scholarly, factual reversals of the conclusions of higher criticism that undermine its own foundations and credibility; and

Fact Ten: Legal and other testimony as to New Testament reliability.

To begin, the historical accuracy of the New Testament can be proven by subjecting it to three generally accepted tests for determining historical reliability. Such tests are utilized in literary criticism and the study of historical documents in general. (These are discussed by military historian Chauncey Sanders in his *An Introduction to Research in English Literary History.*[3]) These involve the 1) bibliographical, 2) internal, and 3) external tests of historical evidence.

Fact One: The Bibliographical Test (corroboration from textual transmission)

The bibliographical test seeks to determine if we can reconstruct the original New Testament writings from the extant copies at hand. We have 5,300 Greek manuscripts and manuscript portions, 10,000 Latin Vulgate, and 9,300 other versions, plus 36,000 early (100–300 A.D.) patristic quotations of the New Testament—so that all but a few verses of the entire text could apparently be reconstructed from these alone.[4]

Few scholars question the general reliability of ancient classical literature on the basis of the manuscripts we possess. Yet this manuscript evidence is vastly inferior to that of the New Testament. For example, of sixteen well-known classical authors (Plutarch, Tacitus, Sentonius, Polybius, Thucydides, Xenophon, etc.), the total number of extant copies is typically less than ten, and the earliest copies date from 750 to 1600 years after the original manuscript was first penned.[5] We need only compare such slim evidence to the mass of biblical documentation involving over 24,000 manuscript portions, manuscripts, and versions, the earliest fragment and complete copies dating between 50 and 300 years after originally written.

Given the fact that the early Greek manuscripts (the Papyri and early Uncials) date much closer to the originals than for any other ancient literature, and the overwhelming additional abundance of manuscript attestation, any doubt as to the integrity or authenticity of the New Testament text has been removed. Indeed, this kind of evidence is the dream of the historian. No other ancient literature has ever come close to supplying historians and textual critics with such an abundance of data.

Dr. F.F. Bruce, former Ryland's Professor of Biblical Criticism and Exegesis at the University of Manchester, asserts of the New Testament: "There is no body of ancient literature in the world which enjoys such a wealth of good textual attestation as the New Testament."[6] Professor Bruce further comments, "The evidence for our New Testament writings is ever so much greater than the evidence for many writings of classical writers, the authenticity of which no one dreams of questioning. And if the New Testament were a collection of secular writings, their authenticity would generally be regarded as beyond all doubt."[7]

Further, Dr. Rene Pache remarks of the great Princeton scholar B.B. Warfield that he "goes on to say that the great bulk of the New Testament has been transmitted to us without, or almost without, any variations. It can be asserted with confidence that the sacred text is exact and valid and that no article of faith and no moral precept in it has been distorted or lost."[8]

It is this wealth of material that has enabled scholars such as Westcott and Hort, Ezra Abbott, Philip Schaff, A.T. Robertson, Norman Geisler, and William Nix to place the restoration of the original text at better than 99 percent.[9] No other document of the ancient period is as accurately preserved as the New Testament.

Hort's estimate of "substantial variation" for the New Testament is one-tenth of one percent, Abbot's estimate is one-fourth of one percent, and even Hort's figure including trivial variation is less than two percent. Sir Frederic Kenyon well summarizes the situation:

> The number of manuscripts of the New Testament...is so large that it is practically certain that the true reading of every doubtful passage is preserved in some one or another of these ancient authorities. This can be said of no other ancient book in the world.

> Scholars are satisfied that they possess substantially the true text of the principal Greek and Roman writers whose works have come down to us, of Sophocles, of Thucydides, of Cicero, of Virgil; yet our knowledge depends on a mere handful of manuscripts, whereas the manuscripts of the

New Testament are counted by hundreds and even thousands.[10]

In other words, those who question the reliability of the New Testament must also question the reliability of virtually every ancient writing the world possesses! How can the Bible be rejected when its documentation is one hundred times that of other ancient literature? Because it is impossible to question the world's ancient classics, it is far more impossible to question the reliability of the New Testament.[11]

In addition, none of the established New Testament canon is lost or missing, not even a verse as indicated by variant readings. By comparison, the books of many ancient authors are filled with omissions: 107 of Livy's 142 books of history are lost, and one-half of Tacitus' 30 books of Annals and Histories. For Polybius, only five complete books remain from the original forty. Finally, the Gospels are extremely close to the events which they record. The first three can be dated within twenty years of the events cited, and this may even be true for the fourth gospel. This means that all four Gospels were written during the lives of eyewitnesses, and that abundant opportunity existed for those with contrary evidence to examine the witnesses and refute them.

The Gospels, then, pass the bibliographical test and must, by far, be graded with the highest mark of any ancient literature we possess.

Fact Two: The Internal Evidence Test (corroboration from content accuracy)

This test asserts that one is to assume the truthful reporting of an ancient document (and not assume either fraud, incompetence or error) unless the author of the document has disqualified himself by his presence. For example, do the New Testament writers contradict themselves? Is there anything in their writing which causes one to objectively suspect their trustworthiness? Are there statements or assertions in the text which are demonstrably false according to known archæological, historic, scientific or other data?

The answer is no. There is lack of proven fraud or error on the part of any New Testament writer. But there is evidence of careful eyewitness reporting throughout. The caution exercised by the writers, their personal conviction that what they wrote was true and the lack of demonstrable error or contradiction indicate that the Gospel authors and, indeed, all the New Testament authors pass the second test as well (Luke 1:1-4; John 19:35; 21:24; Acts 1:1-3; 2:22; 26:24-26; 2 Peter 1:16; 1 John 1:1-3).

For example, the kinds of details the Gospel writers include in their narratives offer strong evidence for their integrity. They record their own sins and failures, even serious ones (Matthew 26:56, 72-75; Mark 10:35-45). They do not hesitate from recording accurately even the most difficult and consequential statements of Jesus (John 6:41-71). They forthrightly supply the embarrassing and even capital charges of Jesus' own enemies. Thus, even though Jesus was their very Messiah and Lord, they not only record the charges that Jesus broke the Sabbath, but that He was born in fornication, a blasphemer and a liar, insane, and demonized (see Matthew 1:19, 26:65; John 7:20, 48; 8:41, 48, 52; 10:20, 33, etc.)! To encounter such honesty in reporting incidents of this nature gives one assurance that the Gospel writers placed a very high premium on truthfulness.

Fact Three: The External Evidence Test (corroboration from reliable sources outside the New Testament)

The test of external evidence seeks to either corroborate or falsify the documents on the basis of additional historical literature and data. Is there corroborating evidence outside the Bible for the claims made in the Gospels? Or are the claims of the New Testament successfully refuted by other competent reports or eyewitnesses?

Any honest investigation will reveal that the New Testament passes the test. For example, we earlier noted the resurrection itself had never been refuted, even by Jesus' own enemies, and that Luke's careful historical writing has been documented from detailed, personal archæological investigation by former critic Sir William Ramsay.[12] A. N. Sherwin-White, the distinguished historian of Rome, stated of Luke: "For [the book of] Acts, the confirmation of historicity is overwhelming. Any attempt to reject its basic historicity even in matters of detail must now appear absurd."[13]

Papias, a student of the Apostle John[14] and Bishop of Hierapolis around 130 A.D., observed that the Apostle John himself noted that Mark, in writing his Gospel, "wrote down accurately...whatsoever [Peter] remembered of the things said or done by Christ. Mark committed no error...for he was careful of one thing, not to omit any of the things [Peter] had heard, and not to state any of them falsely."[15] Fragments of Papias' Exposition of the Oracles of the Lord, ca. 140 A.D. assert that the Gospels of Matthew, Mark, and John are all based on reliable eyewitness testimony (his portion on Luke is missing).[16]

The relevant bibliographic, internal and external evidence for the New Testament force us to concede the historical accuracy and reliability of the Gospel accounts. They pass persuasive tests which determine their integrity. Even two hundred years of scholarly rationalistic biblical criticism have proven nothing except that the writers were careful and honest reporters of the events recorded, and that these methods attempting to discredit them were flawed and biased from the start.[17]

In conclusion, it is not only a demonstrable historical fact that Jesus lived and taught what the New Testament says He lived and taught, it is also a fact that the Bible is the best-documented and most accurately preserved book of ancient history. That means we can trust what the authors say as true. When we examine the evidence for something like the resurrection of Jesus as reported in the New Testament, there is no logical, historical, or other basis upon which to doubt what is written.

Fact Four: Corroboration from Non-Christian Sources

The existence of both Jewish and secular accounts, to a significant degree, confirm the broad picture of Christ we have in the New Testament.[18] For example, scholarly research, such as that by Dr. G. R. Habermas in *Ancient Evidences for the Life of Jesus*, indicates that "a broad outline of the life of Jesus" and His death by crucifixion can be reasonably and directly inferred from entirely non-Christian sources.[19] Even the resurrection of Christ can be indirectly inferred.

> Using only the information gleaned from these ancient extra-biblical sources, what can we conclude concerning the death and resurrection of Jesus? Can these events be historically established based on these sources alone? Of the seventeen documents examined in this chapter, eleven different works speak of the death of Jesus in varying amounts of detail, with five of these specifying crucifixion as the mode. When these sources are examined by normal historical procedures used with other ancient documents, the result is conclusive. It is this author's view that the death of Jesus by crucifixion can be asserted as a historical fact from this data.... The ancient references to the resurrection are fewer and more questionable. Of the seventeen sources, only six either imply or report this occurrence, with four of these works being questioned in our study. Before answering the issue concerning Jesus' resurrection, we will initially address the cognate point of whether the empty tomb can be established as historical by this extra-biblical evidence alone. There are some strong considerations in its favor. First, the Jewish sources which we have examined admit the empty tomb, thereby providing evidences from hostile documents.... Second, there are apparently no ancient sources which assert that the tomb still contained Jesus' body. While such an argument from silence does not prove anything, it is made stronger by the first consideration from the hostile sources and further compliments it. Third, our study has shown that Jesus taught in Palestine and was crucified and buried in Jerusalem under Pontius Pilate. These sources assert that Christianity had its beginnings in the same location. But could Christianity have survived in this location, based on its central claim that Jesus was raised from the dead, if the tomb had not been empty? It must be remembered that the resurrection of the body was the predominant view of the first century Jews. To declare a bodily resurrection if the body was still in a nearby tomb points out the dilemma here. Of all places, evidence was readily available in Jerusalem to disprove this central tenet of Christian belief.[20]

Fact Five: Correlation from Archæology

There also exists detailed archæological confirmation for the New Testament documents as we saw in chapter thirteen.[21] Archæologist Dr. Clifford Wilson, author of *New Light on the New Testament Letters, New Light on the Gospels, Rock, Relics and Biblical Reliability,* and a 17-volume set on the archæological confirmation of the Bible, writes concerning Luke:

> Luke demonstrated a remarkably accurate knowledge of geographical and political ideas. He referred correctly to provinces that were established at that time, as indicated in Acts 15:41; 16:2, 6-8. He identified regions, such as that referred to in Acts 13:49, and various cities, as in Acts 14:6. He demonstrated a clear knowledge of local customs, such as those relating to the speech of the Lycaonians (Acts 14:11), some aspects relating to the foreign woman who was converted at Athens (Acts 17:34), and he even knew that the city of Ephesus was known as "the temple-keeper of Artemis" (Acts 19:35).... he refers to different local officers by their exact titles—the proconsul (deputy) of Cyprus (Acts 13:7), the magistrates at Philippi (Acts 16:20, 35), the politarchs (another word for magistrates) at Thessalonica (Acts 17:6), the proconsul of Achaia (Acts 18:12), and the treasurer at Corinth (Aedile)—which was the title of the man known as Erastus at Corinth (Acts 19:22; Romans 16:23)....
>
> Luke had accurate knowledge about various local events such as the famine in the days of Claudius Caesar (Acts 11:29); he was aware that Zeus and Hermes were worshiped together at Lystra, though this was unknown to modern historians (Acts 14:11, 12). He knew that Diana or Artemis was especially the goddess of the Ephesians (Acts 19:28); and he was able to describe the trade at Ephesus in religious images (Acts 19:26, 27)....
>
> At these points, archæology has had something significant to say, sometimes where the biblical record had previously seemed to be in error. One good example relates to those magistrates at Philippi. In Acts 16:20, 35 we read of the magistrates being referred to as "praetors." Strictly, their title should have been *duumvir*, but it was as though they

called themselves, "senior magistrates" instead of magistrates." Ramsay showed by an inscription recovered in another Roman colony, Capua, that Cicero had spoken of the magistrates: "Although they are called duumvirs in the other colonies, these men wish to be called praetors."

This is a point at which critics had thought Luke was in error, but the fact is Luke was better informed than those who opposed him. His writings constantly bear this impress of authenticity. He was an eyewitness of so much that is recorded in the Acts, and the source documents have now been recognized as first-class historical writings.[22]

This is only a minuscule portion of the data underlying his conclusion that "Those who know the facts now recognize that the New Testament must be accepted as a remarkably accurate source book."[23]

Fact Six: Corroboration from Enemies' Silence

The complete inability of the numerous enemies of Jesus and the early Church to discredit Christian claims (when they had both the motive and ability to do so) also argues strongly for their veracity, especially in light of the dramatic nature of those claims (e.g., concerning Christ's messiahship and resurrection) and the relative ease of disproof (documenting Jesus' failure to fulfill specific prophecies, producing Jesus' body).

Fact Seven: Corroboration from Eyewitnesses

The presence of hundreds of eyewitnesses to the events recorded in the New Testament would surely have prohibited any alteration or distortion of the facts, just as today any false reporting as to the events of the Vietnam War or World War II would be immediately corrected on the basis of living eyewitnesses and historic records.

Some argue that the Gospel writers' reporting of miracles can't be trusted because they were only giving their religiously excited "subjective experience" of Jesus, not objectively reporting real events. They thought Jesus did miracles, but were mistaken. What is ignored by critics is what the text plainly states and the fact that the gospel writers could not have gotten away with this in their own day unless they had been telling the truth. They claimed that these things were done openly, not in a corner (Acts 26:26), that they were literally eyewitnesses of the nature and deeds of Jesus (Luke 1:2; Acts 2:32; 2 Peter 1:16), and that their testimony should be believed *because* it was true (John 20:30,31).

Indeed, the apostles wrote that Jesus Himself presented His miracles in support of His claims to be both the prophesied Messiah and God incarnate. In Mark 2:8-11 when He healed the paralytic, He did so "that you may know that the Son of Man has authority on earth to forgive sins"—a clear claim to being God. In John 10:33, when the Jews accused Jesus of blaspheming because as supposedly only a man He was yet claiming to be God, what was Christ's response? "Do not believe me unless I do what my Father does. But if I do it, even though you do not believe me, believe the miracles, that you may learn and understand that the Father is in me, and I in the Father" (John 10:37-38 NIV).

When John the Baptist was in jail and apparently had doubts as to whether or not Jesus was the Messiah—after all, if Jesus was the Messiah, John probably reasoned, he should not be in jail— what did Jesus do? He told John's disciples to go and report about the miracles that Jesus did, which were in fulfillment of specific messianic prophecy (Matthew 11:2-5). Christ's miracles proved His claim to be God.

The teachings and miracles of Jesus, as any independent reading of the gospels will prove, are so inexorably bound together that if one removes the miracles, one must discard the teachings. It is logically impossible to have any other Jesus than the biblical one. But it is precisely the biblical Jesus—his deeds and teaching—which have such abundant eyewitness testimony, as any reading of the Gospels and Acts proves.

Fact Eight: Corroboration from Date of Authorship

The fact that both conservatives (F. F. Bruce, John Wenham) and liberals (Bishop John A.T. Robinson) have penned defenses of early dating for the New Testament is a witness to the strength of the data on its behalf. For example, in *Redating Matthew, Mark and Luke*, noted conservative British scholar John Wenham presents a convincing argument that the synoptic Gospels are to be dated before 55 A.D. He dates Matthew at 40 A.D. (some tradition says the early 30's), Mark at 45 A.D., and Luke no later than 51-55 A.D.[24] German papyrologist Carsten Peter Thiede has argued that the Magdalen papyrus, containing snippets of three passages from Matthew 26, currently housed at Oxford University, are actually the oldest extant fragments of the New Testament, dating from about 70 A.D. Thiede's book, *Eyewitness to Jesus* (Doubleday, 1995), points out that the Magdalen papyrus is written in Uncial style, which began to die out in the middle of the first century. In addition, the fragments are from a codex, containing writing on both sides of the papyri, which may have been widely used by Christians in the first century since they were easier to handle than scrolls. Further, at three places on the papyri the name of Jesus is written as "KS," which is an abbreviation of the Greek word *kyrios* or "Lord." Thiede argues that this shorthand is proof that early Christians considered Jesus a sacred name just as the devout Jews shortened the name of God to YHWH. This would indicate a very early belief for the deity of Christ. "New papyrus discoveries, Thiede believes, will eventually prove that all four gospels, even the problematic one ascribed to John, were written before 80 A.D. rather than during the mid-second century. He argues that a scroll fragment unearthed at the Essene community of Qumran in 1972 almost certainly contains a passage from Mark's gospel and can be accurately dated to 68 A.D. In Thiede's opinion, recent research has established that a papyrus fragment of *Luke* in a Paris library was written between 63 A.D. and 67 A.D."[25]

Even liberal bishop John A.T. Robinson argued in his *Redating the New Testament* that the entire New Testament was written and in circulation between 40 and 65 A.D.[26] And liberal Peter Stuhlmacher of Tubingen, trained in Bultmann's critical methodology of form criticism, says, "As a Western scripture scholar, I am inclined to doubt these [Gospel] stories, but *as a historian*, I am obligated to take them as reliable." And, "The biblical texts as they stand are the best hypothesis we have until now to explain what really happened."[27] Indeed, it is becoming an increasingly persuasive argument that all the New Testament books were written before 70 A.D.—within a single generation of the death of Christ.

The implications of this are not small. A New Testament written before 70 A.D. virtually destroys the edifice on which higher critical premises regarding the New Testament are based. If true, insufficient time now remains for the early church to have supposedly embellished the records with their own particularist views. What the New Testament reports, it reports accurately.

Fact Nine: Corroboration from Critical Methods Themselves

Even the critical methods themselves indirectly support New Testament reliability. Although higher critical theories in general reject biblical reliability *a priori*, nevertheless, when such theories "are subjected to the same analytical scrutiny as they apply to the New Testament documents, they will be found to make their own contribution to validating the historicity of those records"[28] If 200 years of higher criticisms of the biblical text reveals anything, it is that the higher critical methods are untrustworthy, not the Bible.

Fact Ten: Corroboration from Legal Testimony and Former Skeptics

Certainly we must also concede to the historicity of the New Testament when we consider the fact that many great minds of legal history have, on the grounds of strict legal evidence alone, accepted the New Testament as reliable history—not to mention also the fact that many skeptical intellects of history and today have converted to Christianity on the basis of the historical evidence (Athanagoras, Augustine, George Lyttleton and Gilbert West, C. S. Lewis, Frank Morrison, Sir William Ramsay, and John Warwick Montgomery, to name a few).

Lawyers, of course, are expertly trained in the matter of evaluating evidence and are perhaps the most qualified in the task of weighing data critically. Is it coincidence that so many of them throughout history have concluded in favor of the truth of the Christian religion?

What of the "father of international law," Hugo Grotius, who wrote *The Truth of the Christian Religion* (1627)? Or the greatest authority in English and American common-law evidence in the nineteenth century, Harvard Law School professor Simon Greenleaf, who wrote *Testimony of the Evangelists,* in which he powerfully demonstrated the reliability of the Gospels?[29] What of Edmund H. Bennett (1824–1898), for over 20 years the dean of Boston University Law School, who penned *The Four Gospels from a Lawyer's Standpoint* (1899)?[30] What of Irwin Linton, who in his time had represented cases before the Supreme Court, and who wrote *A Lawyer Examines the Bible* (1943, 1977), in which he stated:

> So invariable had been my observation that he who does not accept wholeheartedly the evangelical, conservative belief in Christ and the Scriptures has never read, has forgotten, or never been able to weigh—and certainly is utterly unable to refute—the irresistible force of the cumulative evidence upon which such faith rests, that there seems ample ground, for the conclusion that such ignorance is an invariable element in such unbelief. And this is so even though the unbeliever be a preacher, who is supposed to know this subject if he knows no other.[31]

What of hundreds of contemporary lawyers who, also on the grounds of strict legal evidence, accept the New Testament as historically accurate? The eminent Lord Chancellor Hailsham has twice held the highest office possible for a lawyer in England, that of lord chancellor. He wrote *The Door Wherein I Went,* in which he upholds the truth of the Christian Religion.[32] What of Jacques Ellul and of Sir Norman Anderson, one of the greatest authorities on Islamic law, who is also a Christian convinced of New Testament authority and reliablilty?

Certainly, such men were well acquainted with legal reasoning and have just as certainly concluded that the evidence for the historic truthfulness of the Scriptures is beyond reasonable doubt. As apologist, theologian, and lawyer John W. Montgomery observes in *The Law Above the Law:* considering the "ancient documents" rule (that ancient documents constitute competent evidence if there is no evidence of tampering and they have been accurately transmitted), the "parol evidence" rule (Scripture must interpret itself without foreign intervention), the "hearsay rule" (the demand for primary-source evidence), and the "cross examination" principle (the inability of the enemies of Christianity to disprove its central claim that Christ resurrected bodily from the dead in spite of the motive and opportunity to do so) all coalesce directly or indirectly to support the preponderance of evidence for Christianity. The legal burden for disproving it rests with the *critic*, who in 2,000 years has yet to prove his case.[33]

We must, then, speak of the fact that to reject the New Testament accounts as true history is by definition to reject the canons of all legitimate historical study. To reject the Gospels or the New Testament is to reject primary historical documentation in general. If this cannot be done, the New Testament must be retained as careful historical reporting. The Scripture has thus proven itself reliable in the crucible of history. It is the critic of Scripture who has been unable to prove his case.

Legal scholar J. N. D. Anderson observes in *Christianity: The Witness of History:*

> ... it seems to me inescapable that anyone who chanced to read the pages of the New Testament for the first time would come away with one overwhelming impression—that here is a faith firmly rooted in certain allegedly historical events, a faith which would be false and misleading if those events had not actually taken place, but which, if they did take place, is unique in its relevance and exclusive in its demands on our allegiance. For these events did not merely set a "process in motion and then themselves sink back into the past. The unique historical origin of Christianity is ascribed permanent, authoritative, absolute significance; what happened once is said to have happened once for all and therefore to have continuous efficacy."[34]

In other words, even if we personally choose to disbelieve what the New Testament teaches, our disbelief changes nothing. Jesus Christ is who the New testament says He is. One day He will either become our Lord and Savior or He will become our Divine Judge.

Conclusion: Where Does the Truth Lead Us?

Whether you are a Christian or a non-Christian, as you read through this book you may have learned a number of things:

- The importance of truth.

- The tremendous influence of Jesus Christ in the world; that leading thinkers have declared Him the greatest person to have ever lived.

- That Jesus' claims for Himself—to be Messiah, God incarnate, sinless, Savior, and Judge—are evidentially true. Logically speaking, no other explanation for Jesus is possible than the Christian explanation.

- That the character, teachings and deeds of Jesus Christ stand far above the founder of any other world religion. When Jesus declared He was the only way to God (John 14:6), the proof of His claim is seen in who He is and what He did.

- That the evidence for Jesus' resurrection is so powerful it can persuade even seasoned critics and stands cross-examination in modern courts of law and public debate forums. Indeed, no other explanation ever proposed for the empty tomb is sufficient; all naturalistic and critical theories are actually more difficult to believe than the resurrection itself.

- That the naturalistic, evolutionary explanation for the existence of the universe and life in it is woefully inadequate, and ultimately irrational. Naturalism requires faith in far more and far greater miracles than the Christian explanation.

- That the evidence for genuine biblical predictions of the future is not only undeniable, it actually proves who the one true God is.

- That when the Bible is tested in the crucible of history through archeology, textual criticism, and other means, it is proven to be accurate and trustworthy. The Bible is truly unique, unlike any other religious book ever written.

- That the doctrine of inerrancy is vital, biblical and proven true or confirmed through the nature and revelation of God, the testimony of Jesus and the Apostles, and historic, prophetic, scientific and other data.

Now that you have finished reading, what do you intend to do with what you have learned? Obviously, if Christianity is not true and Christ did not rise from the dead, then Christianity is a deception and you can forget all about it. But can you honestly believe this in light of all the evidence? If Christianity is true and Christ did rise from the dead, then He is who He claimed to be—God Incarnate (see John 1:1; 5:16-18; 8:58,59; 10:30,31; 14:6-9).

Surely then, it is our duty to follow Him. He is the One who is indeed "the Savior of the world" (John 4:42) who atoned for our sins on the cross:

> And He Himself is the propitiation for our sins; and not for ours only, but also for those of the whole world... (1 John 2:2; see also John 3:16).

> Jesus said "...I am the resurrection and the life; he who believes in Me shall live even if he dies..." (John 11:25).

> If we receive the witness of men, the witness of God is greater; for the witness of God is this, that He has borne witness concerning His Son. The one who believes in the Son of God has the witness in Himself; the one who does not believe God has made Him a liar, because he has not believed in the witness that God has borne concerning His Son. And the witness is this, that God has given us eternal life, and this life is in His Son. He who has the Son has the life; he who does not have the Son of God does not have the life. These things I have written to you who believe in the name of the Son of God, in order that you may know that you have eternal life (1 John 5:10-13).

Our eternal destiny depends on whether or not we believe in Jesus Christ as our personal Savior (Matthew 20:28; 25:46; 26:28; John 3:16-18, 36; 5:24). Jesus Himself emphasized, "I told you that you would die in your sins; if you do not believe that I am the one I claim to be, you will indeed die in your sins" (John 8:24).

The Bible teaches that, "All have sinned and fall short of the glory of God" and that "the wages of sin is death, but the free gift of God is eternal life in Christ Jesus our Lord" (Romans 3:23; 6:23). Because we have sinned and broken God's laws, we need His forgiveness before we can enter into a personal relationship with Him and inherit eternal life. This gift is *free*. Anyone who wishes can receive Christ as his or her personal Savior by praying the following prayer (the exact words are not important, but you may wish to use this as a guide):

> Dear God, I confess I am a sinner who has broken Your laws. I now turn from my sins. I ask Jesus Christ to enter my life. I now choose to make Him my Lord and my Savior. I realize that this is a serious decision and commitment, and I do not enter into it lightly. I believe that on the cross Jesus Christ died for my sins, then rose from the dead three days later. I receive Him as my eternal King. Help me to live my life so it is pleasing to You. Amen.

Again, accepting Christ is a serious commitment. If you have prayed this prayer, we encourage you to write us at "The John Ankerberg Show" for help in growing as a Christian. We suggest the following. Begin to read a modern, easy-to-read translation of the Bible (such as the New International Version or New American Standard Bible). Start with the New Testament, Psalms, and Proverbs and then proceed to the rest of the Scriptures. Also, find a church where people honor the Bible as God's Word and Christ as Lord and Savior. Tell someone of your decision to follow Christ and begin to grow in your new relationship with God by talking to Him daily in prayer. Then continue to read the Bible daily, as well as good Christian literature. This will help you to "grow in the grace and knowledge of our Lord and Savior Jesus Christ" (2 Peter 3:18). In sum, seek out all you can about "the eternal life to which you were called" (1 Timothy 6:12) and which you have just begun. Take your Lord seriously and enjoy Him immensely, since your relationship will last forever and "no eye has seen, no ear has heard, no mind has conceived what God has prepared for those who love him" (1 Corinthians 2:9).

If you are a Christian who has read this book, you should now be *ready with an answer*. So what do you do with the information you have learned? You can share this information with friends and family who may be doubtful or skeptical of your Christian beliefs. You can help other Christians whose faith may be weak through exposure to critical attacks against Christianity or other intellectual intimidation. You can give this book to someone who is close to becoming a Christian but isn't quite sure if it's really true. In short, you can use the information in this book whenever anyone needs to know that Christianity is true, and that being committed to Christ is the most important thing in life. Christianity is not just true for Christians; it's true for everyone. And Jesus is not just the Lord of Christians; He is the Lord of everyone. That is why we would also encourage you to *continue* your studies, not only in apologetics, but in important subjects like Bible doctrine as well. These topics are often neglected in the church.

In today's world, however, no Christian can ever underestimate the relevance of the personal study of apologetics and theology, for learning about God, loving God, spiritual growth, encouragement, and effective evangelism. The Bible is replete with these themes. The law and prophets, for example, concern themselves with commitment to God and discernment. The Psalms and Proverbs concern themselves with wisdom and practical living. The Gospels and Epistles concern themselves with evangelism and apologetic and doctrinal knowledge. Jesus Himself often employed logical thinking and apologetics in His defenses against His enemies (cf., Matthew 11:1-6; 12:2-8; 16:1-4; 19:3-8; 22:22,33, 41-46). In the Book of Acts, the Apostles repeatedly defended their beliefs by appealing to fulfilled prophecy, the resurrection, and biblical authority (Acts 2:14ff.; 3:12-26; 4:7-12; 13:14-42; chs. 15, 22–26). And the New Testament has many commands for us to be informed doctrinally (1 Timothy 1:3, 10; 4:1, 6, 11, 15, 16; 6:3; 2 Timothy 1:13; 2:14, 15; 3:14; 4:3; Titus 1:9; 2:1).

The biblical testimony concerning the importance of apologetics and theology is better understood when we realize that they strengthen the mind by teaching us to think independently and critically. They strengthen our faith and thereby inhibit backsliding whenever our faith is tested. They help us develop a Christian mindset, which covers a multitude of sins. They correct misconceptions people have about Christianity, which makes it easier for them to become Christians. And they encourage evangelism. This explains why God Himself commands Christians to be informed Christians: "But in your hearts set apart Christ as Lord. Always be prepared to give an answer to everyone who asks you to give the reason for the hope that you have. But do this with gentleness and respect" (1 Peter 3:15). And He also tell us, "You must teach what is in accord with sound doctrine" (Titus 2:1). All this is necessary because the most important thing in the life of every Christian is to have his or her priorities straight, so that God may be glorified.

And we pray this in order that you may live a life worthy of the Lord and may please him in every way: bearing fruit in every good work, growing in the knowledge of God, being strengthened with all power according to his glorious might so that you may have great endurance and patience, and joyfully giving thanks to the Father, who has qualified you to share in the inheritance of the saints in the kingdom of light. For he has rescued us from the dominion of darkness and brought us into the kingdom of the Son he loves, in whom we have redemption, the forgiveness of sins. (Colossians 1:10-14)

Not to us, O Lord, not to us but to your name be the glory, because of your love and faithfulness. (Psalm 115:1 NIV)

Bibliography

Listed below are the volumes we recommend for your personal apologetics library.

Adler, Mortimer J. *Truth in Religion: The Plurality of Religions and the Unity of Truth*. MacMillan, 1990.

———. *Ten Philosophical Mistakes*. New York: Collier, 1985.

——— and Charles Van Doren. *How to Read a Book*. Rev. ed. New York: Touchstone, 1972.

Anderson, J. N. D. *A Lawyer Among the Theologians*. Grand Rapids, MI: Eerdmans, 1974.

———. *Christianity: The Witness of History*. Downer's Grove, IL: InterVarsity, 1970.

Anderson, Norman. *Christianity and World Religions*. 2d ed. Downer's Grove, IL: InterVarsity, 1984.

Ankerberg, John and John Weldon. *Encyclopedia of New Age Beliefs*. Eugene, OR: Harvest House Publishers, 1996.

———. *The Facts on Creation v. Evolution* (and other titles in the "Facts On" series). Eugene, OR: Harvest House Publishers.

———. *Knowing the Truth About the Resurrection; Jesus the Messiah; Biblical Inerrancy; Christ as the Only Way of Salvation; The Trinity* (and other titles related to apologetics). Eugene, OR: Harvest House Publishers, 1996.

Barnett, Paul. *Is the New Testament Reliable?* Downer's Grove, IL: InterVarsity, 1986.

Beisner, E. Calvin. *Answers for Atheists, Agnostics, and Other Thoughtful Skeptics: Dialogues About Christian Faith and Life*. Rev. ed. Wheaton, IL: Crossway Books, 1993.

Blomberg, Craig L. *The Historical Reliability of the Gospels*. Downer's Grove, IL: InterVarsity, 1987.

Brown, Colin. *Miracles and the Critical Mind*. Grand Rapids, MI: Eerdmans, 1984.

Bruce, F. F. *The New Testament Documents: Are They Reliable?* Downer's Grove, IL: InterVarsity.

Bush, L. Russ. *The Handbook for Christian Philosophy*.

Chesterton, G. K. *Orthodoxy*. Garden City, NY: Image/Doubleday, 1959.

Craig, William Lane. *Reasonable Faith: Christian Truth and Apologetics*.

———. *The Son Rises*. Chicago: Moody Press.

"Dismantling NonChristian Worldviews," cassette tape from Simon Greenleaf University, (714) 632-3434.

Ferando, Ajith. *The Supremacy of Christ*. Wheaton, IL: Crossway, 1995.

Geisler, Norman L. *Christ: The Theme of the Bible*. Chicago: Moody, 1969.

———. *When Skeptics Ask: A Handbook of Christian Evidences*. Wheaton, IL: Victor, 1990.

———. *Christian Apologetics*. Grand Rapids, MI: Baker, 1976.

———. *Miracles and Modern Thought*. Grand Rapids, MI: Zondervan, 1982.

———, ed. *Inerrancy*. Grand Rapids, MI: Zondervan, 1980.

——— and Ronald M. Brooks. *Come, Let Us Reason: An Introduction to Logical Thinking*. Grand Rapids, MI: 1990.

——— and William Watkins. *Perspectives: Understanding and Evaluating Today's World Views*. San Bernardino, CA: Here's Life Publishers, 1984.

Geivett, Douglas. *Evil and the Evidence for God*. Philadelphia: Temple University Press, 1993.

——— and Gary Habermas, eds. *Miracles: Has God Acted in History?* Downer's Grove, IL: InterVarsity, 1997.

Guinness, Os. *God in the Dark: The Assurance of Faith Beyond a Shadow of Doubt*. Wheaton, IL: Crossway, 1996.

———. *The Dust of Death*. Downer's Grove, IL: InterVarsity, 1973.

Habermas, Gary R. "Resurrection Claims in Non-Christian Religions."*Religious Studies* 25 (1989): 167-77.

Habermas, Gary R. and Anthony G. N. Flew. *Did Jesus Rise from the Dead?* Terry L. Miethe, ed. San Francisco: Harper & Row, 1987.

Hackett, Stuart C. *The Reconstruction of the Christian Revelation Claim: A Philosophical and Critical Apologetic.* Grand Rapids, MI: Baker, 1984.

Hoover, A. J. *Don't You Believe It.* Chicago: Moody Press.

Jaki, Stanley. *God and the Cosmologists.* Washington, D.C.: Regnery Gateway, 1989.

Jastrow, Robert. *God and the Astronomers.* New York: W. W. Norton, 1978.

Johnson, David L. *A Reasoned Look at Asian Religions.* Minneapolis: Bethany, 1985.

Johnson, Phillip E. *Reason in the Balance: The Case Against Naturalism in Science, Law, and Education.* Downer's Grove: InterVarsity, 1995.

Jones, D. Martyn Lloyd. *Truth Unchanged, Unchanging.* London: Evangelical Press, 1973.

Kennedy, D. James and Jerry Newcomb. *What If Jesus Had Never Been Born?* Nashville: Nelson, 1994.

Kreeft, Peter. *Between Heaven and Hell.* Downer's Grove, IL: InterVarsity, 1982.

Kreeft, Peter and Ronald Tacelli. *Handbook of Christian Apologetics.* Downer's Grove, IL: InterVarsity, 1994.

Lewis, C. S. *Mere Christianity.* New York: MacMillan, 1958.

———. *The Problem of Pain.* New York: MacMillan, 1971.

———. *Miracles.*

Lewis, Gordon R. *Decide for Yourself: A Theological Workbook* (1970) and *Think for Yourself.* Downer's Grove, IL: InterVarsity.

Linneman, Eta. *Historical Criticism of the Bible: Methodology or Ideology?* Grand Rapids, MI: Baker, 1990.

Mangalwadi, Vishal. *The World of Gurus.* Rev. ed. New Delhi: Vikas Publishing, 1987.

Martin, Walter. *The Kingdom of the Cults.* Rev. ed. Minneapolis: Bethany.

———. *The New Cults*. Santa Ana: Vision House.

McCallum, Dennis, gen. ed. *The Death of Truth: What's Wrong with Multi-Culturalism, the Rejection of Reason and the New Post-Modern Diversity?* Minneapolis: Bethany, 1996.

McDowell, Josh, *Evidence That Demands a Verdict*. Vols. 1 and 2. San Bernardino, CA: Campus Crusade for Christ, 1972, 1975.

McDowell, Josh and Bill Wilson. *He Walked Among Us: Evidence for the Historical Jesus*. San Bernardino, CA: Here's Life Publishers, 1988.

Montgomery, John Warwick. *Evidence for Faith: Deciding the God Question*. Dallas: Probe Books, 1991.

———. *History and Christianity*.

———. "Is Man His Own God?" and other essays in *Christianity for the Tough-Minded*. Minneapolis: Bethany, 1976.

———. *Myth, Allegory and Gospel*. Minneapolis: Bethany, 1974.

———. *Where Is History Going?*

———. *The Shape of the Past: A Christian Response to Secular Philosophies of History*. Minneapolis: Bethany, 1975.

Moreland, J. P., ed. *The Creation Hypothesis: Scientific Evidence for an Intelligent Designer*. Downer's Grove, IL: InterVarsity, 1995.

———. *Scaling the Secular City*. Grand Rapids, MI: Baker, 1987.

Morey, Robert A. *Introduction to Defending the Faith*.

Morris, Henry M. *The Biblical Basis for Modern Science*. Grand Rapids, MI: Baker, 1984.

Morris, Henry M. with Henry M. Morris, III. *Many Infallible Proofs*. Rev. ed. San Diego: Creation-Life, 1996.

Morris, Thomas V. *Making Sense of It All: Pascal and the Meaning of Life*. Grand Rapids, MI: Eerdmans, 1992.

———. "Pascalian Wagering" in R. Douglas Geivett, Brendan Sweetman, eds., *Contemporary Perspectives on Religious Epistemology*. New York: Oxford University Press, 1992.

Morrison, Frank. *Who Moved the Stone?* Downer's Grove, IL: InterVarsity, 1958.

Nash, Ronald H. *Is Jesus the Only Savior?* Grand Rapids, MI: Zondervan, 1994.

———. *Faith and Reason.* Grand Rapids, MI: Zondervan/Academie, 1988.

Newman, Robert C., ed. *The Evidence of Prophecy: Fulfilled Prediction As Testimony to the Truth of Christianity* (1994) and other materials from the Interdisciplinary Biblical Research Institute, P.O. Box 423, Hatfield, PA 19440-0423.

North, Gary. *Unholy Spirits.* Fort Worth, TX: Dominion.

Pache, Rene. *The Inspiration and Authority of Scripture.* Chicago: Moody, 1969.

Packer, J. I. *Knowing Christianity.* Wheaton, IL: Harold Shaw, 1995.

Payne, J. Barton. *Encyclopedia of Biblical Prophecy.* Grand Rapids, MI: Baker, 1989.

Pinnock, Clark. *Set Forth Your Case.* Chicago: Moody, 1971.

Ramm, Bernard. *Protestant Christian Evidences.* Chicago: Moody Press, 1966.

Schaeffer, Francis. *He Is There and He Is Not Silent.* Wheaton, IL: Tyndale.

Sire, James W. *The Universe Next Door.* 2d ed. Downer's Grove, IL: InterVarsity, 1988.

———. *Why Should Anyone Believe Anything at All?* Downer's Grove, IL: InterVarsity, 1994.

Sproul, R. C. *Basic Training: Plain Talk on the Key Truths of the Faith.* Grand Rapids, MI: Zondervan, 1982.

———. *If There's a God, Why Are There Atheists?: Why Atheists Believe in Unbelief.* Wheaton, IL: Tyndale, 1996.

———. *Not a Chance: The Myth of Chance in Modern Science and Cosmology.* Grand Rapids, MI: 1994.

Story, Dan. *Defending Your Faith.* Nashville: Thomas Nelson, 1992.

Swinebirne, Richard. *The Concept of Miracle.* New York: St. Martin's, 1970.

Swinebirne, Richard. *The Existence of God.* Oxford: Clarendon, 1979.

———. *The Christian God.* Oxford: Clarendon, 1979.

————. *The Coherence of Theism*. Oxford: Clarendon, 1979.

————. *Faith and Reason*. Oxford: Clarendon, 1979.

Virkler, Henry A. *A Christian's Guide to Critical Thinking*. Nashville: Thomas Nelson, 1993.

Walker, James B. *The Philosophy of the Plan of Salvation*. 1887 rpt. Minneapolis: Bethany, n.d.

Wenham, David and Craig Blomberg, eds. *Global Perspectives IV: The Miracles of Jesus*. Sheffield: JSOT, 1986.

Wenham, John. *Christ and the Bible*. 2d ed. Grand Rapids, MI: Baker Book House, 1984.

————. *The Enigma of Evil: Can We Believe in the Goodness of God?* Grand Rapids, MI: Zondervan, 1985.

————. *The Goodness of God*. Downer's Grove, IL: InterVarsity, 1974.

Wilkins, Michael and J. P. Moreland. *Jesus Under Fire: Modern Scholarship Reinvents the Historical Jesus*. Downer's Grove, IL: InterVarsity, 1995.

Wysong, R. L. *The Creation Evolution Controversy*. East Lansing, MI: Inquiry Press, 1976.

Zacharias, Ravi, *Can Man Live Without God?* Dallas: Word, 1994.

Organizations

There are many fine Christian organizations devoted to apologetics including:

Simon Greenleaf University in Anaheim, California with its master's degree in apologetics program.

The Ankerberg Theological Research Institute and The John Ankerberg Show, P.O. Box 8977, Chattanooga, TN 37411, (423) 892-7722.

"The Crossroads Project," 611 E. Weber Road, Columbus, OH 43211, (800) 698-7884 or, on the Internet, http://www.crossrds.org.

Probe Ministries International, P.O. Box 801046, Dallas, TX 75204, (800) 899-7726.

Sequential Index

The following index will assist the reader to find the approximate location of major or important topics.

ationists; Evolution v. Belief in God; Evolution and the Bible; Science Reconsiders God; Materialism vs. Christianity.

Chapter Ten: More False Assumptions about Evolution: The Fossil Record; A Miracle Either Way; Probability, Evolution and Faith; Creation Superiority; The Myth of Chance: Magic with a Vengeance; Only Four Options to Explain the Universe; Scientific Creationism; Predictions v. Data.

Chapter Eleven: Bible Prophecy—Part One: Time Travel; The Purpose of Prophecy; The Importance of Prophecy; Christ: The Theme of the Bible; Difficulty of Fulfillment; Sampling of Jesus' Fulfillment of Messianic Prophecy; Probability and Messianic Prophecy.

Chapter Twelve: Bible Prophecy—Part Two: Prophecy Statistics in Biblical Books; Genesis and Daniel; Categories of Prophecy; Fulfilled Prophecy: King Josiah, Bethlehem, Babylonian Captivity, King Cyrus, Future Kingdoms, Tyre, Israeli Deportation, and Modern Israel.

Chapter Thirteen: Archæology and the Biblical Record: Definition and Apologetic Value of Archeology; Problems of Archeology; Archeology and the Biblical Record: Old Testament, New Testament; Silencing the Critics; Liberal Reversals; Dead Sea Scrolls; Critical Biases; Documentary Hypothesis; Ebla and Politics; Examples of Confirmations.

Chapter Fourteen: Biblical Inerrancy: An Introduction: Statements about the Bible; The Need for Accepting Biblical Authority; The Dangers of Limited Inerrancy; The Iota; Historic Watersheds; Definition/Explanation of Inerrancy; Inspiration and Inerrancy.

Chapter Fifteen: Biblical Inerrancy: The Evidence: The Nature of God; The Bible and Inerrancy; Jesus Christ and Inerrancy; Church History; The Accuracy of the Biblical Text; Uniqueness of the Bible; Scientific Prevision; Lack of Proven Error; Weakness of the Alternate Position.

Chapter Sixteen: The Historic Reliability of Scripture: Critical View; Conservative View; Ten Facts That Establish New Testament Reliability.

Notes

A Note from the Authors

1. See Ecclesiastes 3:11; Acts 17:28; Romans 1:19-22 and our *Knowing the Truth About Salvation: Is Jesus the Only Way to God?* Part 1 (Eugene, OR: Harvest House, 1997).
2. R. C. Sproul, *Choosing My Religion* (Grand Rapids, MI: Baker, 1995), p. 1.6 [pages are renumbered for each chapter]. See Dennis McCallum (gen. ed.), *The Death of Truth* (Minneapolis, MN: Bethany, 1996) for illustrations.

Chapter 1—Why Christianity?

1. Unless otherwise indicated these citations were taken from various books of contemporary or historical quotations, i.e., Rhoda Tripp (compiler), *The International Thesaurus of Quotations;* Ralph L. Woods (compiler and ed.), *The World Treasury of Religious Quotations;* William Neil (ed.), *Concise Dictionary of Religious Quotations;* Jonathan Green (compiler), *Morrow's International Dictionary of Contemporary Quotations.*
2. C. S. Lewis, *The Problem of Pain* (New York: Macmillan, 1962), p. 145.
3. As cited in an interview in *Christianity Today,* November 19, 1990, p. 34.
4. John W. Montgomery (ed.), *Evidence for Faith: Deciding the God Question* (Dallas: Word, 1991), p. 9.
5. Alvin Plantinga, "A Christian Life Partly Lived," in Kelly James-Clark (ed.), *Philosophers Who Believe* (Downer's Grove, IL: InterVarsity, 1993), p. 69, *emphasis added.*
6. As interviewed in the *Chattanooga Free Press,* July 23, 1995, p. A-11.
7. L. Neff, "*Christianity Today* Talks to George Gilder," *Christianity Today,* March 6, 1987, p. 35 cited in David A. Noebel, *Understanding the Times: The Religious Worldviews of Our Day and the Search for Truth* (Eugene, OR: Harvest House, 1994), p. 13.
8. Alister E. McGrath, "Response to John Hick" in Dennis L. Okholm and Timothy R. Phillips (eds)., *More Than One Way? Four Views on Salvation in a Pluralistic World* (Grand Rapids, MI: Zondervan, 1995), p. 68.
9. Ajith Fernando, *The Supremacy of Christ* (Wheaton, IL: Crossway, 1995), p. 109.
10. Norman L. Geisler, "Joannine Apologetics" in Roy B. Zuck (gen. ed.), *Vital Apologetic Issues: Examining Reasons and Revelation in Biblical Perspective* (Grand Rapids, MI: Kregel, 1995), p. 37.
11. Richard N. Ostling, "Who Was Jesus?" *Time,* August 15, 1988, p. 37.
12. Maureen O'Hara, "Science, Pseudo-Science, and Myth Mongering," Robert Basil (ed.), *Not Necessarily the New Age: Critical Essays* (New York: Prometheus, 1988), p. 148.

Chapter 2—Great Minds Speak About Jesus

1. Cited by Douglas Groothuis, "When the Salt Loses Its Savor," *Christian Research Journal,* Winter 1995, p. 50.
2. D. James Kennedy, *What If Jesus Had Never Been Born?* (Nelson, 1994), pp. 1, 8.
3. David Watson, *Jesus Then and Now* (Belleville, MI: Lion, 1986), p. 5.
4. See Ch. 16, the apologetics bibliography and our *Do the Resurrection Accounts Conflict and What Proof Is There Jesus Rose from the Dead?* (Chattanooga, TN: The John Ankerberg Show, 1989).
5. Pope John Paul II, *Crossing the Threshold of Hope* (New York: Alfred A. Knopf, 1994), p. 42.

6. Malcolm Muggeridge, *Jesus: The Man Who Lives* (New York: Harper & Row, 1978), pp. 7, 184, 191
7. Sir Lionell Luckhoo, *What Is Your Verdict?* (Fellowship Press, 1984), p. 12 cited in Ross Clifford, *Leading Lawyers Look at the Resurrection* (Claremont, CA: Albatross, 1991), p. 112.
8. Unless otherwise indicated these citations were taken from various books of contemporary or historical quotations, i.e., Rhoda Tripp (compiler), *The International Thesaurus of Quotations;* Ralph L. Woods (compiler and ed.), *The World Treasury of Religious Quotations;* William Neil (ed.), *Concise Dictionary of Religious Quotations;* Jonathan Green (compiler), *Morrow's International Dictionary of Contemporary Quotations.*
9. See e.g., our "Facts On" series on Mormonism, Jehovah's Witness, Islam, our book *Cultwatch* (Eugene, OR: Harvest House, 1993), and other titles.

Chapter 3—What Does the Bible Say About Jesus Christ?

1. Harvest House is publishing an expanded version in 1997. See *Knowing the Truth About Jesus the Messiah* for a condensed argument.
2. Based upon 1) the Scriptural lunar calendar year of 360 days, 2) the Hebrew word *shabuim* referring to units of seven years, and 3) the decree to "restore and rebuild Jerusalem" referring to the decree of Artaxerxes to Nehemiah in 444 B.C. For documentation see John Ankerberg, John Weldon, *The Case for Jesus the Messiah* (Chattanooga, TN: A.T.R.I.), pp. 66-72, 127-29, or the in-depth treatment by Sir Robert Anderson in *The Coming Prince* (Kregel, 1977).
3. Ibid.
4. J. Barton Payne, *Encyclopædia of Biblical Prophecy* (Grand Rapids, MI: Baker, 1989); Franz J. Delitzsch and Parton J. Gloag, *The Messianic Prophecies of Christ* (Minneapolis: Kloch & Kloch, 1983, rpt.).
5. Delitzsch and Gloag, pp. 123-24 [See book II, pp. 31-38, for additional important literature]
6. Emile Borel, *Probabilities and Life* (New York: Dover, 1962), chs. 1, 3.
7. Gerhard Kittel (ed.,) q.v., "monogenes," *Theological Dictionary of the New Testament* (Grand Rapids, MI: Eerdmans, 1978), Vol. 4, pp. 740-41.
8. Colin Brown (gen. ed.), *The New International Dictionary of New Testament Theology* (Grand Rapids, MI: Zondervan, 1976), Vol. 2, pp. 286-88.
9. In Fernando, *The Supremacy of Christ*, pp. 28-29.
10. Ibid., p. 52.
11. Ibid., p. 64, citing R. T. France, *The Evidence for Jesus* (Downer's Grove, IL: InterVarsity Press: 1986), p. 20.
12. Sura 3:138, "The House of Inram," A. J. Arberry, trans., *The Koran Interpreted* (New York: Macmillan, 1976), 91; Sura, "The Night Journey," in N. J. Dawood, trans., *The Koran* (Baltimore, MD: Penguin, 1972), p. 235.
13. *The Koran*, J. M. Rodwell, trans. (New York: Dutton), pp. 244, 384, 423, 460, 468, etc. (Sura 4:106; 40:57; 47:21; 48:2; 110:3).
14. Robert O. Ballou, *The Portable World Bible: A Comprehensive Selection from the Eight Great Sacred Scriptures of the World* (New York: The Viking Press, 1968), pp. 134, 147, 151.
15. Houston Smith, *The Religions of Man* (New York: Harper & Row, 1965), p. 99.
16. Clive Erricker, *Buddhism* (Chicago, IL: NTC Publishing, 1995), pp. 2-3.
17. Arthur Waley, trans., *The Analects of Confucius* (New York: Vintage, 1938), p. 130.
18. Yasna, 44:11; Moulton, Ez.368; from Robert E. Hume, *The World's Living Religions* (New York: Charles Scribner's Sons, 1959), rev., p. 203.
19. Tao-The-King, 20:3, 20:5-7 cited in Hume, p. 136.
20. In Hume, p. 95.
21. Hume, p. 283.
22. Ibid., pp. 285-86.
23. G. K. Chesterton, *The Everlasting Man* (Garden City, New York: Image, 1985), p. 272.
24. Ibid., p. 274.
25. J. I. Packer, *Knowing Christianity* (Wheaton, IL: Harold Shaw, 1995), p. 1.
26. See also Mortimer Adler, *Truth in Religion* (Macmillan, 1990).
27. A. T. Robertson, *Word Pictures in the New Testament* (Nashville: n.p., 1932), Vol. 5, p. 186.

28. See our *Do the Resurrection Accounts Conflict? And What Proof Is There That Jesus Rose from the Dead?* p. 110.

29. See chs. 5-6 in this text.

30. John Warwick Montgomery, *Faith Founded on Fact* (New York: Thomas Nelson, 1978), 47, *emphasis added*).

Chapter 4—Could Christ Be Who He Claimed?

1. William E. Lecky, *History of European Moral from Augustus to Charlemagne* (New York: D. Appleton and Co., 1903), Vol. 2, 8-9 in Josh McDowell, *More Than a Carpenter* (Wheaton, IL: Tyndale/Living Books, 1983), p. 28.

2. John Warwick Montgomery, *History and Christianity* (Downers Grove, IL: InterVarsity, 1965), p. 63.

3. In McDowell, *More Than a Carpenter*, p. 30.

4. James W. Sire, *Why Should Anyone Believe Anything At All?* (Downer's Grove, IL: InterVarsity, 1994), pp. 133-35.

5. Ernest R. Hilgard, et al., *Introduction to Psychology*, 5th ed. (New York: Harcourt Brace Jovanovich 1971), p. 472.

6. In Montgomery, *History and Christianity*, p. 65.

7. Ibid., pp. 65-66.

8. *Encyclopædia Britannica*, (q.v. *Jesus Christ*, Macropaedia, Vol. 10).

9. Philip Schaff, *History of the Christian Church*, Vol. 1: Apostolic Christianity (Grand Rapids, MI: Eerdmans, 1978), p. 109.

10. Montgomery, *History and Christianity*, pp. 66-67.

11. C. S. Lewis, *Miracles: A Preliminary Study* (London: Collins/Fontana, 1970), p. 113.

12. C. S. Lewis, *Mere Christianity* (New York: Macmillan, 1971), p. 56.

13. Sire, p. 136.

Chapter 5—What Former Skeptics Say

1. John Warwick Montgomery, "The Jury Returns: A Juridical Defense of Christianity" in John Warwick Montgomery (ed.), *Evidence for Faith: Deciding the God Question* (Dallas: Probe/Word, 1991), p. 319.

2. Frederic R. Howe, "The Role of Apologetics and Evangelism" in Roy B. Zuck (gen. ed.), *Vital Apologetic Issues: Examining Reasons and Revelation in Biblical Perspective* (Grand Rapids, MI: Kregel, 1995), p. 26.

3. E.g., cf., John Warwick Montgomery, "How Muslims Do Apologetics" in *Faith Founded on Fact* (New York: Nelson, 1978); David Johnson, *A Reasoned Look at Asian Religions* (Minneapolis, MN: Bethany, 1985); Stuart C. Hackett, *Oriental Philosophy* (Madison, WI: University of Wisconsin Press, 1979); John Weldon, *Buddhism* (MA Thesis) on file at Simon Greenleaf University, Anaheim, CA; and John Ankerberg and John Weldon, *The Facts on Hinduism in America* and *The Facts on Islam.*

4. Henry Morris, *Many Infallible Proofs* (San Diego, CA: Master Books, 1982), p. 1.

5. G. Fernando, *The Supremacy of Christ*, p. 243.

6. Michael Green, *Man Alive!* (Chicago, IL: InterVarsity Christian Fellowship, 1969), p. 40.

7. William Lane Craig, *The Son Rises: Historical Evidence for the Resurrection of Jesus* (Chicago: Moody Press, 1981), pp. 128-30.

8. Ibid., p. 131.

9. Norval Geldenhuys, *Commentary on the Gospel of Luke* (Grand Rapids, MI: Eerdmans, 1975), p. 628.

10. In McDowell, *More Than a Carpenter* (Wheaton, IL: Tyndale/Living Books, 1983), p. 86, citing *Chamber's Encyclopædia* (London: Pergamon Press, 1966), Vol. 10, p. 516.

11. A. Harnack, "Alexandria, School of," *The New Schaff-Herzog Encyclopædia of Religious Knowledge*, Vol. 1 (Grand Rapids, MI: Baker, 1977), pp. 124-25, 347 and L. Russ Bush (ed.), *Classical Readings in Christian Apologetics: AD 100–1800* (Grand Rapids, MI: Zondervan, 1983), p. 31.

12. L. Russ Bush (ed.), *Classical Readings in Christian Apologetics: AD 100–1800* (Grand Rapids, MI: Zondervan, 1983), pp. 195-98.

13. American Antiquarian Society, Early American Imprints, No. 8909 (1639–1800 AD), p. 3.
14. Frank Morison, *Who Moved the Stone?* (Downer's Grove, IL: InterVarsity Press, 1969), pp. 9-10.
15. Ibid., p. 10.
16. Ibid., p. 11.
17. In Josh McDowell, *Evidence That Demands a Verdict* (San Bernardino, CA: Here's Life Publishers, rev. ed. 1979), p. 351.
18. In Ibid., p. 368.
19. C. S. Lewis, *Surprised by Joy* (New York: Harcourt, Brace & World, Inc., 1955), pp. 175, 191.
20. Ibid., pp. 228-29.
21. McDowell, *Evidence*, p. 373.
22. Personal conversations, March 26-28, 1990.
23. The John Ankerberg Show, transcript of a debate between Dr. John Warwick Montgomery and John K. Naland, televised April 1990, p. 39.
24. John Warwick Montgomery, "Introduction to Apologetics" class notes, Simon Greenleaf School of Law, Anaheim, CA, January 1986.
25. Malcolm Muggeridge, *Jesus: The Man Who Lives* (New York: Harper & Row, 1978), pp. 7, 184, 191, *emphasis added*.
26. In McDowell, *Evidence* (1972 ed.), p. 366.
27. William M. Ramsay, *The Bearing of Recent Discovery on the Trustworthiness of the New Testament* (Grand Rapids, MI: Baker Bookhouse, 1959), p. 81, cf. his *Luke the Physician*, pp. 177-79, 222.
28. In W. J. Sparrow-Simpson, *The Resurrection in Modern Thought* (London, 1911), p. 405, from Wilbur M. Smith, *Therefore Stand: Christian Evidences* (Grand Rapids, MI: Baker, 1972), p. 365.
29. Michael Grant, *Jesus: An Historian's Review of the Gospels* (New York: Charles Schribner's Sons, 1977), p. 176.
30. Ibid., pp. 190-91, *emphasis added*.
31. Ibid.
32. James I. Packer, in Terry L. Miethe (ed.), *Did Jesus Rise from the Dead?: The Resurrection Debate* (New York: Harper & Row, 1987), p. 15.
33. Gleason L. Archer, *Encyclopædia of Bible Difficulties* (Grand Rapids, MI: Zondervan, 1982), pp. 23-22.
34. Ibid., p. 23.

Chapter 6—Resurrection on Trial

1. Joseph Thayer, *Thayer's Greek English Lexicon of the New Testament* (Grand Rapids, MI: Baker, 1982), p. 617; James Hope Moulton, George Milligan, *The Vocabulary of the Greek Testament Illustrated from the Papyri and Other Non-Literary Sources* (Grand Rapids, MI: Eerdmans, 1980), p. 628; Spiros Zodhiates, *The Hebrew-Greek Key Study Bible* (Grand Rapids, MI: Baker, 1985), p. 71; Kurt Aland, *et al., The Greek New Testament* (New York: American Bible Society, 1968), p. 179.
2. See the Simon Greenleaf University 1989-1990 and future catalogues.
3. Ibid.
4. In Michael Green, *Man Alive!* (Chicago, IL: InterVarsity Christian Fellowship, 1969), p. 54.
5. In Wilbur M. Smith, *Therefore Stand: Christian Apologetics* (Grand Rapids, MI: Baker, 1972), p. 425, cf., p. 584.
6. q.v., "Hugo Grotius," *Encyclopædia Britannica Micropaedia*, Vol. 4, p. 753, and references.
7. In Josh McDowell, *Evidence That Demands a Verdict* (San Bernardino, CA: Here's Life Publishers, rev. ed., 1979), pp. 201-02.
8. J. N. D. Anderson, *Christianity: The Witness of History* (London: Tyndale Press, 1970), p. 90.
9. Ibid., p. 105.
10. In John Stott, *Basic Christianity* (London: InterVarsity Fellowship, 1969), p. 47.
11. Irwin H. Linton, *A Lawyer Examines the Bible: A Defense of the Christian Faith* (San Diego: Creation Life Publishers, 1977), pp. 13, 196.
12. Ibid., p. 192.
13. Ibid., p. 120.
14. Ibid., p. 50.
15. Ibid., p. 45, cf., pp. 16-17.

16. Ibid., p. 16.

17. Smith, *Therefore Stand*, p. 423.

18. Linton, p. 36.

19. In Josh McDowell, *More Than a Carpenter* (Wheaton, IL: Tyndale/Living Books, 1983), p. 97.

20. In John Warwick Montgomery, *The Law Above the Law* (Minneapolis, MN: Bethany, 1975), pp. 132-33. (Greenleaf's *Testimony of the Evangelists* is reprinted as an appendix.)

21. In Linton, p. XXIV.

22. Ibid., p. XXV. ·

23. Ibid., p. 242; Sherlock's text is reproduced herein.

24. Ibid., p. 277.

25. Sir Lionell Luckhoo, *What Is Your Verdict?* (Fellowship Press, 1984), p. 12, cited in Ross Clifford, *Leading Lawyers Look at the Resurrection* (Claremont, CA: Albatross, 1991), p. 112.

26. Dale Foreman, *Crucify Him: A Lawyer Looks at the Trial of Jesus* (Grand Rapids, MI: Zondervan, 1990), pp. 176-78, cited in Clifford, p. 127.

27. Val Grieve, *Your Verdict* (STL/InterVarsity Press, 1988), p. 17, cited in Clifford, p. 127.

28. Francis J. Lamb, "Miracle and Science: Bible Miracles Examined by the Methods, Rules and Tests of the Science of Jurisprudence as Administered Today in Courts of Justice," *Bibliotheca Sacra*, 1909, p. 284, cited in Clifford, p. 128.

29. Stephen D. Williams, *The Bible in Court or Truth Vs. Error* (Deerborn Publishers, 1925), p. 212, cited in Clifford, p. 130.

30. Clifford, pp. 128-32.

31. Lord Chancellor Hailsham, "The Door Wherein I Went," ("On His Conversion and the Truth of Christian Faith"), "The Simon Greenleaf Law Review," Vol. 4; Lord Diplock, ibid., Vol. 5, pp. 213-16, the Simon Greenleaf School of Law, Anaheim, CA.

32. Thomas Sherlock, "The Trial of the Witnesses of the Resurrection of Jesus" (rpt.) in John Warwick Montgomery, *Jurisprudence: A Book of Readings*, 1974; also in Linton.

33. Linton, p. 186.

34. See Ibid., pp. 14-20 and Stephen D. Williams, *The Bible in Court: A Brief for the Plaintiff* (1925); Judge Clarence Bartlett, *As a Lawyer Sees Jesus: A Logical Analysis of the Scriptural and Historical Record* (Cincinnati, OH: New Life/Standard Publishing, 1960), pp. 127-28; William Webster, "The Credibility of the Resurrection of Christ Upon the Testimony of the Apostles" (1735), *The Simon Greenleaf Law Review*, Vol. 6 (1986-1987), pp. 99-145, Anaheim, CA. Also see our forthcoming book on the resurrection (Harvest House).

35. Cf., the membership of: The Victoria Institute of Great Britain, Christian Medical Society, Creation Research Society, American Scientific Affiliation, Christian Philosophical Society, Evangelical Theological Society, and related professional organizations.

36. See their essays in Kelly James Clark (ed.), *Philosophers Who Believe: The Spiritual Journeys of Eleven Leading Thinkers* (Downer's Grove, IL: InterVarsity, 1993).

Chapter 7—Alternate Theories to the Resurrection

1. Wilbur M. Smith, *The Supernaturalness of Christ* (Grand Rapids, MI: Baker, 1974, rpt.), p. 220.

2. For more thorough descriptions and critcisims of these positions, see Frank Morison, *Who Moved the Stone?* (Downer's Grove: InterVarsity Press, 1969), pp. 88-103; W. M. Smith, *Therefore Stand* (Grand Rapids: Baker, 1972), pp. 359-437; G. E. Ladd, *I Believe in the Resurrection of Jesus* (Grand Rapids: Eerdmans, 1975), pp. 132-42; Josh McDowell, *Evidence That Demands a Verdict*, Vol. 1, 2d ed. (San Bernardino: Here's Life, 1979), pp. 232-59; William Lane Craig, *The Son Rises: Historical Evidence for the Resurrection of Jesus* (Chicago: Moody, 1981), pp. 23-44.

3. J. Orr, "Jesus Christ," *International Standard Bible Encyclopaedia*, Vol. 3, 1st ed., p. 1664; cf. idem., *The Resurrection of Jesus* (Joplin, Mo: College, 1972 repr.), pp. 9-30.

4. James F. Babcock, "The Resurrection—A Credibility Gap?" in John Warwick Montgomery (ed.), *Christianity for the Tough-Minded* (Minneapolis: Bethany, 1973) p. 250.

5. G. Hanson, *The Resurrection and the Life* (New York: Revell, 1911), p. 24.

6. Smith, *Therefore Stand*, p. 451.

7. Craig, *The Son Rises*, p. 43.

8. John Warwick Montgomery, *History & Christianity* (Downer's Grove, IL: InterVarsity, 1965), p. 77.
9. Bernard Ramm, *Protestant Christian Evidences* (Chicago, IL: Moody, 1971), p. 194.
10. J. Lilly, "Alleged Discrepancies in the Gospel Accounts of the Resurrection," *Catholic Biblical Quarterly*, Vol. 2, 1940, p. 99.
11. Smith, *Supernaturalness of Christ*, p. 205
12. Smith, *Therefore Stand*, p. 398.
13. Gary Habermas, *Ancient Evidence for the Life of Jesus: Historical Records of His Death and Resurrection* (New York: Nelson, 1984), pp. 20-21.
14. See Terry L. Miethe (ed.), *Did Jesus Rise from the Dead? The Resurrection Debate* (New York: Harper & Row, 1987), pp. 19-20.
15. Ibid., p. 149.
16. John M. Robertson, *Pagan Christs* (New Hyde Park, New York: University Books, 1967).
17. Kersey Graves, *The World's Sixteen Crucified Saviors or Christianity Before Christ* (New Hyde Park, New York: University Books, 1971).
18. G. A. Wells, *Did Jesus Exist?* (Buffalo, New York: Prometheus Books, 1975).
19. Cf. *Encyclopædia Britannica, Macropædia*, 15th edition, s.v., "Mystery Religions." Some of this material is taken from the author's *The Secret Teachings of the Masonic Lodge: A Christian Perspective* (Chicago: Moody Press, 1991), pp. 244-45.
20. John Allegro, *The Sacred Mushroom and the Cross* (New York: Bantam, 1971), p. 154.
21. Ibid., p. 193.
22. Ibid., p. 192.
23. Ibid., p. 205.
24. J. N. D. Anderson, *Christianity: The Witness of History* (London: Tyndale, 1970), p. 15.
25. Cf., Jack Finegan, *Myth and Mystery: An Introduction to the Pagan Religions of the Biblical World* (Grand Rapids, MI: Baker, 1989).
26. In Tom Snyder, *Myth Conceptions* (Grand Rapids, MI: Baker Books, 1995), p. 191, citing the 1965 ed. p. 42.
27. Samuel N. Kramer, *Mythologies of the Ancient World* (Garden City, New York: Doubleday, 1961), p. 10 from Josh McDowell, *Evidence That Demands a Verdict* (Arrowhead Springs, San Bernardino, CA: Campus Crusade for Christ, 1972), p. 263.
28. P. Lambrechts, "La' Resurrection de Adonis," in *Melanges Isidore Levy*, 1955, pp. 207-40 as cited in Edwin Yamauchi, "The Passover Plot or Easter Triumph?" in Montgomery, (ed.), *Christianity for the Tough-Minded* (Minneapolis: Bethany, 1973).
29. Ibid.
30. *Encyclopædia Britannica*, 1969, Vol. 15, article on Adonis.
31. Wilbur M. Smith, *Therefore Stand* (New Canaan, CT: Keats, 1981), p. 583.
32. Ibid.
33. Ibid.
34. J. N. D. Anderson, *Christianity and Comparative Religion* (Downer's Grove, IL: InterVarsity Press, 1977), p. 38.
35. C. S. Lewis, *Miracles: A Preliminary Study* (London: Collins/Fontana, 1970), p. 119.
36. Ibid., p. 118.
37. Anderson, p. 41, *emphasis added*.
38. Snyder, p. 194.
39. E.g., Anderson, p. 22.
40. Geoffrey W. Bromiley, "Mysticism" in Everett F. Harrison, (ed.), *Baker's Dictionary of Theology* (Grand Rapids, MI: Baker, 1972), p. 366.
41. *Encyclopædia Britannica*, 1969, vol. 15, pp. 604-05.
42. Robert Speer, *The Finality of Jesus Christ* (Grand Rapids, MI: Zondervan, 1968), p. 100.
43. As cited in Paul A. Fisher, *Behind the Lodge Door: Church, State and Freemasonry* (Washington, DC: Shield Press), 1987, pp. 273-74.
44. *Encyclopædia Britannica, Macropedia*, 15th edition, s.v., "Mystery Religions."
45. Ronald H. Nash, *Christianity & the Hellenistic World* (Grand Rapids, MI: Zondervan/Probe, 1984), pp. 171-72.
46. Ibid., pp. 172-73.

47. Ibid., p. 173.

48. Ibid., pp. 192-99; citing Metzger on the cult of Cybele.

Chapter 8—Did He Rise? The Resurrection Debates

1. Terry L. Miethe (ed.), *Did Jesus Rise from the Dead? The Resurrection Debate* (New York: Harper & Row, 1987), xiv.

2. Ibid.

3. Ibid., xv

4. Ibid.

5. Ibid., 254.

6. Ibid., 134-35.

7. Ibid., 142.

8. Ibid., 149.

9. Ibid., 29.

10. Ibid., 33.

11. Ibid., 45.

12. Transcript, The John Ankerberg Show, "Did the Resurrection Really Happen?" (Chattanooga, TN: ATRI, 1990), p. 48

13. Ibid., p. 52.

14. Ibid., p. 50

15. Ibid., p. 66.

16. Ibid., p. 55.

17. Ibid., p. 67.

18. Ibid., pp. 50-51.

19. Ibid., p. 51.

20. Ibid., p. 11.

21. Ibid., p. 17, *last emphasis added.*

22. Ibid., p. 54.

23. Ibid., p. 75.

Chapter 9—False Assumptions Concerning Evolution

1. Ernst Mayr, "The Nature of the Darwinian Revolution," *Science*, Vol. 176 (June 2, 1972), p. 981.

2. James More, *Darwin: The Life of a Tormented Evolutionist* (New York: Warner, 1991), p. xxi.

3. W. R. Bird, *The Origin of Species Revisited: The Theories of Evolution and of Abrupt Appearance*, Vol. 1 (New York: Philosophical Library, Inc., 1989), p. 1.

4. Theodosius Dobzhansky, *Mankind Evolving: The Evolution of the Human Species* (New York: Bantam, 1970), p. 1.

5. Ibid., p. xi.

6. Michael Denton, *Evolution: A Theory in Crisis* (Bethesda, MD: Adler and Adler, 1986), p. 358.

7. Francis A. Schaeffer, *How Should We Then Live?: The Rise and Decline of Western Thought and Culture* (Old Tappan, NJ: Revelle, 1976), p. 19.

8. Henry Morris, *The Long War Against God: The History and Impact of the Creation/Evolution Conflict* (Grand Rapids, MI: Baker, 1989), p. 18.

9. John Ankerberg, John Weldon, *The Facts on Creation vs. Evolution* (Eugene, OR: Harvest House, 1993), pp. 35-44, and our forthcoming book to be published by Harvest House.

10. The term *evolution* is used in reference to the general theory that all life on earth has evolved from nonliving matter and has progressed to more complex forms with time; hence, "macroevolution" and not "microevolution" or minor changes within species illustrated in crossbreeding (e.g., varieties of dogs).

11. J. P. Moreland, *Christianity and the Nature of Science: A Philosophical Investigation* (Grand Rapids, MI: Baker, 1989), p. 21.

12. Ibid., 21-42.

13. Ibid., 17-138.

14. R. L. Wysong, *The Creation/Evolution Controversy* (East Lansing, MI: Inquiry Press, 1976), pp. 40-41.

15. Ibid., 41.
16. Ibid., 44.
17. A. E. Wilder-Smith, *The Natural Sciences Know Nothing of Evolution* (San Diego: Master Books, 1981), p. 133.
18. Willem J. Ouwneel, "The Scientific Character of the Evolution Doctrine," *Creation Research Society Quarterly*, September 1971, p. 109.
19. Ibid., 109-115.
20. Robert T. Clark , James D. Bales, *Why Scientists Accept Evolution* (Grand Rapids, MI: Baker, 1976), pp. 29-95; Ankerberg and Weldon, *Facts on Creation*, pp. 25-42.
21. Pierre-P. Grasse, *Evolution of Living Organisms: Evidence for a New Theory of Transformation* (New York: Academic Press, 1977), p. 3, *emphasis added.*
22. Cited in Bird, Vol. 1, p. 141, *emphasis added.*
23. Dobzhansky, *Mankind Evolving*, pp. 5-6, *emphasis added.*
24. George Gaylord Simpson, *The Meaning of Evolution* (New York: Bantam, 1971), pp. 4-5, *emphasis added.*
25. Carl Sagan, *Cosmos* (New York: Random House, 1980), p. 27, *emphasis added.*
26. Konrad Lorenz, *Intellectual Digest*, February 1974, p. 62, *emphasis added.*
27. Morris, *The Long War*, p. 20, *emphasis added;* citing Rene Dubos, *American Scientist*, March 1965, p. 6.
28. Morris, *The Long War*, p. 24, *emphasis added;* citing Goldschmidt, *American Scientist*, January 1952, p. 84.
29. Julian Huxley in Sol Tax, ed., *Issues in Evolution* (Chicago, IL: University of Chicago Press, 1960), p. 41, from Morris, *The Long War*, p. 322, *emphasis added.*
30. Morris, *The Long War*, p. 32.
31. Arthur Custance, "Evolution: An Irrational Faith" in *Evolution or Creation?* Vol. 4—*The Doorway Papers* (Grand Rapids, MI: Zondervan, 1976), pp. 173-74.
32. Ibid., pp. 174-75.
33. Ibid., p. 179.
34. A. E. Wilder-Smith, *The Scientific Alternative to Neo-Darwinian Evolutionary Theory: Information, Sources and Structures* (Costa Mesa, CA: TWFP Publishers, 1987), p. III.
35. Denton, p. 326.
36. Wilder-Smith, *The Scientific Alternative*, p. iv.
37. Ibid., *second emphasis added.*
38. Bird, Vols. 1 and 2; cf., Vol. 1, p. 45.
39. Denton, p. 348, *emphasis added.*
40. Ibid.
41. Ibid., p. 349.
42. Ibid., *emphasis added.*
43. Ibid.
44. Wilder-Smith, *The Scientific Alternative*, p. I.
45. Denton, p. 358.
46. Ibid.
47. H. Butterfield, *Origins of Modern Science*, 1957, p. 199, cited in Denton, p. 351.
48. Denton, pp. 351-52.
49. Ibid., p. 75.
50. In ibid.
51. Ibid., p. 76.
52. P. Feyerabend, *Beyond the Edge of Certainty*, 1965, p. 176, as cited in Denton, p. 77.
53. Morris, *The Long War*, pp. 109-20.
54. Wysong, *The Creation/Evolution Controversy*, p. 40, citing Dobzhansky, *Heredity, Race and Society*, 1952, p. 63, *emphasis added.*
55. Aldous Huxley, *Ends and Means* (London: Chatto & Windus, 1946), pp. 270, 273.
56. R. J. Rushdoony, *The Mythology of Science* (Nutley, NJ: Craig Press, 1968), p. 13.
57. Ibid.
58. A. E. Wilder-Smith, *The Scientific Alternative*, pp. iii-iv.
59. Jerry Bergman, *The Criterion* (Richfield, MN: Onesimus Publishers, 1984), passim.

60. Ibid., p. vii.
61. Ibid., pp. vii-viii.
62. Ibid., p. xi.
63. Ibid., p. xiii, xv.
64. Ibid., p. xi.
65. Ibid., p. 54.
66. These are taken from ibid., pp. 4-11, 20-24.
67. Ibid., 56-57.
68. Ibid., 7.
69. Ibid.
70. Ibid., 28.
71. Mortimer J. Adler, editor in chief, William Gorman, general editor, *The Great Ideas: A Syntopicon of Great Books of the Western World* (Chicago: IL: Encyclopædia Britannica, 1952), Vol. 1, p. 543.
72. In Sol Tax, ed., *Evolution After Darwin*, Vol. 3 (Chicago, IL: University of Chicago Press, 1960), p. 45.
73. Colin Brown, *Philosophy and the Christian Faith* (Wheaton, IL: Tyndale, 1971), p. 147.
74. Huston Smith, *The Christian Century*, July 7-14, 1982, p. 755, citing *Studies in Comparative Religion*, Winter 1970.
75. John Randall, *Parapsychology and the Nature of Life* (New York: Harper Colophon, 1977), p. 11.
76. J. W. Burrow, introduction in Charles Darwin, *The Origin of Species* (Baltimore, MD: Penguin, 1974), p. 24.
77. Newman Watts, *Why Be An Ape?: Observations on Evolution* (London: Marshall, Morgan & Scott Ltd., n.d.), p. 97.
78. "Humanist Manifesto II," *The Humanist*, September/October 1973, pp. 4-9.
79. E.g., George H. Smith, *Atheism: The Case Against God* (Los Angeles: Nash, 1974), pp. 112-13.
80. Richard Bozarth, *The American Atheist*, September 1978, cited by Richard Bliss, "Evolution Versus Science," *Christian Herald*, July/August, 1985.
81. Ibid.
82. Ravi Zacharias, *Can Man Live Without God?* (Dallas: Word, 1994), p. XVII.
83. Ibid., pp. 22-23.
84. On theistic evolution, see Burt Thompson, *Theistic Evolution* (Shreveport, LA: Lambert, 1977); on the gap theory see Weston Fields, *Unformed and Unfilled: The Gap Theory*, Presbyterian Reformed; in general see Nigel N. de S. Cameron, *Evolution and the Authority of the Bible* (Greenwood, SC: Attic Press, 1983); on the day age theory see note 87; on progressive creationism see Marvin L. Lubenow, "Progressive Creationism: Is It a Biblical Option?" Proceedings of the Third Creation-Science Conference (Caldwell, Idaho: Bible Science Association, 1976) and Marvin L. Lubenow, *Bones of Contention: A Creationist Assessment of Human Fossils* (Grand Rapids, MI: Baker, 1992), ch. 20.
85. Morton O. Beckner in Paul Edwards, editor in chief, *The Encyclopædia of Philosophy* (New York: Macmillian, 1972), Vol. 2, p. 304.
86. In *The Remarkable Birth of Planet Earth*, Appendix B, Henry Morris Lists, 77 New Testaments References to Genesis 1-11, pp. 99-101.
87. Keil and Delitszch, *Commentary on the Old Testament in Ten Volumes*, Vol. 1 (Grand Rapids, MI: Eerdmans, 1978), p. 51; H. C. Lupold, *Exposition of Genesis*, Vol. 1 (Grand Rapids, MI: Baker, 1978), pp. 57-58.
88. Mark Eastman, Chuck Missler, *The Creation Beyond Time and Space* (Costa Mesa, CA: TWFT, 1996), pp. 83, 212.
89. Hugh Ross, "Astronomical Evidence for a Personal Transcendent God" in J. P. Moreland, (ed.), *The Creation Hypothesis: Scientific Evidence for an Intelligent Designer* (Downer's Grove, IL: InterVarsity Press, 1994), pp. 141-42, 160, 171.
90. Kurt P. Wise, "The Origin of Life's Major Groups" in J. P. Moreland, (ed.), *The Creation Hypothesis*, p. 233.
91. Henry Margenau, "The Laws of Nature Are Created by God" in Henry Margenau, Roy Abraham Varghese, (eds.), *Cosmos Bios Theos* (LaSalle, IL: Open Court, 1992), p. 61, cf. p. 59.
92. Ibid., p. 11.

Chapter 10—More False Assumptions About Evolution

1. Good resources are The Creation Research Society in St. Joseph, MO, and The Institute for Creation Research in Santee, CA. To illustrate, W. R. Bird is a summa cum laude graduate of Vanderbilt University and the Yale Law School who argued the major case on the origin's issue before the U.S. Supreme Court. He is a member of the most prestigious legal organization, the American Law Institute, and has published articles on the origins topic in the *Harvard Journal of Law and Public Policy* and the *Yale Law Journal*. He is also listed in the most selective directory, *Who's Who in the World*, plus listings in several others. In *The Origin of Species Revisited*, 2 vol. (New York: Philosophical Library, 1993), he documents how evolutionary scientists are increasingly questioning the validity of standard evolutionary theory. This book was prepared utilizing the research amassed for the 1981 Supreme Court case over the issue of origins (Aguillard, *et al.*, v. Edwards, *et al.*, civil action No. 81-4787, Section H, U.S. District Court for the Eastern District of Louisiana, *Brief of the State in Opposition to ACLU Motion for Summary Judgment*, c., 1984, W. R. Bird). Attorneys for the defendant gathered thousands of pages of information from hundreds of evolutionary scientists who, collectively, had expressed reservations from most scientific fields, in most areas of evolutionary thinking.
2. Pierre-P. Grassé, *Evolution of Living Organisms* (New York: Academic Press, 1977), pp. 3-4, 204.
3. Thomas Huxley in *Three Lectures on Evolution* (1882), 619, from Bird, I, p. 59.
4. Theodosius Dobzhansky, *American Scientist*, 45, 388, 1957, as cited in Stephen Jay Gould, *Wonderful Life: The Burgess Shale and the Nature of History* (New York: W. W. Norton, 1985), p. 3, *second emphasis added*.
5. Charles Darwin, *The Origin of Species*, J. W. Burrow, ed. (Baltimore, MD: Penguin, 1974), pp. 206, 292; cf., pp. 313-16, *emphasis added*.
6. In Phillip E. Johnson, *Darwin on Trial* (Downers Grove, IL: InterVarsity, 1991), p. 46, who gives original references on p. 166, *emphasis added*.
7. Stephen Jay Gould, "The Return of Hopeful Monsters," *Natural History*, June-July, 1977, pp. 22, 24, *emphasis added*.
8. See e.g., Bird, I, pp. 48, 59 citing Stanley, Gould, Eldredge, Kitts and Tattersall. See Steven M. Stanley, *Macroevolution: Pattern and Process* (San Francisco: W. H. Freeman, 1979), pp. 1, 4-9, 23, 74, 84, 88-98.
9. David Raup, "Conflicts Between Darwin and Paleontology," *Field Museum of Natural History Bulletin*, January 1979 at 22, 25 from Bird, I, p. 48.
10. George Gaylord Simpson, *The Major Features of Evolution* (New York: Columbia University Press, 1965), p. 360, emphasis in original. Simpson went on to state that these discontinuities did not require a belief in special creation.
11. Austin Clark, "Animal Evolution," *3 Quarterly Review of Biology*, p. 539, from Bird, I, p. 50.
12. A. Thompson, *Biology, Zoology and Genetics: Evolution Model vs. Creation Model*, 2 (1983), p. 76, emphasis added, from Bird, I, p. 49.
13. Derek V. Ager, "The Nature of the Fossil Record," p. 87, *Proceedings of Geological Association* 133 (1976) from Bird, I, p. 51.
14. G. Simpson, *The Major Features of Evolution* (1953), p. 143, and G. Simpson, *Tempo and Mode in Evolution* (1944), 107, from Bird, I, pp. 49, 57.
15. E. J. H. Corner "Evolution" in A. M. MacLeod and L. S. Cobley, (eds.), *Evolution in Contemporary Botanical Thought* (Chicago: Quadrangle Books, 1961), at pp. 95, 97, from Bird, I, p. 234.
16. See Bird, I, pp. 58-59.
17. Donn Rosen, "Evolution: An Old Debate with a New Twist," in *St. Louis Post Dispatch*, 17 May 1981, quoted by James E. Adams; cf. references in Bird, I, p. 536.
18. For examples, cf., Bird, Vol. 1, passim, and Bolton Davidheiser, *Evolution and Christian Faith* (Nutley, NJ: Presbyterian and Reformed, 1969), pp. 302-09.
19. D. Johansen, M. Edey, *Lucy: The Beginnings of Humankind*, p. 363 (1981); cf., N. Eldgedge and I. Tattersall, *The Myths of Human Evolution*, pp. 7-8 (1982) from Bird, I, p. 55.
20. R. A. Stirton, *Time, Life and Man* (John Wiley and Sons, 1957), p. 416, from Davidheiser, p. 307.
21. Paul B. Weiss, *The Science of Biology* (McGraw Hill, 1963), p. 732, from Davidheiser, p. 303.
22. Pierre-P. Grasse, *Evolution of Living Organisms* (New York: Academic Press, 1977), p. 30.

23. White, "Presidential Address: A Little on Lungfishes" 177, *Proceedings of the Linnean Society*, I, 8 (1966) in Bird, I, p. 62.

24. Colin Patterson in a letter to Luther D. Sunderland, 10 April 1979, cited in Bird, I, p. 59, and by William J. Guste, Jr. in the Plaintiff's Pre-Trial Brief for the Louisiana Trial on Creation vs. Evolution, 3 June 1982.

25. Robert Barnes, book review of *Invertebrate Beginnings, Paleobiology*, 6(3), 1980, p. 365.

26. Earl L. Core, *et al.*, *General Biology*, 4th ed. (John Wiley and Sons, 1961), p. 299, from Davidheiser, p. 309.

27. David Raup and Steven M. Stanley, *Principles of Paleontology* (San Francisco. W. H. Freeman, 1978), p. 372.

28. Steven M. Stanley, *Macroevolution: Pattern and Process* (San Francisco: W. H. Freeman & Co., 1979), p. 39; cf., pp. 47, 62.

29. Stephen Jay Gould, "Evolution's Erratic Pace," *Natural History*, May 1977, p. 12.

30. Ibid., p. 14.

31. Francis Darwin, (ed.), *The Life and Letters of Charles Darwin* (New York: Johnson Reprint, 1969), Vol. 3, p. 248. Apparently is emphasized in the original.

32. Charles Darwin, *The Origin of Species* (ed: J. W. Burrow), p. 292.

33. Stanley, *Macroevolution*, p. 35.

34. Stephen J. Gould, *The Panda's Thumb: More Reflections in Natural History* (New York: W. W. Norton & Co., 1980), 184-85 and note 29, p. 24.

35. Nils Heribert-Nilsson, *Synthetische Artbildung* (Lund, Sweden: CWK Glerups, 1953), p. 11.

36. Ibid., pp. 1142-43.

37. Ibid., pp. 1239-40.

38. Steven M. Stanley, *The New Evolutionary Timetable: Fossils, Genes, and the Origin of Species* (New York: Basic Books, 1981), p. xv.

39. E. Mayr, *Populations, Species and Evolution*, p. 253 (1970) Harvard University Press, in Bird, I, p. 177 (cf., Bird, pp. 168-77).

40. Michael Denton, *Evolution: A Theory in Crisis*, pp. 193-94. See also Stanley, *Macroevolution*, pp. 122-23.

41. E.g., cf., the citations in Bird, I, pp. 155-290 (cf., pp. 134-55).

42. Cf., Coppedge, *Evolution*, p. 113, passim.

43. Ernst Mayr, *Systematics and the Origin of Species*, 1942, p. 296, from Bird, Vol. 1, p. 119.

44. Bird, Vol. 1, p. 75.

45. Denton, p. 351.

46. Francis Crick, *Life Itself: Its Origin and Nature* (New York: Simon & Schuster, 1981), p. 88.

47. Cited in Norman L. Geisler, *Creator in the Classroom—"Scopes 2": The 1981 Arkansas Creation/Evolution Trial* (Milford, MI: Mott Media, 1982), p. 151.

48. Mark Eastman, Chuck Missler, *The Creator Beyond Time and Space* (Costa Mesa, CA: The Word for Today, 1996), pp. 11-12. See especially Alexander Vilenkin, "Did the Universe Have a Beginning?" CALT-68-1772DOE Research and Development Report, California Institute of Technology, Pasadena, November 1992.

49. Ibid., p. 17.

50. Ibid., p. 207.

51. Ibid., p. 27.

52. Hugh Ross, "Astronomoical Evidences for a Personal, Transcendent God" in J. P. Moreland (ed.), *The Creation Hypothesis: Scientific Evidence for an Intelligent Designer* (Downers Grove, IL: Inter-Varsity, 1994), p. 164, citing Paul Davies, *The Cosmic Blueprint: New Discoveries in Nature's Creative Ability to Order the Universe* (New York: Simon & Schuster, 1988), p. 203 and Paul Davies, *Superforce: The Search for a Grand Unified Theory of Nature* (New York: Simon & Schuster, 1984), p. 243.

53. Stephen C. Meyer, "The Methodological Equivalence of Design and Descent: Can There Be a Scientific 'Theory of Creation'?" in Moreland (ed.), *The Creation Hypothesis*, pp. 67-68, citing George Greenstein, *The Symbiotic Universe: Life and Mind in the Cosmos* (New York: William Morrow, 1988), pp. 26-27.

54. Eastman and Missler, p. 28, citing Tony Rothman, "A 'What You See Is What You Beget' Theory," *Discover*, May 1987, p. 99.

55. Ibid., p. 29, citing Henry Margenau and Roy Barghese (eds.), *Cosmos, Bios and Theos* (LaSalle, IL: Open Court, 1992), p. 83.

56. Ibid., p. 156.

57. Carl Sagan, F. H. C. Crick, L. M. Muchin in Carl Sagan, ed., *Communication with Extraterrestrial Intelligence* (CETI) (Cambridge, MA: MIT Press), pp. 45-46.

58. Emile Borel, *Probabilities and Life* (New York: Dover, 1962), chs. 1 and 3; Borel's cosmic limit of 10^{200} changes nothing.

59. Marcel P. Schutzenberger, "Algorithms and the Neo-Darwinian Theory of Evolution," in Paul S. Moorehead and Martin M. Kaplan, *Mathematical Challenges to the Neo-Darwinian Interpretation of Evolution* (Wistar Institute Symposium Monograph No. 5) (Philadelphia, PA: The Wister Institute Press, 1967), p. 75; cf., Bird, Vol. 1, pp. 79-80, 158-65.

60. J. Allen Hynek, Jacque Vallee, *The Edge of Reality* (Chicago, IL: Henry Regenery, 1975), p. 157.

61. Coppedge, *Evolution: Possible or Impossible?* (Grand Rapids, MI: Zondervan, 1973), pp. 118-20

62. Cited in Eastman, Missler, *The Creator Beyond Time and Space*, p. 61.

63. Cf., Frank B. Salisbury, "Natural Selection and the Complexity of the Gene," *Nature*, Vol. 24, October 25, 1969, pp. 342-43, and James Coppedge, Director Center for Probability Research and Biology, North Ridge, California, personal conversation; cf., Coppedge, *Evolution: Possible or Impossible?* passim.

64. George Wald, *The Physics and Chemistry of Life* (New York: Simon & Schuster, 1955), p. 12.

65. Sir Fred Hoyle, "Hoyle on Evolution," *Nature*, Vol. 294, November 12, 1981, p. 105.

66. Jacques Monod, *Chance and Necessity: An Essay on the Natural Philosophy of Modern Biology* (New York: Vintage, 1971), pp. 138-39.

67. E.g., E. J. H. Corner, "Evolution" in Anna M. McLeod, L. S. Cobley, *Contemporary Botanical Thought* (Chicago, IL: Quadrangle, 1961), p. 97.

68. H. S. Lipson, "A Physicist Looks at Evolution," *Physics Bulletin*, Vol. 31, No. 4, May 1980, p. 138. Article reproduced in full in *Creation Research Society Quarterly*, June 1981, p. 14, *emphasis added*

69. A. Thompson, *Biology, Zoology and Genetics* (1983), p. 76, cited in Bird, Vol. 1, p. 49.

70. Austin Clark, "Animal Evolution," *3 Quarterly Review of Biology*, p. 539, from Bird, Vol. 1, p. 50.

71. Bird, Vol. 1, p. 102.

72. Fred Hoyle, Chandra Wickramasinghe, *Evolution from Space* (London: J. M. Denton & Sons, 1981), p. 130.

73. Jacques Monod, *Chance and Necessity* (New York: Vintage, 1972), pp. 112-13, *emphasis added*.

74. R. C. Sproul, *Not a Chance: The Myth of Chance in Modern Science & Cosmology* (Grand Rapids, MI: Baker, 1994), p. xiv; cf., R. J. Rushdoony, *The Mythology of Modern Science*.

75. Ibid., pp. 10-11.

76. Ibid., p. 6.

77. Ibid., p. 9.

78. George Wald, "The Origin of Life" in *The Physics and Chemistry of Life*, ed., the editors of *Scientific American* (New York: Simon & Schuster, 1955), pp. 9, 12.

79. Sproul, pp. 14-15.

80. Ibid., pp. 15-16.

81. Ibid., p. 156.

82. Ibid., pp. 157-58.

83. Ibid., p. 158; cf., p. 12ff

84. Ibid., p. 12.

85. Ibid., pp. 12-13.

86. Ibid., p. 173.

87. Ibid., pp. 159-60.

88. Ibid., pp. 185-86.

89. Ibid., p. 192.

90. Ibid., p. 190.

91. Ibid., p. 214.

92. Stuart C. Hackett, *Oriental Philosophy*, (Madison, WI: The University of Wisconsin Press, 1979); David L. Johnson, *A Reasoned Look at Asian Religions*, (Minneapolis, MN: Bethany, 1985); R.C. Sproul, *Lifeviews*, (Revelle, 1986); David Ehrenfeld, *The Arrogance of Humanism*, (New York: Oxford University Press, 1978); Ravi Zacharias, *Can Man Live Without God?*; R.C. Sproul, *If*

There's a God, Why Are There Atheists? (Wheaton, IL: Tyndale, 1978); Phillip E. Johnson, *Reason in the Balance: The Case Against Naturalism in Science, Law and Education* (Downer's Grove, IL: Inter-Varsity, 1995).

93. Norman L. Geisler William Watkins, *Perspectives: Understanding and Evaluating Today's Worldviews* (San Bernardino, CA: Here's Life), 1984.

94. David L. Hull, *Darwin and His Critics: The Reception of Darwin's Theory of Evolution by the Scientific Community* (Cambridge, MA: Harvard University Press, 1974) p. 7, *emphasis added.*

95. Roy Abraham Varghese, introduction in Henry Margenau and Roy Abraham Varghese, (eds.), *Cosmos Bios Theos: Scientists Reflect on Science, God, and the Origin of the Universe, Life, and Homo Sapiens* (LaSalle, IL: Open Court, 1992), p. 5.

96. Moreland, (ed.), *The Creation Hypothesis*; Bird, passim; Norman L. Geisler, J. Kirby Anderson, *Origin Science: A Proposal for the Creation-Evolution Controversy* (Grand Rapids, MI: Baker, 1987); Henry M. Morris, Gary E. Parker, *What Is Creation Science?* (San Diego, CA: Creation Life, 1982).

97. Bird, Vol. 1, p. xvi.

98. Morris and Parker, p. III.

99. Ibid., p. 3.

100. Bird, Vol. 1, pp. 44-45.

101. A. E. Wilder-Smith, *A Basis for a New Biology* and *The Scientific Alternative*; cf., p.V.

102. Arthur N. Shapiro, review in *Creation/Evolution*, Vol. 14, no. 2, pp. 36-37.

103. The religious and/or unscientific nature of evolutionary theory has been pointed out in the following articles by creationists in *The Creation Research Society Quarterly*: Arthur Jones, "The Nature of Evolutionary Thought," Vol. 8, No. 1; William J. Ouwenell, "The Scientific Character of the Evolution Doctrine," Vol. 8, No. 2; Gary L. Schoephlin, "On Assumptions and Their Relation to Science," Vol. 9, No. 2; Raymond C. Telfar II, "Should Macroevolution Be Taught as Fact?" Vol. 10, No. 1; John N. Moore, "Retrieval System Problems with Articles in Evolution," Vol. 10, No. 2; Glenn W. Wolfram, "Evolution, Science and Religion," Vol. 12, No. 2; John N. Moore, "An Estimate of the Current Status of Evolutionary Thinking," Vol. 18, No. 4; Randall Hedtke, "The Divine Essence in Evolutionary Theorizing: An Analysis of the Rise and Fall of Evolutionary Natural Selection, Mutation and Punctuated Equilibria as Mechanisms of Megaevolution," Vol. 21, No. 1; Ralph E. Ancil, "On the Importance of Philosophy in the Origins Debate," Vol. 22, No. 3; Robert E. Kofahl, "Correctly Redefining Distorted Science: A Most Essential Task," Vol. 23, No. 3; John N. Moore, "Properly Defining 'Evolution,' " Vol. 23, No. 3; W. R. Bird, "Expostulated Evidence for Macroevolution and Darwinism: Darwinian Arguments and the Disintegrating Neo-Darwinian Synthesis, Part 2," Vol. 24. No. 2.

104. R. L. Wysong, *The Creation/Evolution Controversy* (East Lansing, MI: Inquiry Press, 1976), p. 422.

105. Cf., *The Wall Street Journal*, June 15, 1979; Dennis Dubay, "Evolution Creation Debate," *Bioscience*, Vol. 30, January 1980, pp. 4-5.

106. Bird, Vol. 1, p. 8.

Chapter 11—Biblical Prophecy—Part One

1. J. Barton Payne, *Encyclopædia of Biblical Prophecy* (Grand Rapids, MI: Baker, 1989), p. 10.

2. Ibid., p. 13.

3. Ibid., p. 681.

4. Ibid., p. 13.

5. John Wesley White, *Re-Entry* (Grand Rapids, MI: Zondervan, 1971), p. 14; cf. ibid., p. 680.

6. Payne, p. 7.

7. Norman Geisler, *Christ: The Theme of the Bible* (Chicago: Moody Press, 1969), pp. 31-110.

8. Ibid., p. 88.

9. Chart adapted from Norman Geisler, *A Popular Survey of the Old Testament* (Grand Rapids, MI: Baker, 1978), pp. 24-25; see also Arthur Pink statement in ch. 12 and Christopher J. H. Wright, *Knowing Jesus Through the Old Testament* (Downer's Grove, IL: InterVarsity, 1992) and E. W. Hengstenberg, *Christology of the Old Testament* (MacDill AFB, FL: McDonald Pub. Co., n.d.).

10. In our book *The Case for Jesus the Messiah* we discuss these verses in detail.

11. See below for Edersheim; Dr. James Smith, *What the Bible Teaches About the Promised Messiah* (Nashville: Thomas Nelson Publishers, 1993); Payne, p. 680 (cf., pp. 665-72).

12. Alfred Edersheim, *The Life and Times of Jesus the Messiah* (one volume edition) (Grand Rapids, MI: Eerdmans, 1972), pp. 160-63.

13. Ibid., p. 163; cf., 710-41.

14. Ibid., p. 165.

15. Peter W. Stoner, *Science Speaks: Scientific Proof of the Accuracy of Prophecy and the Bible* (Chicago: Moody Press, 1969), p. 4.

16. Ibid., p. 107.

17. Ibid., p. 109.

18. James Coppedge, *Evolution: Possible or Impossible?* (Grand Rapids, MI: Zondervan, 1973), p. 120.

Chapter 12—Biblical Prophecy—Part Two

1. Quote from Carl Henry in Sherwood Eliot Wert, *Living Quotations for Christians* (New York: Harper & Row, 1974), p. 191.

2. J. Barton Payne, *Encyclopædia of Biblical Prophecy: The Complete Guide to Scriptural Predictions and Their Fulfillment* (New York: Harper & Row, 1973), p. 27.

3. Ibid., p. 674.

4. Ibid., p. 682.

5. Ibid., pp. 645-50, 665-70, 682.

6. For a critique see John Ankerberg, John Weldon, *Astrology* (Eugene, OR: Harvest House, 1989) and *The Facts on Psychic Readings* (1997).

7. Payne, p. V.

8. Ibid., pp. 154-55.

9. Ibid., p. 369.

10. Sir Robert Anderson, *The Coming Prince* (Grand Rapids, MI: Kregel, 1977 rpt., 10th ed.), pp. 81-82.

11. Ibid.

12. John F. Walvoord, *Armageddon: Oil and the Middle East Crisis—What the Bible Says About the Future of the Middle East and of the End Western Civilization* (Grand Rapids, MI: Zondervan, 1990 Rev.), p. 14.

13. E.g., Arnold G. Fruchtenbaum, *The Footsteps of the Messiah: A Study of the Sequence of Prophetic Events* (San Antonio, TX: Ariel Press, 1982), pp. 120, 254, 266.

14. Payne, p. 27.

15. Ibid., p. 11.

16. Ibid., p. 13.

17. Charles Boutflower, *In and Around the Book of Daniel* (Grand Rapids, MI: Kregel, 1977, rpt.), p. 1370.

18. Gleason Archer, Jr., *A Survey of Old Testament Introduction* (Chicago, IL: Moody Press, 1974, Rev.), pp. 326-51.

19. John C. Whitcomb, *Darius the Mede* (Mutley, NJ: Presbyterian and Reformed, 1961).

20. Josh McDowell, *Evidence That Demands a Verdict* (San Bernardino, CA: Campus Crusade for Christ, 1976), p. 308; cf. Peter Stoner, *Science Speaks* (Chicago, IL: Moody Press, 1975), pp. 93-95.

21. Gleason Archer, "Daniel," in Frank E. Gaeblein (ed.), *The Expositors Bible Commentary*, Vol. 7., p. 1298; cf. Payne, p. 372.

22. Josh McDowell, *Daniel in the Critic's Den: Historical Evidence for the Authenticity of the Book of Daniel* (San Bernardino, CA: Campus Crusade for Christ, 1973), p. 31.

23. John Ankerberg, *et al., One World: Bible Prophecy and the New World Order* (Chicago, IL: Moody Press, 1991).

24. See ibid.

25. Gleason L. Archer, *Encyclopædia of Bible Difficulties* (Grand Rapids, MI: Zondervan, 1982), pp. 11-12, and personal conversation.

26. Ibid., pp. 24-26.

27. Robert Dick Wilson, *Studies in the Book of Daniel* (Grand Rapids, MI: Baker, 1979, rpt.).

28. Ibid.

29. K. A. Kitchen, *Notes on Some Problems in the Book of Daniel* (London: Tyndale, 1965), pp. 31-79.

30. Boutflower.

31. McDowell, *Daniel in the Critic's Den.*

32. Arthur Custance, "Some Striking Fulfillment of Prophecy" in *Hidden Things of God's Revelation* (Grand Rapids, MI: Zondervan, 1977), pp. 118-19; cf., George T. V. Davis, *Rebuilding Palestine According to Prophecy* and *Fulfilled Prophecies That Prove the Bible.*

33. Ibid., pp. 109-41.

34. Robert W. Manweiler, "The Destruction of Tyre" in Robert C. Newman (ed.), *The Evidence of Prophecy: Fulfilled Prediction as a Testimony to the Truth of Christianity* (Hatfield, PA: Interdisciplinary Biblical Research Institute, 1994), pp. 28-30.

35. Custance, pp. 121-27; McDowell, *Evidence That Demands a Verdict*, pp. 274-80.

36. In McDowell, *Evidence That Demands a Verdict*, p. 275.

37. Ibid., pp. 275-76.

38. Ibid., pp. 275-76.

39. Custance, p. 126.

40. Manweiler, p. 26; cf., Ralph Alexander, "Ezekiel"; Vol. 6 in Gaeblein (ed.), *The Expositors Bible Commentary*, pp. 869-71.

41. Archer, in Gaeblein (ed.), p. 1343.

42. Bernard M. Ramm, *Protestant Christian Evidences* (Chicago, IL: Moody Press, 1971), p. 110.

43. Ibid., p. 101.

44. Edgar James, *Moody Monthly*, March, 1974, p. 103.

45. Taken from Eastman and Missler, *The Creator Beyond Time and Space*, p. 154.

46. Henry Morris, *Many Infallible Proofs* (San Diego, CA: Creation Life Publishers, 1974), p. 191.

47. Fruchtenbaum, p. 67.

48. Ibid., p. 80.

49. Cf., ibid., pp. 69-83.

50. Archer, in Gaeblein (ed.), p. 1227.

51. Paul Lee Tan, *The Interpretation of Prophecy* (Winona Lake, IN: Assurance Publishers, 1978); Fruchtenbaum, *The Footsteps of the Messiah: A Study of the Sequence of Prophetic Events;* John Ankerberg, John Weldon, *The Case for Jesus the Messiah: Incredible Prophecies That Prove God Exists* (Chattanooga, TN: Ankerberg Theological Research Institute, 1988); John Urquhart, *The Wonders of Prophecy* (Harrisburg, PA: Christian Publications, Inc., Ninth ed., n.d.); John Walvoord, *Daniel: The Key to Prophetic Revelation* (Chicago, IL: Moody Press, 1971); Anderson, *The Coming Prince;* Alfred Edershim, *Prophecy and History in Relation to the Messiah* (Grand Rapids, MI: Baker, 1955); Charles Lee Feinberg, *The Prophecy of Ezekiel: The Glory of the Lord* (Chicago, IL: Moody Press, 1969); McDowell, *Evidence That Demands a Verdict;* Payne, *Encyclopedia of Biblical Prophecy: The Complete Guide to Scriptural Predictions and Their Fulfillment;* Wilson, *Studies in the Book of Daniel;* Custance, "Some Striking Fulfillment of Prophecy" in *Hidden Things of God's Revelation;* Alfred Kastler, "The Challenge of the Century," *Bulletin of the Atomic Scientists,* September 1977; Norman Geisler, *Christ: The Theme of the Bible* (Chicago, IL: Moody Press, 1969); Archer, in Gaeblein (ed.), *The Expositors Bible Commentary.*

Chapter 13—Archeology and the Biblical Record

The authors would like to thank Dr. Clifford Wilson for his reading of this chapter and helpful comments.

1. K. A. Kitchen, *The Bible in Its World: The Bible and Archeology Today* (Downer's Grove, IL: Inter-Varsity, 1977), p. 7.

2. Keith N. Schoville, *Biblical Archeology in Focus* (Grand Rapids, MI: Baker, 1978), p. 80.

3. E.g., *Biblical Archeology Review, The Biblical Archeologist, Bible and Spade, American Journal of Archeology, Annual of the American Schools of Oriental Research, Israel Exploration Journal, The Journal of Near Eastern Studies, The Palestine Exploration Quarterly, Quarterly of the Department of Antiquities of Palestine,* as well as encyclopedias such as *Encyclopedia of Archeological Excavations in the Holy Land.*

4. Kitchen, *The Bible in Its World*, p. 9.

5. Edwin Yamauchi, *The Stones and the Scriptures* (New York: J. B. Lippencott, 1972), p. 17.

6. In Schoville, p. 16.

7. Ibid.

8. Ibid.
9. Joseph P. Free, revised and expanded by Howard F. Vos, *Archeology and Bible History* (Grand Rapids: Zondervan, 1992), p. IX.
10. Ibid.
11. K. A. Kitchen, *Ancient Orient and Old Testament* (Chicago: InterVarsity Press, 1973), p. 173.
12. Walter Kaiser, "The Promise of Isaiah 14 and the Single-Meaning Hermeneutic" in John Ankerberg, John Weldon, *The Case for Jesus the Messiah* (Chattanooga, TN: The John Ankerberg Evangelistic Association, 1989), p. 144.
13. Citing Henry Morris, *The Bible and Modern Science* (Chicago: Moody Press, 1956, rev.), p. 95, in Josh McDowell, *Evidence That Demands a Verdict* (San Bernardino, CA: Here's Life, 1979 rev.), p. 70.
14. Free and Vos, p. 13.
15. Yamauchi, p. 21.
16. Ibid., pp. 21-22.
17. Free and Vos, p. IX.
18. Ibid., p. 13.
19. Schoville, p. 154.
20. Ibid., p. 157.
21. Free and Vos, pp. 293-94.
22. Kitchen, *The Bible in Its World*, p. 12.
23. Ibid., p. 11.
24. Ibid., p. 13.
25. Schoville, p. 156; Dr. Bryant Wood's article in the *Biblical Archeological Review* is also relevant.
26. Ibid., p. 157.
27. Ibid., p. 158
28. Ibid., p. 161.
29. Ibid., p. 158.
30. Ibid.
31. Ibid., p. 159.
32. Ibid., p. 165.
33. Norman Geisler and Ron Brooks, *When Skeptics Ask: A Handbook on Christian Evidences* (Wheaton, IL: Victor, 1990), p. 179.
34. Schoville, p. 159.
35. (New York: Bobbs Merrill, 1960), p. 16, a book endorsed by an editorial board comprising American Liberal Clergymen, from Gleason L. Archer, Jr., *A Survey of Old Testament Introduction*, 1974, rev., p. 166.
36. E. M. Blaiklock, "Editor's Preface," *The New International Dictionary of Biblical Archeology* (Grand Rapids, MI: Regency Reference Library/Zondervan, 1983), pp. vii-viii, *emphasis added*.
37. J. A. Thompson, *The Bible and Archeology* (Grand Rapids, MI: Eerdmans, 1975), p. 5.
38. Geisler and Brooks, p. 200.
39. Clifford A. Wilson, *Rocks, Relics and Biblical Reliability* (Grand Rapids, MI: Zondervan/Richardson, TX: Probe, 1977), pp. 98-101.
40. Geisler and Brooks, p. 200.
41. Thompson, pp. 375, 405.
42. Cited in Geisler and Brooks, p. 202.
43. Wilson, pp. 112-13.
44. Merrill C. Tenney, "Historical Verities in the Gospel of Luke," in Roy B. Zuck (Genesis ed.), *Vital Apologetic Issues: Examining Reasons and Revelation in Biblical Perspective* (Grand Rapids, MI: Kregel, 1995), p. 204.
45. John Warwick Montgomery, "The Jury Returns: A Juridicial Defense of Christianity" in John Warwick Montgomery (ed.), *Evidence for Faith: Deciding the God Question* (Dallas: Probe/Word, 1991), p. 326.
46. Wilson, p. 120.
47. Kitchen, *The Bible and Its World*, p. 134.
48. Schoville, p. 156.
49. Thompson, p. 442.

50. Free and Vos, p. 294.
51. Schoville, p. 163.
52. Ibid., p. 163.
53. In Geisler and Brooks, p. 179.
54. Eugene H. Merrill, professor of Old Testament Studies, Dallas Theological Seminar, "Ebla and Biblical Historical Inerrancy" in Roy B. Zuck (Genesis ed.), *Vital Apologetic Issues: Examining Reasons and Revelation in Biblical Perspective* (Grand Rapids, MI: Kregel, 1995), p. 180.
55. A. H. Sayce, *Monument Facts and Higher Critical Fancies* (London: The Religious Tract Society, 1904), p. 23, cited in Josh McDowell, *More Evidence That Demands a Verdict* (Arrowhead Springs, CA: Campus Crusade for Christ, 1975), p. 53.
56. As cited in McDowell, *Evidence That Demands a Verdict*, p. 66.
57. Josh McDowell, *Evidence That Demands a Verdict* (Arrowhead Springs, CA: Campus Crusade for Christ, 1972 edition), p. 366. This statement is not found in the revised 1979 version of *Evidence That Demands a Verdict*. Whether the citation was removed for space or other legitimate considerations or is incorrect in some fashion is unknown to the authors.
58. William M. Ramsay, *The Bearing of Recent Discovery on the Trustworthiness of the New Testament* (Grand Rapids, MI: Baker Bookhouse, 1959), p. 81; cf. William M. Ramsay, *Luke the Physician*, pp. 177-79, 222 from F. F. Bruce, *The New Testament Documents: Are They Reliable?* (Downers Grove, IL: InterVarsity Press, 1971), pp. 90-91.
59. Wilson, *Rocks, Relics*, p. 126.
60. J. Randall Price, *Secrets of the Dead Sea Scrolls* (Eugene, OR: Harvest House, 1996), p. 146.
61. Ibid., p. 159.
62. Ibid., p. 163.
63. Ibid., p. 164; cf. p. 157.
64. E. M. Blaiklock, *Christianity Today*, September 28, 1973, p. 13.
65. Geisler and Brooks, p. 202.
66. Kitchen, *Ancient Orient and Old Testament*, pp. 20, 20n.
67. Kitchen, *The Bible in Its World*, p. 7.
68. Yamauchi, p. 161.
69. Ibid., p. 30.
70. Ibid.
71. Free and Vos, pp. 255-57.
72. Kitchen, *Ancient Orient and Old Testament*, p. 23.
73. Ibid., p. 172.
74. Gleason L. Archer, Jr., *A Survey of Old Testament Introduction* (Chicago: Moody Press, 1974, rev.), pp. 85, 90.
75. Ibid., p. 107.
76. Yamauchi, p. 164.
77. Merrill in Zuck, (ed.), p. 184.
78. Ibid., p. 179.
79. In McDowell, *Evidence That Demands a Verdict* (1975 ed.), p. 65, citing John Warwick Montgomery, "Evangelicals and Archeology," *Christianity Today*, August 16, 1968, pp. 47-48.
80. Merrill in Zuck, (ed.), p. 187.
81. Cf., Free and Vos, pp. 108, 170, passim, and John Whitcomb, *Darius the Mede* (Presbyterian & Reformed, n.d.).
82. Schoville, p. 167.
83. *The New International Dictionary of Biblical Archeology*, p. 441.
84. Wilson, p. 32.
85. Ibid., p. 442.
86. Personal letter, 1996; see also Clifford Wilson, *Ebla: Secrets of a Forgotten City* (San Diego: Master books, 1980).
87. *The New International Dictionary of Biblical Archeology*, p. 441.
88. Merrill in Zuck, (ed.), p. 189.
89. The situation was discussed in some detail in *The Biblical Archaeological Review*. See next note, p. 75 for a listing of articles.

90. James D. Muhly, "Ur and Jerusalem Not Mentioned in Ebla Tablets, Say Ebla Expedition Scholars," *Biblical Archeology Review*, Nov./Dec. 1983, p. 75.
91. Merrill in Zuck, (ed.), p. 185.
92. Ibid., p. 186.
93. Muhly, p. 75.
94. Merrill in Zuck, (ed.), p. 192.
95. Yamauchi, p. 20.
96. Ibid., p. 20.
97. Most of these are taken from Free and Vos, passim, who list them chronologically by subheading, "Archeological Confirmation Concerning..."
98. Free and Vos, p. 14.
99. Norman Geisler, *Christ: The Theme of the Bible* (Chicago: Moody Press, 1969), p. 29n, citing D. J. Wiseman, "Archeological Confirmations of the Old Testament" in Carl F. Henry, (ed.), *Revelation and the Bible* (Grand Rapids, MI: Baker, 1958), pp. 301-02.
100. Published by Pacific Christian Ministries, P.O. Box 311, Lilydale 3140, Victoria, Australia, and available from Pacific International University and Archaeology Center, P.O. Box 1717, Springfield, Missouri, 65801 (417-831-7515).
101. John Ankerberg, John Weldon, *Behind the Mask of Mormonism* (Eugene, OR: Harvest House, 1996, 2d ed.), pp. 282-90; Jerald and Sandra Tanner, *Archeology and the Book of Mormon* (Salt Lake City, UT: Utah Lighthouse Ministry, 1969).
102. Wilson, *Rocks, Relics,* pp. 124-25.

Chapter 14—Biblical Inerrancy: An Introduction

1. Cited in Carl Hatch, The Charles A. Briggs Heresy Trial, p. 33.
2. Preface, p. 13.
3. Gleason Archer, Jr., *Encyclopedia of Bible Difficulties* (Grand Rapids, MI: Zondervan, 1980), pp. 119-20.
4. Henry M. Morris, *Biblical Creationism* (Grand Rapids, MI: Baker, 1993), p. 14.
5. Harold Lindsell, *The Battle for the Bible* (Grand Rapids, MI: Zondervan Publishers, 1977), p. 23.
6. Gleason Archer, "Alleged Errors and Discrepancies in the Original Manuscripts of the Bible" in Norman Geisler, (ed.), *Inerrancy* (Grand Rapids, MI: Zondervan, 1980), p. 59.
7. Harold O.J. Brown, "The Arian Connection: Presuppositions of Errancy" in Gordon Lewis and Bruce Demarest, *Challenges to Inerrancy: A Theological Response* (Chicago: Moody, 1984), pp. 386-87.
8. Paul Feinberg, "The Meaning of Inerrancy" in Geisler, (ed.), *Inerrancy*, p. 294.
9. James M. Boice, *Does Inerrancy Matter?* (Wheaton, IL; Tyndale House Publishers, 1980), p. 15.
10. See our *The Facts on the King James Only Debate.*
11. Charles Ryrie, *What You Should Know About Inerrancy* (Chicago: Moody Press, 1981), p. 30.
12. See our *The Facts on the King James Only Debate.*
13. Lindsell, *The Battle for the Bible*, p. 31.
14. Harold Lindsell, *The Bible in the Balance* (Grand Rapids, MI: Zondervan, 1979), p. 31.
15. Edward J. Young, *Thy Word Is Truth* (Grand Rapids, MI: Eerdmans Publishing Co., 1970), pp. 206-07.
16. Lindsell, *The Bible in the Balance*, p. 133.
17. Walter C. Kaiser, Jr., "Legitimate Hermeneutics" in Geisler, (ed.), *Inerrancy*, pp. 140-41, cf., pp. 460n., 46. (See also Hebrews 6:13-18, citing Genesis 12, 15, 17, 22 and 1 Corinthians 9:8-10 citing Deuteronomy 25:4 and Romans 4:23; Matthew 23:31-32; 1 Corinthians 10:11; Hebrews 10:15).

Chapter 15—Biblical Inerrancy: The Evidence

1. Clark Pinnock, "Three Views of the Bible in Contemporary Theology" in Jack Rogers, (ed.) *Biblical Authority* (Waco, TX: Word, 1978), p. 64.
2. John W. Montgomery, "Biblical Inerrancy: What Is at Stake?" in John W. Montgomery, (ed.) *God's Inerrant Word* (Minneapolis, MN: Bethany, 1974), p. 21.

3. Benjamine B. Warfield, *The Inspiration and Authority of the Bible* (Phillipsburg, NJ: Presbyterian and Reformed, 1948), p. 442.

4. Harold O. J. Brown, "The Arian Connection: Presuppositions of Errancy" in Gordon Lewis and Bruce Demarest, *Challenges to Inerrancy: A Theological Response* (Chicago: Moody, 1984), p. 389.

5. See Feinberg's comments on the exegetical evidence for inerrancy based on five scriptural phenomena in Norman Geisler, (ed.), *Inerrancy* (Grand Rapids, MI: Zondervan, 1980), pp. 276-87. We may also observe here that several excellent texts may be consulted on biblical inspiration and inerrancy: Rene Pache, *The Inspiration and Authority of Scripture* (Moody); Norman Geisler, (ed.), *Inerrancy* (Zondervan); Carl Henry, (ed.), *Revelation and the Bible* (Baker); Gordon Lewis and Bruce Demarest, *Challenges to Inerrancy* (Moody); Clark Pinnock, *Biblical Revelation* (Moody); John Warwick Montgomery, *God's Inerrant Word* (Bethany); Geisler and Nix, *A General Introduction to the Bible* (Moody); R. L. Harris, *Inspiration and Canonicity of the Bible* (Zondervan); L. Gaussen, *Divine Inspiration of the Bible* (Kregel); E. J. Young, *Thy Word Is Truth* (Eerdmans); Merrill Tenney, (ed.), *The Bible: The Living Word of Revelation* (Zondervan).

6. Pinnock, Rogers, (ed.), *Biblical Authority*, p. 63.

7. Cf. the discussion in Geisler, (ed.) *Inerrancy*, pp. 45-45, 277-82, as to why "all" is the best translation, not "every"; cf., H. Wayne House, "Biblical Inspiration in 2 Timothy 3:16" in Roy B. Zuck, (gen. ed.), *Vital Apologetic Issues* (Grand Rapids: Kregel, 1995).

8. Edward J. Young, *Thy Word Is Truth* (Grand Rapids, MI: Eerdmans Publishing Co., 1970), pp. 86-87.

9. Harold Lindsell, *The Battle for the Bible* (Grand Rapids, MI: Zondervan Publishers, 1977), p. 67.

10. See e.g., John Wenham, *Christ and the Bible* (Downers Grove, IL: InterVarsity, 1973), chs. 1-2, 5 and his chapter in Geisler, (ed.) *Inerrancy*, pp. 3-38; the classic work is Benjamine B. Warfield's *The Inspiration and Authority of the Bible;* Pierre Ch. Marcel "Our Lord's Use of Scripture" in Henry, (ed.), *Revelation and the Bible* (Grand Rapids, MI: Baker, 1969), pp. 119-34 and Rene Pache, *The Inspiration and Authority of Scripture* (Chicago: Moody Press, 1966), ch. 18.

11. John Wenham, "Christ's View of Scripture," in Geisler, (ed.), *Inerrancy*, pp. 14-15.

12. John Murray "The Attestation of Scripture" in N. B. Stonehouse and Paul Woolley, (eds.), *The Infallible Word: A Symposium* (Grand Rapids, MI: Baker Book House, 1967, Third rev. edition), p. 22.

13. Ibid., pp. 26-27.

14. Ibid., p. 28.

15. Charles Ryrie, *The Bible Truth Without Error* (booklet, rev. ed.) (Dallas: Dallas Theological Seminary, 1977), p. 7.

16. Montgomery in Montgomery, (ed.), *God's Inerrant Word*, p. 31.

17. Ibid., p. 38.

18. See, for example, John Woodbridge, *Biblical Authority* (Zondervan); George D. Barry's *The Inspiration and Authority of Holy Scripture, A Study in the Literature of the First Five Centuries;* Harold Lindsell, *The Battle for the Bible*, chapter 3 (Zondervan); Norman Geisler, *Decide for Yourself* (Zondervan); John W. Montgomery, (ed.), *God's Inerrant Word*, chs. 3-5; Norman Geisler, (ed.), *Inerrancy*, chs. 12-13; J. M. Boice, *The Foundation of Biblical Authority*, chapter 1 (Zondervan).

19. Lindsell, *The Battle for the Bible*, p. 69. This, of course, included matters of science and history, cf., Harold Lindsell, *The Bible in the Balance* (Grand Rapids, MI: Zondervan, 1979), p. 205; cf., R. D. Preus, (ed.), *Inerrancy*, p. 357.

20. John D. Woodbridge, "Does the Bible Teach Science?" in Zuck, (gen. ed.), p. 49.

21. Brown, "The Arian Connection: Presuppositions of Errancy" in Lewis and Demarest, p. 389.

22. James I. Packer, *Beyond the Battle for the Bible* (Westchester, IL: Cornerstone Books, 1980), p. 43.

23. Ryrie, *The Bible Truth Without Error*, p. 10.

24. John Wenham, "Christ's View of Scripture," in Geisler, (ed.), *Inerrancy*, p. 453.

25. R. C. Sproul, "The Case for Inerrancy: A Methodological Analysis" in Montgomery, (ed.), *God's Inerrant Word*, pp. 242-62.

26. J. W. Montgomery, *The Shape of the Past* (Minneapolis, MN: Bethany, 1975), pp. 138-52.

27. Charles Feinberg in Geisler, (ed.), *Inerrancy*, pp. 269-87.

28. E.g., Warfield, Arthur Holmes, and J. I. Packer. See Geisler's comments in Geisler, (ed.), *Inerrancy*, p. 242, who sees some validity in each approach—inductive, deductive, adductive, and retroductive.

29. See ch. 15 notes 5 and 10 for additional information.

30. Norman Geisler,(ed.), *Biblical Errancy: An Analysis of Its Philosophical Roots* (Grand Rapids, MI: Zondervan, 1981).

31. A major work on the subject of the inspiration of Scripture is planned for 1998.

32. Cf. our *The Facts on False Views of Jesus.*

33. J. W. Montgomery, *The Shape of the Past* (Minneapolis, MN: Bethany, 1975), pp. 138-39; R. C. Sproul, "The Case of Inerrancy: A Methodological Analysis" in Montgomery, (ed.), *God's Inerrant Word*, p. 248, cf., 248-60.

34. Norman Geisler, Ron Brooks, *When Skeptics Ask: A Handbook of Christian Evidences* (Wheaton, IL: Victor Books, 1990), p. 143.

35. Mark Eastman, Chuck Missler, *The Creator Beyond Time and Space* (Costa Mesa, CA: The Word for Today, 1996), p. 23.

36. Ibid., p. 87.

37. Ibid., p. 84.

38. Taken from Eastman and Missler, pp. 87-97. A far more detailed analysis is found in Henry Morris, *The Biblical Basis for Modern Science* (Grand Rapids, MI: Baker, 1984).

39. Ibid., pp. 26-27.

40. Ibid., p. 94.

41. Henry M. Morris with Henry M. Morris III, *Many Infallible Proofs* (Santee, CA: Master Books, 1996 rev.), pp. 250-51.

42. Eastman and Missler, p. 156.

43. Ibid., p. 101.

44. Gleason L. Archer, *Encyclopedia of Bible Difficulties* (Grand Rapids, MI: Zondervan, 1982), pp. 11-12.

45. Robert Dick Wilson, *A Scientific Investigation of the Old Testament*, pp. 13, 20, 130, 162-63; David Otis Fuller, (ed.), *Which Bible?* (Grand Rapids, MI: Grand Rapids International Publications, rev. 1971), p. 44.

46. Montgomery, *The Shape of the Past*, p. 176.

47. John W. Haley, *Alleged Discrepancies of the Bible* (Grand Rapids, MI: Baker, 1982), rpt., p. vii.

48. William Arndt, *Does the Bible Contradict Itself?* (St. Louis: Concordia, 1955), rpt., p. XI.

49. R. C. Sproul in Montgomery, (ed.), *God's Inerrant Word*, p. 257.

50. Charles Ryrie, *What You Should Know About Inerrancy* (Chicago: Moody Press, 1981), p. 17.

51. Lindsell, *The Battle for the Bible*, p. 203.

52. George H. Smith, *Atheism: The Case Against God* (Los Angeles: Nash, 1974), pp. 112-13.

53. Woodbridge, "Does the Bible Teach Science?" in Zuck, (gen. ed.), p. 40.

54. Lindsell, *The Battle for the Bible*, p. 97.

55. Ibid., p. 98.

56. Murray in Stonehouse and Woolley, (eds.), pp. 4-5.

57. Lindsell, *The Bible in the Balance*, p. 214.

58. In Woodbridge, "Does the Bible Teach Science?" in Zuck, (gen. ed.), p. 40.

59. Archer, *Encyclopedia of Bible Difficulties*, pp. 23-24.

60. Millard J. Erickson, "Presuppositions of Non-Evangelical Hermeneutics" in Earl Rodmacher and Robert Preus, (eds.), *Hermeneutics, Inerrancy and the Bible* (Grand Rapids, MI: Academie Books, Zondervan, 1984), p. 607.

61. Paul Feinberg in Geisler, (ed.), *Inerrancy*, p. 285.

Chapter 16—The Historic Reliability of Scripture

1. James W. Sire, *Why Should Anyone Believe Anything at All?* (Downer's Grove, IL: InterVarsity, 1994), p. 221, citing Thomas C. Oden, *The Word of Life*, Systemic Theology, 2 (San Francisco: Harper & Row, 1989) from Sire, pp. 223-24.

2. Chauncey Sanders, *An Introduction to Research in English Literary History* (New York: Macmillan, 1952), p. 160. His comments were specifically in reference to the authenticity or authorship of a given text.

3. C. Sanders, *Introduction and Research in English Literary History* (New York: Macmillan, 1952), pp. 143ff.

4. J. McDowell, *Evidence That Demands a Verdict*, rev. 1979, pp. 39-52; and N. Geisler, W. Nix, *A General Introduction to the Bible* (Chicago: Moody Press, 1971), pp. 238, 357-67.

5. McDowell, *Evidence That Demands a Verdict*, p. 42; Robert C. Newman, "Miracles and the Historicity of the Easter Week Narratives," in Montgomery, (ed.), *Evidence for Faith*, pp. 281-84.

6. F.F. Bruce, *The Books and the Parchments* (Old Tappan, NJ: Revell, 1963), p. 78.

7. F.F. Bruce, *The New Testament Documents: Are They Reliable?* (Downer's Grove, IL: InterVarsity Press, 1971), p. 15.

8. Cited in Rene Pache, *The Inspiration and Authority of Scripture*, tr. Helen I. Needham (Chicago: Moody Press, 1969), p. 193, citing Benjamin B. Warfield, *An Introduction to the Textual Criticism of the Old Testament*, p. 12ff.; "The Greek Testament of Westcott and Hort," *The Presbyterian Review*, Vol. 3 (April 1982), p. 356.

9. J. McDowell, *Evidence That Demands a Verdict*, pp. 43-45; Clark Pinnock, *Biblical Revelation: The Foundation of Christian Theology* (Chicago: Moody Press, 1971), pp. 238-39, 365-66.

10. Newman, p. 284.

11. See John Warwick Montgomery, *Faith Founded on Fact* (New York: Nelson, 1978); F.F. Bruce, *The New Testament Documents: Are They Reliable?*; John Warwick Montgomery, *History and Christianity*, Norman Geisler, *Christian Apologetics* (Grand Rapids, MI: Baker, 1976), pp. 322-27.

12. William M. Ramsay, *The Bearing of Recent Discovery on the Trustworthiness of the New Testament* (Grand Rapids, MI: Baker, 1959), p. 81, cf. William F. Ramsay, *Luke the Physician*, pp. 177-79, 222, as given in F.F. Bruce, *The New Testament Documents: Are They Reliable?* pp. 90-91.

13. A.N. Sherwin-White, *Roman Society and Roman Law in the New Testament* (Oxford: Clarendon Press, 1963), from N. Geisler, *Christian Apologetics*, p. 326.

14. Gary R. Habermas, *Ancient Evidence for the Life of Jesus: Historical Records of His Death and Resurrection* (New York: Nelson, 1984), p. 66.

15. Philip Schaff, Henry Wace, (eds.), *A Select Library of Nicene and Post-Nicene Fathers of the Christian Church*, 2d series, Vol. 1, Eusebius: Church History, Book 3, Chapter 39, "The Writings of Papias" (Grand Rapids, MI: Eerdmans, 1976), pp. 172-73, *emphasis added*.

16. Gary R. Habermas, *Ancient Evidence for the Life of Jesus*, pp. 66, 177.

17. E.g., Gerhard Meier, *The End of the Historical Critical Method* (St. Louis, MO: Concordia, 1977); and J. McDowell, *More Evidence That Demands a Verdict* (San Bernardino, CA: Campus Crusade for Christ, 1972).

18. Habermas, *Ancient Evidence for the Life of Jesus*, p. 115.

19. Ibid., pp. 112-13.

20. Gary Habermas, *Ancient Evidence for the Life of Jesus* (Nashville, TN: Thomas Nelson, 1973); cf., F. F. Bruce, *The New Testament Documents: Are They Reliable?* (Downers Grove, IL: InterVarsity, 1971), chs. 9-10.

21. See our chapter on archæology and F.F. Bruce, "Are the New Testament Documents Still Reliable?" *Christianity Today*, October 28, 1978, pp. 28-33; F.F. Bruce, *The New Testament Documents: Are They Reliable?* chs. 7-8; Sir William Ramsay, *The Bearing of Recent Discoveries on the Trustworthiness of the New Testament* (Grand Rapids, MI: Baker Books, 1979); C.A. Wilson, *Rocks, Relics and Biblical Reliability* (Grand Rapids, MI: Zondervan, 1977), ch. 2; *New Light on New Testament Letters* and *New Light on the Gospels* (Grand Rapids, MI: Baker, 1975); Edwin Yamauchi, *The Stones and Scriptures*, Section II (New York: Lipincott, 1972).

22. Clifford Wilson, *Rocks, Relics and Biblical Reliability*, pp. 112-14.

23. Ibid., p. 120.

24. John Wenham, *Redating Matthew, Mark and Luke*, (Downer's Grove, IL: 1992), pp. 115-19, 136, 183, see pp. xxv, 198, 147, 200, 223, 238-39, 243-45.

25. John Elson, "Eyewitness to Jesus?" *Time*, April 8, 1996, p. 60.

26. John A. T. Robinson, *Redating the New Testament* (Philadelphia: Westminster, 1976).

27. In Richard S. Ostling, "Who Was Jesus?" *Time*, August 15, 1988, p. 41, *emphasis added*.

28. F. F. Bruce "Are the New Testament Documents Still Reliable?" p. 33.

29. See J. W. Montgomery, *The Law Above the Law*, (Minneapolis, MN: Bethany, 1975), appendix, pp. 91-140.

30. *The Simon Greenleaf Law Review*, Vol. 1, (Orange, CA: The Faculty of the Simon Greenleaf School of Law, 1981-1982), pp. 15-74.

31. Irwin Linton, *A Lawyer Examines the Bible* (San Diego: Creation-Life-Publishers, 1977), p. 45.

403

32. *The Simon Greenleaf Law Review,* Vol. 4, 1984-1985, pp. 28-36.
33. Montgomery, *The Law Above the Law,* pp. 87-88.
34. J. N. D. Anderson, *Christianity: The Witness of History* (Downer's Grove, IL: InterVarsity, 1970), pp 13-14.

Other Books by
John Ankerberg and John Weldon

BEHIND THE MASK OF MORMONISM

The Church of Jesus Christ of Latter-day Saints (Mormons) is the largest, wealthiest, and most influential cult in America. This accurate, comprehensive guide to Mormonism covers the pertinent aspects of the history, beliefs, and practices of this religious organization. With nearly 500 information-packed pages, *Behind the Mask of Mormonism* comprehensively traces the roots of Mormonism from its early schemes to its modern deceptions.

CULT WATCH

Now you can know the historical background and vital facts on the major beliefs of modern religious movements! *Cult Watch* takes a close look at the reasons people become entrapped in cults and what keeps them there. Drawing on years of research and interaction with representatives of each movement, the authors offer penetrating analysis on how each religious system clearly contrasts with the essential doctrines of biblical Christianity.

ENCYCLOPEDIA OF NEW AGE BELIEFS

This comprehensive volume of in-depth information is specially designed to help you understand New Age beliefs and how they contrast with biblical Christianity. With thoroughly researched articles that provide insights into recently popularized practices such as dream work and channeling, the *Encyclopedia of New Age Beliefs* is a valuable reference book for students, teachers, and everyone interested in the New Age and the emerging spiritual trends of our nation.

"KNOWING THE TRUTH ABOUT" SERIES

Knowing the Truth About Jesus the Messiah
Knowing the Truth About the Resurrection
Knowing the Truth About Salvation
Knowing the Truth About the Trinity

THE "FACTS ON" SERIES

The Facts on Abortion
The Facts on Angels
The Facts on Astrology
The Facts on Creation vs. Evolution
The Facts on the Faith Movement
The Facts on False Teaching in the Church
The Facts on Halloween
The Facts on Hinduism
The Facts on Holistic Health and the New Medicine

The Facts on Homosexuality
The Facts on Islam
The Facts on the Jehovah's Witnesses
The Facts on the King James Only Debate
The Facts on Life After Death
The Facts on the Masonic Lodge
The Facts on the Mind Sciences
The Facts on the Mormon Church
The Facts on Near-Death Experiences
The Facts on the New Age Movement
The Facts on the Occult
The Facts on Rock Music
The Facts on Roman Catholicism
The Facts on Self-Esteem, Psychology, and the Recovery Movement
The Facts on Spirit Guides
The Facts on UFOs and Other Supernatural Phenomena

Other Good
Harvest House Reading

THE GOD MAKERS
by Ed Decker and Dave Hunt

This unique exposé on Mormonism is factual, carefully researched, and fully documented. *The God Makers* provides staggering insights that are beyond the explosive film of the same title. An excellent tool in reaching Mormons.

CHRISTIANITY IN CRISIS
by Hank Hanegraaff

Christianity in Crisis confronts head-on a cancer that is ravaging the body of Christ. Influential teachers are utilizing the power of the airwaves as well as scores of books, tapes, and magazines to distort the biblical concept of the Creator and promote antibiblical doctrines. In addition to exposing darkness to light, *Christianity in Crisis* provides solutions for restoring a Christianity centered in Christ. The *Christianity in Crisis Study Guide* is also available.

DECKER'S COMPLETE HANDBOOK ON MORMONISM
by Ed Decker

In this informative book, the differences between Mormonism and Christianity are clearly presented. Through a series of conversations between neighbors, Ed Decker presents the basic tenets of Mormonism and the countering truths of the Bible.